# THE MAKING OF MODERN THEOLOGY

### 19th and 20th CENTURY T̶

This series of theological texts is des̶
of readers — theological students, stu̶
and the interested general reader –
Christian theologians who, since the
had a formative influence on the development of Christian theology. Each
volume in the series is intended to introduce the theologian, to trace the
emergence of key or seminal ideas and insights, particularly within their
social and historical context, and to show how they have contributed to the
making of modern theology. The primary way in which this is done is by
allowing the theologians chosen to address us in their own words.

There are three sections to each volume. The Introduction includes a
short biography of the theologian, and an overview of his or her theology in
relation to the texts which have been selected for study. The Texts, the
bulk of each volume, consist largely of substantial edited selections from
the theologian's writings. Each text is also introduced with information
about its origin and its significance. The guiding rule in making the
selection of texts has been the question: in what way has this particular
theologian contributed to the shaping of contemporary theology? A Select
Bibliography provides guidance for those who wish to read further both in
the primary literature and in secondary sources.

## Available in this series

1 Friedrich Schleiermacher: Pioneer of modern theology
2 Paul Tillich: Theologian of the boundaries
3 Dietrich Bonhoeffer: Witness to Jesus Christ
4 Rudolf Bultmann: Interpreting faith for the modern era

Paul Tillich 1886-1965

THE MAKING OF MODERN THEOLOGY

19th and 20th CENTURY TEXTS

General Editor: John de Gruchy

# PAUL TILLICH

## Theologian of the Boundaries

MARK KLINE TAYLOR

COLLINS

Collins Liturgical Publications
8 Grafton Street, London W1X 3LA

Collins Liturgical in USA
Icehouse One — 401
151 Union Street, San Francisco, CA 94111-1299

Collins Liturgical in Canada
c/o Novalis, Box 9700, Terminal,
375 Rideau St, Ottawa, Ontario K1G 4B4

Distributed in Ireland by
Educational Company of Ireland
21 Talbot Street, Dublin 1

Collins Liturgical Australia
PO Box 316, Blackburn, Victoria 3130

Collins Liturgical New Zealand
PO Box 1, Auckland

Library of Congress Cataloging-in-Publication Data

Taylor, Mark Kline, 1951-
    Paul Tillich: theologian of the boundaries.

    (The Making of modern theology)
    Bibliography: p.
    Includes index.
    1. Tillich, Paul, 1886-1965.    I. Title.    II. Series.
BX4827.T53T44 1987    230'.092'4    87-18269
ISBN 0-00-599059-9
ISBN 0-00-599978-2 (pbk.)

ISBN 0 00 599978 2

Introduction, notes and compilation copyright © 1987
Collins Publishers

First published 1987

Typographical design Colin Reed
Typeset by Swains Glasgow
Printed in Great Britain by
Richard Clay, Bungay

# CONTENTS

———

# CONTENTS

# ACKNOWLEDGMENTS

The publishers acknowledge with thanks permission to reproduce the following copyright texts from works by Paul Tillich:

by permission of The University of Chicago Press and Dr. Mutie Tillich Faris:
   from *The Protestant Era*, trans. with a concluding essay by J. L. Adams,
      © 1984, The University of Chicago
   from *Systematic Theology*, volume 1 (© 1951 by The University of Chicago),
      volume 2 (© 1957 by The University of Chicago), volume 3 (© 1963 by
      The University of Chicago)
   from *The Journal of Religion*, vol. xxvii, no. 1, January 1947, "The Problem of
Theological Method"; vol. xxxv, no. 2, April 1935, no. 2 "What is wrong with the
'dialectic' theology?" © 1935 and 1947, The University of Chicago

by permission of Harper & Row, Publishers, Inc.:
   pp. 80-94 from *The Future of Religions*, copyright © 1966 by Hannah Tillich
   pp. 1-10 from *The Socialist Decision*, trans. Franklin Sherman, copyright © 1977
by Harper & Row, Publishers, Inc.
   pp. 58-88 (passim), from *Political Expectations*, copyright © 1971 by Harper &
Row

by permission Verlag Alfred Topelmann, Berlin:
   "The Right to Hope", from *Neue Zeitschrift für systematische Theologie and
Religionsphilosophie 7*(1965), pp. 371-77

by permission Andrea Bocherer:
   translation (unpublished) of "The Church and the Third Reich: Ten Theses"

by permission Wayne State University Press:
   translation printed as footnote on pp. 40-41

# AUTHOR'S NOTE

Introducing texts for an anthology is an act of interpretation nurtured by a network of other people. I cannot trace out here the intricacies of that entire network, noting contributions of each colleague, but my place in communities of learning and teaching requires some specific acknowledgments.

I especially thank those who studied in my courses on Paul Tillich. Suspicious as well as appreciative readings were made by Rebecca Brenner, Clarence Carmichael, Charles B. Casper, Mark Cladis, Daniel Dupree, Bill Goldsmith, Galen Guengerich, Brenda Halbrooks, John E. Kelso, Catherine McCullough, John Prager, John Yuu Zhong Qiu, Jeffrey Thompson, Lois Wolff, and many others who journeyed through Tillich's *Systematic Theology* and other writings. Thanks also to Greg Boyd whose able role as teaching assistant made one semester's study a more dialogical endeavor.

Several took time out from their schedule to read my own introductory remarks on Tillich: James Luther Adams, Alexander McKelway, David Mosoma and Peter Paris. I have learned much from each, though surely I have not been able to introduce Tillich in a way that completely accords with their own perspectives. Lowell Livezey and Lois Gehr Livezey made a considerable contribution to this project by giving me the use of their Vermont home for a week of essential preparation.

A number of scholars responded to my request for suggestions about the selections from Tillich's corpus that should be included here: James Luther Adams, Mary Daly, Joseph M. Kitagawa, Victor Nuovo, Peter Paris, Robert P. Scharlemann, Nathan A. Scott, Jr., John E. Smith, Ronald Stone, and Ann Belford Ulanov. I have tried to remain faithful to the suggestions each has offered, but I am acutely aware of how I may have compromised each one of these Tillich scholars' ideals for such an anthology.

Special acknowledgment must go also to institutions: to The University of Chicago Divinity School, whose teachers taught me to appreciate Tillich's work without assuming an uncritical "Tillich school" posture; and to Princeton Theological Seminary, whose gracious provision of a Research Leave in the academic year of 1986-1987 freed up time that went, in part, for work on this collection.

At the Seminary, I received the very able assistance of Joe Herman, who carefully typed the manuscript through its several revisions and whose high caliber, secretarial expertise was invaluable.

A special word of thanks to this series' General Editor, John W. de Gruchy, whose warmth, theological wisdom, and exemplary Christian practice regularly found their way here from South Africa to nurture this book.

While learning from this network of scholars and students, I keep learning also from Anita Kline, whose insights and life remain sources of creative suspicion and strong motivation for the reading of theology.

Mark Kline Taylor
Princeton, New Jersey
March, 1987

# INTRODUCTION

## THE THEOLOGICAL DEVELOPMENT AND CONTRIBUTION OF PAUL TILLICH (1886-1965)

"Hell rages around us. It's unimaginable." Paul Tillich, 28-year-old theologian and German Army chaplain, wrote those words to his father from the trenches of World War I at the battle of Verdun. Even amid his grim despair and breakdowns worked by "the sound of exploding shells, of weeping at open graves, of the sighs of the sick, of the moaning of the dying", Tillich remained both preacher and professor — delivering sermons at the Western front of battle and lectures in front of academics at the University of Halle.[1]* Whether facing bombshells of battle in World War I, political oppression and social chaos after the war, the specter of nuclear warfare after World War II, the threatening character of world capitalist economy, or the deep-running *angst* in personal life — in the face of all these, Tillich sought sustenance for his theology not only from the Christian scriptures and tradition, but also from his culture's art and the literature of Friedrich Nietzsche, Karl Marx, Sigmund Freud and others.

Tillich's writings had power because in them he risked being in touch with the unrepeatable tensions of his present. Our reading and writing about him must likewise risk a view of him through an awareness of the unrepeatable tensions of our own era.

But the very notion of "*our* own era" is problematic. Given the intense plurality of thought, religions, and cultures in our times, to invoke the first person plural is often, at best, to risk misleading generalizations. At worst, it is to exclude others from our conversation and life. When I write here in the plural, the "we" I have in mind are precisely those who know the problems with such writing. There may be many who work within communities that inspire little suspicion about the collective "we". But there are also many of us who see theology as entering an age of increasing consciousness of theologians' locations, whether these be described in terms of gender, class, ethnicity, or of some cultural

* Numbered notes will be found on pp. 337ff.

11

amalgam of those factors. Pragmatic philosophies on both sides of the Atlantic, from Ludwig Wittgenstein to Richard Rorty, reinforce the sense of communal particularity. In these times when women and men are wrestling with the implications for theology of a radically self-locating consciousness, why read Paul Tillich, who for all his talk of concreteness, loved also his ontology, his essence-language, his universals, and a theology of "culture"?

When Tillich's works are studied in my classes, rarely do they receive ready endorsement. Tillich's writing engages the problems of human life, even making specific references to the lives of Central American rural Indians and North American college students, for example, but such references are connected to a demanding philosophical analysis that plunges readers into a world of technical terms. In addition, women, Afro-Americans, and international students bring to Tillich's texts a set of suspicions and issues that Tillich often does not directly address. But rarely does Tillich fail to provoke and equip us in some way for reflecting on, and acting in relation to, the distinctive problems we discern, even if, finally, this may mean rendering negative judgments about Tillich's work.

Not all of the main features of Tillich's theology have been represented in this book. Many other occasional writings of his, which may dramatically display his personal engagement with history and politics, also could not be included. But if the selections found here enable others to be provoked and equipped in some way for Christian theological reflection, then this volume will bear much of the fruit hoped for it.

To this end, I have devoted my Introduction to a sketch of Tillich's intellectual contributions in relation to key developments in his context. After the first section, each subsequent section of the Introduction corresponds to sections of the Tillich material found in the rest of this volume. Within each section, I highlight a particular tension in his thought that has remained salient for theology after Tillich's death and into this last quarter of the twentieth century.

## TILLICH: OF THE BOUNDARIES

The context that formed Tillich's theology may be seen as a set of many places: the geographical places of Germany and the United States; the cultural-historical places of late nineteenth-century imperial Germany, of post-World War I Berlin, of New York City in the decades of the thirties, forties and fifties; the institutional places of the Universities of Breslau, Halle, Berlin, Marburg, Leipzig, Frankfurt, Union Theological Seminary in New York, Harvard University and the University of Chicago. There are the city places and the country places, the manor places of the well-to-do, and proletarian places of workers in Berlin's Moabit district. There were the ecclesial spaces and the scientific spaces, the places philosophical and theological. His context included the political spaces of socialist rallies, and the intellectual ones in wood-paneled halls of academe.

Tillich's writing was formed and nurtured by tensions arising from such varied contexts. After Tillich emigrated from Germany to the United States, he introduced himself to his American public with an autobiographical statement entitled *On the Boundary*. That work was actually his commentary on at least twelve different boundaries that he experienced (between two temperaments, between social classes, between theory and practice, between reality and imagination, *et al.*). The title of this book, then, features the plural term, "boundaries". Further, I have chosen to characterize Tillich as "of" these boundaries rather than "on" them, in part because the latter often can suggest staying uninvolved on a boundary line or with a foot in each camp. Tillich was a theologian "of the boundaries" in the sense of one whose life and thought were derived from experiences of the boundaries. He was engaged with the boundaries and stood *in* them to speak to others who may or may not have shared his kind of experience. Tillich was also a theologian "of the boundaries" in the sense of one who reflected *about* boundary experiences, as when he drew on Hebrew narratives about Abraham to illumine the boundary-crossing life of all emigrants, or when he fashioned a view of God related to experience of the infinite in the boundaries of human life.

Tillich's life-journey through and between so many diverse places began with his birth in 1886 in Starzeddel, Germany (now part of Poland). His father, a leading Lutheran pastor and superintendent, was a Prussian father who cut an authoritarian figure and who, as Tillich recalls, "heightened consciousness of duty and sin". Less is known about his mother. Though she has been characterized as "inflexible" and a "Calvinist", Tillich adored her and later wrote how he received from her elements of a temperament different from that received from his father. From her came a "zest for life, love of the concrete, mobility, rationality, and democracy".[2]

Eight years elapsed between the time of Tillich's beginning his theological studies at the age of 18, and the time of his ordination in his twenty-sixth year in the Evangelical Church of the Prussian Union in Berlin. During these eight years he not only completed three years of academic theological study, he also wrote his first dissertation on F.W.J. von Schelling and submitted it to the University of Breslau to receive the degree of Doctor of Philosophy at the age of 24. His second Schelling dissertation enabled his being awarded the Licentiate in Theology, then the highest theological degree that could be earned in Germany. During this time he received ministerial training of several forms: eight months of pastoral work and occasional preaching in a rural town near Berlin, a full year in another training school for preachers, a short vicarage in a Berlin suburb.

The strong interest in Schelling, which was never to leave him, was especially nurtured in him by one of his teachers at the University of Halle, Fritz Medicus. From Schelling, Tillich developed his own vision of a "Christian philosophy of existence", in which both philosophical and theological impulses would find distinctive place and enrich one another in Christian thought.[3] Such a vision even permeated his early years of ministry when, just after ordination in his twenty-sixth year, Tillich sought to communicate the Christian message to the poor of the Moabit workers' district in Berlin. Tillich found the traditional languages of church and theology not sufficient to convey the meaning of Christian terms, even those as familiar as "faith".[4] Both Schelling's vision and also what Tillich saw to be the demands of ministry would nurture in him a lifelong "apologetic" concern, i.e. a concern to render the Christian message in new terms that effectively convey its meaning.

Another teacher, indeed the most influential, was Martin Kähler, who confirmed in him the impulses to develop a theology that would mediate between ecclesiastical belief and the claims of reason and experience. Through Kähler's influence, Tillich may be seen as one who in his own ways continued the perspectives of nineteenth century "theologies of mediation" — a phrase referring to diverse attempts by theologians to link Christian faith with emerging worldviews of nineteenth century life.[5] But Kähler also conveyed to Tillich a suspicion of mediation efforts, especially those which merely baptized cultural forms with Christianity or those which compromised Christianity's distinctive message. Tillich received from Kähler, then, a more profound, albeit emphatic, impetus to formulate a theological perspective mediating between theology and forms of cultural existence. Certain doctrines elaborated by Kähler, especially the Pauline-Lutheran idea of justification and his christology, also were influential on Tillich because of their special power to mediate between Christian faith and cultural experience.

But Tillich's greatest teacher was his life-journey; and beginning in 1914, after his ordination and early ministries in Berlin, that journey was to bring some hard lessons. Already, along the way of his education and early ministry, some had been learned. Compared with the journey that lay ahead of him, this period seems to have been one of "dreaming innocence"; but there were important struggles and anxieties set in motion during these years.

His very day of birth was a precarious one, as he lay in a death struggle then for nearly seven hours, subjecting his parents to both despair and hope. After his mother died of cancer in his seventeenth year, he repressed her death and would not speak of her to anyone. The Paucks write, "he sought her ever after in every Demeter or Persephone he pursued. He continued to worship her by transferring his love to the sea and to the sun."[6] Tillich's biographers are not all of the same mind on this matter, but her repressed early death was one of many factors contributing to an erotic lifestyle that left his spouse, closest friends and others, writing about it long after his death.[7] The early tensions in Tillich's relationship with his father intensified until he wielded the very philosophy his father had taught him to love against the authoritarian pressure his father held over him.[8]

In January 1914, Tillich's late-blooming emotional life issued in a serious love for Margarethe Wever whom he married. But the year of 1914 was not a happy one for anyone to begin a career, a marriage or a family. World War I would constitute a major turning point in Tillich's life — according to his biographers, the "first, last, and only one."[9] Passing through the boundary experience of this war, Tillich would emerge a very changed man.


## THE STRUGGLE FOR A NEW THEONOMY*

The first two selections in this volume are taken from the years just following the end of World War I. Tillich had been no exception to the many young German men who with nationalistic fervor went off to fight

* For texts, see below pp. 35ff.

the Kaiser's war. Tillich went as a chaplain, serving in the trenches at the front lines where once he was stationed for six months. He was celebrant of Christian worship and retriever of his dying and wounded friends in battle — both pastor and gravedigger. He had at first displayed occasional bravado, but later knew the grimness, resignation and despair that I cited at the outset of this Introduction. Though his nerves gave out more than once, he was awarded the Iron Cross.

Much later, Tillich would portray his experience of the eclipse of civilization in World War I as his "personal *kairos*", meaning that it was "the right time" for the breaking into his life of something new. His intense suffering in the face of battle-deaths was a brokenness seen as ripeness for renewal and action. In his personal life, postwar turbulence meant coping with a wife who left him through an affair with his friend, and then his own entry into what he termed his nonconformist, "Bohemian" lifestyle. Postwar Berlin was a period of experiment, struggle and creativity in almost every facet of existence — personal, sexual, social, economic, political. Tillich was steeped in this milieu, as was Hannah Werner Gottschow whom he met during this time and married in 1924.

Amid all the turbulence, his intellectual vitality persisted. He had worked on lectures and studied art even in the trenches. He emerged amid all the postwar chaos with his determination to be a professor still fiercely intact, though now more intensely directed toward the issues of his day.

It is in his writing at this time that a first significant tension can be indentified: *a tension between being a theologian of culture and being a church theologian.* Tillich's earliest work was marked, on the one hand, by use of his philosophical and theological skills for analysis of a general cultural community. But this early work also featured Tillich's need to speak and write as the ordained minister and chaplain he had become, responding out of his particular church community. Tillich could not give up the demands incumbent upon a theologian of culture to address a whole capital city in the aftermath of war — its people nervous and hungry, its streets filled with beggars and cripples, citizens expecting or debating new political forms. Nor could he overlook the demand that he acknowledge how his theological response to the general culture had its place of origin and nurture in the church. Being a theologian of culture meant using terms drawn from the public he addressed, and risked loss of the distinctive concerns of the church community. Being a church theologian meant using the distinctive narratives, doctrines, practices of his tradition and risked a kind of specificity that is often an obstacle to the church theologian's ability to communicate with the wider society. Amid this tension, with its dual commitment and distinctive risks, Tillich faced the challenge of developing a new theological language that would address clearly the urgencies of the general culture and yet remain faithful to Christian church communities. Like another Berliner before him, the theologian Friedrich Schleiermacher, Tillich sought to address both church and culture, though he was perhaps less interested than was Schleiermacher in defending religion against its "cultured despisers."[10]

At the center of his search for a new theological language was his struggle for "theonomy", a term that can be understood in light of this tension. Tillich claimed that the church had often imposed on its culture a damaging "heteronomy", i.e. a set of alien laws and languages that violate the dynamics and structures proper to human life. Against that kind of heteronomy, Tillich discerned the frequent, often-justifiable, will to "autonomy", i.e. a culture's celebration of itself, of its own structures and dynamics, against all imposed, alienating laws. Because both heteronomy and autonomy can destroy cultural life, Tillich pointed beyond them both toward a "theonomy", a realm in which the structures and dynamics of culture are allowed to be themselves but as transformed and fulfilled in the divine life, in a religious experience of the unconditioned. According to Tillich, the structures imposing "heteronomy" and the champions of "autonomy" were both responsible for unleashing the destructive forces that had worked the end of the European civilization and ushered in the chaos of the war's aftermath. In this situation, Tillich as a church theologian not only felt it necessary to write theology for the church, but also theology of and for the general culture — thus struggling with it toward a new "theonomy", toward a religio-cultural situation in which the human forms of culture are pervaded by a religious meaning.

The tension between a theology of culture and church theology is still salient for theology in the late twentieth century. Since Tillich's death, there has developed a renewed sense of both the necessity and the risks of a "theology of culture" that seeks to relate the church theologian's tradition to categories drawn from philosophy, literature, science or other disciplines. North American theologians have used for their theologies of culture a hermeneutical phenomenology (David Tracy, Sallie McFague),[11] process thought (John Cobb),[12] general philosophy of science (Langdon Gilkey),[13] feminist theories of gender and culture (Rosemary Radford Ruether)[14] or various social sciences (Gregory Baum, Gustavo Gutierrez).[15] In Germany, Wolfhart Pannenberg's theology is probably the clearest example of a theologian using concepts drawn from a wide range of natural and human sciences in order to discern a religious dimension to which theological concepts are then related.[16]

However many may be such cultural-theological analyses, other voices continue to remind theologians of the risks attending such efforts. On the North American scene especially, theologians such as Hans Frei, George Lindbeck, and the theologian and ethicist Stanley Hauerwas, warn how easily a sense of Christianity's distinctive narrative text and cultural-linguistic tradition can be lost when theologians give themselves to use of extra-biblical or non-theological categories for linking Christian theologies to their cultures.[17] These Americans voice suspicions similar to those articulated in Tillich's own day by Karl Barth, who not only uttered his resounding "Nein!" to natural theology, but also registered his profound suspicion of endeavors in a "theology of culture". These "church theologians" are just as committed to addressing their culture as are the "theologians of culture", but they insist that the address is more effective and faithful to Christian faith when it proceeds from the distinctive text, belief and practice of the church rather than when it proceeds from or in tandem with various kinds of cultural analysis.

In the aftermath of World War I, then, for a society in personal and social upheaval, Tillich launched a theological project that sought a place for both theology-of-culture analyses and for church theology. He dwelled in that tension, affirmed the need for both exercises, and pursued both throughout his career. For those theologians who still dwell in this tension Tillich's successes and failures at both theological efforts may be instructive.

## PROTESTANT THEOLOGY AMID SOCIALIST CRISIS*

With the selections in the second part of this volume, we do not really move into a new period of Tillich's life, for he remained very much the young scholar seeking to consolidate his postwar, academic career. As he worked toward full professorship in the German academic world,

* For texts, see below pp. 67ff.

however, Tillich moved beyond programmatic pieces like "On the Idea of a Theology of Culture" and "Basic Principles of Religious Socialism" by deepening and extending his vision of a distinctively *Protestant* faith and theology.

Especially while serving as professor of philosophy and religious studies at the Dresden Institute of Technology, Tillich developed essays on Protestantism that clarified its distinctive traits: its attitude of "self-transcending realism", its "historical realism", its emphasis on "the Word" with a strong sacramental sense. Tillich also maintained this Protestant theology's connection to Religious Socialism, further elaborating that notion in his 1932 book, *The Socialist Decision* (New York: Harper & Row, 1977).

At the same time that Tillich was fashioning a Protestantism related to Religious Socialism, he had to dissociate himself from National-Socialism. Ultimately, the conflict with the Nazis made him a target and they banned *The Socialist Decision.* Tillich lost a later professorship at the University of Frankfurt, where as Dean he publicly defended left-wing and Jewish students while demanding the expulsion of Nazi students causing violence on campus. As affairs worsened, Tillich decided he could not even work effectively in Germany by going underground. After much vacillation, he therefore emigrated to the United States, accepting an invitation conveyed by Reinhold Niebuhr in 1933 to teach at Union Theological Seminary and Columbia University in New York City.

The tension that is distinctive from this period of his writings is *the tension between Protestant theology's affirmation of socialism, on the one hand, and its critique of it, on the other.* The socialism Tillich advocated was a "theonomous" one, i.e. one in which socialist political forms were rooted in a religious substance characterized by an experience of the unconditioned. Using both Karl Marx and the early Christian prophetic tradition, Tillich was devoted to "uncovering the element of faith in socialism and making it explicit." This uncovering of the faith dimension of socialism was crucial, Tillich believed, to resolving its own inner conflicts.[18]

Tillich was not the only theologian in this period to stand in the tension between theological affirmation of socialist vision and the theological critique of it. Karl Barth, especially in his early writings but also later, identified and highlighted areas of mutual concern between the very different socialist and church communities.[19] Dietrich Bonhoeffer, though critical of Tillich's Religious Socialism, also tried to articulate "the 'affinity' between socialism and the Christian idea of community."[20] Reinhold Niebuhr, in the United States, developed a theological anthropology that nurtured both affirmation and critique of socialist projects.[21] Further, these theologians were hardly the first to take on the tension. As the industrial revolution had left its marks everywhere by the end of the nineteenth century, "social gospels" and diverse movements responded to the new kinds of alienation in workers' lives by calling forth theological efforts in Britain, Germany and the United States.[22]

The clash of Tillich's Religious Socialism with the Nazis and with Christians who would lend support to the ideology, is clearly and succinctly formulated in the "Ten Theses" which conclude Tillich's writings in this book's second part. They are not simply condemnations of Nazi evil; they are also an expression of the Protestant theology, philosophical anthropology and Religious Socialism that Tillich formed in his earlier writings. It is in this political context also that Paul Tillich's theological disagreement with Karl Barth can be grasped. Karl Barth also helped formulate vigorous opposition to the Nazi regime. Tillich always felt, however, that this was done by Barth and his supporters from the vantage point of a "supranaturalist" theology that arrived on the scene too late and had not been working, as had his Religious Socialist effort, at laying long-term conditions for genuine and fulfilling socialist practice.[23] Tillich's essay, "What is Wrong with the 'Dialectic' Theology", is one of his more succinct yet appreciative critiques of Barth.

There are in Tillich's writings no ready resolutions for present theological efforts to both affirm and criticize contemporary socialist practice. But Tillich did set himself with full seriousness in that tension, and in that way the tension he faced may be a salient one for current reflection. He minced no words in advocating, as a Christian and as a theologian, the need to say Yes to socialist vision and practice, Yes to Marx, and Yes to the needs of the proletariat suffering from what he termed the "Leviathan" of capitalist economy.[24] But he also knew when to say No to socialism's demonic distortions, No to any uncritical allegiance to it, No to its tyrannical forms. In Tillich's struggle to utter an informed and elaborate Yes and No, contemporary theologians find one important example for forging their own stances in church and theology.[25]

The tension is clearly salient for a number of current Christian thinkers whose reflections on it are well under way and will no doubt continue throughout this century. Some Christian thinkers tend to opt out of the tension by uttering an evermore extensive No to the socialist vision.[26] Many more of them are wrestling to say a Yes to socialist vision and practice in the face of the complex, international apparatus that capitalism has erected. Many of these do so out of new social and political experiences of being the church. Most notably, the *communidades de bases* throughout Latin America, forged for survival in regions of suffering, giving rise to socialist dreaming and practice. Theologians speaking from these communities, such as Gustavo Gutierrez, affirm the socialist vision but also proclaim that their affirmation is sustained by a Christian religious faith that is able to generate prophetic critique of socialism.[27]

Other theologians working in close contact with alienated and oppressed groups also dwell in this creative tension. James Cone and Cornel West do so in connection with the aspirations of Afro-American groups,[28] Rosemary Radford Ruether from experience of diverse groups of women suffering in patriarchal systems, and a number of North Atlantic theologians, male and female, who say Yes and No by sifting through the Western Marxisms of Lukacs, Gramsci, Goldmann, or Habermas.[29] Each in their own way forge new Christian approaches to socialist visions. Where Tillich saw the socialist vision being dreamed, he saw real signs, albeit fragmentary ones, of the fulfillment of the kingdom of God.

## IN THE SACRED VOID: BEING AND GOD*

Our next set of writings begins in the aftermath of another war, World War II. After Tillich's emigration to the United States, he gave himself to study of the English language and extensive travel throughout North America and occasionally to Europe. His writing in the periods before and during the Second World War took up a whole range of subjects: German emigration, the church and economic order, churches in wartime, postwar reconstruction, as well as theological issues like the historical Jesus, faith, the idea of a personal God, existentialism and the Christian message.

The first selection here, "Religion and Secular Culture", is a noteworthy autobiographical piece, displaying what several writers have

* For texts, see below pp. 119ff.

called a shift by Tillich away from concrete Religious Socialist analyses to general existentialist theology.[30] More accurately, it is Tillich's attempt to focus on what, given the postwar, world-political situation, he considered to be the pervasive existential trauma. Perhaps his writings of this period turn away from concrete Religious Socialist analyses because of the difficulty of mastering the political situation in the United States. That, however, can only be a partial explanation. Tillich felt that the culture demanding theological address was one now haunted by a dramatic existential void or vacuum. In that situation, the challenge for a theologian of culture was both to identify that void as a potential source of new demonic eruptions, but also to interpret its sacred possibilities.

Moreover, this was not only the task of a theologian of culture. It was also Tillich's task as a church theologian. Tillich, therefore, further presented a theological "method of correlation" by which essential symbols of Christian tradition could be correlated with human being and existence. The method of correlation can be misunderstood as one that in all too sanguine a fashion seeks "similarities" between the Christian message and the human situation. Actually, as Tillich himself stressed, the method is "a genuine pragmatism that refuses to close any door" and, hence, may heighten awareness of radical dissimilarity between Christian message and human situations. Tillich's method of correlation has remained one of his most influential notions in twentieth-century theology, evident in theologians of different persuasions: David Tracy, Rosemary Radford Ruether, Hans Küng, Edward Schillebeeckx, George Lindbeck.[31] This method was refined and practiced in his highly acclaimed, first volume of *Systematic Theology*, which articulated his fundamental approaches to religious thought and theology. Central to this volume is his presentation of a doctrine of God correlated with the structures of human being — a being always in tension and in anxiety, threatened by nonbeing but finding courage and wholeness, a "courage to be", in God.

The God Tillich presented for humans who sensed the void, who knew "the shock of nonbeing", was dramatically formulated. As he stressed time and again, God was not *a* being, but "Being-Itself" or "the power of Being". And with this stress there emerges in Tillich's writing *another distinctive tension, between the immanence and transcendence of God.* To understand Tillich's treatment of this tension, one really needs to work through his complete doctrine of God. Tillich is not unusual in the history of the Christian tradition in highlighting that God is immanent "as well as" transcendent. But his ways of interpreting these two classic spatial metaphors for relating God and world were controversial for many. This was due to the radically immanental themes that Tillich played out in his doctrine. Everything finite (natural, social and personal) according to Tillich, participates in Being-Itself, in God. While Tillich also stressed that God as the power of being transcends every being and the totality of beings (the world), his transcending God was in fundamental tension with many traditional theisms. Indeed, he was aware of this, affirming atheism's protest againt God as "a highest being" and speaking of his doctrine of God as pointing toward a "God beyond the God of theism".[32] Tillich's understanding of transcendence was so thoroughly immanental that many remained perplexed about his meaning of God's "otherness" or "transcendence".

Tillich's doctrine of God, as Malcolm Diamond so well points out, tends to give short shrift to the complexities of theistic discussions.[33] Tillich was convinced, though, that no amount of talk about God's caring for finite existence was effective or healing so long as God was conceived as "a Supreme Being" occupying the highest realm of a hierarchically structured cosmos. His own faith, as well as the intellectual challenges to classic belief in God posed by Immanuel Kant and masters of suspicion like Karl Marx, Sigmund Freud and Friedrich Nietzsche, led him to risk tracing out God's transcendence so deep in the fabric of existence (at times, even in the abyss) that the meaning of "transcendence" was stretched beyond recognition.

This tension is again a salient one in our time. As Christian communities confront the profanations of history and nature, the faithful are driven beyond both history and nature to seek diverse experiences of divine transcendence. When we recall the profanations of history and nature in the violation of Native American land and culture, of Africans brought in slavery to the Americas, of Jews at Auschwitz, of women's bodies and lives in patriarchal societies, of the ecosystem, indeed of all life trembling in this nuclearist era, then and especially then do our religious quests for transcendence seem vital. History and nature seem to be failing us, or we are failing them. Late twentieth century religious revitalizations of many kinds testify to the hunger for transcendence, even if this is only an affirmation of mysteries beyond history and nature.

At the same time, it must be stressed that these impulses to transcendence also stimulate a renewed and radical sense of divine immanence. When lands, bodies, cultures, whole peoples, and life itself, are threatened or violated, then these tangible realities are often intensely revalued. They become laden with sacredness. Nowhere does this seem more dramatic than in the feminist movements and theologies of our day. In resisting the patriarchal systems that engender the physical abuse of women's bodies, that isolate women from one another, that silence women's voices, feminist spiritualities rarely turn to a higher deity to find a "transcendence" of the brokenness forced upon women. Instead, in a radically immanental way, they affirm the sacred *in* the created and very human realm: in the many dimensions of their bodiliness, in their coming together as women, in their coming to speech.[34] Whether we note feminist spiritualities, or Native Americans' revaluation of land and culture, Jews' intensification of their sense of land, the poor gaining needed life-sustaining goods — in all these, we can see how drives to transcend the profanations of nature and history often entail radically immanental spiritualities.

There have been and will remain many ways to interpret the immanence and transcendence of God. Tillich's own form of immanental transcendence will surely not satisfy all who struggle with these themes. Feminists, in particular, may resonate with Tillich's immanental turn and critique of a one-sided male-determined symbolism in Christianity,[35] but often view his dichotomizing, polar tensions and talk of penetrating to the dimension of depth, as modes of phallocentric discourse.[36] Whatever the criticism, the tension here, in which Tillich dwelled, may remain salient for many in our time.

## AMID STRUCTURES OF DESTRUCTION:
## CHRIST AS NEW BEING*

Tillich's writings in this section are all drawn from volume 2 of his *Systematic Theology* (1963). It is in this volume that he presented his theology of the brokenness of human existence, of the human quest for Christ and then of Christ as New Being. After a selection on the links between existentialism and theology, additional readings display his approaches to the doctrines of sin and evil and of the Christ.

In both the doctrine of sin and evil, and also in his doctrine of Christ, there is a distinctive tension that has always accompanied Christian thought, but which Tillich's work handled in striking ways. *It is a tension between historicist and presentist interpretations of these doctrines.*

* For texts, see below pp. 186ff.

Historicist impulses tend to stress views of the fall, sin, evil, and of Jesus Christ in terms of historical events and persons. Indeed, a Christian theology that takes its cues from the temporal sequence of its scriptural narratives cannot help but heed the historicist impulse and, thereby, speak of sin and evil as acts by responsible agents of history, and of Jesus the Christ as an active historical subject. Interpreting the force or effect of these events and figures of history for present life has not been easy. Historicist approaches to sin and evil will refer to a historical event of disobedience and fall that issues in a train of similar disobediences and false-turnings that continue into the present human situation. In christology, historicist impulses often emphasize the historical deeds, words and attitudes of Jesus. Methodologically, these impulses are evident in biblical scholars' "quest" or "new quest" for the historical Jesus, or in the various contemporary attempts to display Jesus' personality, consciousness and actions.

What I am terming "presentist" impulses move interpretation of sin, evil, and of Jesus the Christ, toward focus on Christian believers in their present situation. Certain historicist impulses in methods may here be preserved, but the emphasis is on the present meaning and meaningfulness of the doctrines. Sin and evil, therefore, whatever we may say about historical origins and development in a history of responsible human agents, are valued as ways for speaking of aspects of contemporary experience. Schleiermacher's doctrine of sin is an example. "*Original* sin", for him, refers not so much to historical "origins", during which responsible agents departed from a state of innocence and so inaugurated the train of evil extending into the present; rather, it refers more to "origins" as the deep wellsprings of human life or as fundamental qualities of human existence.[37] Presentist readings of a doctrine of "original sin" will stress less a "first fall" of humans in history and more the "universal fallenness" operative in the structures of human being and action from the very beginning and in every moment. In christology, presentist approaches focus less on the historical Jesus constructed by historians' research, and more on this Jesus as received in the present faith of the community of Christians.

Tillich located himself within the tension between historicist and presentist impulses, but with what many have read as a leaning toward the presentist side. In his doctrines of sin and evil, for example, Tillich did not deny the historicist sensitivity to the biblical depiction of sin as a fall of responsible human moral agents. This was, as he called it, "the moral element" in the doctrine of sin and evil that must be emphasized.

But his distinctive and controversial claim was that there is also a "tragic element". Based on his presentist reading of the doctrine, highlighting a universal sinfulness etched into the very structure of actualized humanity, human sinfulness is tragically inevitable. Hence it is not sufficient to say that sin and evil are only due to human moral responsibility. Tragically, they must be seen as just being there, as well as involving human will. Tillich's sensitivity to existentialist analyses made him highly conscious of this tragic element in personal, social and political realms.[38]

In Tillich's christology, the historicist/presentist tension is clear, again with a marked emphasis on the presentist aspect. This is evident in his claim that "Jesus Christ" is an event with both historicist and presentist sides. In his terms, Jesus the Christ is "both fact and reception"; not only the Jesus of history witnessed to by the Bible and of which historical scholars may provide us a glimpse, but also the Jesus who was received as the Christ by believers. It is the unity of fact and reception by believers that has created Christianity and from which christology is built. Ultimately, for Tillich, this meant that completion of his own christology could not begin until he took up an ecclesiology, a theological interpretation of concrete group life in the Christian communities which take Jesus as the Christ. ". . . Christ would not be the Christ without those who receive him as the Christ."[39]

Tillich's unique way of fusing historicist and presentist impulses in christology may be seen in the way he refers to the biblical witness as a work of art, as an expressionist portrait of Jesus. In doing so, he relied on what he had long found to be the powers of German expressionist style: both to intimate the concreteness of historical life and also to nourish the deep existential, present concern of its viewers. The "biblical picture of Jesus", understood in this expressionist way, mediated between historicist and presentist sensibilities.[40] While he did not jettison historicist concerns, this approach of his also refused to subordinate the presentist concerns of believers to historicist presentation. Instead he made personal and social concerns of the present intrinsic to the very being of Jesus the Christ whom we know in the Bible's expressionist portrait.

In our late twentieth century period, the tension between historicist and presentist impulses continues in views of sin and evil and in christology, and may even call for increasing theological cultivation of presentist impulses as we see in Tillich's handling of the tension. Late twentieth century doctrines of sin and evil must be formulated with consciousness of the magnitude of human sin and evil manifest in the holocaust suffered by European Jews in the Nazi period, and in the nuclear holocaust that threatens and is always present to our consciousness. The enslavement of Black men and women, the genocides in a Cambodia, a Guatemala or an Afghanistan are also reminders of the magnitude of human sin and evil, achieving dimensions that defy all Christian theodicies that, in various ways, combine notions of divine permission and human, moral culpability. Those notions will not fall completely by the wayside, but they are now dwarfed by the sheer magnitude and intensity of evil — evil seeming now to be a *mysterium tremendum* for us, as Arthur Cohen has written about the Holocaust.[41] The tragic element of human existence, which Tillich kept to the fore in the presentist aspects of his view of sin and evil, seems an inevitable feature of current theological agendas. Full sensitivity to the immensity of the tragic will require more subtle and comprehensive accounts of the divine presence in history and of the sociohistorical conditions of human moral accountability and evil.

Just as urgent today are the christological forms of the historicist/presentist tension. In North Atlantic regions, historicist impulses flourish in the historical-critical guilds of academies which probe the life and times of Jesus or the "original intentions" of those who wrote about Jesus. Liberationists throughout the world also nurture historicist impulses when they focus on the humanness of Jesus of Nazareth in his social and political contexts.[42] But the Jesus of history today is especially refracted by diverse presentist concerns. Aware as we are in this late twentieth century of the ways a Christian's location (specified in terms of gender, ethnicity, class, culture) inevitably affects historical research and affects Christian life and practice, we have many interpretations of this human Jesus. There is the "Black Messiah" of Albert Cleague, and the carefully formulated considerations of Jesus as Black by Afro-American theologian James Cone and South African theologian and activist, Allan Boesak.[43] There are the recollections of Jesus as Sophia or as Mother, and new suggestions for appropriating these feminist interpretations.[44] Throughout the Third World, there are testimonies to experience of Jesus as the one who lives in solidarity with the socioeconomically disenfranchised. Writings may also focus on "the unacknowledged Christ of Hinduism" or on the "Christ in a Philippine context".[45]

    In these times we find it more difficult to view these refractions of Jesus as simply some people's ideological or personal distortions of the reality of Jesus. Antifoundationalist and antiessentialist reflections sow in us suspicions of our own or anyone's powers to go behind cultural and personal appropriations to some essential or foundational reality and, hence, these diverse ways of locating Jesus in our cultural-historical present impose themselves on us with their own integrity and seriousness. Tillich's work, as he himself admitted, did not study the Christ symbol in its many possible, local refractions, but he did understand the Christ symbol as having its reality because of the nature of its present, concrete "reception", as well as because of the historical "fact" of Jesus' life in history and society. If it is true that "Christ would not be the Christ without those who receive him as the Christ", then christology becomes what Tillich calls a "function of soteriology",[46] i.e. a function of the experiences of those who experience healing in the spiritual community that develops after Jesus and on into our present. In his insistence on cultivating these presentist elements as well as historicist impulses in christology, Tillich foreshadows an important theological agenda that is still being formulated.

## AMONG THE AMBIGUITIES OF LIFE: SPIRIT AND THE CHURCHES*

The readings in this section of the book are all taken from volume 3 of *Systematic Theology* (1963). Tillich's renown increased measurably in the time following his retirement from Union Theological Seminary in 1955 and during the years when the final two volumes of *Systematic Theology* appeared in 1957 and 1963. Tillich retired in 1962 from an appointment on the Harvard University faculty and accepted a position in The Divinity School at the University of Chicago. During this period, too, the first volume of his *Gesammelte Werke* was published, he made visits to Greece and Japan, and received the Peace Prize at the German Publisher's Association in Frankfurt (1962).

The theological public in the United States, already aware of Tillich through several small books in addition to the *Systematic Theology*, received also a collection of his essays in a book entitled *Theology of Culture* (1959). In 1963, he published his thinking on *Christianity in the Encounter of World Religions*. In addition, Tillich was writing for a wide array of periodicals on a diverse set of topics. He wrote essays not only in

---

* For texts, see below pp. 223ff.

many church periodicals and theological journals, but also in journals of psychotherapy, art and architecture, dance, philosophy, social work, Asian cultural studies. Essays or interviews appeared in such popular literature as *The Saturday Evening Post, Esquire,* and *Glamour.* Topics he addressed included pastoral care, space exploration, science and theology, American culture, the theology of ministry, the demonic, religious socialism, art, the nuclear dilemma, birth control, Japanese religion, Protestant architecture.

In 1963, he was the main speaker at *Time* magazine's 40th anniversary dinner. Tillich spoke before the audience of 284 personalities of past *Time* cover stories. His address, occurring between an invocation by Francis Cardinal Spellman and a benediction by President Henry van Dusen of Union Theological Seminary, and delivered while standing near to Adlai Stevenson and Douglas MacArthur, was entitled "The Ambiguity of Perfection". In it he stressed themes central to the third volume of his *Systematic Theology:* the persistent ambiguities of human life, the "inseparable mixture of good and evil, of creative and destructive forces" in individual and social life. His biographers, Wilhelm Pauck and Marion Pauck, summarized the way his own comments on the ambiguities of life applied to his own career at this stage of fame:

> He was aware that his belated fame was itself ambiguous, an inseparable mixture of good and evil, of creative and destructive forces. The capitalist society which he characterized as lacking in depth was the same society that had enabled him to reap unusual and manifold benefits, the very epitome of which was his appearance at the *Time* dinner. As if unaware of all he had said on many occasions about the crisis of capitalism and bourgeois culture, the avowed religious socialist willingly mingled with the wealthy, influential men who represented this civilization, accepting their applause and favors.[47]

Volume 3 of the *Systematic Theology,* which appeared when Tillich's fame was at its height, has as its central theme the ambiguities of life in relation to the divine Spirit. In the third volume, Tillich developed new ideas in terms of the structures discussed in the previous two volumes, and also brought to fulfillment the themes set out in Volumes 1 and 2. Volume 3 not only offers his doctrines of divine spirit, of the Kingdom of God, and of Eternal Life, it is also the culmination of his doctrine of God and his christology. It is easy to lose sight of the place of the third volume within the whole of Tillich's *Systematic Theology* because of its many commentaries on issues ranging from subatomic particles in life's "inorganic dimensions" to church functions of worship, prayer, missions, education and evangelism; to empire-building and atomic warfare.

I have edited the third volume so as to highlight a tension that pervades the entire volume's treatment of life's ambiguities and their relation to the divine Spirit. *It is the tension between structure and ecstasy.* Tillich developed a notion of the divine Spirit that highlighted its presence in accord with, and as fulfillment of, the structures of human being. Not surprisingly, then, he articulates his notions of *what* the Spirit does in terms of certain structural "functions of life" that bring healing to the elemental polarities of being he set out in volume one, and then described as torn asunder in volume two. The Spirit does not disrupt these structural functions, but grounds and heals them. Personal, social, political, ecclesial structures of human formation are, therefore, intrinsic to experience of the divine spirit.

Tillich insists just as strongly, however, against ecclesiasticism or any other absolutizing of structures, that ecstasy is just as intrinsic to Christian experience of Spirit. "This whole part of the present system is a defense of the ecstatic manifestation of the Spiritual Presence against its ecclesiastical critics; in this defense, the whole New Testament is the most powerful weapon."[48] "Ecstasy" in life's structures is another way of formulating "self-transcendence", "the drive toward the infinite" or the "ultimate concern" that Tillich sees as immanent to all being and process. In each structured function of life, and while commenting on a host of ambiguities, Tillich charts his way toward a Christian spiritual experience that affirms structure without becoming structuralist, and that yields to ecstasy without succumbing to the destructiveness of mere frenzy.

This tension is also salient not because of the banal counsel that our lives need both structure and also a certain flexibility. More significantly, we can observe that many in our time reflect on contemporary crises out of a double-consciousness of late twentieth century failures. On the one hand, many cite the failures of our structures — bureaucratic, sociopolitical, economic, technological. To be sure, these failures are ambiguous. Tillich was highly conscious of that, acknowledging the gains in communication, world peace, standards of health and increased wealth that have come with the elaboration and extension of those structures. But the sense of failure is intense, especially for the many who do not benefit from the flow of human goods through those structures, and for many others — doctors of medicine and nuclear physicists among them — who lament the possiblity of species' destruction that is bound up with our structural achievements.[49]

On the other hand, there is also consciousness of the destruction and alienations worked by antistructural enthusiasms, evident to those who must dwell in societies of permanent revolution and who thus hunger for a life-nourishing structure whether it be brought by "rightist" or "leftist" groups; evident in those whose personal life fails to endure in connection with others due to personal ecstasy become individualist arbitrariness, or (perhaps, a very powerful symbol in the United States) evident in the deaths at Jonestown where antiecclesial and antistructural religious enthusiasm united with loss of human life. Again, a consciousness of these enthusiasms as somehow "failure" is itself ambiguous; for, revolution, individual expression (even abandon), and distinctively religious enthusiasms are essential to personal and social life. Though such ambiguity persists, we are often as conscious of the failures of antistructural ecstasies as we are of the failures of late twentieth century structures.

What is needed is what Tillich sought in the third volume: analyses of human personal and social life that present a view of its essential structures while also discerning and affirming the essential, untameable dimension (ecstasy) through which those structures are fulfilled. This is far more complex a task than merely combining structure and ecstasy in some sort of "balance". Tillich saw it as a task that presupposed the ontology and existentialist analysis of the previous volumes, and then the more intricate phenomonology of personal, group and historical life attempted in this third volume. Where structure and ecstasy united, there is to be found the realm where the divine Spirit thrives, and it is there that, for Tillich, God works through the communities and churches that mediate the New Being of Jesus the Christ.

## IN THE END: REVISIONING AND HOPE*

Into the last year of his life Tillich's work attracted vigorous criticism as well as the tribute that had brought fame. His biographers report that in public he accepted the criticism with grace, but in private was irritated at the "ignorance and nonunderstanding" revealed in the criticisms.[50]

* For texts, see below pp. 312ff.

Nevertheless, his genius for friendship and a certain childlike playfulness remained unspoiled in him. Concerning his written work, this playfulness found its counterpart in a willingness to be open to revisioning his own thought and work. Amid the risk and openness that such revisioning involved, Tillich never relinquished his "right to hope" — a hope, as the sermon at the close of this book displays, nourishing his sense of the Eternal ever unfolding in the here and now.

His openness and hope is especially evident in his last public lecture, given at the University of Chicago in 1965, and included here, "The Significance of the History of Religions for the Systematic Theologian." In the early morning hours after the lecture he was taken to a hospital for heart failure, and he died there ten days later on October 22, 1965. Referring to this last lecture and to the way Tillich had participated in a History of Religions seminar with him, the renowned historian of religions Mircea Eliade remarked: "Paul Tillich did not die at the end of his career . . . he died at the beginning of another renewal of his thought."[51] The openness that marked his increasing study of other religions and cultural forms did not signal any diminishing of his commitment as a Christian theologian. But that openness did intensify a final noteworthy tension in his thought that has remained salient long after Tillich's death. *This tension is one between pluralism and commitment*; between "pluralism" as the affirmation of the enriching facts of cultural and religious plurality, and "commitment" as a clear advocacy of the distinctive symbols and perspectives of the Christian tradition centered in Jesus the Christ. This tension is evident from the beginning of Tillich's career. In several of his early essays and in his *Systematic Theology*, for example, he formulated various typologies of religions in relation to his discussion of Christian faith and doctrine.[52] In addition, he had addressed the issue in his book *Christianity and the Encounter of World Religions* (1963).

But in the last lecture he anticipates the need for a more intensive revisioning. Here, he acknowledges (with a note of "self-accusation") the particularity of his own systematic theological effort, appealing as it did largely to a North Atlantic, theological culture conscious of scientific and philosophical criticisms of Christianity. As early as 1952, John Herman Randall, Jr. suggested that Tillich's readers inquire into the "cultural conditions" in which Tillich assumes our lives dwell. Randall suggested that the "ontological anxiety of finitude", which underlies so much of Tillich's theology in Volumes 1 and 2, primarily expressed "the way many Continental Europeans feel these days".[53] The Tillich of this final lecture, if not readily admitting the truth of this particular suspicion, most surely acknowledged the culturally conditioned character of his own, indeed of all, theology. He hoped now for an "emphasis on the particular" in future systematic theology, so that the religious symbols developed in theology would appear as having their "roots in the totality of human experience, including local surroundings, in all their ramifications, both political and economic."[54]

Eliade reported that in his seminars Tillich welcomed the strangeness of other cultural religious forms, studied in all their locality. He welcomed also the opportunity, as he had before, to be in dialogue with other traditions and religions. We do not know the precise forms Tillich's theological response to religious and cultural plurality might have taken, i.e. what it would have meant for him to formulate a systematic theology highly conscious of the local surroundings in which religious symbols thrive. We do know that this affirmation of plurality, for Tillich, required not a lessening of Christian commitment, but in fact an intensification of a christological approach. In particular, this approach would take the event of the cross as the criterion for Christian participation in dialogue with and in affirmation of others. In that event Tillich saw a negation of all demonic or absolutistic claims — be they made by Christians or by others. In the dialogues that have been published, we can note Tillich not compromising his hope for this Christian criterion, however much he was committed to the give and take of dialogical conversation.[55]

There could hardly be a more salient tension for Christian theologians in the late twentieth century than that between pluralism and commitment. It is one that is shared by many North Atlantic theologians whose theologies are variously characterized as liberal, evangelical, postliberal, revisionist.[56] Among Christian liberation theologians — whether in North Atlantic or other regions — the tension is also present, as when Afro-American theologians enter into conversations with South African, Latin American and then with feminist theologians, Asian theologians or theologians seeking liberation for gay and lesbian Christians.[57] Though we may justifiably write and talk of our "global village" or "planetary culture", this often makes all the more intense our sense of being particular and our sense of the diversity of religious and cultural forms existing in the global village. Except in the most recalcitrant of absolutistic communities, commitment in all its vitality includes, and exists in tension with, affirmations of plurality. We in this age can hardly avoid being theologians of the global village, who yet speak persuasively to the whole only by acknowledging the local and specific character of our theological discourses.

In our period, the adjectives used for characterizing theology (Feminist, Latin American, Black, White, *et al.*) have been growing both in number and in the complexity of groupings they signal. "Black theology", for example, has become Afro-American, South African, African — indeed Ghanaian or Kenyan; better, Akan or Kikuyu. Latin Americans' theology has likewise grown in a complexity that focuses themes and symbols in terms of local surroundings: writing of Peru, Nicaragua, Guatemala, or more specifically of Mam, Zapotec, or Quechua peoples. Feminist approaches in North America display spiritualities that vary as one moves from the Hispanic feminist reflections of Ada Maria Isasi-Diaz or Delores Huerta,[58] to the Black feminist or womanist writings of Katie G. Cannon and Delores S. Williams,[59] to those feminisms that assign different kinds of emphasis to a "lesbian aesthetic" in their theological writing.[60]

Tillich's ontology and theology will hardly adapt to the specific local needs of these self-consciously particular theological discourses. But it is to his credit that he pointed future theologians not back to the general ontology he had formulated, but forward to the systematic theologian's necessary "emphasis on the particular." That vision will require ever more careful, multidisciplinary analyses of the places at which theologians are located and the difference those places make to what they do. It will also require just as vital a commitment to the distinctive symbols and narratives of the Christian tradition. Much of the challenge for the future of theology lies in the question of whether persuasive correlations can be articulated between a multidisciplinary affirmation of plurality, on the one hand, and the distinctive resources of the Christian tradition, on the other. Many see in the affirmation of plurality the looming of a relativistic abyss or of a new void. Others see in any will to maintain vital commitment the risking of new dogmatisms or absolutisms. We should not wonder that a thinker like Tillich would send theologians toward renewed Christian hope along a journey where risk, the abyss and the void attend each step they take.

# SELECTED TEXTS

# 1

---

## THE STRUGGLE FOR A NEW THEONOMY*

### ON THE IDEA OF A THEOLOGY OF CULTURE

*Given on April 16, 1919, this first public presentation of his own thinking was well received by the Kant Society in Berlin who heard the address within the turbulent milieu of post-World War I Berlin. As a* Privatdozent *of theology at the University of Berlin (1919-24), Tillich had turned his intellectual skills toward the concrete tensions of his period, teaching as his first course, "Christianity and the Present Social Problems." Tillich himself later described the situation toward which his theology of culture was directed and which he himself felt as a chaplain who had survived war in the trenches, who now knew the pain of broken marriage and the struggles of a whole set of similarly displaced friends: "The political problems determined our whole existence; even after revolution and inflation there were matters of life and death. The social structure was in a state of dissolution, human relations with respect to authority, education, family, sex, friendship and pleasure were in a creative chaos" (Kegley,* The Theology of Paul Tillich, *p. 13). Tillich here presents basic notions retained throughout his career: his view of religion and its relation to culture, "theonomy", the relationships of theology of culture to philosophy, religion and to church theology. The essay first appeared in* Religionsphilosophie der Kultur *(Berlin: Reuther & Reichard, 1919). The first English translation by William Baillee Green is reprinted here from Paul Tillich,* What is Religion?, *edited and with an Introduction by James Luther Adams (New York: Harper & Row, 1969), pp. 155-181.*

### 1. THEOLOGY AND RELIGIOUS PHILOSOPHY

In the empirical sciences one's own standpoint is something that must be overcome. Reality is the criterion by which what is right is measured, and reality is one and the same. As between two contradictory standpoints, only one can be right, or both can be wrong. The progress of scientific experience must decide between them. It has decided that the earth is a body in space and not a flat, floating plate, and that the five

---

* See also pp. 15-18 above.

Books of Moses stem from various sources and not from Moses himself. Standpoints opposed to this are wrong. Scientific progress has not yet decided who is the author of the Epistle to the Hebrews. Among the various hypotheses only one, or none, is correct.

The situation is different in the systematic cultural sciences; *here the standpoint of the systematic thinker belongs to the heart of the matter itself.* It is a moment in the history of the development of culture; it is a concrete historical realization of an idea of culture; it not only perceives but also creates culture. Here the alternative "right or wrong" loses its validity, for there is no limit to the number of attitudes which the spirit can adopt toward reality. There is a Gothic and a baroque style in aesthetics; a Catholic and a modern Protestant dogmatic theology; a romantic and a puritanical code of ethics; but in none of these pairs of alternatives is it possible simply to call one right and the other wrong. Therefore it is also impossible to form useful universal concepts of cultural ideas. The true nature of religion or art cannot be learned through abstract reasoning. Abstraction destroys what is essential, the concrete forms, and necessarily neglects any future concretizations. *Every universal concept in cultural science is either useless or a normative concept in disguise;* it is either an alleged description of something that does not exist or an expression of a standpoint; it is a worthless shell or it is a creative act. A standpoint is expressed by an individual; but if it is more than individual arbitrariness, if it is a creative act, it is also, to a greater or lesser degree, a creative act of the circle in which the individual moves. This circle, with its peculiar spiritual quality, has no existence apart from the cultural groups that surround it and the creative acts of the past on which it rests. Thus, in the same way even the most individual standpoint is firmly embedded in the ground of the objective spirit, the mother soil from which every cultural creation springs. From this soil the concrete standpoint derives the universal forms of spirit. And viewed from there, it finds its own concrete limitation through the ever narrower circles and historical components of concrete spiritual quality, until, by its own creative self-expression it develops the new individual and unique synthesis of universal form and concrete content. There are three forms of nonempirical cultural science which correspond to this: philosophy of culture, which is concerned with the universal forms, the a priori of all culture; the philosophy of the history of cultural values, which, through the abundance of concretizations, constitutes the transition from the universal forms to one's own individual standpoint and by so doing justifies the latter; and finally, the normative science of culture, which provides the concrete standpoint with a systematic expression.

Thus the following distinctions must be made: between the philosophy of art, i.e., a phenomenology of art, and a presentation of art within a philosophy of value concerned with the essence or value of "art" on the one hand, and "aesthetics", i.e., a systematic and normative presentation of what must be considered as beautiful, on the other hand. Or between moral philosophy — which asks "What is morality?" — and normative ethics, which asks "What is moral?" The same distinction must be made between philosophy of religion on the one hand and theology on the other. *Theology is thus the concrete and normative science of religion.* This is the sense in which the concept is used here, and in my opinion it is the only sense in which it is entitled to be used in any scholarly context. By this means two allegations are refuted. First, theology is not the science of one particular object, which we call God, among others; the *Critique of Reason* put an end to this kind of science. It also brought theology down from heaven to earth. Theology is a part of science of religion, namely the systematic and normative part. Second, theology is not a scientific presentation of a special complex of revelation. This interpretation presupposes a concept of a supernaturally authoritative revelation; but this concept has been overcome by the wave of religious-historical insights and the logical and religious criticism of the conception of supernaturalism.

It is therefore the task of theology, working from a concrete standpoint, to draw up a normative system of religion based on the categories of philosophy of religion, with the individual standpoint being related to the standpoint of the respective confession, the universal history of religion, and the cultural-historical standpoint in general. This is no hidden rationalism, for it recognizes the concrete religious standpoint. Nor is it hidden supernaturalism, such as may still be found even in our historical-critical school of thought, for it is the breaking down of all the authoritarian limitations upon the individual standpoint by means of a philosophy of history. It is oriented to Nietzsche's notion of the "creative" on the basis of Hegel's concept of "objective-historical spirit".

One final word on the relation between a philosophy of culture and a normative systemization of culture: they belong together and each exercises an influence over the other. Not only is theology oriented to philosophy of religion, but the reverse is also true. As indicated at the outset, any universal philosophical concept is empty unless it is at the same time understood to be a normative concept with a concrete basis. Accordingly, this does not constitute the difference between philosophy and the science of norms, but the fact that each works in a different direction. Philosophy provides universal, a priori categorical thought forms on the widest empirical basis and in systematic relationship with other values and essential concepts. The normative sciences provide each cultural discipline with its content, with what is peculiar to it, with what is to be regarded as valid within the specific system.

Out of the power of a concrete, creative realization the highest universal concept gains its validity, full of content and yet comprehensive in form; and out of a highest universal concept the normative system acquires its objective scientific significance. In every useful universal concept there is a normative concept; and in every creative "norm" concept there is a universal concept. This is the dialectic of the systematic science of culture.

## 2. CULTURE AND RELIGION

Traditionally, systematic theology has included theological ethics as well as dogmatics. Modern theology usually divides the system into apologetics, dogmatics, and ethics. What is this peculiar kind of knowledge which assumes a place beside the general philosophical subject of ethics under the name of theological ethics? To this one can give various answers. One can say that philosophical ethics is concerned with the nature of morality and not with its norms; in which case the two differ from each other as do moral philosophy and normative ethics. But why should normative ethics be theological ethics? Philosophy, or better the science of culture, cannot refrain from producing a system of normative ethics of its own. Insofar as both now claim to be valid, we would then have admitted in principle the existence of the old double truth in the sphere of ethics. But one can also say: the moral life likewise tends to become concrete, and in ethics, too, there must be a standpoint that is not only the standpoint of an individual but also stems from a concrete ethical community in historical contexts. The church is such a community.

This answer is correct wherever the church is the dominating cultural community or wherever culture is under the leadership of the church and not only ethics but also science, art, and social life are controlled, censored, kept within limits, and systematized by the church. In Protestant areas, however, the church has long ago abandoned any claim to do this. It recognizes an overlapping cultural community outside the church, where the individual viewpoint is rooted in the contemporary viewpoint of the cultural community in general. There is no more room for a system of ethics, aesthetics, science, or sociology based on theological principles than there would be for a German or Aryan or bourgeois system of the same kind, although these concretions naturally play an important part in the actual shaping of the individual standpoint. Once a secular culture has been recognized in principle by the church, there is no longer any question of a theological system of ethics — nor of a theological system of logic, aesthetics, and sociology.

My assertion now is the following: *What was essentially intended in the theological system of ethics can only be realized by means of a theology of culture applying not only to ethics but to all the functions of culture. Not a theological system of ethics, but a theology of culture.* This calls for a few remarks on the relation of culture to religion. Religion has the peculiarity of not being attributable to any particular psychic function. None of the theories advanced either by Hegel, who assigned religion to the theoretical sphere of the mind, or by Kant, who assigned it to the practical sphere, or by Schleiermacher, who assigned it to the realm of feeling, has survived. The last theory is the one nearest to the truth, inasmuch as it signifies the indifference of the genuinely religious realm toward its cultural expressions. But feeling accompanies *every* cultural experience without necessarily justifying its being described as religious. However, if a *definite* feeling is meant, then with this certainty a theoretical or practical element is already given. Religion is not a feeling; it is an attitude of the spirit in which practical, theoretical, and emotional elements are united to form a complex whole.

In my opinion, the following is the way of systematizing which most nearly approaches the truth. If we now divide all cultural functions into those through which the spirit absorbs the object into itself — i.e., intellectual and aesthetic functions, grouped together as theoretical or intuitive — and those through which the spirit tries to penetrate into the object and mold it after itself — i.e., the individual and the socioethical functions (including law and society), which is the practical group, we find that religion can become operative only in relation to a theoretical or practical attitude. The religious potency, i.e., a certain quality of consciousness, is not to be confused with the religious act, i.e., an independent theoretical or practical act containing that quality.

The connection between religious principle and cultural function now enables a specifically religious-cultural sphere to emerge: a religious perception — myth or dogma; a sphere of religious aesthetics — the cultus; a religious molding of the person — sanctification; a religious form of society — the church, with its special canon law and communal ethic. In forms like these, religion is actualized; the religious principle only exists in connection with cultural functions outside the sphere of religion. The religious function does not form a principle in the life of the spirit beside others; the absolute character of all religious consciousness would break down barriers of that kind. But the religious principle is actualized in all spheres of spiritual or cultural life. This remark, however, seems to have set new boundaries. In every sphere of cultural life there is now a special circle, a special sphere of influence of "the religious". How are these spheres to be defined? Here indeed is the field of the great cultural conflicts between church and state, between the religious community and society, between art and cultic form, between science and dogma — conflicts which occupied the first centuries of the modern era and which have not yet entirely ceased. No conflict is possible as long as the cultural functions are held by a heteronomy dominated by religion; and it is overcome as soon as the cultural functions have won complete autonomy. But what happens then to religion? The autonomy of the cultural life is threatened, and even abolished, as long as science stands in any way side by side with dogma; or society side by side with a "community"; or the state side by side with a church — all of them claiming definite spheres for themselves alone. For through this a double truth, a double morality, and a double justice come into being, and one out of each pair has its origin not in the legitimacy of the cultural function concerned but in an alien kind of legitimacy dictated by religion. This double existence must be abolished at all costs; it is intolerable as soon as it enters consciousness, for it destroys consciousness.

The solution can only be found through the concept of religion. Without offering proof, for that would mean writing a miniature philosophy of religion, I shall present the concept of religion I presuppose here. Religion is directedness toward the Unconditional. Through existing realities, through values, through personal life, the meaning of unconditional reality becomes evident; before which every particular thing and the totality of all particulars — before which every value and the system of values — before which personality and community are shattered in their own self-sufficient being and value.* This is not a new

* This translation of the previous two sentences omits important phrases from the German original. Victor Nuovo has provided a much improved translation of this passage:

"Religion is the experience of the unconditioned, and this means the experi-

reality, alongside or above other things: that would only be a thing of a higher order which would again fall under the No. On the contrary, it is precisely through things that that reality is thrust upon us which is at one and the same time the No and the Yes to everything. It is not a being, nor is it the substance or totality of beings; it is — to use a mystical formula — that which is above all things which at the same time is the absolute Nothing and the absolute Something. But even the predicate "is" already disguises the facts of the case, since we are here dealing not with a reality of existence, but with a reality of meaning, and that indeed is the ultimate and deepest meaning — reality which shakes the foundation of all things and builds them up anew.

At this point it now becomes clear without further reference that one cannot speak of special religious spheres of culture in the true sense of the term. If it is the nature of fundamental religious experience to negate the *entire* cognitive sphere and affirm it through negation, then there is no longer any place for a special religious cognition, a special religious object, or special methods of religious epistemology. The conflict between dogma and science is overcome. Science is in full possession of its autonomy, and there is no possibility of a rule of heteronomy exercised by religion; but in exchange for this, science as a whole is subordinated to the "theonomy" of a fundamental religious experience which is paradoxical. The same holds good of ethics. It is impossible for a special code of personal or communal ethics in relation to the religious object to exist side by side with an individual or social code of ethics. Ethics, too, is purely autonomous, entirely free of all religious heteronomy and yet "theonomous" as a whole in the sense of the fundamental religious experience. The possibilities of conflict are radically eliminated. By that the relation of religion to culture is clarified in principle. The specifically religious spheres of culture have in principle ceased to exist. The question of what importance may still be attached to them can only be decided after the question of the meaning of a theology of culture has been answered.

------

ence of absolute reality founded on the experience of absolute nothingness. One experiences the nothingness of entities, the nothingness of values, the nothingness of the personal life. Wherever this experience has brought one to the nothingness of an absolute radical No, there it is transformed into an experience, no less absolute, of reality, into a radical Yes."
For the entire, new translation of Tillich's "On the Idea of a Theology of Culture" see Victor Nuovo, *Visionary Science*, Detroit: Wayne State University Press, forthcoming (1987).

## 3. THEOLOGY OF CULTURE

Various references have been made in the last few pages to an autonomy and theonomy of cultural values. We have to follow these up still further: that is, I would like to propose the hypothesis that the autonomy of cultural functions is grounded in their form, in the laws governing their application, whereas theonomy is grounded in their substance or import, that is, in the reality which by these laws receives its expression or accomplishment. The following law can now be formulated: The more the form, the greater the autonomy; the more the substance or import, the greater the theonomy. But one cannot exist without the other; a form that forms nothing is just as incomprehensible as substance without form. To attempt to grasp import disengaged from form would constitute a relapse into the worst kind of heteronomy; a new form would immediately come into being, now opposing the autonomous form and limiting it in its autonomy. The relation of import to form must be taken as resembling a line, one pole of which represents pure form and the other pole pure import. Along the line itself, however, the two are always in unity. The revelation of a predominant import consists in the fact that the form becomes more and more inadequate, that the reality, in its overflowing abundance, shatters the form meant to contain it; and yet this overflowing and shattering is itself still form.

The task of a theology of culture is to follow up this process in all the spheres and creations of culture and to give it expression. Not from the standpoint of form — that would be the task of the branch of cultural science concerned — but taking the import or substance as its starting point, as theology of culture and not as cultural systematization. The concrete religious experiences embedded in all great cultural phenomena must be brought into relief and a mode of expression found for them. It follows from this that in addition to theology as a normative science of religion, a theological method must be found to stand beside it in the same way that a psychological and a sociological method, etc., exist alongside systematic psychology. These methods are universal; they are suited to any object; and yet they have a native soil, the particular branch of knowledge in which they originated. This is equally true of the theological method, which is a universal application of theological questioning to all cultural values.

We have assigned to theology the task of finding a systematic form of expression for a concrete religious standpoint, on the basis of the universal concepts of philosophy of religion and by means of the classifications of philosophy of history. The task of theology of culture corresponds to this. It produces a general religious analysis of all cultural creations; it provides a historical-philosophical and typological classification of the great cultural creations according to the religious substance realized in them; and it produces from its own concrete religious standpoint the ideal outline of a culture penetrated by religion. It thus has a threefold task, corresponding to the threefold character of the cultural-systematic sciences in general and the systematic science of religion in particular:

1. *General religious analysis of culture*
2. *Religious typology and philosophy of cultural history*
3. *Concrete religious systematization of culture*

Attention must be paid to two things in regard to the cultural-theological analysis. The first is the relation between form and substance. *Substance or import* is something different from content. By content we mean something objective in its simple existence, which by form is raised up to the intellectual-cultural sphere. By substance or import, however, we understand the meaning, the spiritual substantiality, which alone gives form its significance. We can therefore say: *Substance or import is grasped by means of a form and given expression in a content.* Content is accidental, substance essential, and form is the mediating element. The form must be appropriate to the content; so there is no opposition between the cultivation of form and the cultivation of content; it is rather that these two represent one extreme, and the cultivaton of substance represents the other. The shattering of form through substance is identical with the loss of significance of content. Form loses its necessary relation to content because the content vanishes in the face of the preponderance of the substance. Through this, form acquires a quality of detachment, as of something floating freely in space; it is directly related to substance; it loses its natural and necessary relation to content; and it becomes form in a paradoxical sense by allowing its natural quality to be shattered by the substance. This is the first point to which attention must be paid; for it is precisely in the substance that the religious reality appears with its Yes and No to all things. And this is the second point: the relation between the Yes and the No, the relation and the force in which both find expression. There are innumerable possibilities here, because the relations and the reciprocal interactions are infinitely rich in possibilities.

But there is also a certain limitation: and this leads us to the second task assigned to theology of culture, the typological and historical-philosophical task. A limitation is given by the aforementioned image of the line with the poles of form and substance (or import) respectively. This image leads us to three decisive points representing the three fundamental types: the two poles and the central point where form and substance are in equilibrium. From this may be derived the following fundamental classifications for typology: the typically profane or secular and formal cultural creation; the typically religious-cultural creation in which the substance or import is predominant; and the typically well-balanced, harmonious, or classical cultural creation. This universal typology now leaves room for intermediate stages and transitions and is extraordinarily varied by reason of the different concrete forms of religion which it covers. If this doctrine of types is applied to the present and systematically related to the past, a historical-philosophical classification develops which then leads us directly to the third and, properly speaking, systematic task of theology of culture.

How far can the theologian of culture be at the same time a religious-cultural system-builder? The question has to be answered first from its negative side. It is impossible as far as the form of the cultural functions is concerned; that would be a forbidden infringement and would amount to cultural heteronomy. It is possible only from the side of substance, but substance only attains cultural existence in forms; to this extent it must be said that the theologian of culture is not directly creative with regard to culture. The theologian of culture as such is not productive in the sphere of science, morals, jurisprudence, or art. But he adopts a critical, negative, and affirmative attitude toward autonomous productions on the basis of his concrete theological standpoint; he draws up with the material at hand a religious system of culture by separating this material and unifying it again in accordance with his theological principle. He can also go beyond the material at hand, but only in making demands and not in fulfillment; he can reproach the existing culture because he finds nothing in its creative acts which he can acknowledge as an expression of the living substance in himself; he can indicate in a very general way the direction in which he visualizes the realization of a truly religious system of culture, but he cannot produce the system himself. If he attempts to do so, he ceases to be a theologian of culture and becomes in one or more ways a creator of culture; but in so doing he steps over to the full and completely autonomous criticism of cultural forms, which often leads him with compelling force to goals quite different from those he wished to attain. Herein lies the limitation of the task of systematization assigned to the theologian of culture: but his universal significance also originates here. Far removed from every restriction to a special sphere, he can give expression from the standpoint of substance to the all-embracing unity of the cultural functions and demonstrate the relations that lead from one phenomenon of culture to another, through the substantial unity of the substance finding expression in them; he can thereby help, from the viewpoint of substance, to bring about the unity of culture in the same way that the philosopher helps from the viewpoint of pure forms and categories.

Cultural-theological tasks have often been posed and solved by theological, philosophical, literary, and political analysts of culture (e.g., Simmel); but the task as such has not been understood or its systematic meaning recognized. It has not been realized that in this context it is a matter of a cultural synthesis of the greatest importance, a synthesis that not only embraces the various cultural functions but also overcomes the culture-destroying opposition of religion and culture by a design for a religious system of culture in which the opposition of science and dogma is replaced by a science religious in itself; the distinction between art and forms of cultus is replaced by an art religious in itself; and the dualism of state and church is replaced by a type of state religious in itself, etc. The task of theology of culture is only understood if it is seen within so wide a scope. Some examples should serve to explain and lead further.

## 4. CULTURAL-THEOLOGICAL ANALYSES

In what follows I want to limit myself mainly to the first, or analytical, part of cultural-theological work, with occasional references to the second, or typological part, since I do not wish to introduce at this point a concrete theological principle without offering proof; that, however, would be necessary for the completion of the historical-philosophical and systematic task of theology of culture. One or two indications with regard to systematization, however, will make some appearance in the course of the analysis.

I begin with a cultural-theological consideration of art — to be precise, with the Expressionist school of art in painting, because it seems to me to offer a particularly impressive example of the above-mentioned relation between form and substance; and because these definitions were worked out partly under its influence.

To start with, it is clear that in Expressionism content has to a very great extent lost its significance, namely content in the sense of the external factuality of objects and events. Nature has been robbed of her external appearance; her uttermost depth is visible. But, according to Schelling, horror dwells in the depths of every living creature; and this horror seizes us from the work of the Expressionist painters, who aim at more than mere destruction of the form in favor of the fullest, most vital and flourishing life within, as Simmel thinks. In their work a form-shattering religious import is struggling to find form, a paradox that most people find incomprehensible and annoying; and this horror seems to me to be deepened by a feeling of guilt, not in the properly ethical sense, but rather in the cosmic sense of the guilt of sheer existence. Redemption, however, is the transition of one individual existence into the other, the wiping out of individual distinction, the mysticism of love achieving union with all living things.

This art therefore expresses the profoundest No and Yes; but the No, the form-destroying element, seems to me still to be predominant, although this is not what the artists, with their passionate will toward a new and absolute Yes, intend.

Many of the remarks made by these artists confirm the existence of a strong religious passion struggling for expression. It is no accident that in the lively debates carried on about these pictures, the enthusiastic representatives of Expressionism make constant references to philosophy and religion and even to the Bible itself. The religious meaning of this art is to a large extent consciously affirmed by its representatives.

And now for an example taken from philosophy. The autonomous forms of knowledge achieve perfect clarity in the Neo-Kantian school. Here we have a truly scientific — and unreligious — philosophy. Form rules absolutely. There are contemporary attempts to go beyond this, but that is harder in this field than in any other; during the idealistic period the experience of reality had engulfed the form too brutally. Not only that: Neo-Kantianism had forged for itself a new form, which in the name of intuition opposed the autonomous forms of knowledge. This was not a struggle between the different fields of knowledge; it was the old struggle between a particular religious mode of cognition and a profane and secular one. It was a piece of heteronomy which science was compelled to counteract, and did counteract, most vigorously. If now a new movement toward intuition succeeds in gaining influence when the fight against the materialistic shadow of idealism has been completely won, then a mistrust on the part of science is understandable, but not necessary. For a new intuitive method can never attempt to compete with the autonomous methods of science; it can only find an opening where the substance itself shatters the form of these methods and where the way into the realm of the metaphysical opens up. Metaphysics is nothing but the paradoxical attempt to fit into forms the experience of the Unconditional which is above and beyond all form; and if at this point we look back to Hegel, there still being no outstanding metaphysics at present, we find one of the most profound accounts of the unity of negation and affirmation, though it must be admitted that it has a strong optimistic tendency to raise affirmation above everything else. It does not include the experience of horror which is a fundamental part of Schelling's and Schopenhauer's work and should not be lacking in any modern metaphysics.

We come now to the sphere of practical values: first, to individual ethics. Nietzsche could serve as a splendid and characteristic example for a theology of culture in this sphere. His apparently totally anti-religious orientation makes it particularly interesting to analyze, from the theological point of view, his doctrine of the shaping of the human personality. It should now be recognized that the opposition between the ethics of virtue and the ethics of grace is contained in his message and that, since Jesus' fight against the Pharisees and Luther's fight against Rome, there is hardly a parallel case where the personal forms of ethics are shattered by the substance with such violence.

"What is the greatest experience you can have? The hour in which you say: What does my virtue matter? It has not yet made me rage!" But the virtue that makes men rage is beyond virtue and sin. The theological sentence of destruction hangs mightily over each individual: "Thou shalt wish to consume thyself in thine own flame. How wouldst thou be new again if thou wert not first burned to ashes?" But almost at the same moment the affirmation arises, with unparalleled fervor and passion, whether as a sermon by the *Übermensch* or as a hymn to the marriage ring of rings, the ring of eternal return. This experience of reality which Nietzsche gained and contrasted with the personal goes so far beyond the individual-ethical form that he could be called the antimoralist *kat' exokēn* (par excellence), just as Luther has to be stigmatized as the great libertine by all those whose personal thinking takes place within the categories of virtue and reward.

From the standpoint of form, it is simply paradoxical how an overwhelming metaphysical substance deprives the ethical contents (norms) of significance, shatters the form adapted to them, and then still, of its own volition, presents within this shattered form a higher order of becoming a person than would have been possible within those others forms. The person who, according to Nietzsche, is beyond good and evil, is just "better" from the absolute viewpoint, even if he is "worse" from the relative, formal-ethical viewpoint, than the "good and righteous man". The former is "pious", whereas the righteous man is "impious".

In social ethics, it is the new mysticism of love now stirring everywhere that signifies a theonomous overcoming of the autonomous ethical forms without a relapse into the heteronomy of a specifically religious community of love. If you take the speeches of the idealistic socialists and communists, the poems of Rilke and Werfel, Tolstoi's new interpretation of the Sermon on the Mount — everywhere the formal system of ethics of reason and humanity oriented to Kant is being eliminated. Kant's formulae of ethical autonomy, his demand that man should do good for the sake of good itself, and his law of universal validity are unassailable principles of autonomous ethics; and no interpretation of ethics as a divine  commandment or of love as the overcoming  of the law can be allowed to shake this foundation; but the content of love overflows the narrow cup of this form in an inexhaustible stream. The world that merely exists and is split up into individual beings is destroyed and experienced as an empty, unreal shell. The man who thinks in terms of the individual can never attain to love, for love is beyond the individual; the man who thinks in terms of the end to be attained does not know what love is: for love is pure experience of being, pure experience of reality. The man who tries to impose a limit or a condition upon love does not know that love is universal, cosmic, simply because it affirms and embraces everything that is real as something real.

Now we pass on the theology of the state. This theology shows the substance embedded in the different forms of the state; it shows how this substance outgrows the form of the state, or, alternatively, how the form of the state stifles the substance. The rational theories of the state from which the autonomous state developed in the struggle against theocracy led to an abstract state floating above society, described in *Thus Spake Zarathustra* as "the coldest of all cold monsters". "Faith and love create a people, but the sword and a hundred greedy desires create the state" is a magnificent characterization of the unreligious power-state or utility-state. Nor does it help matters if we adorn this abstract, autonomous state with all the functions of culture and turn it into God on earth, as does Hegel; for then the spirit itself becomes a power-object or utility-object. The religious substance shatters the autonomous form of the state: that is the profoundest meaning of idealistic "anarchism", not to make way for a new theocracy but in favor of a theonomy built up from communities themselves and their spiritual substance. Even this is still a form of society — a state, but one created by negation, by the destruction of the autonomous form pertaining to a state; and this very paradox is the form of "anarchy". Such a state, built up from cultural communities, a "state" in the paradoxical sense of the term, is what must be termed "church" in the sense of the theology of culture: the universal human community, built up out of spiritual communities and bearing with it all cultural functions and their religious substance, with the great creative philosophers for its teachers, artists for its priests, the seers of a new ethic of the person and the community for its prophets, men who will lead it to new community goals for its bishops, leaders and recreators of the economic process for its deacons and almoners. For the economy, too, can be shattered in its pure autonomy and in its quality of being an end in itself, through the substance of the religious mysticism of love, which produces not for the sake of production but for the sake of the human being. Yet it does not curtail the process of production in accord with the principles of heteronomy, but directs it along the lines of theonomy as the universal form of the earlier, specifically ecclesiastical care of the poor which has been eliminated on socialist territory along with the concept of poverty.

With this we want to close the list of examples. I have given so many of them that they amount almost to the outline of a system of theology of culture. They will in any case serve to illustrate what is meant. At this point now the question could be raised why the whole of the work is limited to the analysis of culture and why nature (or technology) is excluded. The answer is that for us nature can only become an object through the medium of culture, if at all. For us, nature derives its sole importance from the functions of the spirit; and culture is conceived as both the subjective and objective embodiment of these functions. The essence of nature in itself is quite out of our reach, and we cannot even comprehend it sufficiently to be able to speak positively of such an essence. But as nature only becomes a reality to us through culture, we are justified in speaking exclusively of "cultural theology" and in rejecting a concept such as "natural theology". Any religious substance or import that may exist in nature lies in the cultural functions insofar as these are related to nature. The religious substance of a "landscape" is a religious-aesthetic phenomenon; the religious substance of a law of astronomy is a religious-scientific one. Technology can function in a religious way through aesthetic, socioethical, or legal interpretations; but in every case we find ourselves dealing with theology of culture, which unquestionably comprises the whole of nature and of technology. An independent natural theology would have to presuppose the existence of a mythology of "nature in itself", and that is unthinkable.

## 5. THEOLOGY OF CULTURE AND THE THEOLOGY OF THE CHURCH

We still have to deal with a question that has been postponed several times: What happens to the specifically religious culture, to dogma, cultus, sanctification, community, and church? How far does a special sphere of holiness still exist? The answer must be based on the relationship of polarity existing between the profane or secular and the religious aspects of the line of culture. In point of fact, they are never apart; but they are separated *in abstracto*, and this separation is the expression of a universal psychological need. In order to experience anything at all, we are perpetually compelled to separate things that in reality are bound up together, so that our conscious mind may become aware of them.

A specific religious culture must already have come into being before we can experience religious values in culture, or develop a theology of culture, or identify and label the religious elements. Church, cultus, and dogma must already have come into being, and not only that, before we can conceive of the state as church, or art as cultus, or science as theory of faith. To be able somehow to comprehend the Holy and experience it as distinct from the profane or secular, we must take it out of context and bring it into a special sphere of cognition, of worship, of love, and of organization. The profane or secular pole of culture — the exact sciences, formal aesthetics, formal ethics, the purely political and economic aspects — claims our whole attention if it is not balanced by the opposite pole; a universal profanation and desecration of life would be inevitable if no sphere of holiness existed to oppose and contradict it. This contradiction cannot be resolved as long as a distinction must be made between form and content, and as long as we are forced to live in the sphere of reflection and not in the sphere of intuition. This is one of the profoundest and most tragic contradictions of cultural life. But the importance of the progress made in recent centuries is revealed by the fact that we have learned the true nature of this conflict and have ceased to credit it with any real, fundamental significance, so that it has lost its residue of active power.

The relation of the theology of culture to the theology of the church is a consequence of this. Our whole development of this theme has taken culture and its forms as a starting point and has shown how culture as such receives a religious quality when substance or import flows into form, and how it finally produces a specifically religious-cultural sphere in order to preserve and heighten that religious quality. This sphere is one of teleo-logical, not independently logical, dignity. The church theologian now understands this sphere as the expression of a definite religious "concreteness", no longer derived from culture but with an independent history going back much farther than most other cultural creations. It has evolved its own forms, each with its separate history, its independence, and its continuity, in spite of all the influences exerted by autonomous forms of culture. Yes indeed, from its own nature it has exercised the very greatest influence on the evolution of these forms. That is an accurate statement of fact; but it is not adequate to decide the attitude that must be adopted toward theology of culture.

There are three possible attitudes that the church theologian can adopt toward culture. He can group all its aspects together under the heading of "world" and confront this group with the "kingdom of God", which is realized in the church. The result is that the specifically religious-cultural functions, insofar as they are exercised by the church, share in the "absoluteness" of the religious principle; and that there are absolute science, art forms, morality, etc. — i.e., those realized in the church, in its dogma, in its cultus, etc. Starting from this typically Catholic attitude, there is no possible road to a theology of culture.

The second possibility is the old Protestant attitude. Here church, cultus, and ethics are freed and seen in their relativity; but the cognitive tie, the idea of absolute knowledge as a supernatural revelation, is still retained. But since the period of the theology of the Enlightenment this position has been seriously shaken, for it is basically inconsistent; and the preference given to the intellectual sphere could no longer be justified, once the absoluteness of its only possible advocate, the church, had been allowed to lapse.

The task now facing present and future Protestant theology is to arrive at the third attitude. On the one hand, the distinction between religious potentiality and actuality, i.e., between religious principle and religious culture, will be strictly drawn and the character of "absoluteness" assigned only to the religious principle and not to any factor of the religious culture, not even that of its historical foundation. On the other hand, the religious principle will not be defined in purely abstract terms, nor will its concrete fulfillment be entrusted to every fleeting fashion of cultural development. Every effort, however, will be made to ensure the continuity of its concrete religious standpoint. Only if this attitude is adopted can there be any positive relation between theology of culture and the theology of the church.

In this relationship the church theologian is in principle the more conservative and the more selective, looking backward as well as forward. "The Reformation must continue" is his principle; but it is reformation and not revolution; for the substance of his concrete standpoint is preserved and the new mold must be adapted to the old one in every field.

The theologian of culture is not bound by any such considerations; he is a free agent in the living cultural movement, open to accept not only any other form but also any other spirit. It is true that he too lives on the basis of a definite concreteness, for *one can live* only in concreteness; but he is prepared at any time to enlarge and change this concreteness. As a theologian of culture, he has no interest in ecclesiastical continuity; and this of course puts him at a disadvantage as compared with the church theologian, since he is in danger of becoming a fashionable religious prophet of an uncertain cultural development divided against itself.

In consequence, the only relationship possible is one in which each is the complement of the other; and the best way of achieving this is through personal union, which is admittedly not always desirable, as types must be free to develop unhampered. In any case, a real opposition becomes impossible the moment the theologian of culture acknowledges the necessity of the concrete standpoint in its continuity, and the church theologian in turn acknowledges the relativity of every concrete form compared with the exclusive absoluteness of the religious principle itself.

The cultural-theological ideal itself, however, goes farther than the distinction between cultural theology and ecclesiastical theology. Yet it does not demand a culture that eliminates the distinction drawn between the profane or secular pole and the holy, for that is impossible in the world of reflection and abstraction, but it does demand one in which the entire cultural movement is filled by a homogeneous substance, a directly spiritual material, which turns it into the expression of an all-embracing religious spirit whose continuity is one with that of culture itself. In that case, the opposition of cultural theology and church theology is eliminated, for it is only the expression of a split between substance and meaning in culture.

Even in a new, unified culture, however, the task of working on the predominately religious-cultural elements would be entrusted to the theologian, with the idea of producing a specifically religious community that would not differ in reality from the rest of the cultural community. Instead, and precisely in the manner of the pietistic communities in the seventeenth century, which liked to refer to themselves as *ecclesiola in ecclesia*, the church, as far as theology of culture is concerned, will be something like an *ecclesiola in ecclesia* to the cultural community as such. The church is the circle, as it were, to which is assigned — ideally speaking — the task of creating a specifically religious sphere and thus removing the element of contingency from the living religious elements, collecting them, concentrating them in theory and in practice, and in this way making them into a powerful — indeed, into the most powerful — cultural factor, capable of supporting everything else.

Let me add a few closing words on the subject of the most important supporters of cultural-theological work, that is, the theological faculties. What is the meaning of the theological faculties, and what significance do they possess in this particular connection? The theological faculties are regarded by science with suspicion, and rightly so, in two cases. First, when theology is defined as a scientific knowledge of God in the sense of one particular object among others. Second, when theolgy is taken to mean a description of a definite and limited denomination with authoritarian claims. In both instances the autonomy of other functions is threatened, even if outwardly they still seem to run independently side by side. A *universitas litterarum*, considered in terms of systematic unity, is then not possible. These objections at once disappear when theology is defined as a normative branch of knowledge concerned with religion and put on the same level as normative ethics, aesthetics, etc. The meaning of "standpoint" in the cultural branches of knowledge must be made clear at the same time, as was done at the beginning of this lecture. Regarded from the standpoint of theology of culture, however, the theological faculties are not only entitled to the same rights as others, but acquire, as do the purely philosophical faculties also, a universal and outstandingly high cultural significance. The theological faculties then perform one of the greatest and most creative tasks within the scope of culture. The demand for the removal of the theological faculties originated in the age of liberalism and of individualistic and antithetical culture. Socialism, by reason of its enmity toward the existing churches, unhesitatingly took up this demand for removal; although the demand contradicts the nature of socialism, for its nature is that of a cultural unity. It must be admitted that socialism has no room for a hierarchy or theocracy or heteronomy of the religious, but in order to complete its own development it needs the all-embracing religious substance which through theonomy alone can free the autonomy of the individual and also that of the individual cultural function from their self-destroying isolation. For this reason we need theological faculties for the new, unifying culture springing from socialist soil; and the first and fundamental task of these faculties is a theology of culture. For nearly two hundred years theology has been in the unfortunate but unavoidable situation of a defender whose position is finally untenable and who is forced to relinquish point after point, and now must again take the offensive, after abandoning the last trace of its untenable, culturally heteronomous position. It must fight under the banner of theonomy, and under this banner it will conquer, not the autonomy of culture but the profanation, exhaustion, and disintegration of culture in the latest epoch of mankind. It will conquer because, as Hegel says, religion is the beginning and the end of all things, and also the center, giving life and soul and spirit to all things.

*

## BASIC PRINCIPLES OF RELIGIOUS SOCIALISM

*Tillich sustained the struggle for a new theonomy after World War I through participation in the Religious Socialist movement. This movement grew in relation to Tillich's and his colleagues' conviction that the postwar era was a special time, indeed the "right time", a* kairos, *for the emergence of new theonomous forms of culture. Thus, a "Kairos Circle" was founded in 1920 and was the context for the young Tillich's political and theological work. Although he later acknowledged "a slight tinge of romanticism" in this Religious Socialism, and although the political dimension would, for several reasons, seem to diminish in later writings, Tillich insisted late in his career, "If the prophetic message is true, there is nothing 'beyond religious socialism'" (Kegley,* The Theology of Paul Tillich, *p. 13). The following essay sets forth the basic features of this movement, and also introduces Tillich's notions of the* kairos *and of "the demonic", while deepening his notion of theonomy. The selection is taken from the lengthy essay that first appeared in a journal published by the "Kairos Circle"* (Blätter fur Religiosen Sozialismus IV, 8-10 [1923]:1-24), *and was translated into English by James Luther Adams and Victor Nuovo as part of a collection of Tillich's essays entitled,* Political Expectation *(New York: Harper & Row, 1971, pp. 58-69, 86-8).*

## 1. THE INNER ATTITUDE OF RELIGIOUS SOCIALISM

We shall begin by making a distinction between two basic attitudes toward any actual situation: the sacramental attitude that lacks historical consciousness, and the rational attitude that is historically critical. The sacramental attitude is defined by a consciousness of the presence of the divine, be it in the primitive consecration of everything real or in the fixation of the holy upon certain objects and actions. Here lies the root of sacred symbols and forms, of the sacred relationships of community and justice. On this basis we may explain the inviolable connections between man and the soil, between present and past generations, between rulers and the ruled, and between communities based on blood, folk, and race. All of these relationships are founded sacramentally regardless of the occasions that have led to their sacramental consecration. They owe to this character their power, endurance, and invulnerability, but at the same time they also owe to it the abundance of life, which they mediate, and the meaning of life, which they reveal. Here history is viewed as myth. It points out the occasions that have led to sacramental consecration, it contains the divine deeds upon which the import and the value of the present are based. There can be no doubt that even today there are still wide circles, especially of the peasantry, which are unaware of history, and that the sacramental spiritual situation is constantly strengthened by attachment to the soil despite the ongoing influence of the critical spirit. It is a great error if, from the perspective of the urban spiritual situation, one overlooks this fact, and, above all, if one does not grasp its metaphysical claim and its significance for every social structure.

The opposing spiritual situation derives not from import and consecration but, rather, from form and law (*Recht*). There is form and law in the sacramental attitude also, but they do not appear as form. It is directed not toward the right (*das Richtige*) but toward the holy (*das Heilige*), which may agree with the right but may also contradict it. On the other hand, in the rationally critical attitude, the holy that is not at the same time right and formed (*Richtige and Geformte*) is rejected. Spirit is directed toward form and thereby loses the presence of the holy. It becomes separated from everything given and becomes empty and without import. It pursues the unconditioned pure form *ad infinitum* without being able to find it. This critical rational spirit is the genuine heritage of the primitive wanderlust in social conditions that issue from an uprooting from the soil, as in colonies and cities. It is the titanic world-forming will that wants to restore the lost presence of the holy through the creation of form. But this will, from which flows all the creative activity of the spirit, breaks down because of the loss that it necessarily brings about. The holy that is given cannot be replaced by the holy that is demanded. Reflection, creative activity, is endless and is emptied of all that is present in favor of a future that is never realized. This is the tragedy of all reflection, that by itself it necessarily deepens the gulf that separates it from reality, and which it desires to overcome. It is the barrenness of every reflective attitude toward the present that it not only cannot create the future it demands, but it also hinders its coming. Whereas it is hardly necessary in our circle to be critical of the sacramental, unhistorical conception, it is necessary to point out the danger of rational criticism. Numerous contemporary critical movements share the fate of reflection and its sterility, even though they fly from reflection into subjective feeling, as, for example, in the case of the youth movement. The one can create import or meaning (*Gehalt*) as little as the other, for both stand on the same ground of subjective detachment from the immediacy of the holy and its unconditionally meaning-fulfilling power.

In contrast to both of these tendencies, religious socialism adopts the prophetic attitude. It is the unity and a higher form of both of the former tendencies. The demand of the holy that should be arises upon the ground of the holy that is given. Prophetism is neither mantic that predicts the future nor ethics that demands the future. Prophetism grasps the coming that should be from its living connection with the present that is given. It has the holy, but only as it permeates law and form; it is free from sacramental indifference, but it does not succumb to rational purgation. Prophetism is a religious and spiritual function that persists. It can be weaker or stronger, purer or more distorted, but never missing. It is the religious unity of morality and the metaphysics of history, and can be borne by individuals, groups, and movements, indeed, even by the masses. It is susceptible to error to the degree that it becomes mantic, and it is barren to the degree that it becomes moralism.

The prophetic attitude is essential to religious socialism. It exists in socialism even though it is frequently distorted by reflection, rationalism, and political strategy. Everything depends upon whether these elements in socialism are subordinated and its pure prophetic power becomes manifest. The fate of the socialist movement hinges upon the success or failure of this effort. Whether it proceeds from the prophetic attitude or not is decisive for all discussion about religious socialism. Every debate that remains only in the rational plane does not penetrate to the essence. The rational attitude necessarily misunderstands the prophetic. In this way bourgeois science refuted socialism, and the Enlightenment refuted the teachings of faith, successfully in the rational sphere while missing the essence itself. They did not reach the metaphysical and the ethical and their unity, namely, the prophetic element of those creations. Nevertheless, religious socialism should not underrate the rational element. It must radically affirm law and form precisely from its prophetic consciousness. It must demand corrrect form even more strongly than rationalism. But it must recognize that the presence of the Unconditional is the *prius* of all conditioned action, that the unconditioned import of meaning is the *prius* of all forms of meaning, that the development of form (*Gestalt*) is the *prius* of all form-creation (*Gestaltung*).

We have used the word Kairos for the content of the prophetic view of history. It signifies a moment of time filled with unconditioned meaning and demand. It does not contain a prediction of a nearer or more distant future; as far as it does involve this, mantics is joined to prophetism and the possibility of error to unconditioned certainty. But Kairos also does not signify a mere demand or ideal. As far as these are involved, it is discerned either as a momentary trend that is not reality, or as utopian. Kairos is the fulfilled moment of time in which the present and the future, the holy that is given and the holy that is demanded meet, and from whose concrete tensions the new creation proceeds in which sacred import is realized in necessary form. Prophetism is consciousness of Kairos in the sense of the words: "Repent; the time (*kairos*) is fulfilled and the kingdom of God is at hand." Thus the sacramental and the critical attitudes are united in the consciousness of the Kairos, in the spirit of prophetism.

## 2. THE GOAL OF RELIGIOUS SOCIALISM

How are we to understand the "sovereignty of God"? The answer to this question must be given primarily and fundamentally as follows: it is the realization of unconditioned import in unconditioned form according to the saying "God is all in all." But this saying expresses an idea. It expresses the truth about the real, not reality itself. In reality we find a series of creative syntheses in which the eternal idea, the absolute synthesis, is revealed. One such concrete synthesis we call theonomy. It is the content of the prophetic view of history, the creation that is experienced in the Kairos simultaneously as given and as demanded (as near at hand). Theonomy is a condition in which the spiritual and social forms are filled with the import of the Unconditional as the foundation, meaning, and reality of all forms. Theonomy is the unity of sacred form and sacred import in a concrete historical situation. Theonomy transcends the indifference to form of the sacramental attitude of spirit in the same way as it transcends the emptying of import in formal autonomy. It fills the autonomous forms with sacramental substance. It creates a sacred and a just (*gerechte*) reality at the same time.

Theonomy is distinguished in like manner from both other-worldly and this-worldly utopianism. Otherworldly utopianism, the absolute rule of God as a concrete ideal, is usually associated with the sacramental attitude, whereas this-worldly utopianism, the perfect kingdom of reason, is associated with the critical attitude. Otherworldly utopianism is deeper, inasmuch as it sees the unity of form and import in the absolute sovereignty of God and therefore also conceives nature, the basis of all realization of form, as taken up into the condition of perfection. But it confuses idea and appearance, truth and reality. It makes the idea into a higher reality and places the Unconditional merely alongside the conditioned, thereby contradicting the essence of the Unconditional and devaluating the conditioned. Every theology that devaluates this world must be opposed not only from the socialist standpoint, but even more from the religious standpoint. Reality is the locus of the revelation of the Unconditional, in individual as well as in universal history. And no one and no time can have a greater share in the idea than it realizes in the phenomenon. This is the unconditional seriousness which belongs to the conditioned, in individual as well as in communal life. However, affirmation of this world does not imply an affirmation of this-worldly utopianism, which, rather, is to be rejected as emphatically as otherworldly utopianism. It is more utopian than the latter, inasmuch as it leaves nature untouched and wishes to erect a rational social and spiritual structure on an irrational natural foundation. It forgets that the unconditioned form can never be realized as such, that it is an ultimate abstraction, a purely ideal point of direction, but it is not reality. Everything real, however, is the individually creative synthesis of universal form and of the irrational ground of nature. For everything real is concrete. Religious socialism is distinguished from utopianism by the fact that its goal is individually creative, born concretely in history. It desires theonomy, not a rational utopia. In theonomy, however, the individual, the concrete, and the creative are preserved, for import is united with form on the irrational ground of nature only in the creative individual.

The relation of theonomy to religion and culture follows directly from these definitions of the essence of theonomy. In an ideal theonomy, religion and culture cannot exist merely side by side. Every coordination of the Unconditional and the conditioned makes the Unconditional conditioned and the conditioned unconditioned. All culture is actualized religion, and all religion is actualized as culture. There can be no other expression for the direction of the spirit to the Unconditional than conditioned forms, and no other import can give meaning and reality to conditioned forms than the unconditioned meaning upon which they rest. The more a spiritual situation realizes this unity of form and import, the more it is to be characterized as theonomous.

But these definitions are not adequate. Theonomy realizes itself individually and creatively upon the irrational ground of nature from which it wrests its individual form-giving power. Where there is individual creativity, there is also opposition to the creative process and there are also forms that contradict form. We call the embodiment of these forms that oppose the unconditioned form and are therefore destructive and self-destroying, the demonic, in contrast to the unity of forms subjected to the Unconditional, that is, in contrast to the divine. In every culture we find divine and demonic forms intermingled. Consequently, a simple identificaton of religion and culture can never be asserted. Religion always has a dual relation to culture. It contains within itself a No, a *reservatum religiosum*, and a Yes, an *obligatum religiosum*. By virtue of the *reservatum religiosum*, the religious spirit falls back upon itself in the face of the demonically distorted and conditioned forms of an epoch; that is, it falls back upon the sacred personality and the sacred community in a strict sense. In this way, the culturally negative attitude of early Christianity, of mysticism in late antiquity, and of Lutheranism may be interpreted as a religious withdrawal (*Reservat*) before the predominance of the demonic in social, personal, and political life. This religious withdrawal can and must always come into force again; it is the ground for the delimiting of a sacred alongside a secular sphere. But it becomes false, and opens the way to the demonic as soon as it forgets the other side, the *obligatum religiosum*. In reality, religion is never able to do without cultural forms. In the most profound act of religious introspection, forms of cultural creation are operative. Moreover, the religious communities that renounce the world are themselves "world" in the forms of their renunciation and in their own life-forms. The *reservatum* without the *obligatum* is impossible and untrue. Just as untrue, however, is the affirmation of the *obligatum* without the *reservatum*, as is almost the case with autonomous Protestantism. To reduce religion to cultural activity is to forget that all culture lives from the Unconditional, which is intended in religion, and that, therefore, a culture religion not only dissipates religious substance but also robs culture of its import. Therefore, culture is right in renouncing culture-Protestantism, and religion is right in rejecting the identification of religion and socialism. The only proper attitude toward culture and also toward socialism is that characterized by the double demand of *reservatum* and *obligatum religiosum*.

The attitude of theonomy toward the churches and confessions also follows from what has been said. They are the representatives of the *reservatum religiosum*, and from this follows their positive and negative valuation: positive, inasmuch as they are the focal points of the religious spirit; negative, inasmuch as in their forms they are just as much culture as the secular culture that confronts them; positive, inasmuch as it is an impossibility and an error of the critically rational attitude to suppose that symbols can be made; negative, inasmuch as no symbol may make a claim to absoluteness. The churches with their cultic and mythical symbols are absolute neither toward each other nor toward the forms of secular culture. Every religion stands under the No issuing from the Unconditional. Therefore, the exclusiveness of confessionalism is abandoned, but not by criticism of confessionalism in general but, rather, by a deepening of the confession to the point where it negates itself before the Unconditional. Not skeptical and rational criticism, but only profound religious criticism can overcome the hubris of the confessions. Therefore, this ultimate negation before the Unconditional does not at all preclude an emphatic Yes in conditioned circumstances. In the empirically cultural sphere, confessional conflict has the same right as the conflict that prevails in all creative realms of spirit. But the creative, symbol-bearing conviction of the truth of one's own confession is not the same as the certainty of the Unconditional itself, which transcends the entire plane of convictions, even confessional ones. This conception of the duality of certainty and conviction with respect to every religious symbol is the presupposition for a religious consciousness of unity directed toward humanity. It is a consciousness that is far from a critical purgation of the confession and its individually creative symbols. Only a religion that includes in its own symbols this negativity toward itself has the power to become a world religion. The more it negates itself from the point of view of the Unconditional, the more justified a claim to absoluteness by a confession or a church, and the easier for religious socialism to enter into the symbols of such a church. But the No coming from the Unconditional is directed not only against itself as confession, but also against itself as a specifically religious sphere. Religion is truer the more it cancels itself out (*aufheben*) as religion over against culture without thereby losing its specifically religious power. Likewise it is truer the closer it stands to theonomy in which religious symbols are the ultimate and most universal expression of autonomous cultural consciousness, and in which autonomous culture-forms radiate the fullness of the import of the Unconditional. The closer a religion stands to this ideal of theonomy, the more easily can an autonomously born religious socialism unite with it. For theonomy is the goal of religious socialism.

## 3. THE STRUGGLE OF RELIGIOUS SOCIALISM

Theonomy, as it is represented in the contemporary era, receives its clearest expression through the understanding of what at present opposes its realization. The goal of religious socialism becomes most conspicuous through its struggle. Theonomy stands in opposition to the predominance of the demonic. The struggle of a religious movement can never direct itself against the secular or the irreligious. The secular abides in the religious and has just as much reality as there is religious substance within it. Rather, religion struggles against anti-divine religion, against the demonic. Therefore, a profound and creative identification of the object of the struggle of religious socialism must begin with a conception of the general nature of the demonic, and proceed to an understanding of the demonry of this Kairos.

The demonic is the contradiction of unconditioned form, an eruption of the irrational ground of any realization of form that is individual and creative. The irrational can contradict unconditioned form only when it clothes itself in forms and opposes these to unconditioned form. The demonic is never formless. In this respect it is like the divine. It is also like it in the fact that it is not reduced to form (that is, is not exhausted in it) but, rather, filled with import, it bursts form open. The demonic, like the divine, is perceptible in the ecstatic, the overwhelming, and the dreadful. But whereas the ecstatic element of the divine affirms the unconditioned form and therefore creates forms, the ecstatic element of the demonic destroys form. We can distinguish between the divine and the demonic by their relation to unconditioned form.

In the immediacy of the sacramental spiritual situation, the divine and the demonic are mixed. We call theocratic the rising of the divine against the demonic and the consequent dissolution of sacramental immediacy. By this concept we do not mean the external appearance of a priestly or religious dominion but, rather, the will to conquer the sacred reality of the demonic in the name of sacred unconditioned form. It would not be difficult to show that the deepest root of even external theocracy is this inner theocratic tendency, which, to be sure, is often enough again misdirected into the demonic. In this sense, therefore, theocratic movements are antidemonic inwardly religious reform movements, like Jewish prophetism, Mohammedanism, monastic reform, Calvinism, and the socioethical sects. In this sense, religious socialism is also a theocratic movement.

The goal of theocratic movements is the sovereignty of the unconditioned form, of the right and the just. But as soon as this goal is reached, the danger threatens that sacred import will be lost. Formalism and emptiness always threaten. Form frees itself from sacramental constraint and from its fullness of import. It becomes profane or secular. Theocracy passes over into autonomy. Autonomy is able to elaborate pure forms with rational perfection in every sphere, but, by itself, it cannot bring about the fulfillment of forms in any sphere. It lives on the import of the past and the more it produces abstract forms, the more it becomes separated from life. A complete autonomy would mean the complete destruction of life. But life does not let itself be destroyed, and as the divine import of theonomy is dissipated, the demonic import that was previously subjected breaks forth from the life ground and uses autonomous form for the destruction of form. This resurgence of the demonic is characteristic of an era purged by autonomy. It is the peculiar form of reaction against the rising theonomy of our time. The result is a two-sided conflict of theonomy rising against the demony of this Kairos. On the one side are the unconquered residues of the old sacramental demonry against which religious socialism must continue the theocratic conflict with the aid of autonomous forms. On the other side are the reappearances of the demonic which find their way into the empty space created by autonomous formal criticism, and which frequently strive for sacramental meaning by the use of autonomous forms. Between the two stands autonomous form. It stands over against both. Nevertheless, it can never be willed as form, but only as an expression of import. The conflict of religious socialism is directed against sacramental and natural demonries. Corresponding to the duality of all form-giving power that creates either ideal or real forms, either theoretical or practical forms, is the substratum of the realization of all forms, the irrational ground. It too can be conceived as a duality: either as a drive to become one with being (*das Seiende*) or as a drive to transcend being, either as will to abandonment or as will to self-assertion. Love and power are polar opposites. Nevertheless, they are basically identical substrata of all creative form-giving power. Therefore, they are the bearers of divine and demonic ecstasy. Both primordial elements of the creative ground have always been recognized, and for the most part, one has been considered more worthy than the other: love above all by Plato, in innumerable appearances of mysticism, in romanticism, and the like; the will to power in voluntarism, in the philosophy of nature of the Renaissance, in Boehme, Schelling, Schopenhauer, Nietzsche, etc.; and both of them in realistic psychology and sociology, above all in poetry, but also in science. Essential to a clearer view of these two powers as symbols of the creative ground is their intrinsic dialectical character, their capacity to break out into divine and demonic ecstasy. Both powers are contained in every creative reality; it is not possible to separate will-to-power from love or love from will-to-power. Yet in every phenomenon one or the other can be recognized more clearly. The dominion of pure form seeks to drive out both. The perfected autonomy of form would create a rational reality without the erotic and the dynamic. It would be without the demonic, but also without divinity. However, no such reality is possible, for the erotic and the dynamic powers are the real in every actuality, forming its ground and its abyss. It would be a misunderstanding if one tried to take these concepts, in the universal application that they are given here, strictly and objectively in a psychological or sociological sense. One would thereby become guilty of poor metaphysics. Rather, they are to be taken symbolically as an expression of the creative ground that reveals itself with great symbolic force through the phenomena designated by them. The irrational ground they are supposed to symbolize is, however, no longer logically but only metalogically conceivable.

The basic definitions have now been given with which it is possible to approach an interpretation of the contemporary Kairos from the point of view of the Unconditional. In all spheres, religious socialism must lead the struggle against the demonries of the sacramental spiritual situation and against the natural demonry that emerges for the first time. In this struggle it must avail itself of pure rational form, offered to it by the autonomous culture of previous centuries. But, beyond that, it must strive for the revelation of a new sacred import by which autonomous form is fulfilled. . . . It must combat the demonic in the naturalistic as well as in the sacramental sense, and it must strive for theonomy in the sense of the unity of form and import. These are its tasks: the conquest of sacramental demonry through a theocratic struggle, and the pursuit of autonomous form, but not in order to come to a halt when it reaches autonomous form, for that is not possible — autonomous form is emptied of divine import, and forthwith it is a prey to demonic import — but in order to permit autonomous form to be filled with theonomous import. Its opponent is the demonic. But this does not mean that the irrational forces, that is, power and eros, which support the demonic must be annihilated; the attempt to do this is either rational utopianism or the mystical destruction of form. On the contrary, the same element that is destructive in the demonic (because it is manifestly destructive of form) will come to be seen as the divine, that is, as form-fulfilling, in theonomy. This corresponds to the idea of Kairos, which also does not lead to rational utopianism or to the mystical negation of the world but, rather, to a new and creative fulfillment of forms with an import borne by power and eros but penetrated by obedience to unconditioned form. It is therefore not demonic but divine. . . .

The decisive element . . . the new breakthrough of import, is not a matter of work. Rather, it is fate and grace. Belief in the Kairos is the expression of the consciousness of existing in that fate and of being touched by a new breakthrough of the Unconditional. All rational work in theory and practice can have no other meaning than to give expression to this import in every sphere of life.


## 4. THE WAY OF RELIGIOUS SOCIALISM

The consciousness of Kairos in the sense of an emerging theonomy creates a community of those who are filled with the same import and who strive for the same goal. It is a community of those who hear the call of the Kairos and understand themselves in it. Such a community is not a church in the sacramental spiritual sense, for it does not proceed from fixed sacred forms and symbols. Rather, it stands in theocratic and autonomous criticism before the given symbols whose demonic distortion it fights. This applies to all existing confessions but not to all in the same way. Religious socialism stands nearest to that confession that bears within itself the critical-theorcratic element most strongly, although it knows that it is nearer in terms of goal to those confessions in which the theonomous idea has found expression, though a demonically degenerate one. This determines its peculiar double attitude toward the Reformed and the Catholic expressions of the Christian idea. Thus, in its critical attitude it must go along with the radical forms of the Reformation, and in the theonomous idea it must go along with a Catholicism set free from demonic heteronomy. Moreover, it follows from this that religious socialism cannot be identified directly with any of the confessions. Still less is the community of those supported by the Kairos a separate confession, a religious sect. The formation of new religious communities does not proceed from autonomy and criticism but only from a new apprehension and transformation of old symbols. New religious creations stand in living connection with the creations of the past. They burst forth only out of the deepest tensions within a confession. Religious socialism, however, is born on the soil of critical autonomy. It has in itself no power to create symbols and it can therefore form no religious community in a special concrete sense. Whether in coming developments it will join in the formation of a religious community is a question that at present is without significance.

Religious socialism is no more identical with a cultural movement or a political party than it is with a religious confession. Religious socialism is therefore not identical with political socialism, nor does it form a party alongside it. It calls itself "socialism" because it has adopted the antidemonic socialist criticism historically and substantially and because it supports the political struggle of socialism as far as it intends to break the domination of political and social demonries. But religious socialism does not overlook the extent to which political socialism itself in possessed by these demonries, and, above all, it knows that the socialist idea should not be equated with the goal of political strategy. It must therefore repudiate giving religious consecration to a party as such or to an economic program as such. It keeps its eye open for the theonomous elements in other parties and movements as well. It cannot make fellowship with itself depend positively or negatively upon membership in a party. But it certainly calls for the recognition of the socialist criticism of culture and of the socialist struggle against sacramental and naturalistic demonries.

Religious socialism is a community of those who understand themselves in the consciousness of the Kairos and who struggle for the fate, that is, the grace, of theonomy. They can work in every party, confession, movement, so far as the latter make room for their work and allow for the struggle against the demonic elements within themselves. Only in this way can religious socialism protect itself from premature objectification, from becoming heteronomous, and thus from becoming subject to its own criticism. Certainly there can be more or less close alliances of those conscious of the Kairos. But they must retain a provisional character until symbols and forms are found that are the immediate expression of the total spiritual situation and which, therefore, do not operate rationally and heteronomously. The overcoming of the provisional, however, and the development of a new theonomy can occur only through a new creative breakthrough of the import that has been revealed in the symbols of the past. Without such a breakthrough a theonomous spiritual situation is impossible. However, when it has happened — and it is the Kairos faith that it is happening — then it pours forth into the forms that have been created out of its spirit, forms that religious socialism must help to create.

# 2

## PROTESTANT THEOLOGY AMID SOCIALIST CRISIS*

### REALISM AND FAITH

*As more powerful forces, especially Nazism, prevailed against Religious Socialism, Tillich continued his effort to forge a Protestantism that would fully engage the tumults of history while preserving its own critical and prophetic spirit. Taking his cues from expressionist painting, Tillich calls here for a historical realism that is also "self-transcending." Transcendence, for this Protestant, is never to be detached from the real that is "here and now." This "belief-ful realism", as he termed it in his earlier work (*Die religiöse Lage der Gegenwart, *1926) is another expression for the attitude and knowledge of theonomy. The following essay first appeared in* Religiöse Verwirklichung *(Collected Essays. Berlin: Furche, 1929) and then was included in* The Protestant Era *(Chicago: The University of Chicago Press, 1948, pp. 66-8, 69-82), the latter being the book that gained Tillich a substantial hearing in the United States after World War II.*

### 1. THE IDEA OF A SELF-TRANSCENDING REALISM

For those who have followed with sympathy or enthusiasm the development of painting in the first three decades of the nineteenth century, two events will stand out in memory: first, the emergence and success of "expressionism", then the flagging of its energies and the rise of a style called *neue Sachlichkeit* ("the new objectivity"). When expressionism appeared, it was largely rejected as repulsive, dark, and ugly. But slowly it began to fascinate many people because of the riddle implied in it and the radicalism of its solutions. Finally, it won most enthusiastic adherence from groups who saw it in a new mysticism or the way to a new religious cultus. This is understandable. Expressionism was a revolution against the realism of the nineteenth century. It was a rebellion against the naturalistic-critical, as well as against the idealistic-conventional wing of realism, and it also trespassed the limits of the subjective-

* See also pp. 18-21.

impressionistic realism from which it came. Things were interpreted by the expressionistic painters in their cosmic setting and their immeasurable depth. Their natural forms were broken so that their spiritual significance could become transparent. Colors, expressing divine and demonic ecstasies, broke through the gray of the daily life. It seemed as if the period of the myth had returned, and developments in other realms seemed to confirm the visions of the artists. But this feeling lasted no longer than to the middle of the third decade. At this time, works of art appeared which kept much closer to the natural forms of things than the expressionists did. They could, however, not be considered as a relapse to the nineteenth-century naturalism. They represented a post-expressionistic, not a pre-expressionistic style. They repudiated the elements of subjectivism and romanticism in the preceding period without giving up the depth and cosmic symbolism of their predecessors. Those who expected from this development a return to the idealizing naturalism of bourgeois liking were destined to disappointment, for the new realism was not interested in the natural forms of things for their own sake but for their power of expressing the profounder levels and the universal significance of things. Nineteenth-century realism had deprived reality of its symbolic power; expressionism had tried to re-establish this power by shattering the surface of reality. The new realism tries to point to the spiritual meaning of the real by using its given forms. In these movements art is driving toward a self-transcending realism. There is no guaranty that this goal will be reached; many tendencies in our period work against it, some of them honest, some of them merely ideological. But it is a tendency which should be understood and supported by Protestantism because it has a genuinely Protestant character.

Self-transcending realism is a universal attitude toward reality. It is neither a merely theoretical view of the world nor a practical discipline for life; it lies underneath the cleavage between theory and practice. Nor is it a special religion or a special philosophy. But it is a basic attitude in every realm of life, expressing itself in the shaping of every realm.

Self-transcending realism combines two elements, the emphasis on the real and the transcending power of faith. There seems to be no wider gap than that between a realistic and a belief-ful attitude. Faith transcends every conceivable reality; realism questions every transcending of the real, calling it utopian or romantic. Such a tension is hard to stand, and it is not surprising that the human mind always tries to evade it. Evasion is possible in two ways — in the way of a realism without self-transcendence or in the way of a self-transcendence which is not realistic. For the latter I want to use the word "idealism", for the former the word "self-limiting realism". Neither of these attitudes is necessarily irreligious. Positivism, pragmatism, empiricism — the different forms of realism which refuse self-transcendence — may accept religion as a realm beside the philosophical and scientific interpretation of reality, or they may connect the two realms in terms of a theology of immanent experience (the former more an English, the latter more an American, type). Idealism, on the other hand, in its different forms, such as metaphysical, epistemological, moral idealism (the first a classical German, the second a universal bourgeois, the third an Anglo-Saxon type) is essentially religious but in such a way that genuine religion must be critical of it. Faith is an ecstatic transcending of reality in the power of that which cannot be derived from the whole of reality and cannot be approached by ways which belong to the whole of reality. Idealism does not see the gap between the unconditional and the conditioned which no ontological or ethical self-elevation can bridge. Therefore it must be judged from a prophetic and Protestant point of view as religious arrogance and from the point of view of a self-limiting realism as metaphysical arrogance. In this double attack, from the side of faith and from the side of realism, idealism breaks down, historically and systematically, practically and theoretically. It is the glory of idealism that it tries to unite an autonomous interpretation of reality with a religious transcending of reality. Idealism is always on the way to "theonomy". Most of the theological, philosophical, and political critics of idealism have not even understood its problems. Their feeling of superiority over idealism is based on their ignorance about the depth of its questions and answers. The limitation and tragedy of idealism lie in the fact that it idealizes the real instead of transcending it in the power of the transcendent, i.e., in faith. Hence we are led to the result that faith and realism, just because of their radical tension, belong together. For faith implies an absolute tension and cannot be united with any attitude in which the tension is weakened. Idealism relativizes, self-limiting realism denies, but self-transcending realism accepts the tension.

## 2. THREE TYPES OF REALISM

.... The unity of rationality and the power of being may be interpreted in different ways. Since the power of being is discovered by thought, the thinking subject may become, intentionally or unintentionally, the bearer of all power. In this case the things are subjected to control and use by the rational man. They become powerless means for him who analyzes them or enjoys them or transforms them or rises above them or retires from them. From the critical and ethical schools of Greek philosophy this attitude is transmitted through late nominalism to modern technical science and the technocratic world view. One concedes to things only so much power as they should have in order to be useful. Reason becomes the means of controlling the world. The really real (*ousia*) of things is their calculable element, that which is determined by natural laws. Anything beyond this level is without interest and not an object of knowledge. This relation to reality is called "realistic" today. Through technical science and its economic utilization this realism is so predominant in our social and intellectual situation that the fight against it seems romantic and almost hopeless. Later Neo-Kantianism and, more consistently, positivism are the philosophical expressions of this radical reduction of the power of things to their theoretical calculability and their practical utility. Even theology was largely drawn into the orbit of this "technological realism".

But reason as the way of grasping the power of things may be understood in a quite different way. The power of being within reality may be preserved also in a rationalized and spiritualized form. In this case the true being, discovered by the logos, becomes a matter of contemplation and union. There are degrees of the power of being (Plato, Aristotle, and Plotinus agree on this point), and on these degrees the human mind climbs theoretically and practically to the highest one, the supreme power of being. Mere vital existence, the control and transformation of reality, practice generally, and even physical and mathematical knowledge are transcended, and the eternal essences and their unity and ground are sought. Here "matter" exercises a permanently retarding and often preventive influence on the ascending mind. Matter, although without form or essential being, has a negative, half-demonic power which cannot be overcome in the material world. Therefore, the mind must transcend the visible cosmos as a whole, in order to find the ultimate power of being in that which is beyond being, the "good", the "pure actuality", "the One". Their longing for the true power of being drives the Greeks into a flight from the ambiguous half-demonic power of things. This is the conceptual foundation of Neo-Platonic asceticism and of that type of realism which we should call "mystical realism".

Mystical realism was dominant in the early and high Middle Ages before its nominalistic disintegration. It was not a radical, but a moderate, realism which the Middle Ages accepted. On the basis of biblical religion it was impossible to follow Greek mysticism in its ultimately negative attitude toward individuality and personality. But mystical realism was "realism" and not romanticism or idealism. Although our present terminology makes it difficult for us to use the word "realistic" for something that seems to be just the opposite of what the word generally means today, we must understand that medieval realism was as much right in using the word "real" for its attitude as modern realism is in using it for its attitude. In both cases realism gives an answer to the question of the really real or the essential power of things, but the place where this power is sought and found is different. We are prevented, however, from acknowledging this if we interpret the belief that the universals are the really real merely as a logical theory (which it also is) instead of understanding it primarily as the ontological expression of a social and spiritual situation.

The mystical realism of the Middle Ages is still alive in our time. The technological concept of reality is permanently challenged by the mystical concept, which reappears in many transformations. Theories of intuitive knowledge, classicist and romantic revivals of ancient or medieval forms of thought, phenomenology, the philosophy of life (aesthetic or vitalistic), the "theory of Gesalt", some types of the psychology of the "unconscious" — all these seek for the inner power of things beyond (or below) the level at which they are calculable and dominable. The fight between the two types of realism is continuously going on, with changing results. On the whole, however, technological realism is victorious because the real situation of the man of today, his personal and his social situation, and his relation to things are determined by its effects. But though not yet victorious, the struggles of the modern offsprings of mystical realism have not been in vain, as is noticeable in all fields of knowledge. The fate of our culture is, in the long run, bound up with this conflict and with our ability to go forward to a new kind of realism.

Both technological and mystical realism have, according to their Greek origin, one thing in common. They do not look at concrete existence, its "here and now", in order to discover the power of things. They

71

abstract from it — technological realism for the sake of means and ends, mystical realism for the sake of essence and intuition. It is, of course, a necessary quality of all thinking to go beyond the given as given, but it is possible to seek for the power of reality within the concreteness of its existence. This is the nature of historical knowledge on which a third type of realism, namely, "historical realism", is based. Historical realism is a creation of the Occident, and especially of the Occident in so far as it stands under Protestant influence. The really real is asked for in time and space, in our historical existence, in that sphere from which all Greeks had taken flight. It was now no longer necessary to flee, since the world is divinely created and no demonic ambiguity can be found in the material world as such.

For historical realism the really real appears in the structures created by the historical process. Historical logic is still in a beginning stage, but this much is already clear: History cannot be understood in terms of technological realism. It cannot become an object of calculation and control like some levels of natural objects. History, on the other hand, cannot be grasped in a mystical contemplation of its essence. It is open to interpretation only through active participation. We can grasp the power of historical being only if we are grasped by it in our own historical existence. Detached observation of historical events and registration of assumed historical laws removes us from the possibility of approaching history.

Historical realism transcends technological, as well as mystical, realism. Its decisive characteristic is consciousness of the present situation, of the "here and now". It sees the power of being, in the depth of "our historical situation". It is contemporaneous, and in this it differs from the technological, as well as from the mystical, idea of reality.

Neither technological nor mystical realism knows the principle of contemporaneity. The technological does not, because it relates every moment in the historical process to a purpose the fulfillment of which lies in the future. There is no "present" in the vicious circle of means and ends, as the doctrine of infinite progress clearly indicates. Life, in so far as it occurs in the present, is concerned only with the surface, the accidental, with the experience of pleasure and pain, the mere impression. It is just the lack of contemporaneity that subjects us to the bondage of the passing moment. There is no contemporaneity in mystical realism either. It transcends the concrete historical existence and tries to create a union of the mind with the eternal essences in which individual things and events participate in a transitory way and for which they are only examples. The Christian, especially the Protestant, understanding of history as the history of salvation, has overcome this attitude of indifference toward our historical existence. The prophetic-Christian interpretation of history is the background of historical realism.

Contemporaneity is not bondage to the passing moment, it is not living in mere impressions. Not only historical realism but every intellectual penetration into things transcends the accidental, the mere flux of events. Such a transcending is presupposed in all our relations to reality, even before philosophy has created methods and discovered categories. Our very being as "minds" divides our world into essential and accidental elements, into that level which contains the power of being and that level which is without power. But what is the power of the here and now? It is its unique, unrepeatable, and fateful character. It is the merging of the still actual past and the already actual failure in the present moment which creates the power of a historical situation. Even nature has one side which makes a historical interpretation of it possible. Although the particular event in nature is subject to the law of repetition, the natural process as a whole runs forward and is irreversible.

## 3. HISTORICAL REALISM AND KNOWLEDGE

The principle of contemporaneity as emphasized by historical realism has important consequences for the relation of the cognitive sphere to the whole of human existence. Neither mystical nor technological realism demands the participation in all elements of life, the mystical because of its ascetic attitude toward the dynamics of life, the technological because of its domineering attitude toward reality. Only historical realism makes the participation in the whole of human existence a condition of true knowledge.

This applies to the personal, as well as to the social, reality of man in history. Nobody is able to penetrate into the deeper levels of a historical situation without penetrating into the deeper levels of his personality. Knowing the really real of our historical existence presupposes the knowledge of the really real in ourselves. But knowing one's self on this level is transforming one's self. Detached observation of one's self is here impossible. And knowing our historical situation on this level transforms our historical situation. Detached observation of our historical situation is here impossible. He who knows in terms of historical realism is he who is creative in himself and in history. Even technological realism has a certain awareness of this situation. Through its educational methods and its public communications it has shaped the forces of intellect and will through which man controls things, scientifically and technically. A psychological type has been created, in Europe as well as in America, which is powerful and empty at the same time and is feared by those Europeans and Asiatics who are still under the influence of some form of mystical realism. The latter, on the other hand, has in connection with the scientific ideals of the Occident produced that type of theoretical detachment from history and of scholarly asceticism which has transformed the scholar into an apparatus for the registration of facts, without critical or creative passion. I do not want to underestimate the heroism of scientific self-surrender in every inquiry, an attitude that corresponds to the immovable, eternal element in all knowledge. But this is only *one* element. The other one is the change, the movement, and here and now. While the elder generation of scholars (e.g., Max Weber) emphasized the ascetic element, thus producing an estrangement from life in the academic world, the scholars of the younger generation have more and more emphasized the active element in knowledge and the need for participation in all sides of life. *The ideal of knowledge in historical realism is the union of scientific objectivity with passionate self-interpretation and self-transformation.*

Contemporaneity in knowing demands not only the penetration into the depth of our personal being but also into the depth of our social being. Mystical realism is far from admitting such an attitude. It uses the cognitive function for the sake of escaping the historical and political reality through an intuition of the immutable truth. All those, therefore, who are directly or indirectly dependent on mystical realism (as is, for instance, recent neoclassicism) disregard the historical constellation to which they are bound, in its significance for knowledge. The situation is different with technological realism. It has always been aware of the connection between technical science and the structure of industrial society. The attitude of the proletariat and its political expression, the socialist movement, toward the scholars and their work is rooted in this awareness. The proletarians look at knowledge as a means of power in the class struggle, in which they find themselves strongly criticized by those members of the intelligentsia who are unable to imagine such a necessity and viciously attacked by those members of the ruling groups who use knowledge as a means of power without any inhibition. It is understandable that in this situation socialism accuses the *bourgeoisie* of producing not ideas which are true but ideologies which idealize and justify the power of the ruling class, and this through concepts and values that belong to the past and have no actuality today. Our scholars have seldom understood the seriousness of this attack. The concept of ideology in its polemical sense is a symbol for the volcano over which our society lives. If an intellectual system is successfully interpreted as a mere ideology, it has lost its formative power. The official representatives of science and religion have not even noticed how far advanced this undermining process has gone, and not only in the proletariat. These people will face the coming catastrophe of their intellectual world as unprepared as they faced the catastrophe of their political world after the First World War. It is pathetic and provoking to see the naïveté with which many highly educated people absolutize their own favored position in society, without realizing the general structure which gives them this position. Although it is the duty of scientific honesty to reject any propagandistic abuse of the search for truth, it is also a duty of honesty to know the power of the social structure to which one belongs, for one cannot escape it. It determines one's cognitive functions as much as the system of values in which one lives. He who wants to know the power of reality in the depth of his historical existence must be in actual contact with the concrete, unrepeatable tensions of the present. *The ideal of knowledge in historical realism is the union of scientific objectivity with a passionate understanding and transformation of the historical situation.*

Historical realism repudiates any attempt to escape the present for the sake of an unreal past or an unreal future. Romanticism which turns toward the past (a past that never did exist) and utopianism which turns toward the future (a future that never will exist) are equally wrong from the point of view of historical realism. Both lose the present and do not reach the really real in the historical existence, for the past can be reached only on the basis of an active participation in the present, and the future can be molded only in concrete decisions about actual historical problems. This does not lead to the so-called *Realpolitik* which was proposed by the imperialistic *bourgeoisie* in the Bismarckian and prewar epochs and was readily — much too readily — accepted by large sections of the German intelligentsia. *Realpolitik* has nothing to do with historical realism. It is a product of a merely technological realism and derives its goal not from a penetration into the meaning of the present but from the so-called "demands of the moment". Therefore, it is finally self-destructive.

There is no conflict between the principle of contemporaneity and the validity of the ethical norms. "Ethical instinct" can never replace the ethical principles, the criteria of good and evil. Historical realism is not without principles and criteria. It presupposes them on its way to the depth of a historical situation. Without universal criteria of justice, no profound analysis of a historical situation is possible. Without principles of the ideal, the real cannot be interpreted in its depth. But historical realism prevents the principles from becoming abstract. It expresses them in the light of the present and as answers to the questions implied in a historical situation.

## 4. HISTORICAL REALISM AND FAITH

The question now arises: What is the relation of historical realism to what we have called "self-transcending realism"? Historical realism strives to grasp the power of reality or the really real in a concrete historical situation. But the really real is not reached until the unconditioned ground of everything real, or the unconditioned power in every power of being, is reached. Historical realism remains on a comparatively unrealistic level if it does not grasp that depth of reality in which its divine foundation and meaning become visible. Everything before this point has preliminary, conditioned reality. Therefore, historical realism has truth to the degree that it reaches the ultimate ground and meaning of a historical situation and, through it, of being as such.

But it is the character of the unconditional that it cannot be grasped; its power includes its unapproachable mystery. It we try to grasp it, it is no longer the unconditional that we have in our hands — even if it has the highest religious or ontological names. Idealism is the philosophy that makes this mistake. It confuses the world of essences and values and their unity with the unconditionally real. It fails to transcend this sphere of pure reason, a sphere that can be transcended only by accepting that which is "before reason", the *Unvordenkliche*, as Schelling has called it ("that before which thinking cannot penetrate"), the originally given, the ground and abyss of everything that is. There was a feeling for this limit in all Greek philosophy. Indeed, pure realism is not Greek, because the ancient mind could not overcome the belief in the eternally resisting matter, the negative, restricting power of which excludes an unconditional divine power. Genuine idealism is possible only on Christian soil, on the basis of the idea of creation which affirms the essential goodness and unity of the world. Perfect systems like those of the great idealists presuppose the Christian victory over the remnants of religious dualism in Greek thought. But they arise only because the other Christian idea is disregarded, the gap between God and man through finitude and sin.

In this respect positivism is more Christian than idealism. It accepts the limited and fragmentary character of the human situation and tries to remain in the sphere of the conditioned. It shows more humility than idealism in taking the given as it is and rejecting romantic or utopian syntheses which have no reality. But positivism does not see the problem of self-transcendence. It restricts itself to the immanence, not because of the unapproachable mystery of the transcendent, but because of its unwillingness to trespass the limits of the empirically given. Positivism is realism without self-transcendence or faith.

Self-transcending realism is the religious depth of historical realism; therefore, it is opposed to mystical and technological realism. Mysticism is not aware of the unapproachable nature of the divine ground of reality (including the "soul"). It tries to reach the unconditional in conditioned steps, in degrees of elevation to the highest. Mystical self-transcendence is a continuous approximation to the ultimate; it does not realize the infinite gap between the finite and the infinite; it does not realize the paradoxical character of faith and of a realism which is united with faith. This does not mean that mystical realism excludes faith. In every mystical experience an act of self-transcendence or faith is implicit. The complete union with the ultimate is, according to all mystics, a gift to be received and not a perfection to be achieved. Therefore, it is a mistake when Protestant theologians, from Ritschl to Barth, establish an absolute contrast between mysticism and faith. It is true, however, that mysticism tries to transcend faith in the experience of mystical union and that it disregards the historical situation and its power and depth. This is different in a self-transcending, historical realism which experiences the ultimate in and through a concrete historical situation and denies any degrees of approximation to it, knowing that it is always, at the same time, unconditionally near and unconditionally far.

Technological realism is even less capable of becoming self-transcendent. It separates realism and faith. In later Ritschlianism, faith became the means of elevating the ethical personality above nature to moral independence, leaving nature to technical control. The technological interpretation of nature, its complete subjection to human purposes, was accepted but not transcended. And domineering personality used faith as a means for maintaining this position of independence and control. This theology expresses very well the difficulty of combining faith with technological realism. Although the faith of which, for instance, a man like William Hermann speaks, is in itself warm, powerful, and passionate, its function in the context of a technological interpretation of reality is the creation of the personality of the victorious *bourgeoisie.* In English positivism no attempt is made to unite faith and realism. "Faith" is the conventional or serious acceptance of the creeds and institutions of the church. And realism is the technological attitude to nature and society. But there is no union between this kind of faith and this kind of realism. They are two worlds, connected only by a powerful social and intellectual conformism.

Self-transcending realism is based on the consciousness of the "here and now". The ultimate power of being, the ground of reality, appears in a special moment, in a concrete situation, revealing the infinite depth and the eternal significance of the present. But this is possible only in terms of a paradox, i.e., by faith, for, in itself, the present is neither infinite nor eternal. The more it is seen in the light of the ultimate power, the more it appears as questionable and void of lasting significance. So the power of a thing is, at the same time, affirmed and negated when it becomes transparent for the ground of its power, the ultimately real. It is as in a thunderstorm at night, when the lightning throws a blinding clarity over all things, leaving them in complete darkness the next moment. When reality is seen in this way with the eye of a self-transcending realism, it has become something new. Its ground has become visible in an "ecstatic" experience, called "faith". It is no longer merely self-subsistent as it seemed to be before; it has become transparent or, as we could say, "theonomous". This, of course, is not an event in nature, although — as always in spiritual matters — words and pictures have to be used which are taken from the spatial sphere. But it is the whole of the personality, including its conscious center, its freedom and responsibility, which is grasped by the ultimate power that is the ground also of every personal being. We are grasped, in the experience of faith, by the unapproachably holy which is the ground of our being and breaks into our existence and which judges us and heals us. This is "crisis" and "grace" at the same time. Crisis in the theological sense is as much a matter of faith as grace is. To describe the crisis as something immanent, open for everybody at any time, and grace as something transcendent, closed to everybody and to be accepted only by a personal decision, is bad theology. Neither crisis nor grace is in our reach, neither grace nor crisis is beyond a possible experience. The present situation is always full of "critical" elements, of forces of disintegration and self-destruction. But it becomes "crisis" in the religious sense, i.e., judgment, only in unity with the experience of grace. In this way historical realism becomes self-transcendent; historical and self-transcending realism are united.

## 5. SELF-TRANSCENDENT REALISM AND THEOLOGY

Every religious word is an interpretation of the tension between the conditionally and the unconditionally real, between "realism" and "self-transcendence". Religious terms are the more adequate, the more they express this paradox in its depth and power. The same is true of theological terms. In the phrase "unconditioned power", for instance, the word "power", which, in connection with being ("power of being"), points to the most general characteristic of everything that "is", is used for that which transcends everything that is. A quite different power of being is meant if we speak of "unconditioned power" in the sense of "almightiness" or "omnipotence". Religious and theological words lose their genuine meaning if they are used as terms to designate finite objects under the control of the categories which constitute the world of objects. If this happens, the religious words express too much and too little at the same time: too much in so far as they elevate *one* object (called "God") above all the others; too little in so far as they do not attribute to God the unconditioned power which makes him God (and not a highest being only). The criterion of all theology is its ability to preserve the absolute tension between the conditional and the unconditional.

Religion tries to surpass the given reality in order to approach the unconditional. The means for achieving this is rapture and ecstasy. Wherever we transcend the limits of our own being, moving toward union with another one, something like ecstasy ("standing outside one's self") occurs. Ecstasy is the act of breaking through the fixed form of our own being. In this sense of the term we must say: Only through ecstasy can the ultimate power of being be experienced in ourselves, in things and persons, and in historical situations. Plato in the *Phaedrus* fights against the soberness and the lack of *eros* in the immanent realism of the Sophists. Even in the feeling of unlimited power over nature in technological realism an enthusiastic element is noticeable. There is ecstasy in love and communion, in the penetration of one's own depths, in the experience of freedom and of the sublime greatness of the categorical imperative. This gives a key to the use of intoxicating foods and drinks in primitive cults, and it makes understandable the ecstasy of asceticism and the "rapture" of mysticism. It cannot be said that all this is the opposite of the attitude of faith as expressed in the Bible. It is hard not to hear the ecstatic element in the words and the attitude of the great prophets; in the radicalism of the words of Jesus and the description of his visionary experiences; in the mystery sermons of the Fourth Gospel; in the "holy legend" as conceived by the Synoptic Gospels; in Paul's witness to the effects of the Spirit (especially in its main effect, love); in the triumphant words of Luther about the victory over law, death, and the devil. And even in some utterances of the "theology of crisis" (which wants to be a theology of faith exclusively) the ecstasy of the paradox and the ascetic self-sacrifice of reason and autonomy are unmistakably present.

He who refuses to see all this and fights against the ecstatic element in religion is motivated by a justified fear. He is afraid of the confusion between genuine ecstasy and artificial self-intoxication, for not every kind of enthusiasm is a participation in the unconditioned power, not everything that calls itself ecstasy is an experience of being grasped by the really real. An ecstasy that drives us away from the reality and the demands of the present is destructive, and, if it pretends to be holy, it is demonic. In true ecstasy we receive ultimate power by the presence of the ultimate; in a false ecstasy one section of our being overwhelms the whole of our personality, emptying it and leaving it in a state of disintegration. Any attempt to force the unconditioned power upon us necessarily creates a false ecstasy, for there is no way to reach the ultimate that we can manipulate. It grasps us when and where it will, for it is always also darkness, judgment, and death for us. Cults, sacramental power, pure doctrines, mystical or moralistic theologies that give us a way by which we seem to grasp what is beyond grasp lead us away from the real power of reality, from the depth of the here and now. They betray us in trying to elevate us. True ecstasy is united with faith, and faith transcends what seems to be real, because it is the presence of the really, the ultimately, real.

False ecstasy can be found in many places, even in a religion that is based on the principle of "faith alone" and that often produces an anti-ecstatic morality, as in Protestantism. This refers to the Protestant cultus, or to what is left of it, and even to what purports to reform and enrich it. Protestant liturgy contains very few elements in which the ecstasy of being grasped unconditionally is expressed. But those elements that it does contain are far removed from the depth of the present. They do not really concern us, and, consequently, they are strange and unreal to most of our contemporaries; it is of no use to introduce the "treasures of the past" into our liturgies if they are not able to express the depth of our present situation.

This is true also of the spoken word, which is abundant in Protestantism, in and outside the cultus. "Word of God" is an ambiguous term. It is often used in the sense of the written word of the Bible. But no biblical word is the word of God for us so long as we have to give up our historical reality in order to understand it. Not even the biblical word can reach us religiously if it does not become contemporaneous. The "Word of God" is every reality through which the ultimate power breaks into our present reality, a person (e.g., the Christ), a thing (e.g., a sacramental object), a written text (e.g., the Bible), a spoken word (e.g., a sermon). It is the greatest emergency of the Protestant churches of today that they have not yet found a way of preaching in which contemporaneity and self-transcending power are united. The ecclesiastical, and to a great extent the biblical, terminology is removed from the reality of our historical situation. If it is used, nevertheless, with that attitude of priestly arrogance which repeats the biblical word and leaves it to the listeners to be grasped by it or not, it certainly ceases to be the "Word of God" and is rightly ignored by Protestant people. And the minister who feels himself to be a martyr of "divine" frustration — and even becomes ecstatic about this frustration — is guilty of a lack of contemporaneity.

The noncontemporary interpretation of the Bible is based on a noncontemporary understanding of revelation. Revelation is revelation to me in my concrete situation, in my historical reality. If I am asked to make a leap from my situation into a situation of past history in order to receive revelation, what I receive is no longer revelation *for me*, but a report about revelations received by others, for instance, in A.D. 30-33, by people in Palestine. Either I must become a real contemporary of those people, which is impossible, or something must be in the revelation which they received that can become contemporary with me and with every historical situation. At the same time, the denial of contemporaneity endangers the transcendent element in revelation. The leap from my present to a past situation is the "work" I have to do and am able to do in order to receive revelation. In this way revelation is dependent on me in so far as I have to move out of my concrete historical situation into the situation in which I can meet the "historical Jesus". Historical criticism, however, has shown that this is impossible, even if it were theologically admissible. There is no way of meeting the "historical Jesus" (i.e., the product of historical criticism) because the Jesus of whom we have reports was from the very beginning the "Christ of faith". This result of scientific honesty, religious courage, and an indomitable desire for historical truth agrees entirely with the demands of self-transcendent realism. It prevents theology from confusing the venerating

81

intuition of a character of the past with the manifestation of the unconditional in the present. He who is the Christ is contemporaneous, or he is not the Christ.

Self-transcending realism requires the criticism of all forms of supranaturalism — supra-naturalism in the sense of a theology that imagines a supra-natural world beside or above the natural one, a world in which the unconditional finds a local habitation, thus making God a transcendent object, the creation an act at the beginning of time, the consummation a future state of things. To criticize such a conditioning of the unconditional, even if it leads to atheistic consequences, is more religious, because it is more aware of the unconditional character of the divine, than a theism that bans God into the supra-natural realm. The man of today, who feels separated by a gulf from the theistic believer, often knows more about the "ultimate" than the self-assured Christian who thinks that through his faith he has God in his possession, at least intellectually. A Christian who unites his supra-naturalistic belief with the continuous denial of his historical situation (and the historical situation of many others for whom he is responsible) is rejected by the principles of a self-transcendent realism that is always also historical realism. This is the Protestant solution of the problem: faith and reality.

\*

## NATURE AND SACRAMENT

*Tillich's lecture "Nature and Sacrament" illustrates why his Protestant theology retained appeal to Roman Catholics with whom he insisted on a dialogue done in "listening love". While Tillich never retracted claims that the Protestant principle is the criterion of every sacramental experience, he also never ceased emphasizing that Protestantism lives from and needs "the Catholic substance". As Tillich states in the following selection so clearly, the very destiny of Protestantism depends on an appropriate view of the sacramental in Protestant thought and practice. This essay was a lecture originally delivered at a conference of the Berneuchen group, which was committed to rigorous reforms of ritual in the German churches. Led by Wilhelm Stählin and Karl Ritter, the group shared Tillich's sense that no church was possible without sacramental symbols and rituals of the holy. Tillich moved away from this group only when it focused exclusively on archaic, liturgical forms (see Tillich, On the Boundary, pp. 72-4). First published in Religiöse Verwirklichung, this essay was another of the important contributions in The Protestant Era (Chicago, 1948, pp. 94-112).*

No other question in Protestantism has from the beginning offered so much difficulty as has the question of the sacraments, and no other has received such uncertain answers. This is no mere accident, for the whole protest of the Reformation was in fundamental opposition to the sacramental system of Catholicism. Indeed, all sides of the Protestant criticism may be interpreted as an attack of the Protestant spirit upon the Catholic tendency to a sacramental objectivation and demonization of Christianity. The teachings of the Reformed churches represent the most thoroughgoing application of this principle of Protestantism. The famous answer of the Heidelberg Catechism to the effect that the Mass is "an accursed idolatry" expresses the vigorously antidemonic attitude of the Reformed churches in their battle against the Roman Catholic view of the sacraments. Luther broke with Zwingli, because Zwingli's hostile attitude toward the sacraments was strange to the mystical element in Luther's faith (though Luther did not himself succeed in working out a clear and consistent theory of the sacraments). The situation in the church today reflects the same tensions. Many ministers who are in a position to judge the situation as it really is remark with anxiety the "death of the sacraments". Nor are strong countertendencies visible, not even in theory. Yet the problem of the sacraments is a decisive one if Protestantism is to come to its full realization. A complete disappearance of the sacramental element (not the same thing, be it noted, as the particular sacraments) would lead to the disappearance of the cultus and, finally, to the dissolution of the visible church itself. For this reason Protestantism must deal seriously with the whole sacramental aspect of religion, an aspect that is fundamental for an understanding of the way in which Protestantism can gain a strong historical form. The aspect of the question with which we shall deal here is, in spite of its importance, often neglected. It is the problem of the relation between nature and sacrament. Bearing in mind the concrete situation in which we find ourselves, I should like to begin with an analysis of the two sacraments still alive in Protestantism and of the significance of the word in its relation to them.

## 1. THE SACRAMENT OF BAPTISM

We begin with baptism not only because it is the basic sacrament but also because it is the easiest to analyze. The sacrament of baptism has only one element, and this element is a simple element, water. It is through water that baptism becomes a sacrament. Without water there would be no baptism. But, on the other hand: "Without the Word of God, the water is simply water and no baptism." This statement from Luther's Catechism raises a whole series of profound theological and historical problems. Among these problems we must first ask the question as to what is meant by the phrase "simply water". And if water as such is to be described as "simply water", why use water at all? Why is not the "Word of God" sufficient without water, why need there be a sacrament? There are three possible answers to this question, which is the question concerning the natural element in the sacrament.

The first answer gives a symbolic-metaphoric interpretation of the element. It considers water as a symbol, say, for purification or for drowning or for both together and speaks of the dying of the old, the unclean, and the resurrection of the new, the pure. On this interpretation, sprinkling by water or baptism by immersion serves the purpose of setting forth in an understandable picture the idea that is expressed also by the accompanying word. The act of baptism is thus a visible representation of the idea of baptism. Obviously, other pictorial actions could serve as representation of the same idea, such as passing through fire, going down into a cave and the like, as are, in fact, familiar in votive ceremonies or in the mystery religions. The use of water may also have a rational motivation, on the ground that water is easy to use, or it may have some justification in the fact of its traditional use. But neither of these explanations suggests any necessary, intrinsic relationship between water and baptism.

The second answer may be characterized as the "ritualistic" interpretation of the element. Here it is asserted that the relation between water and baptism is merely accidental. The connecting of the two is dependent on a divine command. Because of this command, water acquires its sacramental significance as soon as it is employed in the properly celebrated rite of baptism. A residue of this conception, which is fundamentally nominalistic in character, is evident in the Protestant claim that the sacrament had to be instituted by Christ himself according to the biblical reports. The ritualistic conception does not even hint that there might be an intrinsic relationship between water and baptism.

The third answer gives a realistic interpretation of the element. It explicitly raises the question as to whether there is not a necessary relationship between water and baptism. It questions Luther's view that water is "simply water", although accepting his repudiation of the magical conception of the sacraments. A special character or quality, a power of its own, is attributed to water. By virtue of this natural power, water is suited to become the bearer of a sacral power and thus also to become a sacramental element. A necessary relationship between baptism and water is asserted. This realistic conception seems to me to be adequate to the true nature of the sacrament. It rejects the idea that there is a merely arbitrary connection between the idea and the material document.

## 2. THE SACRAMENT OF THE LORD'S SUPPER

The analysis of the Lord's Supper is much more difficult and complicated. To begin with, we have here two perceptible elements, bread and wine. In the second place, neither of these elements is an original natural element; both are rather the result of an artificial changing of natural products. In the third place — and this is the most important point — the two together represent the body of Christ, the basic element of the Lord's Supper. And in the fourth place, whereas the body of Christ as a body belongs to nature, as a transcendent body it is beyond nature.

The meaning of the Lord's Supper as a sacrament is that it is the sacramental appropriation of the exalted body of Christ. The human body is the highest creation of nature, containing within itself all other natural elements and, at the same time, surpassing them all. The eating of a real body is, of course, out of the question. The anthropophagism of a primitive cultus had already been eliminated by the antidemonic struggles of early religious periods. And the body of Jesus Christ, in so far as it existed at a particular time in history, is obviously inaccessible to us.

But it is just this body that becomes accessible to us through the fact that it has become transcendent. It remains a body; it does not become spirit; it becomes rather a "spiritual" body. As such it is accessible. But as such it lacks perceptibility. It lacks the natural element without which a real celebration of the sacrament is impossible. The problem is solved by substituting organic substances for the body, substances that nourish the body and that have the form of artificially prepared means of nourishment. That is, in place of the body we have the elements that nourish the body.

We may now make use of the various interpretations of the sacrament which we have derived from our analysis of baptism. If we apply the results of this analysis to the elements of the Lord's Supper, first, to the basic elements of the Supper — the body of Christ — it is evident that the body of Christ can be understood only by means of the third, the realistic interpretation. What is it supposed to symbolize? The spirit of Christ? In that case we should be attempting to symbolize black by white. The body of Christ itself is what is referred to. A natural reality is elevated to transcendent, divine meaning. Participation in the divine power is a participating also in the divine power in nature. It seems to me as if Luther's (logically absurd) theory of the ubiquity of the body of Christ was an attempt to give expression to this idea.

It is a more difficult question if we try to determine the precise significance of the secondary elements, the bread and wine. The Catholic doctrine of transubstantiation is the simplest answer to the question. Through transubstantiation, the bread and the wine — the secondary elements — are in substance annulled and replaced; there remains only one element, the body of Christ, which, by means of the transubstantiation, assumes the bread and wine into its own mode of being. Among Protestants, on the other hand, the independence and separate character of the secondary elements are maintained. Hence the question as to their significance is all the more difficult, and especially the question as to the reason for the choice of just these elements. A ritualistic conception of the sacrament would center attention upon the words of institution, for ostensibly they contain a command of Jesus. The command would be responsible for the linking-together of the primary with the two secondary elements, and thus the association of the body of Christ with bread and wine would be explained as the mere accident of a historical situation. But this interpretation would practically eliminate the primary element of the Lord's Supper, the exalted body of Christ; for neither the pouring and drinking of the wine nor the breaking and eating of the bread have any symbolic relation to the transcendent Christ, although at least the breaking of the bread is a clear and adequate symbol for the event on Golgotha. Beyond this the ritualistic interpretation cannot go. The realistic interpretation, on the other hand, can explain bread and wine as representing the natural powers that nourish the body and support in the human body the highest possibility of nature. They point to the presence of the divine saving power in the natural basis of all spiritual life as well as in the spiritual life itself.

### 3. THE WORD AND THE SACRAMENT

The classical combination "word and sacrament" means, in the first place, "the word as well as the sacrament". Next it signifies, "the sacrament through the word". And it has often been used, especially in Protestantism, as "word without sacrament". This variety of implications is inevitable so long as the two concepts are understood as being qualitatively contrasted or, more concretely expressed, so long as it is denied that the word by itself can have a sacramental character. But there is no justification for such a denial. The word is, first of all, a natural phenomenon. As such, it can, like other natural elements, become a part of a ritual act in which it functions as the bearer of a transcendent power: it can become sacramental.

The word as breath, as sound, as something heard, is a natural phenomenon. At the same time, however, a word is the bearer of a meaning. There are two possible ways of understanding the relation between the word as a natural phenomenon and the word as a bearer of meaning. The one possibility is to deprive the word of its intrinsic power and to deny any essential relation between the word and the meaning it bears. The power, the significance, the penetrating force of words is then attributed to the meaning which could be expressed as well by other words. The words are thought of as arbitrarily interchangeable. The other possibility is to consider the sound and the meaning as bound together in such a way that the natural power of words becomes the necessary bearer of its power of meaning, so that the one is not possible without the other. Where this is asserted, words by their natural power are potential bearers of a transcendent power and are suitable for sacramental usage.

Sacramental words that definitely exhibit this character are to be found in Protestantism in connection with the administration of the sacraments and also in the pronouncing of the words of absolution. In these cases the following questions arise: Are the words that are here used only signs that indicate and communicate a meaning? Or are they words in which sound and meaning are so united that the speaking of the words, and therefore the natural process of speaking as such, has a power through which they can become bearers of a transcendent power? If the second question is answered in the affirmative, a realistic interpretation of the sacramental word would be implied, and the ritualistic conception, which traces the words back only to commands, as well as the symbolic-metaphorical interpretation, which makes words only empty tokens, would be precluded.

We have shown in our analysis of the two Protestant sacraments, as well as of the words used in them, that the "realistic" interpretation alone provides an adequate explanation of their nature. We must, however, raise the question as to whether such an interpretation is logical and justifiable and as to what significance its application would have for a theory of the sacraments and for the shaping of the cultus in Protestantism. Above all, we must ask: What conception of nature is implied in such a realism and how can it be shown that such a conception of nature is necessary?

## 4. WAYS OF INTERPRETING NATURE

The concept of nature has a number of very different meanings, depending upon what it is contrasted with. The *formal* concept of nature contrasts the natural with everything nonnatural (the unnatural or the supernatural). It therefore also includes soul and mind as results of natural growth. The *material* concept of nature contrasts the natural with everything in which freedom is involved. The concepts antithetical to the material concept of nature are spirit and history. Theology places a negative value-judgment upon the natural in the formal sense, which is viewed as corrupted, sinful, and fallen, in opposition to the supernatural, which is the redeemed, the restored, the perfected. In this study we are concerned with nature in its material sense as the bearer of sacramental meaning and power.

The conception of nature that we find earliest in history, so far as we have knowledge of it, is the magical-sacramental conception. According to it, everything is filled with a sort of material energy which gives to things and to parts of things, even to the body and the parts of the body, a sacral power. The word "sacral" in this context, however, does not signify something in opposition to the profane. Indeed, at this phase of cultural development the distinction between the sacred and the profane is not a fundamental one. The natural power in things is, at the same time, their sacral power, and any commerce with them is always both ritualistic and utilitarian. One could characterize this primitive view as pan-sacramentalism, but, if this is done, one must remember that what we today call the "sacramental" is not thought of by the primitive mind as a separate or special religious reality. The primitive man holds to a magical interpretation of nature; the technical control of reality is supposed to be effected without reference to what we call "natural law". The control of reality is accomplished through the operations of magical energy without using the circuitous methods of rational manipulation. It should be pointed out, however, that there has never been a merely magical relation to nature. The technical necessities somehow always assert themselves and create certain areas in which rational objectivity prevails.

When this occurs, generally the magical view of nature disappears and is replaced by the rational-objective attitude. Only when the latter view of nature is reached may we speak of "things" in the strict sense, that is, as entities completely conditioned. Mathematical physics and the technical control of nature based on it are the most impressive and the most consistent expressions of this view. Nature is brought under control, objectified, and stripped of its qualities. No sacramental conception can find a root in this soil. Nature cannot become the bearer of a transcendent power, it can at most be an image of it, a witness to it. But the rational-objective view of nature is also never fully applicable. The qualities of things resist any attempt at their complete eradication. Even in the structure of the atom there is something primordial, a Gestalt, an intrinsic power. And the highly complicated machines created by the applied sciences are, in many ways, analogous to the basic organic forms; they can gain a new magical power over the minds of those who serve them.

The technical attitude toward nature and its merely quantitative analysis have been opposed since the times of Greek philosophy by the vitalistic interpretation of nature. Here an immediate power of being is attributed to things. Everything, the whole world-process, is envisaged as an expression of life: *élan vital,* "the vital urge", the "creative power of life", and the like are the characteristic phrases used. The modern Gestalt theory has given unexpected scientific confirmation to these ideas. But vitalistic philosophy goes beyond this justified protest. Even the mind is subjected to the principle of unbroken vitality and is branded as a sort of disease and fought against as a degenerate form of life. In this vitalistic philosophy nature recovers its power again, but it is a power without meaning; and power without meaning is ultimately impotent. Sacramental trends on the basis of the "vitalistic" philosophy of nature can be seen in the attempts of some semipagan movements to re-establish the symbolism of the religions of nature by using elements and forms of the natural world (fire, water, light) as powerful in themselves without relationship to spirit and transcendence.

The symbolic-romantic interpretation of nature attempts to give back to nature its qualitative character, its depth, its meaningfulness, by interpreting nature as a symbol of the spirit. The power of things is the power of soul or spirit in them. It is clear that this provides rich possibilities for the symbolic interpretation of sacraments. In the place of pan-sacramentalism we have here a pan-symbolism. But it should be pointed out that this view is very little aware of the real structure of nature. It gives us the creations of an arbitrary imagination. The quantitative, calculable "nature" of physics is certainly not overcome by it; only subjective imagination has been added. For this reason the symbolic-romantic interpretation of nature cannot provide a solid basis for a new theory of the sacrament.

The unsatisfactory character of all the interpretations of nature mentioned thus far drives us to a view which we may call "new realism", a term in which elements of the medieval and of the modern use of the word "realism" are united. Thinkers like Schelling and Goethe and Rilke in our day, have proposed this way of penetrating into the depth of nature. We must follow them with the means of our present knowledge of nature and man. The power and meaning of nature must be sought within and through its objective physical structures. Power and physical character, meaning and objective structure, are not separated in nature. We cannot accept the word of mathematical science as the last word about nature, although we do not thereby deny that it is the first word.

The power of nature must be found in a sphere prior to the cleavage of our world into subjectivity and objectivity. Life originates on a level which is "deeper" than the Cartesian duality of *cogitatio* and *extensio* ("thought" and "extension"). It was the wish of the vitalistic interpretation of nature to reach this level. But a philosophy of life that denies intellect and spirit has deprived life of its strongest power and its ultimate meaning, as even Nietzsche realized when he said: "Spirit is life which itself cutteth into life." The difficult problem for all attempts to reach the uncleft level of reality is the necessity to penetrate into something "nonsubjective" with categories of a subjective mind and into something "nonobjective" with categories of objective reality. This necessarily falsifies the pictures, which can be corrected only by a strict understanding of the indirect, symbolic character of terms used for the description of the power and meaning of nature.

A realistic interpretation of nature such as we have outlined would be able to provide the foundation of a new Protestant theory of sacraments. But this alone is not sufficient. No sacrament, in Christian thought, can be understood apart from its relation to the new being in Jesus as the Christ; and, consequently, no sacrament can be understood apart from history. Nature, in being adapted to sacramental use in Christianity, and especially in Protestantism, must be understood historically and in the context of the history of salvation. Obviously, there are historical elements in nature. Nature participates in historical time, that is, in the time that proceeds in an unrepeatable and irreversible way. The structure of the cosmos, of atoms, of stars, of the biological substance, is changing in an unknown direction. Although the historical element in nature is balanced with the nonhistorical one (the "circle of genesis and decay," the self-repetition in nature, the circular movement which dominated Greek thinking), Christianity, following old mythological visions in Persia and Israel, decided for the historical element and included nature in the history of salvation.

If nature is interpreted in this realistic and, at the same time, historical way, natural objects can become bearers of transcendent power and meaning, they can become sacramental elements. The Protestant criticism against any direct magical or mythological use of nature as the bearer of the holy is heeded. Nature, by being brought into the context of the history of salvation, is liberated from its ambiguity. Its demonic quality is conquered in the new being in Christ. Nature is not the enemy of salvation; it does not have to be controlled in scientific, technical, and moral terms or be deprived of any inherent power, in order to serve the "Kingdom of God," as Calvinistic thinking is inclined to believe; rather, nature is a bearer and an object of salvation. This is the basis for a Protestant rediscovery of the sacramental sphere. . . .

## 6. SACRAMENTAL OBJECTS

Any object or event is sacramental in which the transcendent is perceived to be present. Sacramental objects are holy objects, laden with divine power. From the point of view of the magical interpretation of nature, any reality whatsoever may be holy. Here the distinction between "the holy" as divine or as demonic, as clean or unclean, is not yet known. At this stage the unclean and the holy can still be looked upon as identical. The significance of prophetic criticism lies in the fact that it dissolves the primitive unity between the holy and the real. To the prophets the holy is primarily a demand. Nothing can be holy apart from the fulfillment of the law. Holiness and purity are brought together. The "unclean" is eliminated from the idea of the holy. To the extent to which this process takes place the original sacramental interpretation of nature disappears. The holy is now transformed into an unconditional demand, transcending any given reality. Nature as such is deprived of its sacred character and becomes profane. Immediate intercourse with nature no longer possesses religious significance. Ritualistic demands are transformed into ethical (and utilitarian) demands. Nevertheless, the sacramental attitude does not lose its power. Indeed, it can never entirely vanish from the consciousness. Unless the holy has some actuality, its character as a demand becomes abstract and impotent. In Hegel's view that the "idea" is not lacking in the power to realize itself we can still discern a residue of the sacramental attitude, in contrast to the antisacramental, critical, and moralistic attitude of the Enlightenment. If this holds true for the secular sphere, it is all the more true for the religious sphere. No church can survive without a sacramental element. However effectively prophetic criticism serves to make impossible an absolute reliance upon the holy at present, however effectively it opposes every fixation and every objectification of the sacrament, it cannot do away with the sacramental background; indeed, prophetic criticism itself is possible only by virtue of this background. Just as Old Testament prophecy in its vehement attack upon the demonic sacramentalism into which the old worship of Yahweh had fallen continued to hold to the sacramental idea of the covenant between God and nation, so the Protestant fight against Roman Catholic sacramentalism remained bound to the Scripture as an expression of the presence of the divine in Jesus Christ. Any sacramental reality within the framework of Christianity and of Protestantism must be related to the new being in Christ. No Protestant criticism would be conceivable in which this foundation was denied.

But if the presence of the holy is the presupposition of any religious reality and any church, including the Protestant churches, then it follows that the interpretation of nature in sacramental terms is also presupposition of Protestantism, for there is no being that does not have its basis in nature. This holds true also for personality. If the holy is seen as present in a personality, if the personality shows that transparence for the divine which makes the saint a saint, then this is expressed not only in his spiritual life but also in his whole psychological organism, in "soul and body". The pictures and sculptures of the saints would be meaningless without the presupposition that their sainthood is expressed in their bodies and especially in their faces. Sainthood is not moral obedience but "holy being", a substance out of which moral and other consequences follow. The "good tree" precedes the "good fruit". But where the "holy being" is accepted as the "prius" of the holy act, there the basic principle of all sacramental thinking is also accepted: the presence of the divine, its transparence in nature and history.

## 7. PROTESTANTISM AND SACRAMENT

Protestant thinking about sacraments must not revert to a magical sac-ramentalism, such as has been preserved by Catholicism down to our own time. No relapses to a pre-prophetic or pre-Protestant attitude should occur on Protestant soil.

This means, first of all, that there can be no sacramental object apart from the faith that grasps it. Apart from the correlation between faith and sacrament, there can be no sacrament. From this it follows that a sacrament can never be made into a thing, an object beside other objects. The intrinsic power of nature as such does not create a sacra-ment. It can only become a *bearer* of a sacramental power. Of course, without such a bearer there can be no sacramental power, the holy cannot be felt as present. But the bearer does not in and of itself constitute the sacrament. Moreover, we must remember that for a Christian the idea of a purely natural sacrament is unacceptable. Where nature is not related to the events of the history of salvation its status remains am-biguous. It is only through a relation to the history of salvation that it is liberated from its demonic elements and thus made eligible for a sacra-ment. However, their relationship does not deprive nature of its power. If it did, that would mean that being itself would be destroyed; for the intrinsic power of things is their power of being, and for them to be with-out power would mean that they were without being. When the term "being" is employed other than as an abstract category, it means the power to exist. To say that the world has been created is to say that power of being has been given to the world. And the world retains this power, even if it is demonically distorted. It is not because of an alleged powerlessness of nature that Christianity cannot recognize purely nat-ural sacraments; it is rather because of the demonization of nature. In so far, however, as nature participates in the history of salvation, it is liber-ated from the demonic and made capable of becoming a sacrament.

It could be inferred from this that the Protestant interpretation of nature would attribute sacramental qualities to everything. No finite object or event would be excluded as long as it was the bearer of a tran-scendent power and integrally related to the history of salvation. This is true in principle, but not in our actual existence. Our existence is deter-mined not only by the omnipresence of the divine but also by our separa-tion from it. If we could see the holy in every reality, we should be in the Kingdom of God. But this is not the case. The holy appears only in spe-cial places, in special contexts. The concentration of the sacramental in special places, in special rites, is the expression of man's ambiguous situation. The holy is omnipresent in so far as the ground of being is not far from any being; the holy is demonized because of the separation of the infinite ground of being from every finite reality. And, finally, the holy is manifest in its power to overcome the demonic at special places, ultimately at one place, in Jesus as the Christ. The danger of this situation is that the "special places," the peculiar materials, the ritual performances, which are connected with a sacrament claim holiness for themselves. But their holiness is a representation of what essentially is possible in everything and in every place. The bread of the sacrament stands for all bread and ultimately for all nature. This bread in itself is not an object of sacramental experience but that for which it stands. In Protestantism every sacrament has representative character, pointing to the universality of the sacramental principle.

The representative character of sacramental objects and events does not imply, however, that it is possible to create a sacrament arbitrarily or that these objects or events are interchangeable at will. Sacraments originate when the intrinsic power of a natural object becomes for faith a bearer of sacramental power. Sacraments cannot be created arbitrarily; they originate only by virtue of historical fate. All sacramental realities depend upon a tradition which cannot be abandoned arbitrarily or exchanged with some other tradition. But it can be destroyed by prophetic criticism. Most of the sacramental features of the Catholic tradition have been radically questioned by Protestantism; indeed, they have been abandoned on Protestant soil. And the process of reduction has not stopped with this. In the course of its history Protestantism has become so indifferent to sacramental thinking that even the two remaining sacraments have lost their significance, with the result that only the word has retained a genuinely sacramental character. In the revival of Reformation theology in our day, the word plays an immense role, whereas the sacraments play no role whatsoever. It is fairly evident that the Protestant sacraments are disappearing. To be sure, they can still have a long life simply because of the conservative character of all sacral forms. And then, too, renaissances of one sort or another are by no means beyond the range of possibility. But the one thing needful is that the whole Protestant attitude toward the sacraments be changed. Of primary importance for such a development is a new understanding of the intrinsic powers of nature which constitute an essential part of the sacraments. We need also to realize that the word has its basis in nature, and hence that the usual opposition between word and sacrament is no longer tenable. We must recognize the inadequacy of "Protestant personalism" and overcome the tendency to focus attention on the so-called "personality" of Jesus instead of on the new being that he expresses in his person. We must consider the unconscious and subconscious levels of our existence so that our whole being may be grasped and shattered and given a new direction. Otherwise these levels will remain in a state of religious atrophy. The personality will become intellectualistic and will lose touch with its own vital basis. The phenomenal growth of secularism in Protestant countries can be explained partly as a result of the weakening of the sacramental power within Protestantism. For this reason the solution of the problem of "nature and sacrament" is today a task on which the very destiny of Protestantism depends. But this problem can be solved only by an interpretation of nature which takes into account the intrinsic powers of nature. If nature loses its power, the sacrament becomes arbitrary and insignificant. Of course, the power of nature alone does not create a Christian sacrament. Nature must be brought into the unity of the history of salvation. It must be delivered from its demonic bondage. And just this happens when nature becomes a sacramental element.

*

## THE TWO ROOTS OF POLITICAL THOUGHT

The Socialist Decision, *from which the following selection is taken, was a book that both called for concrete political decision and also offered a speculative philosophy. The former helps explain why the book was banned when Hitler came to power, why Tillich lost his German professorship at the University of Frankfurt and ultimately had to emigrate (see Wilhelm and Marion Pauck,* The Life and Thought of Paul Tillich, *pp. 123-38); the latter foreshadows the later writings on ontology that remained essential to Tillich's social and political views. This book represented an end to what some of his friends (e.g. Max Horkheimer) considered his hesitance to denounce Nazi Socialism publicly. It was a critique of both communism and National Socialism, and a defense of a "localized socialism" that sketched how such socialism could further the liberation of women and the empowerment of minorities within a nation-state (see Stone,* Paul Tillich's Radical Social Thought, *pp. 81-2). Below is the important introduction to* Die sozialistische Entscheidung, *first published in 1933 and translated by Franklin Sherman in 1977 from the text printed in Tillich's* Gesammelte Werke, *vol. 2 (Stuttgart: Evangelisches Verlagswerk, 1962) which the translator then corrected in light of the 1933 text. This essay displays Tillich's way of relating a view of human being to political thought, his early use of Heidegger, his convictions about justice as "the true power of being", and the meaning of the term "principle", which he used extensively when writing of "the socialist principle" or "the Protestant principle". For Tillich's other writings on relationships between Christianity and socialism, Marxism and Communism, see Paul Tillich,* Political Expectation, *ed. J.L. Adams (New York: Harper & Row, 1971) and Paul Tillich, "The Protestant Principle and the Proletarian Situation" in* The Protestant Era *(1948). (Reprinted from Paul Tillich,* The Socialist Decision, *trans. Franklin Sherman. New York: Harper & Row, 1977, pp. 1-10.)*

## 1. HUMAN BEING AND POLITICAL CONSCIOUSNESS

It is not always necessary to inquire into the roots of a spiritual or social phenomenon. When sturdy growth shows us that the roots are unimpaired, such an inquiry is superfluous. But if the plant begins to become bent and twisted, if growth ceases and life begins to fade away, then it is essential to ask: What is the condition of the roots? This is the situation of socialism, particularly of its strongest branch, German socialism. The political events of recent months have found it in a gravely weakened state. And this situation is caused not only by the events of recent years. The causes go back much farther, back to the second half of the nineteenth century, and partly even to the historical situation at the time of socialism's origin. The most urgent task in these coming years of self-examination is to seek the causes of this weakening. This can only be accomplished by answering the question of roots.

However, as soon as we ask the question regarding the roots of socialist thought, it becomes necessary to go further. For socialism is a countermovement, in a double sense: it is directly a countermovement against bourgeois society, and indirectly — together with bourgeois society — a countermovement against feudal-patriarchal forms of society. Therefore in order to understand socialism in terms of its roots, it is necessary to uncover also the roots of the political thinking opposed to it.

*The roots of political thought must be sought in human being itself.* Without some notion of human nature, of its powers and tensions, one cannot make any statements about the foundations of political existence and thought. Without a doctrine of human nature, there can be no theory of political tendencies that is more than a depiction of their external form.

A doctrine of human nature, however, cannot be worked out here. It must be presupposed, and at best it can create for itself a favorable hearing by its capacity to illuminate political thought.

Human beings differ from nature in that they are creatures with an internal duality. No matter where nature ends and humanity begins, no matter whether there are gradual transitions or a sudden leap between them, somewhere the difference becomes visible. Nature is a unified life-process, unfolding itself without question or demand, and bound by what it finds in itself and its environment. Humanity is a life-process that questions itself and its environment, placing demands on itself and its environment, which therefore is not one with itself. Rather, it has these two aspects: to exist in itself and simultaneously to stand over against itself, thinking about itself and knowing about itself. Human beings possess self-consciousness, or to contrast this with nature, they are beings who are internally dualized by virtue of their self-consciousness. Nature lacks this duality. We are not implying in these statements that human beings are composed of two independent parts, for example, of nature and spirit, or body and soul; rather, there is *one* being but twofold in its unity.

Even these very general definitions have consequences for any investigation of political thought. They make it impossible to derive political thinking from purely mental processes, from religious and moral demands or ideological judgments. Political thinking proceeds from human nature as a whole. It is rooted simultaneously in being and in consciousness, more precisely in the indissoluble unity of the two. *Therefore it is impossible to understand a system of political thought without uncovering the human and social reality in which it is rooted,* that is, the interrelation of drives and interests, of pressures and aspirations, which make up social reality. But it is equally impossible even to conceive of this reality as separate from consciousness, that is, to view consciousness and along with it political thought as mere by-products of being. *Every element of human and social being, down to the most primitive emotional drive, is shaped by consciousness.* Any effort to dissolve this connection ignores the first and most important characteristic of human nature, and therefore results in distortions in the total picture of that nature.

To point out that there is a consciousness that does not correspond to being, the so-called "false consciousness", proves nothing against the unity of being and consciousness. For the very concept of a "false consciousness" is only possible and such a thing is only knowable if there is a true consciousness. A true consciousness, however, is one that arises

97

out of being and at the same time determines it. It is not one without the other. For human nature is a unity in its duality, and the two roots of all political thinking grow out of this unity.

Human beings find themselves in existence; they find themselves as they find their environment, and as this latter finds them and itself. But to find oneself means that one does not originate from oneself; it means to have an origin that is not oneself, or — in the pregnant phrase of Martin Heidegger — to be "thrown" into the world. The human question concerning the "Whence" of existence arises out of this situation. Only later does it appear as a philosophical question. But it has always been a question; and its first and permanently normative answer is enshrined in myth.

The origin is creative. Something new springs into being, something that did not previously exist and now is something with its own character over against the origin. We experience ourselves as posited, yet also as independent. Our life proceeds in a tension between dependence on the origin and independence. For the origin does not let us go; it is not something that was and is no longer, once we become independent selves. Rather, we are continually dependent on the origin; it bears us, it creates us anew at every moment, and thereby holds us fast. The origin brings us forth as something new and singular; but it takes us, as such, back to the origin again. Just in being born we become involved in having to die. "It is necessary that things should pass away into that from which they are born", declares the first saying handed down to us in Western philosophy.* Our life runs its course in terms of birth, development and death. No living thing can transcend the limits set by its birth; development is the growing and passing away of what comes from the origin and returns to it. This has been expressed in myth in infinitely diverse ways, according to the things and events in which a particular group envisages its origin. In all mythology, however, there resounds the cyclical law of birth and death. Every myth is a myth of origin, that is, an answer to the question about the "Whence" of existence and an expression of dependence on the origin and on its power. *The consciousness oriented to the myth of origin is the root of all conservative and romantic thought in politics.*

But human beings not only find themselves in existence; they not

---

* Fragment of Anaximander, as rendered in Werner Jaeger, *Paideia: The Ideals of Greek Culture,* trans. Gilbert Highet (New York: Oxford University Press, 1945), vol. I, p. 159 — TRANS.

only know themselves to be posited and withdrawn in the cycle of birth and death, like all living things. They experience a demand that frees them from being simply bound to what is given, and which compels them to add to the question "Whence?" [*Woher*] the question "Whither?" [*Wozu*]. With this question the cycle is broken in principle and humankind is elevated beyond the sphere of merely living things. For the demand calls for something that does not yet exist but should exist, should come to fulfillment. A being that experiences a demand is no longer simply bound to the origin. Human life involves more than a mere development of what already is. Through the demand, humanity is directed to what ought to be. And what ought to be does not emerge with the unfolding of what is; if it did, it would be something that is, rather than something that ought to be. This means, however, that the demand that confronts humanity is an unconditional demand. The question "Whither?" is not contained within the limits of the question "Whence?" It is something unconditionally new that transcends what is new and what is old within the sphere of mere development. Through human beings, something unconditionally new is to be realized; this is the meaning of the demand that they experience, and which they are able to experience because in them being is twofold. For the human person is not only an individual, a self, but also has knowledge about himself or herself, and thereby the possibility of transcending what is found within the self and around the self. This is human freedom, not that one has a so-called "free will", but that as a human being one is not bound to what one finds in existence, that one is subject to a demand that something unconditionally new should be realized through oneself. Thus the cycle of birth and death is broken; the existence and the actions of human beings are not confined within a mere development of their origin. Wherever this consciousness prevails, the tie to the origin has been dissolved in principle and the myth of origin has been broken in principle. *The breaking of the myth of origin by the unconditional demand is the root of liberal, democratic, and socialist thought in politics.*

Yet we cannot stop with a simple opposition between these two aspects of human existence. The demand that human beings experience is unconditional, but it is not alien to human nature. If it were alien to our nature, it would be of no concern to us and we could not perceive it as a demand upon us. It affects us only because it places before us, in the form of a demand, our own essence. Therein alone is grounded the unconditionality and inescapability with which the demand confronts us and must be affirmed by us. But if the demand is our own essence, it is grounded in our origin. The questions "Whence?" and "Whither?" do not belong to two different worlds. And yet, the demand is something unconditionally new over against the origin. This indicates that *the origin is ambiguous.* There is a split in it between the true and the actual origin. *The actual origin is not the origin in truth.* It is not the fulfillment of what is intended for humanity from the origin. The fulfillment of the origin lies rather in what confronts us as a demand, as an ought. The "Whence" of humanity finds its fulfillment in the "Whither". The actual origin is contradicted by the true origin, not absolutely and in every respect, for the actual origin — in order to be actual at all — must participate in the true origin; it expresses it, but at the same time both obscures it and distorts it. The mentality oriented solely to the myth of origin knows nothing of this ambiguity of the origin. Therefore it clings to the origin and feels that it is a sacrilege to go beyond it. The ambiguity of the origin is first revealed to it when the experience of the unconditional demand frees this consciousness from bondage to the origin.

The demand is directed towards the fulfillment of the true origin. Now a person experiences an unconditional demand only from another person. The demand becomes concrete in the "I-Thou" encounter. The content of the demand is therefore that the "thou" be accorded the same dignity as the "I"; this is the dignity of being free, of being the bearer of the fulfillment implied in the origin. This recognition of the equal dignity of the "Thou" and the "I" is justice. *The demand that separates from the ambiguous origin is the demand of justice.* From the unbroken origin proceed powers that are in tension with one another; they seek dominion and destroy each other. From the unbroken origin there comes the power of being, the rising and perishing of forces that "pay one another the penalty and compensation for their injustice according to the ordinance of time", as is asserted in the already quoted first statement of Greek philosophy. The unconditional demand transcends this tragic cycle of existence. It confronts the power and impotence of being with justice, arising from the demand. And yet, the contrast is not absolute, for the ought is the fulfillment of the is. *Justice is the true power of being.* In it the intention of the origin is fulfilled.

The result is that the two elements of human being and the two roots of political thought are related in such a way that the demand is superior to mere origin and justice is superior to the mere power of being. The question "Whither?" is of higher rank than the question "Whence?" *Only when the myth of origin is broken and its ambiguity disclosed may it enter into political thinking.*

## 2. APPROACH AND STANDPOINT

The relationship between the two roots of political thought is not one of simple juxtaposition. The demand is superior to the origin. Therefore, a consideration of political trends cannot proceed on the assumption that they are typically human attitudes of equal justification. *The concept of the typical is not applicable where decisions are required.* But this is the case when an unconditioned demand is made. One cannot do it justice by a comparative or typological approach; already by using such an approach one has avoided the demand and in fact has conceded that the alternative is justified, by placing it on the same level with the demand in an allegedly neutral description. At bottom this holds true of every attempt to understand spiritual things. One cannot be a spectator of the spirit; it makes demands, it calls for decisions. No one can understand socialism who has not experienced its demand for justice as a demand made on oneself. *Whoever has not struggled with the spirit of socialism can speak about it only from the outside, which is to say, in fact not at all.*

It is otherwise in the case of political trends in which the bond of origin is predominant. They also must be understood; in them, too, spirit speaks to spirit and requires a decision. But here the decision is to lead precisely in the direction of renouncing inquiry and decision and reverting to mere being. In affirming the origin, one seeks by its help to avoid what is demanded. To be sure, one uses the mind, but against the mind; one inquires, but against the spirit of inquiry; one demands, but against the demand. One seeks by spiritual means to draw the spirit back into the bondage of being. This is the inner contradiction of political romanticism in all its forms. For this reason it is basically impossible to decide for it intellectually. As long as the bond of origin remains unbroken, no decision can be made, because no choice exists. But once it is broken, a decision in its favor can only mean the suspension of all free decision. No attempt to establish a spiritual basis for political romanticism can escape this contradiction.

The roots of political thought do not lie in ideas but in human being, that is, being that is twofold, conscious being. This means that political thinking is necessarily an expression of political being, of a social situation. Thought itself cannot be understood without taking into account the social realities out of which political thought arises. The roots of political thinking cannot be equally effective in every period and every group. The predominance of one side or the other is dependent on a particular social situation, on particular groups and forms of authority.

It is further dependent on particular social-psychological structures which interact with the objective social situation. By means of their social-psychological effects (by which they in turn are influenced), the economic and governmental forms of a given period tend to make certain elements of human being predominate at that time.

This interconnection between social being and political consciousness gives rise to a question that must be answered before we can undertake the discussion of political problems, and especially the problems of socialism. Socialism, as will be demonstrated, is the direct expression of the proletarian situation. How then is it possible, one could ask, to criticize socialism or to argue for it from a position that is not itself proleterian? The answer is that consciousness is indeed dependent on being, but they are interconnected in a functional, not a biographical way. Certain ideas, whether they were set forth by aristocrats or bourgeoisie, had the function of expressing bourgeois being. And certain ideas, whether set forth by bourgeoisie or proletarians, have the function of expressing proletarian being. The fact that it was primarily aristocrats who prepared the way for bourgeois society, and the bourgeois who gave to the proletariat its self-consciousness, shows how little depends on the biographical relationship. Indeed, the distance between being and consciousness can become the very condition for the raising of being to consciousness. *Knowledge entails not only relationship to being but also distance from it.* Therefore the person whose confidence in his or her own group and class situation has been deeply shaken is in the best position to provide an alien class with its self-consciousness. The best examples of this are Marx and Lenin. They serve at the very outset to lift the correlation of social situation and political thought from the biographical to the functional sphere.

### 3. PRINCIPLE AND REALITY

The word *principle* is used to refer to the summarizing characterization of a political group. The following considerations have been decisive in the choice of this term. It is the task of thinking to select from a variety of phenomena that which makes them belong together and which makes the individual intelligible from the standpoint of the whole. This task is usually accomplished by means of a concept of the "essence" of a thing. Since Plato, epistemology in the West has been dominated by the problem of the relation between essence and appearance. But now it has been shown that the logic of essence is inadequate in face of historical realities. The "essence of a historical phenomenon" is an empty abstraction from which the living power of history has been expelled. Nevertheless, we cannot dispense with summarizing characterizations when we are dealing with a coherent movement. It is not enough to refer to historical continuity, since some selection must be made out of the infinite abundance of continuously linked events. Therefore we must seek another method of historical characterization. In place of the concept of essence, which is derived from the knowledge of nature, we must introduce a dynamic concept, in accordance with the character of history. *A concept is dynamic if it contains the possibility of making understandable new and unexpected realizations of a historical origin.* I should like to call such concepts "principles". A principle does not contain the abstract universality of a mass of individual phenomena; it contains the real possibility, the *dynamis*, the power of historical reality. The principle can never be abstracted from the multiplicity of its individual realizations, for it always stands in a critical and judging relation to its reality, and not only in a foundational and supporting relation. There can be no contradiction between essence and appearance, but there can be a contradiction between principle and realization. It is possible to have access to a principle, therefore, only through an act of understanding that always contains at the same time an element of decision. No one understands, for example, the Protestant principle on the basis of everything that has ever happened in and to Protestantism. It can be understood only on the basis of a decision, from the standpoint of which the whole history of Protestantism is not only grasped but also criticized. This consideration is bound up with the other consideration, that spirit can be understood only by a spiritual decision. Thus socialism also is to be understood only in terms of a socialist principle that is gained only by a socialist decision, and which is the standpoint both for interpreting and for judging socialist reality.

Principle must not be confused with idea or with universal concept or the like. A principle is the real power that supports a historical phenomenon, giving it the possiblity to actualize itself anew and yet in continuity with the past. The principle of political romanticism is the inner power of the groups bearing political romanticism, expressed in concepts and understood in terms of the roots of human and historical being. The principle of socialism is not a socialist idea; it is the proletarian situation interpreted in terms of its dynamics. "Principle", therefore, is not an ideological concept, but one that is descriptive of reality. *A principle is the power of a historical reality, grasped in concepts.*

# WHAT IS WRONG WITH THE "DIALECTIC" THEOLOGY?

*More than once Tillich addressed himself to the "dialectic" or "neo-ortho-dox" theology of Karl Barth and others. In 1923, he registered his disagree-ments with Barth, lamenting the latter's "supranaturalist" tendency to privilege Christianity's own distinctive revelation while giving insufficient attention to the manifestation of God in cultural movements, philosophy and history. With this kind of criticism, Tillich anticipated Bonhoeffer's critique of Barth's thought as a "positivism of revelation".\* Even when Barth helped mobilize the church's opposition to Nazism, Tillich believed that Barth showed in his letter to the British Christians that "it was not the common fight of people of all religions and creeds against the National-Socialist distortion of humanity that interested him, but the defense of the church as the finger pointing only to heaven and not to earth. . . . He, like all pessimistic supranaturalists, is not interested in history as such nor in a social transformation for the sake of humanity."\* (Tillich, "Trends in Reli-gious Thought that Affect Social Outlook," pp. 24-5.) The 1936 essay reprinted here is from* The Journal of Religion *XV (1935): 127-45.*

When I am asked, What is wrong with the "dialectic" theology? I reply that it is not "dialectic". A dialectic theology is one in which "yes" and "no" belong inseparably together. In the so-called "dialectic" theology they are irreconcilably separated, and that is why this theology is not dialectic. Rather, it is paradoxical, and therein lies its strength; and it is supernatural, which constitutes its weakness. All that follows in this discussion is devoted to the proof of these two statements.

## I

To ask what is wrong with the "dialectic" theology presupposes the conviction that it contains something that is right. Only because this is presupposed, could I entertain the question proposed to me. It is, indeed, my conviction that there is not only something that is right in the "dialectic" theology, but something quite definitive for theology and equally fundamental for the church. Not until that fact is emphatically established does significant criticism become possible.

Perhaps it is worth while at this point to recall the historical origin of

---

\* On Bonhoeffer's relationship to Karl Barth and in the National Socialist period, see John W. de Gruchy, *Dietrich Bonhoeffer*, The Making of Modern Theology: 19th and 20th Century Theological Texts, General Editor: John W. de Gruchy (London and San Francisco: Collins, 1987).

the "dialectic" theology. Karl Barth, its theological founder and head, with whom we are principally concerned in our exposition and criticism, comes from the Swiss religious-socialist movement. The most important advocates of this movement — Ragaz and Kutter and their Württemberg predecessors, the older and the younger Blumhard — worked out *one* determinative idea which, in spite of all variation through which it has passed, has remained decisive also for Barth. That idea is the notion that God stands as sovereign, not only over against the world, but also over against the church and piety, and consequently he has the power to make more of his will known through a contemporary secular movement — even through an atheistic movement like that of social democracy — than through ecclesiastical activities and the churchly forms of piety. . . .

The Blumhards and the religious socialists taught that God's will is most clearly manifest not in subjective piety and the rescue of individual souls but in the administration of the world, the vanquishing of the demonic powers therein, the coming of the Kingdom of God. . . . The work of the religious-socialist movement that emerged in this setting had extraordinary theological significance notwithstanding the political shipwreck of the movement. It produced an awareness of the limitations of churchliness and piety; it weakened the church's Pharisaic attitude toward the unchurched masses. But there was also a danger hidden in religious socialism. Just as was formerly the case with the church and its secular activity, the will of God could now be identified with political and social forms of activity. The Kingdom of God could be understood as a mundane social reality, and the struggle to realize the Kingdom of God could be interpreted as a political struggle for social righteousness. But the sovereignty of God, denied to the church, was thereby surrendered to a political movement. The Swiss religious socialism did not entirely escape this danger. Therefore Barth withdrew from the movement and retained only the notion of the unconditioned sovereignty of God over against both the church and the world.

Barth laid hold upon this notion with the whole force of his theological thinking and volition. Fundamentally, his entire theology is contained in the first commandment, "I am the Lord thy God; thou shalt not have any other gods beside me." Every single sentence of his writings can be understood as the application of this notion to a particular phase of the relation between God and the world. Any teaching that draws God into the sphere of human possibility is rebellion against the first commandment. This is the theme of Barth's commentary on the

Epistle to the Romans, which is his most radical and most strongly provocative book and is the one in which his prophetic spirit is most in evidence. God is "impossible possibility"; that is, he is beyond human possibilities. From the human point of view every statement about him is a paradox — a statement regarding that about which nothing can be said. Such statements as "impossible possibility" have given rise erroneously to the name "Dialectic theology". For such statements are not dialectical but are paradoxical. They do not yield a process of thought in which "yes" and "no" are mutually involved, but they permit only a constant repetition in other words of the idea expressed in the paradox. The choice of words depends upon the particular sphere in which the fundamental paradox is to be used.

The relation between God and man is expressed in the sentence "God is in heaven and thou art on earth." Between God and man there is a hollow space which man is unable of himself to penetrate. If it were possible for him to do this, he would have power over his relation to God, and thus would have power over God himself. But no creature has such power. The contention that the creature possesses this power is idol-worship. . . .

Every type of natural and cultural theology is condemned along with the philosophy of religion because it attempts to discover immediate knowledge of God from nature on the one hand, and from philosophy, science, art, and history on the other. Culture and history are the spheres in which man stands by himself alone; they express human concerns and are subject to human, not to theological, criteria. Nature also can be interpreted only in a human, not in a theological, way. Human and divine possibility are radically separated, for man is a sinner and the possibility of natural sinlessness is an abstraction that can have for us absolutely no meaning.

Therefore, the liberal theology is heresy. In place of the sinner it substitutes the self-developing personality; in place of Christ, the self-developing religious man Jesus; in place of the word of God in Scripture, the self-developing religious consciousness of humanity. From these three positions Barth launches his attack against the liberal theology. For him the creatureliness of man is essentially an expression of his separation from God, an expression of the rigid contrast between the creator and the creation. Not the dignity but the nothingness of the creature is expressed in the doctrine of creation. And Barth does not concede that one can derive from the teaching about creation divine decrees, as a divinely ordered form of nature and of man and of society.

Even if something of this were apparent in the original creation, it has become invisible through sin, for sin has radically transformed nature and man. We are unable to derive from the natural laws of pre-human and human being any norm for natural and human perfection. Sin has made this impossible. Therefore, all human distinctions, from the most perfect to the most imperfect, are subject to the same judgment; they signify nothing before God. Perfection is an eschatological conception, a transcendental "impossible possibility".

The liberal theology's picture of Christ is accorded a like caustic treatment. This does not mean, however, that Barth rejects the historical work of the liberal school of theology. That is so far from true that even the most radical historical critic of the New Testament, Bultmann of Marburg, can be at the same time one of the most active advocates of the Barthian theology. Historical criticism is of so little concern to Barth that he can quite avowedly express his indifference toward the question of the existence or nonexistence of the "historical Jesus". He does not reject the historical research of the liberals, but he treats it as a trifling matter, of which his Christology is independent. His Christology continues to rest explicitly upon the paradoxical formulas of the Chalcedonian council regarding the "inseparability and unmixed quality of the divine and human nature in Christ". For Barth Christ appears in history only in so far as he is above history; he does not participate in the development of human history and of human spiritual life, but is God's insert into history. Viewed historically and psychologically, Christ continues to be the "impossible possibility".

From such a position, the third line of assault upon the liberal theology is capable of being understood. God speaks to us, not *by means of* our spirit and its cultural and historical creations, but he speaks *to* our spirit and that means *against* our spirit, since our spirit is dominated by the law of sin. The form in which God speaks is the word of the Bible. This is his only and his entire communication. But at this point it should be immediately affirmed that Barth does not intend to combat biblical criticism nor to revive the dogma of biblical inspiration. Whether the word of the Bible becomes for one the "word of God", and by what means, depends upon the working of the Holy Spirit. Not the letter of Scripture, not even the religious spirit of the men who wrote it, not the historical account as such, neither a world-picture nor a morality that might be found in the Bible, make it the word of God, but only the fact that it bears testimony to the revelation made in Christ. But no one is capable of understanding this testimony unless God himself makes it possible through the Holy Spirit. Beyond the word of God there is no disposing power. This understanding is mediated neither by the letter of Scripture, nor by preaching on Sunday, nor by theological study. It can occur, but where and when the event happens is not under our control. It is linked with the Bible, but we do not possess it when we possess the Bible. Like everything else that we can say and learn of God, it is "impossible possibility".

The same paradox holds also for the relation of the Kingdom of God to human action. The Kingdom of God is a purely transcendental quantum which is not constructed by men but which comes to men. It is a purely eschatological quantum entirely distinct from human culture and history. Culture is a human possibility, and in history man stands by himself alone. Therefore, culture and history can furnish us neither standards for Christian teaching nor norms for Christian conduct. Nor can any single procedure in culture and history lay claim to being entirely or partly a realization of the Kingdom of God. The Kingdom of God is never present in history, either in a utopian perfection, or in the real or imagined progress of history. Even the church is not the Kingdom of God. The church is commissioned to bear testimony to God and his Kingdom, yet it is not identical therewith. . . .

The total result is, finally, that theology can be nothing but the exercise of a critical self-consciousness upon the content of the Christian pronouncement, in which the word of Scripture is the ultimate standard of criticism. Any mingling of philosophical ideas in this task is rejected. The use of any sort of natural theology as a preliminary to reflection on God, the world, or man is stoutly resisted. Philosophy, like religion, belongs in human culture and in the sphere of human possibilities. Theology rests on revelation, which is humanly impossible. And there is no bridge spanning the gulf between the divine and the human.

Thus the Barthian theology, from first to last, preserves the sovereign prerogative of God as expressed in the first commandment. God's sovereignty is not blended with any form of human existence and action. Unquestionably, this seems to me to be the truth that is preserved not only in the Barthian theology but in any theology that deserves the name. A criticism of this position would be not only a criticism of Barth but of the Bible, the church, and theology in general.

II

If Barth must be criticized, criticism is possible only when it deals with that which escapes Barth when judged by his own standard. Does

Barth's interpretation of the Christian paradox protect it from the distortion of its meaning? Or does not his interpretation directly weaken the paradox and restrict the sovereign prerogative of God? I believe that to be the case, and it results from Barth's attempt to establish the paradox by means of supernaturalism rather than by dialectics.

Again I would approach the subject by recalling history. When Barth's commentary on Romans was published, a wide circle of theologians of the same age attached themselves to the school for which Barth had prepared the way. Some did so publicly, and some — like the author of this article — in a "subterranean" group of fellow-laborers. In the course of a decade the situation has been completely changed. As the supernaturalistic trend of the Barthian thinking became more clearly evident, it became necessary for me to give up the "subterranean" fellowship. The same was true of Bultmann, who had taken his stand for Barth in a much more open fellowship but whose attachment to the "existential" philosophy brought about his separation from Barth. Gogarten also turned aside. He joined the political reaction and his theological justification for this move made clear the gulf between him and Barth. Finally, last year, a sharp controversy broke out between Brunner and Barth over the possibility of a natural theology. It is, of course, understood that these happenings in themselves prove nothing against the truth of the Barthian theology. But they constantly press home to us the question, What is it in Barth's elaboration of his fundamental idea that has forced these friends and fellow-laborers to seek other ways? What, in their opinion, is wrong with Barth's theology? We are asking about *their* opinions, not about the opinion of those who have never been gripped by the force of Barth's thinking and who have never understood the larger truth of his fundamental paradox. Therefore, the criticism that follows is to be understood as coming from the former "subterranean" fellowship and not from the originally antagonistic group.

The paradox of the "impossible possibility" is an impossibility from the standpoint of men but is a possibility from the standpoint of God. And it is not only a possibility but is also a reality. For only because it has become a reality can we speak of it as a possibility. Theology is the methodical form of speaking of the human impossibility, and of the divine possibility, which has become reality. Now there are two ways of speaking of this event — of this reality — the supernatural and the dialectical. The supernatural way seeks to protect the divinity of the event from being diluted with human possibilities, while attaching it to definite temporal and spatial procedures, persons, words, writings, societies, and actions, such as the events of the years one to thirty, the history of Jesus and the Apostles and their language, the writings of the Bible, the church, and preaching and sacraments. Barth never means that these procedures as such, as human and historical procedures, are the divine event. He does not even deny it as a possibility of thought that God could have happened to use other procedures for the realization of his action, but he does maintain that God chose only one of these procedures and no other, and has restricted revelation to this. He emphasizes in a genuinely nominalistic way the contingency of the divine activity.

It is otherwise with dialectic thinking. It denies, just as does the supernatural way of thinking, that what is a purely divine possibility may be interpreted as a human possibility. But dialectic thinking maintains that the *question* about the divine possibility is a human possibility. And, further, it maintains that no question could be asked about the divine possibility unless a divine answer, even if preliminary and scarcely intelligible, were not always already available. For in order to be able to ask about God, man must already have experienced God as the goal of a possible question. Thus the human possibility of the question is no longer purely a human possibility, since it already contains answers. And without such preliminary half-intelligible answers and preliminary questions based thereon, even the ultimate answer could not be perceived. Were an event only a foreign substance in history it could neither be absorbed by history nor could it continue to be operative in history. It is as far from right to call history purely God-abandoned as to call it simply God's revelation. Indeed, when speaking of revelation, one must say that history is always equipped with revelation because it always contains divine answers and human questions. Thus there can be a "fullness of time", a moment in history when history by means of preliminary procedures has become capable of realizing the ultimate — a moment when history has become ripe for the event, which does not originate from history and also is not injected into it as a foreign substance, but breaks out within it and is capable of being received in history. Liberalism speaks of this as an event arising out of history, and supernaturalism calls it a foreign injection into history. In his radical opposition to the possibility affirmed by the liberals, Barth has made his decision in favor of the supernatural rather than the dialectic interpretation. This is his limitation.

Criticism of the details of the Barthian theology follows from this fundamental criticism which, from the standpoint of the dialectical explanation, must be applied to the supernatural explanation of the Christian paradox.

Certainly God is in heaven and man is on earth. But man can make this statement only in case heaven and earth have touched one another time and again, not only once, but in a process of history in which statements and then doubts have been expressed about gods who are thought to be on earth and men who are thought to be in heaven. That statement can be made and accepted only as the expression of a preliminary erring knowledge about God and man. Erring knowledge is not utter ignorance, especially when it begins to doubt its accuracy and to ask for true knowledge.

Since Barth does not recognize the dialectical value of erring knowledge about God, but makes it identical with ignorance, the whole history of religion is transformed by him into a "Witches' Sabbath" of ghostly fancies, idolatry, and superstition. A warning against the literary frivolities of religious syncretism was certainly appropriate; also religio-historical relativism is dangerous, indeed disastrous; and it is impossible to identify the history of religion with the history of revelation. Yet it seems to me to be just as certain that the church fathers' doctrine of the Logos, which has scattered its seed everywhere, giving answers and inspiring questions, is not only truer from the standpoint of dialectic but in the end signifies much more for every unbiased contact with extra-Christian piety than does Barth's de-divinizing of the history of religion. The liberal interpretation confuses history of religion with revelation; the supernatural interpretation makes them mutually exclusive; the dialectical interpretation finds in the history of religion answers, mistakes, and questions which lead to the ultimate answer and without which the ultimate answer would have to remain something unasked, unintelligible, and alien.

Certainly Barth is right when he measures nature, culture, and history by a human standard. In all three areas man stands apart — even though he is within nature. For nature can give man only that which it has in common with him and not some other thing that is eternally foreign to him. But the question arises, What is this human entity? Can it be thought of only as something without the divine, without the capacity for receiving answers from the divine and for asking questions of the divine? One thing is certain. Creations of culture in which none of these questions and answers are to be found we call superficial. The measure of a culture's depth and power is the measure of its sensitivity to such questions. Every unbiased contact with original cultural creations compels recognition of the fact that they concern themselves neither solely with God as a remote reality nor solely with human self-glorification, but with erring and questioning knowledge about God. I doubt whether there is any meaning in applying to this way of knowing God the term "natural" knowledge of God. As employed in this connection, "natural theology" has very little to do with natural human wisdom in the general and formal sense. Perhaps the conception "natural theology" is itself the product of a faulty supernaturalism.

Certainly culture is not revelation, as a naïve theory of culture assumes it to be. Culture is a human possibility, while revelation is impossibility, which means a divine possibility. Yet revelation would not be even a divine *possibility* — revelation is indeed revelation to man — if it could not be received by means of forms of culture as human phenomena. It would be a destructive foreign substance in culture, a disruptive "nonhuman" entity within the human sphere, and could have had no power to shape and direct human history. It would not convey any message to man, who is ever a historical and culturally sensitive being. It could communicate only with a ghostly and empty form of man, the content of whose being would have to be self-engendered.

Criticism of Barth's repudiation of philosophy of religion and of so-called "natural theology" follows immediately from what has just been said. Barth is right in combating the identity in nature of God and man and in rejecting all attempts to find a point in man where he may be able to find and lay hold of God. He is correct in his resistance to all mysticism, which would permit union with God in the depths of man's own human nature. Apart from the Augustinian *transcende te ipsum* there is no access to God. But this precept does contain within itself the demand to proceed *through* self *beyond* self. Therefore, the other statement, *in interiori anima habitat veritas*, is more basal in the dialectic of Augustine. We can find God *in* us only when we rise *above* ourselves. This transcendentalizing act does not signify that we possess the transcendental. The point is that we are in quest of it. But on the other hand this quest is possible only because the transcendental has already dragged us out beyond ourselves as we have received answers which drive us to the quest. The development of this dialectic is the proper aim of philosophy of religion and of the improperly so-called "natural theology". Only it should not be supposed that this can be a substitute for the theology of revelation. Theology is not anthropology and when studied as if it were it surrenders itself into the hands of Feuerbach and his psychological and sociological followers. But theology is the solution of the anthropological question, which is the problem of the finiteness of man. Again, the question itself is possible only because man has already received answers to it, and therefore can have knowledge about his finiteness.

But Barth will answer that finiteness is not sin. In so far as sin cannot be defined in terms of finiteness, he is correct. But guilt and despair belong to finiteness and are understood as sin in the revelation of God against whom they are guilt and for whose sake they are despair. Sin could never be experienced as sin without the anthropological possibility of guilt and despair. Otherwise they would be empty words, an unintelligible communication, and not a revelation of man's status before God. Therefore it is not correct to say that sin makes impossible any knowledge of God. On the contrary, in the experience of guilt and despair the question of perplexing knowledge about God is as radically presented as it ever can be apart from revelation. And only because of that fact is the answer "sin and grace" a real answer and not an utterly meaningless formula.

In so far as the liberal theology puts human development in the place of revelation, Barth's criticism also holds good for dialectic thinking. But when he deprives the human of any relation to the divine, as he does in his teaching about the God-likeness of man, about Christ, about God's word, and about the Bible, Barth's peculiar formulations are objectionable or wrong. On that account all these ideas become unintelligible. Assuredly the God-likeness of man is not an unfolding of personality independent of revelation; but it cannot be understood merely as a work of the Holy Spirit. The Holy Spirit bears witness to our spirit — a witness that we are able to understand, since this witnessing takes place not beyond our spiritual life, but in response to the quest for a relation to God. The answer is, that we are God's children not through our humanity but through grace; yet the demand for this answer, and the capability of asking and perceiving it, come through humanity. Without this antecedent God-likeness of man no consequent God-likeness would be possible. Without it the witness of the Holy Spirit to his spirit would not concern him. In general, Barth leaves unexplained how revelation can communicate anything to man if there is nothing in him permitting him to raise questions about it, impelling him toward it, and enabling him to understand it.

Barth quite properly makes his Christology and his teaching about the word of God independent of the results of historical criticism. Revelation can neither be called in question nor established by means of historical criticism. But the content and the manner of interpreting that which is called the occurrence of revelation in the New Testament are intelligible only for one who is informed about the questions which are implicit in the New Testament answers. The terms used by the authors of the biblical books were produced by the religious tradition by which they were determined, and the original meaning of these terms must first be understood. At the same time the fact that the ideas when applied to the Christian paradox instantly transcend both these traditions and the individual reworking of tradition by particular authors brings out the revelatory character of the ideas. Yet they would reveal nothing, but would be only alien conglomerations of words, if they did not carry along, so to speak, their traditional usage in the service of revelation. In this fact lies the great theological significance of historical and religio-historical criticism and interpretation of the Bible, and likewise the impossibility of divorcing the word of the Bible from cultural history. With that fact established, the genuinely supernatural notion of verbal inspiration is no longer a remote idea. And, actually, the younger disciples of Barth are moving in this direction. The consequences of this supernaturalistic tendency are evident. That has been true for a long time in the preaching of many pastors of this school who repeat the biblical text in the Barthian way without taking the trouble to treat in a vital way the higher problem to which the word of the Bible is the answer. Barth is right in protesting that preaching has been devoted to displaying religious experience, personal piety, cultural and social convictions. It ought to bear witness to God and not to man. Yet, it must witness *for* man, and it ought to take pains to vitalize the human means, not waiting for a miracle to enable the message to become God's word for the hearer.

Barthian teaching about the relation of the Kingdom of God to human activities is also subject to criticism. It is a fact of church history that Barth made an end of the naïve identification of the Kingdom of God with ecclesiastical activities, social programs, political reconstruction, or human progress. Thus, and only thus, was he able to save German Protestantism from dissolving into a worldly political movement embodying strongly extra-Christian elements. That outcome would scarcely have been possible without Barth's radical and one-sided emphasis upon the separation of the divine from the human. But an instrument that is a mighty weapon in warfare may be an inconvenient tool for use in the building trade.

According to the supernatural way of thinking the Kingdom of God as an eschatological phenomenon is absolutely nonexistent in the present world. But dialectic thinking seeks to derive the nature of eschatology from the words of Jesus, "the Kingdom of God is at hand". "At hand" means that it is here and not here, it is "in your midst", but it cannot be seen and handled. It is qualitatively different from everything that is known to us. But, with this distinctively qualitative difference, it breaks into our world. Therefore, we can never say that it is present in this or that ecclesiastical and social activity, form of human progress, charitable deed, or conception of truth. When we would lay hold upon it, we find that everything is always under the dominion of the demons and never does the dominion of God alone come to realization. Yet we cannot say that the Kingdom of God is not present at all, as though only the dominion of the demons and not the dominion of God prevailed. What we can say is that in this or that act of the church or of society there is a hint at what is meant by "Kingdom of God", namely, "righteousness, peace and joy in the Holy Spirit". Now hints of the Kingdom of God can occur only where the power of this kingdom has broken through into human existence. Because Barth is not acquainted with this dialectic method of interpreting the presence and absence of the Kingdom of God, he would have to conclude that without the insert of revelation as a foreign entity, the world must stand exclusively under the dominion of demons. But he does not draw this conclusion, for the forceful New Testament and early Christian thinking about demons has remained undeveloped in Barth's Calvinistic theology. He believes in a godless objectivity of human action ravaged by sin and without any relation whatever either to the divine or to the demonic. This seems to me to be one of the weakest points in Barthian teaching; and on this ground his refusal to recognize a theological ethics is also based. Now belief in an objective existence, indifferent with respect to both divine and human dominion, is an illusion. We never live merely in the first and second dimension of our existence (in dead matter and in the form we give to it), but we also live constantly in the third dimension (on the divine mountain-top and in the demonic abyss). That holds true of all our activities, even of those that are apparently the most secular. One who does not recognize that fact and who, mistakenly holding to the belief in a two-dimensional reality renounces the religious conflict against psychical, social, and spiritual demonic forces, does in truth forward demonic interests. In this respect the Barthian theology is in effect undeniably guilty. But the liberal theology is liable to the same condemnation, for it, too, through its belief in progress, has obscured the power of the demonic element in human existence. But while liberalism arrives at this erroneous conclusion by identifying a continuity of humanly valuable activities with the realization of the Kingdom of God, Barth arrives at it by the severance of human activities from both divine and demonic powers. Both deny the realism of dialectic, that is three-dimensional thinking.

By his mighty proclamation of the Christian paradox Barth has saved theology from forgetting the deity of God and has saved the church from lapsing into secularism and paganism. This positive value is more important than all the objections that may be urged against Barth. But there is this defect: although he has been called a dialect theologian, he does not think dialectically, but supernaturally.*

\*

## THE CHURCH AND THE THIRD REICH:
## TEN THESES

*The ten theses on the church in Nazi Germany provide a crisp summary of Tillich's Protestant thought as it found expression in critique of National Socialism and of the German Christians who would compromise with it. Tillich's own opposition to Nazism was fueled by his Religious Socialist struggle for theonomy, his theology, and the way he had fused the two in a theology of culture displaying its strong political dimension. These theses were published in 1932, in a book that was sent to Hitler,* Die Kirche und das Dritte Reich: Fragen und Forderungen deutscher Theologen, *Ed. Leopold Klotz (Gotha: Klotz, 1932). J. Stark, a professor of Hitler's, wrote against the book: "The book in question affords a valuable commentary on the intellectual level of numerous 'evangelical' academic theologians. Never have I seen such an accumulation of ignorance, superficiality, presumption and malicious enmity to the German Freedom Movement." (Quoted from Ronald Stone,* Paul Tillich's Radical Social Thought, *pp. 84-5.) The "Ten Theses" appear in English here for the first time, translated by Andrea Böcherer, in a course at Pittsburgh Theological Seminary with Professor Ronald Stone.*

* For Barth's own testimony concerning his response to National Socialism, see Clifford Green, *Karl Barth*, The Making of Modern Theology: 19th and 20th Century Theological Texts, General Editor: John W. de Gruchy (London and San Francisco: Collins, forthcoming, 1988).

1 Protestantism, which opens itself up to National Socialism and rejects Socialism, once more is going to betray its commission to the world.

2 Seemingly obedient to the phrase that the Kingdom of God is not of this world, Protestantism proves itself to be submissive to the victorious forces and their demonic power — as Protestantism often has done in its history.

3 Insofar as Protestantism justifies nationalism and the ideology of blood and race by a doctrine of the divine order of creation, it abandons its prophetic foundation in favor of a new apparent or veiled paganism. It also betrays its commission to testify to the one God and the one human race.

4 Insofar as Protestantism gives the consecration of God-given authority to the capitalistic-feudal form of rule — which National Socialism actually protects — it promotes the perpetuation of class conflict, and it betrays its commission to bear witness against violations and to testify for justice as a measure of every social order.

5 Protestantism is in the utmost danger of going that way, which will be fatal in the long run. From its beginning, Protestantism has lacked a dominating group independent of secular powers and national separations. It lacks a prophetically founded principle of social criticism. On Lutheran ground, Protestantism lacks the will to shape reality according to the image of the Kingdom of God. In Germany, Protestantism is supported sociologically almost exclusively by the groups that advocate National Socialism, and is therefore ideologically and politically bound to them.

6 Official declarations of neutrality by ecclesiastical authorities don't alter the actual attitudes of most Protestant groups, theologians, or lay persons. These declarations become totally worthless if at the same time the church takes actions against socialist ministers and congregations, and if theologians who resist the pagan National Socialism find no protection in the church.

7 Protestantism must prove its prophetic-Christian character by setting the Christianity of the cross against the paganism of the swastika. Protestantism must testify that the cross has broken and judged the "holiness" of nation, race, blood, and power.

117

8  According to its nature, Protestantism cannot present itself in a certain political movement. It must prove that it is free by allowing Protestants to be members of any political party, even of those that oppose Protestantism as it realizes its religious life. But Protestantism must submit every party — as well as all human and religious activities — to the judgment and hope of the prophetic, early Christian proclamation of the Kingdom of God.

9  In this way, Protestantism can direct the political wills of those groups that are allied in supporting National Socialism to a goal that is true, just, and appropriate for their social needs. Protestantism can liberate the movement from the demonic powers that today subdue it and that destroy nation and humanity.

10  After a present increase in church power, an open or clandestine alliance between Protestant churches and the National-Socialist Party to suppress Socialism and oppose Catholicism inevitably will lead to future disintegration of German Protestantism.

# 3

## IN THE SACRED VOID: BEING AND GOD*

### RELIGION AND SECULAR CULTURE

*After World War II, Tillich stunned a gathering of his Religious Socialist friends in the United States with a vision of human life that emphasized the feeling of "the void", more than the political expectation that infused his earlier Religious Socialism. The demonisms of German Nazism and of World War II had run their course and now Tillich saw humankind suspended in an inner void, a vacuum, laden with an angst that theologians of culture must address. As the following essay shows, however, the sense of the void, which included a theology of this void as "sacred", was itself related to a momentous historical-political development: the use and continuing threat of nuclear weaponry. Tillich's subsequent ontology and theology for an age of anxiety never lost their reference to the realities of sociopolitical oppression, but more and more the focus seemed to be on the existential anguish of the general human situation. The following essay provides his remarks as presented in a lecture in January, 1946, for the Hiram W. Thomas Foundation at the University of Chicago, appearing in the Journal of Religion (XXVI [1946]: 79-86) and then in The Protestant Era (pp. 55-65). It begins with very valuable autobiographical reflections on his own religious thought between the wars.*

I

The technical problem of a lecture on religion and secular culture is the implicit demand to give in one paper the content of at least two volumes, namely, that of a philosophy of religion and that of a philosophy of culture. Since this cannot be done except in terms of an abstract and unconvincing summary, I intend to limit myself to one central concept, namely, that of a "theonomous" culture, and to develop this concept in a kind of autobiographical retrospect from the end of the First World War to the end of the Second, adding some systematic analyses of the theonomous character of symbols.

When we returned from the First World War, we found a deep gap between the cultural revolution and the religious tradition in central

* See also pp. 21-24 above.

and eastern Europe. The Lutheran and the Roman and Greek Catholic churches rejected the cultural and — with some exceptions on the part of Roman Catholicism — the political revolutions. They rejected them as the rebellious expression of a secular autonomy. The revolutionary movements, on the other hand, repudiated the churches as the expression of a transcendent heteronomy. It was very obvious to those of us who had spiritual ties with both sides that this situation was intolerable and, in the long run, disastrous for religion as well as for culture. We believed that it was possible to close the gap, partly by creating movements such as religious socialism, partly by a fresh interpretation of the mutual immanence of religion and culture within each other. History, however, has shown that it was too late for such an attempt to be successful at that time. It proved impossible to break down the secular ideology and the mechanistic (non-Marxist) materialism of the labor parties. The Old Guard prevailed against us and against the youth of their own movement. In the religious realm not only the conservative representatives of "ruling-class Christianity" (the European counterpart to American "suburban Christianity") ostracized us; we were also attacked by that dynamic theology which in this country is called "neo-orthodoxy" and which united prophetic powers with a non-prophetic detachment from culture, thus confirming and deepening the gap. Our attempt was frustrated; but we did not and do not accept defeat in so far as the truth of our conception is concerned; for we do not accept the idea, which a consistent pragmatism can hardly avoid, that victory is a method of pragmatic verification.

The first of my attempts to analyze the mutual immanence of religion and culture was made in a lecture which I read in Berlin immediately after the end of the war, entitled "The Idea of a Theology of Culture". It was written with the enthusiasm of those years in which we believed that a new beginning, a period of radical transformation, a fulfilment of time, or, as we called it with a New Testament term, a kairos had come upon us, in spite of breakdown and misery. We did *not*, however, share the feeling of many American religious and secular humanists of the twenties; we did *not* believe that the Kingdom of God, consisting in peace, justice, and democracy, had been established. Very early we saw those demonic structures of reality which during the past months have been recognized by all thoughtful people in this country. But we also saw a new chance, a moment pregnant with creative possibilities. The breakdown of bourgeois civilization in central and eastern Europe could pave the way for a reunion of religion and secular culture. That was what we hoped for and what religious socialism fought for, and to it we tried to give a philosophical and theological basis. The idea of a "theonomous culture" seemed to be adequate for this aim; it became the principle of philosophies of religion and of culture which proposed to fill the gap from both sides.

The churches had rejected the secularized autonomy of modern culture; the revolutionary movements had rejected the transcendent heteronomy of the churches. Both had rejected something from which, in the last analysis, they themselves lived; and this something is theonomy. The words "autonomy", "heteronomy", and "theonomy" answer the question of the *nomos* or the law of life in three different ways: Autonomy asserts that man as the bearer of universal reason is the source and measure of culture and religion — that he is his own law. Heteronomy asserts that man, being unable to act according to universal reason, must be subjected to law, strange and superior to him. Theonomy asserts that the superior law is, at the same time, the innermost law of man himself, rooted in the divine ground which is man's own ground: the law of life transcends man, although it is, at the same time, his own. Applying these concepts to the relation between religion and culture, we called an autonomous culture the attempt to create the forms of personal and social life without any reference to something ultimate and unconditional, following only the demands of theoretical and practical rationality. A heteronomous culture, on the other hand, subjects the forms and laws of thinking and acting to authoritative criteria of an ecclesiastical religion or a political quasi-religion, even at the price of destroying the structures of rationality. A theonomous culture expresses in its creations an ultimate concern and a transcending meaning not as something strange but as its own spiritual ground. "Religion is the substance of culture and culture the form of religion." This was the most precise statement of theonomy.

With these distinctions it was possible to create a theonomous analysis of culture, a "theology of culture", so to speak, which shows its theonomous ground not only where it is clearly indicated, as in the archaic periods of the great cultures and the early and high Middle Ages of our Western civilization, but also in those periods in which heteronomy was victorious, as in the latter Middle Ages and in Arabic and Protestant orthodoxy, and even in autonomous or secular epochs, such as classical Greece, the Renaissance, the Enlightenment, and the nineteenth century. No cultural creation can hide its religious ground or its rational formation. Against ecclesiastical heteronomy it is always possible to show that all the rites, doctrines, institutions, and symbols of a religious system constitute a religious culture which is derived from the surrounding general culture — from its social and economic structure, its character traits, its opinions and philosophy, its linguistic and artistic expressions, its complexes, its traumas, and its longings. It is possible to show that, if such a special religious culture be imposed on dissenters or foreign cultures, it is not the ultimate, with its justified claim to grasp the hearts of men, but something provisional and conditioned which uses the religious ultimacy for *its* claims. The Thomistic philosophy, as well as the Protestant ideal of personality, is a transitory form of religious culture, but neither has any claim to ultimacy and finality; and the same holds true of the Greek concepts in the dogma of the church, of the feudal pattern of the Roman hierarchy, of the patriarchalistic ethics of Lutheranism, of the democratic ideals of sectarian Protestantism, and even of the cultural traditions which, for instance, are embodied in the biblical language and world view. Theonomous thinking sides with autonomous criticism, if such forms of religious culture present themselves as absolutes.

But more important in our situation was and is the other task of a theonomous analysis of culture: to show that in the depth of every autonomous culture an ultimate concern, something unconditional and holy, is implied. It is the task of deciphering the style of an autonomous culture in all its characteristic expressions and of finding their hidden religious significance. This we did with all possible tools of historical research and comparative interpretation and empathic understanding and with a special effort in regard to such stages of civilization as were utterly secular, as, for instance, the later nineteenth century. Autonomous culture is secularized in the degree to which it has lost its ultimate reference, its center of meaning, its spiritual substance. The Renaissance was a step toward autonomy, but still in the spiritual power of an unwasted medieval heritage. The Enlightenment quickly lost its Protestant and sectarian substance and became in some — though not in many — of its expressions completely secular. The later nineteenth century, with its subjection to the technical pattern of thought and action, shows the character of an extremely emptied and secularized autonomy in an advanced stage of disintegration. But even here the religious substance, a remnant of something ultimate, was noticeable and made the transitory existence of such a culture possible. However, more than in the disintegrating bourgeois autonomy, the religious reference was effective in the movements which protested — often with a prophetic passion — against this situation. Theonomous analysis was able to decipher puzzling experiences, such as the visionary destruction of bourgeois idealism and naturalism in art and literature by expressionism and surrealism; it was able to show the religious background of the rebellion of the vital and unconscious side of man's personality against the moral and intellectual tyranny of consciousness; it was able to interpret the quasi-religious, fanatical, and absolutistic character of the reactions of the twentieth century as against the nineteenth. It was able to do all this without special reference to organized religion, the churches being only a part of the whole picture, but with a decisive reference to the religious element which was and is hidden in all these antireligious and anti-Christian movements. In all of them there is an ultimate, unconditional, and all-determining concern, something absolutely serious and therefore holy, even if expressed in secular terms.

So the gap between religion and culture is filled: religion is more than a system of special symbols, rites, and emotions, directed toward a highest being; religion is ultimate concern; it is the state of being grasped by something unconditional, holy, absolute. As such it gives meaning, seriousness, and depth to all culture and creates out of the cultural material a religious culture of its own. The contrast between religion and culture is reduced to the duality of religious and secular culture with unnumerable transitions between them. The revolutionary movements, for instance, represent an ultimate concern, a religious principle, hidden but effective within them. The Lutheran churches, for example, represent a special cultural period in which an ultimate concern, a religious principle, has embodied itself manifestly and directly. Both are religious and both are cultural at the same time. Why, then, the difference? The answer can only be that the Kingdom of God has not yet come, that God is not yet all in all, whatever this "not yet" may mean. Asked what the proof is for the fall of the world, I like to answer: religion itself, namely, a religious culture beside a secular culture, a temple beside a town hall, a Lord's Supper beside a daily supper, prayer beside work, meditation beside research, *caritas* beside *eros*. But although this duality can never be overcome in time, space, and history, it makes a difference whether the duality is deepened into a bridgeless gap, as in periods in which autonomy and heteronomy fight with each other, or whether the duality is recognized as something which should not be and which is overcome fragmentarily by anticipation, so to speak, in a theonomous period. The kairos which we believed to be at hand was the coming of a new theonomous age, conquering the destructive gap between religion and secular culture.

But history took another path, and the question of religion and culture cannot be answered simply in those terms. A new element has come into the picture, the experience of the "end". Something of it appeared after the First World War; but we did not feel it in its horrible depth and its incredible thoroughness. We looked at the beginning of the new more than at the end of the old. We did not realize the price that mankind has to pay for the coming of a new theonomy; we still believed in transitions without catastrophes. We did not see the possibility of final catastrophes as the true prophets, the prophets of doom, announced them. Therefore, our theonomous interpretation of history had a slight tinge of romanticism, though it tried to avoid any kind of utopianism. This has come to an end because the end itself has appeared like a flash of lightning before our eyes; and not only among the ruins of central and eastern Europe but also within the abundance of this country has it been seen. While after the First World War the mood of a new beginning prevailed, after the Second World War a mood of the end prevails. A present theology of culture is, above all, a theology of the end of culture, not in general terms but in a concrete analysis of the inner void of most of our cultural expressions. Little is left in our present civilization which does not indicate to a sensitive mind the presence of this vacuum, this lack of ultimacy and substantial power in language and education, in politics and philosophy, in the development of personalities, and in the life of communities. Who of us has never been shocked by this void when he has used traditional or untraditional secular or religious language to make himself understandable and has not succeeded and has then made a vow of silence to himself, only to break it a few hours later? This is symbolic of our whole civilization. Often one gets the impression that only those cultural creations have greatness in which the experience of the void is expressed; for it can be expressed powerfully only on the basis of a foundation which is deeper than culture, which is ultimate concern, even if it accepts the void, even in respect to religious culture. Where this happens, the vacuum of disintegration can become a vacuum out of which creation is possible, a "sacred void", so to speak, which brings a quality of waiting, of "not yet", of a being broken from above, into all our cultural creativity. It is not an empty criticism, however radical and justified such criticism may be. It is not an indulgence in paradoxes that prevents the coming-down to concreteness. It is not cynical detachment, with its ultimate spiritual dishonesty. It is simple cultural work out of, and qualified by, the experience of the sacred void. This is the way — perhaps the only way — in which our time can reach a theonomous union between religion and culture.

One thing is clear: the experience of the end by no means undermines the idea of theonomy. On the contrary, it is its strongest confirmation. Two events may illustrate this. The first is the turn of Karl Barth from a theology of radical detachment from culture, religious as well as secular, to an equally radical attachment to the fight against a demonically distorted cultural system. Barth suddenly realized that culture can never be indifferent toward the ultimate. If it ceases to be theonomous, it first becomes empty, and then it falls, at least for a time, under demonic control. The demand for a merely matter-of-fact culture is dishonesty or illusion, and a catastrophic illusion at that. This leads to the second event to which I want to refer: the change of attitude toward culture in this country. It was truly symbolic for the collapse of our secular autonomy when the atom scientists raised their voices and preached the end, not unconditionally but with conditions of salvation which present-day humanity is hardly willing to fulfill. It was and is a symptom of a changed mood when some of these men and others with them, statesmen, educators, psychologists, physicians, sociologists, not to speak of artists and poets, whose visions anticipated our cultural predicament long ago — when these people cry for religion as the saving power of our culture. They do it often in the ugly and false phraseology which demands the undergirding of culture by religion, as if religion were a tool for a higher purpose. But even in this inadequate form the ideal of a theonomous culture is transparent. . . .

II

. . . I want to close with a few words concerning that realm of culture which is not an independent realm but is the way of communicating all other realms to those who are to be shaped by them, namely, education. In doing so, I give, at the same time, homage to the genius of this place. The theonomous word for education is "initiation". While the word "education" points to the *terminus a quo*, the "where from", the word "initiation" points to the *terminus ad quem*, the "where to". Secular culture has lost an ultimate and commanding *terminus ad quem*, because it has lost an ultimate and unconditional concern. In the Diotima speech in Plato's *Symposium* we see, still retained, the steps of initiation into the ultimate wisdom. And in his myth of the cave in the *Republic* we learn that the way to wisdom implies a radical transformation, a liberation from bondage and darkness. Such ideas presuppose that there is a level in life, the most and ultimately the *only* important one, which cannot be approached directly. It is the level of gnosis or *sapientia* or "wisdom", in distinction from the level of *episteme* or *scientia* or "science". It is the level of Being and truth as such before they split into subject and object; and, therefore, it has the character of a mystery. Everything which is merely object can be approached directly with scientific reasoning and techni-cal tools. That which precedes mere objectivity needs initiation. Innu-merable rites of initiation in all nations up to Christian baptism and confirmation show that mankind was conscious of the sacred depth in things which cannot be approached in ordinary ways. When the ele-ment of initiation was lost, education lost the *terminus ad quem* and is now desperately looking for it. But no abundance of highest possibility shown to the coming generations can replace something ultimate that is necessary. Are we able to show it to them by initiation as well as by edu-cation? We *cannot* do it today in terms of special contents, whether they be religious or secular. But we *can* do it by accepting the void which is the destiny of our period, by accepting it as a "sacred void" which may qualify and transform thinking and acting. I have not tried to present a well-balanced synthesis between religion and secular culture. I have tried to show their *one* theonomous root and the void which necessarily has followed their separation, and perhaps something of the longing of our time for a new theonomy, for an ultimate concern in all our concerns.

\*

## THE PROBLEM OF THEOLOGICAL METHOD

*In 1947, Tillich offered this statement of his theological method, showing relationships between his earlier call to a "self-transcending realism" and his later effort in systematic theology. Here Tillich's realism, his sense that human experience of transcendence is to be found in the unrepeatable ten-sions of the present, issues in a theological method that "correlates" the symbols of the Christian tradition with the tensions of the human situation: "God" with essential being, "Christ" with estranged existence, "Spirit" with the ambiguities of life, "Kingdom of God" with history. This essay makes clear that the method of correlation is not the mere juxtaposing of a Christian answer with a human problem; it is an interpretive art requiring sensitive readings of both human situations and also of Christian symbols in the tradition. It is a continual tacking back and forth between a situation and a Christian message that are always already in some kind of mutual interrelation. At the heart of this method, then, is a theological interpretive style that Tillich terms "a genuine pragmatism which refuses to close any door". This essay first appeared in the* Journal of Religion *XXVII, 1 (January 1947):16-26, and then in* Will Herberg, ed., *Four Existentialist Theologians: A Reader from the Works of Jacques Maritain, Nicholas Berdyaev, Martin Buber and Paul Tillich (Garden City, N.Y.: Doubleday, 1958): 263-82.*

## 1. METHOD AND REALITY

Method is the systematic way of doing something, especially of gaining knowledge. No method can be found in separation from its actual exercise; methodological considerations are abstractions from methods actually used. Descartes's *Discours de la méthode* followed Galileo's application of the method of mathematical physics and brought it to general consciousness and philosophical definiteness. Schleiermacher's method, as used in the *Glaubenslehre,* followed the mystical-romantic reinterpretation of religion and established methodology of inner experience. The methodological remarks made in this paper describe the method actually used in my attempts to elaborate a theology of "self-transcending Realism" (*gläubiger Realismus*), which is supposed to overcome supra-naturalism as well as its naturalistic counterpart.

It is not a sound procedure to borrow a method for a special realm of inquiry from another realm in which this method has been successfully used. It seems that the emphasis on the so-called "empirical" method in theology has not grown out of actual theological demands but has been imposed on theology under the pressure of a "methodological imperialism", exercised by the pattern of natural sciences. This subjection of theology to a strange pattern has resulted in an undue extension of the concept "empirical" and the lack of a clear distinction between the different meanings of "experience" in the theological enterprise. For some it is the general human experience on the basis of which they try to approach inferentially the religious objects; for others it is the religious experience of mankind, empathically interpreted. Sometimes it is the religious experience of the theologian and the group to which he belongs that gives the material for an "empirical" theology. Sometimes an ontological intuition is called "experience". Certainly, every concrete reality is open to many methods, according to its different "levels" or "functional potentialities". And each of the ways mentioned (besides some others) can contribute something to the investigation of a phenomenon as complex as religion. But the confusing term "empirical" should not be imposed on all of them; nor should the attempt be made to establish a methodological monism which includes chemistry as well as theology. Reality itself makes demands, and the method must follow; reality offers itself in different ways, and our cognitive intellect must receive it in different ways. An exclusive method applied to everything closes many ways of approach and impoverishes our vision of reality. A world construed according to the model of classical mechanics or Hegelian dialectics or behavioristic protocols is not the cognitive fulfillment of the potentialities of reality. In this respect a genuine pragmatism which refuses to close any door is much more realistic than a dogmatic empiricism with which it is sometimes confused — even by its own followers.

We encounter reality — or reality imposes itself upon us — sometimes in a more complex way, sometimes in definite and distinguishable elements and functions. Whenever we encounter reality in the one or the other way, it challenges our cognitive power and brings it into action. The way in which the cognitive power works is dependent on three factors: its own structure, the structure of the reality it encounters, and the relation of the two structures. In a methodical approach these three factors are noticed, analyzed, and evaluated. But the *prius* of all this is the encounter itself; and nothing is more destructive for knowledge than the establishment of methods which, by their very nature, prevent the actual encounter or prejudice its interpretation. (It is my opinion that the term "encounter" is more adequate for our pretheoretical relation to reality than the term "experience", which has lost so much of its specific meaning that it needs to be "saved", namely, restricted to a theoretically interpreted encounter.)

The presupposition of theology is that there is a special encounter with reality — or a special way in which reality imposes itself on us — which is ordinarily called "religious". And it is the presupposition of this paper that "having a religious encounter with reality" means "being ultimately concerned about reality".

## 2. THEOLOGY AND PHILOSOPHY OF RELIGION

The ultimate concern or the religious encounter with reality can be considered in two ways. It can be looked at as an event beside other events, to be observed and described in theoretical detachment; or it can be understood as an event in which he who considers it is "existentially" involved. In the first case the philosopher of religion is at work, in the second the theologian speaks. The philosopher of religion notices the ultimate concern, which he cannot help finding in the history of religion as a quality of practically all representative personalities, symbols, and activities that are called "religious". But in his dealing with this characteristic of religion he himself is only theoretically, but not existentially, concerned. The religious concern is not his concern in so far as he is a philosopher of religion. He points to it, he explains it, but his work is not an expression of the religious encounter with reality. This is different in the theologian. He applies his ultimate concern to everything, as an *ultimate* concern demands — even to his theoretical interpretation of the religious encounter. For the theologian the interpretation of the ultimate concern is itself a matter of ultimate concern, a *religious* work.

But this distinction is not unambiguous. There is an element in every philosophy (not only in every philosopher) which is "existential", i.e., which has the character of an ultimate decision about the meaning of reality. The less technical and the more creative a philosophy is, the more it shows, at least implicitly, an ultimate concern. No creative philosophy can escape its religious background. This is the reason for the tremendous influence that philosophy has had not only on theology but also on the history of religion and vice versa; for, as the philosopher cannot escape his theological background, so the theologian cannot escape his philosophical tool. Those who try to do so deceive themselves: their language, which is shaped through philosophy, betrays them (as even Barth has admitted).

Nevertheless, the distinction between theology and philosophy of religion is valid and cannot be obliterated without dangerous consequences. It is very unfortunate that the so-called "Continental" theology has brought into disregard the function of an independent philosophy of religion, thus creating an intolerable theological absolutism; and it is equally unfortunate that American (nonfundamentalistic) theology was not able to protect itself from being dissolved into a general philosophy of religion, thus producing a self-destructive relativism.

Theology is the existential and, at the same time, methodical interpretation of an ultimate concern. The interpretation of an ultimate concern is "existential" if it is done in the situation of concern. The interpretation of an ultimate concern is methodical if it relates the concern rationally to the whole of experience. Theology, literally and historically, unites these two elements. Theological propositions, therefore, are propositions which deal with an object in so far as it is related to an ultimate concern. No object is excluded from theology if this criterion is applied, not even a piece of stone; and no object is in itself a matter of theology, not even God as an object of inference. This makes theology absolutely universal, on the one hand, and absolutely definite, on the other hand. Theology has to deal with everything, but only under the theological criterion, the ultimate concern.

The concept "ultimate concern" is itself the result of a theological procedure. It expresses two sides of the religious experience: (1) The one side is the absolute or unconditional or ultimate element in religious experience. Every religious relation, attitude, symbol, and action is unconditionally *serious; decisive* in an absolute sense; *transcending* any preliminary, transitory, and dependent value. The whole history of religion confirms this side of religious experience. Where there is a living religion, it makes an absolute claim; it claims the "whole heart"; it does not admit anything ultimate besides itself. (2) The other side is the dynamic presence of the "ultimate" as a continuous, never ceasing, concrete, and universal concern, always demanding and giving, always threatening and promising. As an actual concern it expresses itself in the actualities of life, qualifying every section of existence and using every section of existence for its own embodiment in symbols and actions; for the religious or ultimate concern refers to the ultimate foundation of our being and the ultimate meaning of our existence. Therefore, we can formulate the abstract criterion of every theological work in this way: Those propositions are theological which deal with a subject in so far as it belongs to the foundation of our being and in so far as the meaning of our existence depends on it.

## 3. THE POSITIVE ELEMENT IN THE THEOLOGICAL METHOD

The ultimate concern is a concrete concern; otherwise it could not be a concern at all. Even mysticism lives in concrete traditions and symbols in order to express, in action and thought, that which transcends everything concrete. Theology, therefore, must interpret the totality of symbols, institutions, and ideas in which an ultimate concern has embodied itself; theology is, first of all, *positive*. It works on the basis, in the material, and for the purpose of an actual religion. The participation in a religious reality is a presupposition of all theology. You have to be within the circle of a concrete religion in order to interpret it existentially. This is the "theological circle" which theology cannot (and never should try to) escape. This circle is not vicious, but its denial is dishonest, for it could be denied only in the name of an assumedly higher ultimate, which immediately would establish the same circle.

Traditionally, the theological circle has been expressed in the assertion that faith is the precondition of theology. (*Pistis* precedes *gnosis*, as the Alexandrians said; *credo ut intelligam*, as Anselm, following Augustine, formulated it.) Faith, in this context, means a convinced and active participation in the life of a religious group, its traditions, its tensions, its activities. It is not the individual belief of the theologian to which they refer (as we are inclined to misinterpret the *credo ut intelligam*); but it is the spiritual substance out of which a theologian must create, even if he is aware of the weakness of his personal faith (otherwise there would be no honest theologian).

The ultimate concern out of which *we* are working as theologians is embodied in Christianity. If a Christian theologian says that for him Christianity is one among other elements in the religion he intends to interpret, this can mean two things — either that he is not a theologian but a philosopher of religion or that he belongs to a new religious synthesis which is, like everything concrete, inclusive and exclusive at the same time and which therefore establishes a theological circle, just as Christianity does. Since such a concrete synthesis has not yet appeared within my own theological circle and since I am convinced that Christianity is able to take all possible elements of religious truth into itself without ceasing to be Christianity, I am going to speak now about Christian theology, as the only one which is within my essential reach.

Christian theology is a work of the Christian church. The theological function is one of its essential functions, which never can be lost so long as there is the church. Christian theology, moreover, cannot be carried on except by the church. The positive character of the ultimate concern makes "individual theology" impossible. The individual theologian can and should find more adequate methods of interpretation. But he cannot find that which he is asked to interpret. Concretely speaking: Christian theology is the interpretation of the message that Jesus is the Christ, and of the symbols and institutions based on this message. Theology is the methodical self-interpretation of the Christian church (1) in the direction of its foundation, the "new reality" which has become manifest in Jesus as the Christ, and (2) in the direction of the life, past and present, which is determined by this new reality. The original document of the new reality is the Bible; the expression of the life determined by this new reality is the Tradition.

### 4. THE THEOLOGICAL METHOD WITH RESPECT TO BIBLE AND TRADITION

Bible and Tradition give the material in which the theologian works. The Bible implies three elements which have different impacts on the theological method. First, and basically, it contains the decisive manifestation of what concerns us ultimately, in the picture of Jesus as the Christ. This is the criterion of all Christian theology, the criterion also of the theological use of the Bible, for the Bible contains, second, the reception of this manifestation in the original church. Every biblical writer is, at the same time, a witness to the new reality in Jesus as the Christ and a witness of the way in which he and the group to which he belongs have received the new reality. In the latter sense they have started the Tradition. In the first sense they point to that which judges the Tradition, including their own contribution to it. (This is the meaning of Luther's statement that the Bible is the "Word of God" in so far as it *Christum treibet;* in the power of this criterion he himself judged the canon.) From this it follows that not the Bible as such, as a part of the history of religion, is the norm of Christian theology but the Bible in so far as it is the genuine witness to the new reality. It is the permanent task of Christian theology (in unity with the developing religious and historical understanding of the Bible) to elaborate the norm of Christian theology out of the whole of the biblical material and to apply the norm equally to Bible and Tradition. The third element in the biblical literature that is important for theological method is the preparation for the decisive manifestation of the new reality and for its reception by the church. In the Old as well as in the New Testament we find in language, rites, and ideas a large element of general revelation as it has occurred and continuously occurs within human religion generally. Our eyes have been opened to this element by the work of the *religionsgeschichtliche Schule* in historical theology. So far as method goes, this means that in every theological statement we must take into consideration the religious substance which is transformed and purified in the prophetic and apostolic message. Only in this sense, but in this sense definitely, the *history of religion* belongs to the positive element in Christian theology. The universality of the Christian claim implies that there is no religion, not even the most primitive, which has not contributed or will not contribute to the preparation and reception of the new reality in history. In this sense the theologian always must be a "pagan" and a "Jew" and a "Greek" (humanist) and bring their spiritual substance under the criterion of the theological norm. For instance, the terms "Son of Man", "Messiah", "Son of God", "Kyrios", "Logos", appear in the history of religion; and, if they are used for the interpretation of the new reality, they contribute to it with their previous connotations, but in such a way that their meaning is judged and saved at the same time. This method of *judging and saving the history of a religion* is exercised by all the biblical writers. It must be done methodically and creatively by the theologian.

Methodologically, the Tradition (the beginning of which is the biblical literature) is not normative but *guiding*. This is a rejection of the Roman Catholic point of view; just as the subordination of the biblical literature to the theological norm implied in it is a rejection of orthodox Protestantism. Tradition cannot be normative in Christian theology because there is always an element in Tradition which must be judged and cannot be the judge itself. But Tradition can and must be guiding for the theologian, because it is the expression of the continuous reception of the new reality in history and because, without tradition, no theological existence is possible. It is rather a naïve illusion of some Protestants to believe that by jumping over two thousand years of Christian tradition they can come into a direct and existential (more than philological) relation to the biblical texts. The guiding function of the Tradition has a positive and a negative side. Positively, the Tradition shows the questions implied in the Christian message, the main possibilities of answers, and the points in which Christians have agreed and have disagreed. Negatively, the Tradition shows answers which have generally been avoided and, above all, answers which have been characterized by the church as "heretical". He who takes the Tradition seriously must take heresies seriously. He knows that a heresy is supposed to be, not a deviating opinion, but an existential attack on, or a distortion of, the theological norm in the name of theology. He will not easily — not without the consciousness that he risks his participation in the new reality — promote a view which has been characterized as heretical by the church as a whole. This, of course, should not prevent anyone from following his theological conscience (as Luther did in Worms); but it should sharpen that conscience.

The positive element in theological method is historically given. But nothing is more ambiguous than the concept "historical". When the Anglican church accepted the apostolic succession as one of its basic doctrines, it meant to emphasize the historical continuity of the manifestation of the new reality in history. In this sense the doctrine emphasized the historical element in church and theology. But when Anglican theologians, answering Roman attacks, tried to justify the apostolic character of their episcopate by an 8,000 to 1 documentary probability that there was a real apostolic succession, they introduced another meaning of "historical", namely, the probabilities (which never can become religious certainties) of historical research. In that moment their religious position was scientifically undermined because they confused the two meanings of "historical". The same is true of biblical criticism. If the Christian faith is based even on a 100,000 to 1 probability that Jesus has said or done or suffered this or that; if Christianity is based on possible birth-registers of Nazareth or crime-registers of Pontius Pilate, then it has lost its foundation completely. Then the historical event, that a new reality has appeared in mankind and the world (a reality which is reflected in the picture of Jesus as the Christ), has become a matter of empirical verification, ideally through a competent reporter, armed with a camera, phonograph, and psychograph. Since such a reporter, unfortunately, was not available in the year A.D. 30, we have to replace him by more or less probable conjectures. But this is not the historical character of Jesus as the Christ. It is regrettable that one of the greatest events in the history of religion — the radical criticism of the holy legend of Christianity by Christian theologians, which destroyed a whole system of pious superstition — has been abused for the purpose of giving a pseudo-scientific foundation to the Christian faith. The historical foundation of theological method does not mean that the theologian has to wait, with fear and trembling, for the next mail which may bring him a new, more critical, or more conservative statement about some important facts of the "life of Jesus" according to which he has to change his faith and his theology. But it does mean that his theology is determined by the event of the appearance of the new reality in history, as reflected in the *full* biblical picture of Jesus as the Christ and as witnessed by all biblical writers and by the whole tradition of Christianity.

## 5. THE ELEMENT OF IMMEDIACY IN THE THEOLOGICAL METHOD

The positive element in theology, as discussed above, gives the *content* of theological work; the rational element, to be discussed later, gives the *form* of theological work; and the element of immediacy, to be discussed now, gives the *medium* of theological work. Without participation in the reality within which theology speaks, no theology is possible; it is the air in which theology breathes. We call this participation "experience" in the larger sense of the word, in which it covers the mere encounter as well as the cognitively conscious encounter. "Experience" in both senses is the medium, the element in which theology lives. But the religious experience of the theologian is not a positive source and not a norm of systematic theology. Everybody's religious experience is shaped by the denominational group to which he belongs. The education in his own church opened the door to religious reality for every theologian. Later he has personal experiences which confirm or transform his earlier ones. But his intention should never be to make his earlier or later experiences the content of his theology; they certainly will enter into it, but this is an event, not an intention. It is the function of the medium to mediate, not to hold fast. It was the danger of Schleiermacher's theology that his concept of "religious consciousness" became confused with "experience". But it contradicts the basic principle of the Reformation to look at one's self instead of looking beyond one's self at the new reality which liberates man from himself. Our experience is changing and fragmentary; it is not the source of truth, although without it no truth can become *our* truth.

It might be said that the whole history of religion, including the biblical religion and the development of Christianity, is the reservoir of man's religious experience and that the positive element of theology is identical with the contents of this experience. Such a statement is correct, but ambiguous. A content, e.g., of the experience of the prophet Isaiah, is the paradoxical acting of God in history. This divine acting transcends every immediate experience. It has become manifest to the prophet in a situation which we should call "revelation". Of course, the prophet is aware of this situation, and to that extent it is an "experience". Not the experiential side, however, is significant for the prophet and for the theologian, but the revelatory side. The word "revelation" has been distorted into "supra-natural communication of knowledge"; it is hard to save the word (and many others) from this state of corruption into which it has been brought by both supra-naturalism and naturalism.

135

Nevertheless, "revelation" points to something for which no other adequate word is available — certainly not "religious experience". Revelation is the manifestation of the ultimate ground and meaning of human existence (and implicitly of all existence). It is not a matter of objective knowledge, of empirical research or rational inference. It is a matter of ultimate concern; it grasps the total personality and is effective through a set of symbols. Revelation is not restricted to a special period of history, to special personalities or writings. It occurs whenever it "wills". But we can speak of it only if it has become revelation *for us,* if we have experienced it existentially. Not experience, but revelation received *in* experience, gives the content of every theology.

There is, however, one point (which is only a point, without length or breadth) in which medium and content are identical, because in this point subject and object are identical: It is the awareness of the ultimate itself, the *esse ipsum,* which transcends the difference between subject and object and lies, as the presupposition of all doubts, beyond doubt; it is the *veritas ipsa,* as Augustine has called it. It is wrong to call this point "God" (as the ontological argument does), but it is necessary to call it "that in us which makes it impossible for us to escape God". It is the presence of the element of "ultimacy" in the structure of our existence, the basis of religious experience. It has been called "religious *a priori*"; but if we use this phrase (in the sense of *anima naturaliter religiosa*), we must remove every content from it and reduce it to the pure potentiality of having experiences with the character of "ultimate concern". Every content of such an experience is dependent on revelation, namely, on the special way, form, and situation in which this potentiality is actualized by a concern which is concrete and ultimate at the same time. While the certainty of the pure ultimacy is ultimate, conditioned by nothing, its concrete embodiment in symbols and acts is a matter of destiny and venturing faith. Whenever we speak of religious experience, it is important to distinguish these (inseparable) elements: (1) the "point" of immediate awareness of the unconditional which *is* empty but unconditionally certain; and (2) the "breadth" of a concrete concern which is full of content but has the conditional certainty of venturing faith. Theology deals with the second element, while presupposing the first and measuring every theological statement by the standard of the ultimacy of the ultimate concern.

## 6. THE ELEMENT OF RATIONALITY IN
## THE THEOLOGICAL METHOD

Theology is the rational "word" about God; it is the methodical inter-pretation of our ultimate concern. The rational element is not a source of theology. It does not give the content. But it gives the form; and the relation between form and content is extremely complex and demands careful analysis.

Theology is often identified with systematic theology. Although this terminology is bad, because it excludes historical and practical theol-ogy from their full part in the whole world of theology, it indicates that theology is essentially systematic. The word "system" has a narrower and a larger meaning. In its narrower sense the word points to the ideal of a deductive method in which a whole of interdependent presupposi-tions is derived from highest principles. Attempts have been made to develop such a system in the history of Christian thought. But the posi-tive element in theology utterly resists a "system" in this sense; it includes openness and undermines a closed system. But "system" has also a larger sense. It designates a whole of propositions which are con-sistent, interdependent, and developed according to a definite method. In this sense all classical theology was systematic, and no theology, however fragmentary its actual work may be, can surrender the system-atic idea. Every meaningful fragment is an implicit system, as every system is an explicit fragment; for man, and especially the theologian, lives in fragments, in reality as well as in thought.

It is obvious that the positive character of theology excludes a rational or natural theology, if these terms mean that, without existential partici-pation in an ultimate concern, a detached analysis of reality can pro-duce theological propositions. Even the rational substructure on which, according to scholasticism, the revealed superstructure is built, has convincing power only in the situation of faith. Even if (with Thomas and against Duns Scotus) the logical necessity and correct-ness of the arguments of natural theology are acknowledged, their existential significance without revelation is not asserted.

The terms "natural religion" or "natural revelation" or "natural the-ology" are extremely misleading. If religion is the state of being grasped by an ultimate concern, "natural religion" can only mean that the ulti-mate concern is experienced in an encounter with nature. This, of course, is not only possible and real, but it is a necessary part of every ultimate concern; but it cannot be separated from other elements which also belong to every ultimate concern, such as personal and social elements. The concepts "natural revelation" and "natural theology" are often used for a knowledge of God which is inferentially derived from the structure of reality. But, whether such conclusions are valid or not, in neither case have they the character of "revelation", and they should not be called "theological", for there is no meaningful speaking of God if he is taken as an object which is not, at the same time, the ground of the speaking about him. There is no meaningful speaking of God except in an existential attitude or in the situation of revelation. In any other attitude the religious word "God" is used after it has been deprived of its genuine, namely, its religious, meaning. So we can say: There *is* revelation through nature; but there is no natural (rational) revelation. And there *is* theology dealing with nature; but there is no natural theology. Reason elaborates but does not produce theological propositions.

But the question arises as to whether the "elaboration" of the positive element in theology does not introduce a rational element into the substance itself. The urgency of this question is obvious when we look at the large number of philosophical concepts which have been used for theological purposes throughout the whole history of Christian thought.

It is possible to make a distinction between two types of theology, the *kerygmatic* and the *apologetic* type. In the kerygmatic type the kerygma — the message — is reproduced, interpreted, and organized either in predominantly biblical terms or in terms taken from the classical tradition. In the apologetic type the kerygma is related to the prephilosophical and the philosophical interpretations of reality. An apology "makes answer" — answers the questions asked of, and the criticisms directed against, a concrete religion. But an answer is possible only if there is a common ground between the one who asks and the one who answers. Apologetic theology presupposes the idea of a universal revelation, to which reference can be made because it is acknowledged by both sides. Here the rational element in theological method becomes most important and most intimately connected with the positive element. The way in which this connection has been and should be carried through can be called the "method of correlation".

## 7. THE METHOD OF CORRELATION

Wherever theology is understood in "existential" terms, all theological statements have the character of "correlation". Luther has expressed this principle very often and very strongly: "As you believe, so you have." This does not mean that the belief produces its contents; such an idea would have been utterly blasphemous for Luther. But it does mean that the objective and the subjective side of faith are interrelated, for faith is the expression of the impact of an ultimate concern on the human personality; it is the expression of an "existential situation" and not the acceptance of an objective assertion. Therefore, it is always subjective and objective in a strict interdependence. It is the beginning of a process of disintegration in theology if the objective side is isolated as a quasi-scientific assertion and the subjective side as an emotional "will to believe" in spite of a lack of evidence. The problem of truth in theology cannot be solved in terms of objective evidence. It can be solved only in terms of existential criteria. In the prophetic, as well as in the mystical, literature one criterion always appears: the unconditional character of the unconditional. Symbolically, it is called the "majesty of God"; or his exclusiveness against all finite claims (idols) or the unconditional dependence of every power on the divine power; or the "justification by grace alone". Every genuine heresy is an attack on the divinity of the divine. It gives to something finite infinite validity. It conditions the unconditional, for instance, by human morality or rationality. The "truth" of the Reformation theology against the canons of the Council of Trent is its emphasis on the ultimacy of the ultimate concern; it is not a "scientific" superiority of the Protestant over the Catholic propositions. It is an "existential", not an "objective", truth. This is the reason why the struggle of theologians is significant. They discuss, at least in principle, questions of "to be or not to be".

The method of correlation is especially the method of apologetic theology. Question and answer must be correlated in such a way that the religious symbol is interpreted as the adequate answer to a question, implied in man's existence, and asked in primitive, prephilosophical, or elaborated philosophical terms. For instance, the question implied in human finitude is answered in the symbols which constitute the idea of God; or the symbol of revelation answers the questions which drive reason to its own boundary; or the question implied in man's existential disruption and despair is answered in the symbol of the Christ and his appearance under the conditions of existence; or the idea of the divine Spirit is interpreted as the answer to the question implied in the tragic ambiguities of life, especially man's spiritual life; or the problems of the meaning of history are answered in the symbol of the Kingdom of God. In all these cases the method of correlation establishes a mutual interdependence between questions and answers. The questions implied in human existence determine the meaning and the theological interpretation of the answers as they appear in the classical religious concepts. The form of the questions, whether primitive or philosophical, is decisive for the theological form in which the answer is given. And, conversely, the substance of the question is determined by the substance of the answer. Nobody is able to ask questions concerning God, revelation, Christ, etc., who has not already received some answer. So we can say: With respect to man's ultimate concern the questions contain the substance of the answers, and the answers are shaped by the form of the questions. Here the rational element in theological method has a determining influence on theological propositions — not on their substance but on their form. But there is no way of saying a priori how much substance is hidden in the form. This can be said only in the process of theological work, and never fully. The reception of the "new reality", is always conditioned by the "old reality", which is conquered and fulfilled by it. This is the reason why early Christianity formulated the doctrine of the Logos, who has appeared in a unique way in Jesus as the Christ and is, at the same time, the universal principle of revelation in religion and culture. In this way the old reality can be considered as preparation for the new one; and the philosophical form is ultimately related to the substance of the theological answer instead of being alien to it. It seems to me that, without some form of a Logos doctrine (even if the term "Logos" is not used), no theology — certainly no apologetic theology — is possible.

A few examples may suffice to give a concrete impression of the method of correlation. If the question implied in human finitude is the question of God and the idea of God is the answer to this question, then modern existential analysis of human finitude becomes extremely valuable for the theological treatment of the idea of God. God becomes the correlate to human anxiety and contingency. He becomes the symbol of a "transcendent courage", in which the characteristics of finitude, as essential insecurity, loneliness, having to die, etc., are overcome. In this way the idea of God receives existential significance. The meaningless and self-contradictory question about the "existence of God" is replaced by an intensely meaningful question concerning our participation in an infinite communion, security, power, and meaning in the divine life.

In the same way the question implied in the self-destructive trends of man's personal and social life is to be understood as the question to which the central Christian statement that Jesus is the Christ gives the answer. If Christology is treated on the basis of this correlation, it interprets the picture of Jesus Christ as the ultimate manifestation of saving power in life and history, as the appearance of a "new reality", a power of wholeness and reconciliation conquering the "demonic" mechanisms in personal and social existence. Then our recent rediscovery of the contradictory structures in soul and community determines the form of our christological answer and makes this answer existential for our time. The method of correlation liberates Christology from a historism which tries to base the Christian faith in the new reality on doubtful historical probabilities, and it also liberates Christology from the "alchemy" of the doctrine of two natures, interpreting its meaning as a statement of the paradox of the victorious maintenance of the divine-human unity in a personal life against all the disruptive attacks of man's existential situation.

The method of correlation, as these examples show, is at no point forced into the vicious debate between naturalism and supra-naturalism. It describes things as they show themselves to the religious consciousness in the light of the human situation, the questions implied in it, and the answers given to it by the Christian message. Theology has rediscovered its correlative and existential character. It has overcome a theology of objective statements and subjective emotions. It has become again a way of giving answers to the questons which are our ultimate concern.

*

## THE ONTOLOGICAL STRUCTURE AND ITS ELEMENTS

*A reading of Tillich's* Systematic Theology *requires understanding Tillich's view of the "basic ontological structure" (self and world) and of the "ontological elements" (the polarities of individualization and participation, dynamics and form, freedom and destiny). The story he tells about the elemental polarities, in particular, is what weaves together the human situation with the major Christian symbols throughout his theology and ethics. In this our first selection from the* Systematic Theology *(Chicago: The University of Chicago Press, 1951, pp. 168-70, 179-201) Tillich delineates humans' essential being (what we are in essence and ought to be) in terms of the person's having a self and having a world, and in terms of the taut, anxiety-laden polarities of our finite being. The tenor of Tillich's entire theology is revealed here in these claims that finitude, anxiety and tension*

141

*are each pervasive aspects of our "essence". Our finite essence's drive toward the infinite recalls the self-transcending realism of his earlier work (see "Realism and Faith" above), and anticipates the major symbol, "God", that Tillich will correlate with essential being.*

## 1. MAN, SELF AND WORLD

Man experiences himself as having a world to which he belongs. The basic ontological structure is derived from an analysis of this complex dialectical relationship. Self-relatedness is implied in every experience. There is something that "has" and something that is "had", and the two are one. The question is not whether selves exist. The question is whether we are aware of self-relatedness. And this awareness can only be denied in a statement in which self-relatedness is implicitly affirmed, for self-relatedness is experienced in acts of negation as well as in acts of affirmation. A self is not a thing that may or may not exist; it is an original phenomenon which logically precedes all questions of existence.

The term "self" is more embracing than the term "ego". It includes the subconscious and the unconscious "basis" of the self-conscious ego as well as self-consciousness (*cogitatio* in the Cartesian sense). Therefore, selfhood or self-centeredness must be attributed in some measure to all living beings and, in terms of analogy, to all individual *Gestalten* even in the inorganic realm. One can speak of self-centeredness in atoms as well as in animals, wherever the reaction to a stimulus is dependent on a structural whole. Man is a fully developed and completely centered self. He "possesses" himself in the form of self-consciousness. He has an ego-self.

Being a self means being separated in some way from everything else, having everything else opposite one's self, being able to look at it and to act upon it. At the same time, however, this self is aware that it belongs to that at which it looks. The self is "in" it. Every self has an environment in which it lives, and the ego-self has a world in which it lives. All beings have an environment which is *their* environment. Not everything that can be found in the space in which an animal lives belongs to its environment. Its environment consists in those things with which it has an active interrelation. Different beings within the same limited space have different environments. Each being *has* an environment, although it belongs *to* its environment. The mistake of all theories which explain the behavior of a being in terms of environment alone is that they fail to explain the special character of the environment in terms of the special character of the being which *has* such an environment. Self and environment determine each other.

Because man has an ego-self, he transcends every possible environment. Man has a world. Like environment, world is a correlative concept. Man *has* a world, although he is *in* it at the same time. "World" is not the sum total of all beings — an inconceivable concept. As the Greek *kosmos* and the Latin *universum* indicate, "world" is a structure or a unity of manifoldness. If we say that man has a world at which he looks, from which he is separated and to which he belongs, we think of a structured whole even though we may describe this world in pluralistic terms. The whole opposite man is *one* at least in this respect, that it is related to us perspectively, however discontinuous it may be in itself. Every pluralistic philosopher speaks of the pluralistic character of the *world*, thus implicitly rejecting an absolute pluralism. The world is the structural whole which includes and transcends all environments, not only those of beings which lack a fully developed self, but also the environments in which man partially lives. As long as he is human, that is, as long as he has not "fallen" from humanity (e.g., in intoxication or insanity), man never is bound completely to an environment. He always transcends it by grasping and shaping it according to universal norms and ideas. Even in the most limited environment man possesses the universe; he has a world. . . .

## 2. THE ONTOLOGICAL ELEMENTS

### a. Individualization and participation

According to Plato, the idea of difference is "spread over all things". Aristotle could call individual beings the *telos*, the inner aim, of the process of actualization. According to Leibniz, no absolutely equal things can exist, since precisely their differentiation from each other makes their independent existence possible. In the biblical creation stories God produces individual beings and not universals, Adam and Eve rather than the ideas of manhood and womanhood. Even Neo-Platonism, in spite of its ontological "realism", accepted the doctrine that there are ideas (eternal archetypes) not only of the species but also of individuals. Individualization is not a characteristic of a special sphere of beings; it is an ontological element and therefore a *quality* of everything. It is implied in and constitutive of every self, which means that at least in an analogous way it is implied in and constitutive of every being. The very term "individual" points to the interdependence of self-relatedness and individualization. A self-centered being cannot be divided. It can be destroyed, or it can be deprived of certain parts out of which new self-centered beings emerge (e.g., regeneration of structure in some lower animals). In the latter case either the old self has ceased to exist and is replaced by new selves or the old self remains, diminished in extension and power for the sake of the new selves. But in no case is the center itself divided. This is as impossible as the partition of a mathematical point. Selfhood and individualization are different conceptually, but actually they are inseparable.

Man not only is completely self-centered; he also is completely individualized. And he is the one because he is the other. The species is dominant in all nonhuman beings, even in the most highly developed animals; essentially the individual is an examplar, representing in an individual way the universal characteristics of the species. Although the individualization of a plant or an animal is expressed even in the smallest part of its centered whole, it is significant only in unity with individual persons or unique historical events. The individuality of a nonhuman being gains significance if it is drawn into the processes of human life. But only then. Man is different. Even in collectivistic societies the individual as the bearer and, in the last analysis, the aim of the collective is significant rather than the species. Even the most despotic state claims to exist for the benefit of its individual subjects. Law, by its very nature, is based on the valuation of the individual as unique, unexchangeable, inviolable, and therefore to be protected and made responsible at the same time. The individual is a person in the sight of the law. The original meaning of the word "person" (*persona*, *prosopon*) points to the actor's mask which makes him a definite character.

Historically this has not always been acknowledged by systems of law. In many cultures the law has not recognized everyone as a person. Anatomical equality has not been considered a sufficient basis for the valuation of every man as a person. Personal standing has been denied to slaves, children, women. They have not attained full individualization in many cultures because they have been unable to participate fully; and, conversely, they have been unable to participate fully because they have not been fully individualized. No process of emancipation was begun until the Stoic philosophers fought successfully for the doctrine that every human being participates in the universal *logos*.

The uniqueness of every person was not established until the Christian church acknowledged the universality of salvation and the potentiality of every human being to participate in it. This development illustrates the strict interdependence of individuality, and participation on the level of complete individualization, which is, at the same time, the level of complete participation.

The individual self participates in his environment or, in the case of complete individualization, in his world. An individual leaf participates in the natural structures and forces which act upon it and which are acted upon by it. This is the reason why philosophers like Cusanus and Leibniz have asserted that the whole universe is present in every individual, although limited by its individual limitations. There are microcosmic qualities in every being, but man alone is *microcosmos*. In him the world is present not only indirectly and unconsciously but directly and in a conscious encounter. Man participates in the universe through the rational structure of mind and reality. Considered environmentally, he participates in a very small section of reality; he is surpassed in some respects by migrating animals. Considered cosmically, he participates in the universe because the universal structures, forms, and laws are open to him. And with them everything which can be grasped and shaped through them is open to him. Actually man's participation always is limited. Potentially there are no limits he could not transcend. The universals make man universal; language proves that he is *microcosmos*. Through the universals man participates in the remotest stars and the remotest past. This is the ontological basis for the assertion that knowledge is union and that it is rooted in the *eros* which reunites elements which essentially belong to each other.

When individualization reaches the perfect form which we call a "person" participation reaches the perfect form which we call "communion". Man participates in all levels of life, but he participates fully only in that level of life which he is himself — he has communion only with persons. Communion is participation in another completely centered and completely individual self. In this sense communion is not something an individual might or might not have. Participation is essential for the individual, not accidental. No individual exists without participation, and no personal being exists without communal being. The person as the fully developed individual self is impossible without other fully developed selves. If he did not meet the resistance of other selves, every self would try to make himself absolute. But the resistance of the other selves is unconditional. One individual can conquer the entire world of objects, but he cannot conquer another person without destroying him as a person. The individual discovers himself through this resistance. If he does not want to destroy the other person, he must enter into communion with him. In the resistance of the other person the person is born. Therefore, there is no person without an encounter with other persons. Persons can grow only in the communion of personal encounter. Individualization and participation are interdependent on all levels of being. . . .

Without individualization nothing would exist to be related. Without participation the category of relation would have no basis in reality. Every relation includes a kind of participation. This is true even of indifference or hostility. Nothing can make one hostile in which one does not somehow participate, perhaps in the form of being excluded from it. And nothing can produce the attitude of indifference whose existence has not made some difference to one. The element of participation guarantees the unity of a disrupted world and makes a universal system of relations possible. . . .

### b. Dynamics and form

Being is inseparable from the logic of being, the structure which makes it what it is and which gives reason the power of grasping and shaping it. "Being something" means having a form. According to the polarity of individualization and participation, there are special and general forms, but in actual being these never are separated. Through their union every being becomes a definite being. Whatever loses its form loses its being. Form should not be contrasted with content. The form which makes a thing what it is, is its content, its *essentia*, its definite power of being. The form of a tree is what makes it a tree, what gives it the general character of treehood as well as the special and unique form of an individual tree.

The separation of form and content becomes a problem in man's cultural activity. Here given materials, things, or events which have their natural form are transformed by man's rational functions. A landscape has a natural form which is, at the same time, its content. The artist uses the natural form of a landscape as material for an artistic creation whose content is not the material but rather what has been made of the material. One can distinguish (as Aristotle did) between form and material. But even in the cultural sphere a distinction between form and content cannot be made. The problem of formalism is a problem of attitude.

The question is not whether a certain form is adequate to a certain material. The question is whether a cultural creation is the expression of a spiritual substance or whether it is a mere form without such substance. Every type of material can be shaped by every form as long as the form is genuine, that is, as long as it is an immediate expression of the basic experience out of which the artist lives — in unity with his period as well as in conflict with it. If he fails to use such forms and instead uses forms which have ceased to be expressive, the artist is a formalist irrespective of whether the forms are traditional or revolutionary. A revolutionary style can become as formalistic as a conservative style. The criterion is the expressive power of a form and not a special style.

These considerations point to the other element in the polarity of form and dynamics. Every form forms something. The question is: What is this "something"? We have called it "dynamics", a very complex concept with a rich history and many connotations and implications. The problematic character of this concept, and of all concepts related to it, is due to the fact that everything which can be conceptualized must have being and that there is no being without form. Dynamics, therefore, cannot be thought as something that is; nor can it be thought as something that is not. It is the *me on*, the potentiality of being, which is nonbeing in contrast to things that have a form, and the power of being in contrast to pure nonbeing. This highly dialectical concept is not an invention of the philosophers. It underlies most mythologies and is indicated in the chaos, the *tohu-va-bohu*, the night, the emptiness, which precedes creation. It appears in metaphysical speculations as *Ungrund* (Böhme), will (Schopenhauer), will to power (Nietzsche), the unconscious (Hartmann, Freud), *élan vital* (Bergson), strife (Scheler, Jung). None of these concepts is to be taken conceptually. Each of them points symbolically to that which cannot be named. If it could be named properly, it would be a formed being beside other beings instead of an ontological element in polar contrast with the element of pure form. Therefore, it is unfair to criticize these concepts on the basis of their literal meaning. Schopenhauer's "will" is not the psychological function called "will". And the "unconscious" of Hartmann and Freud is not a "room" which can be described as though it were a cellar filled with things which once belonged to the upper rooms in which the sun of consciousness shines. The unconscious is mere potentiality, and it should not be painted in the image of the actual. The other descriptions of "that which does not yet have being" must be interpreted in the same way, that is, analogically.

In Greek philosophy nonbeing, or matter, was an ultimate principle — the principle of resistance against form. Christian theology, however, has had to try to deprive it of its independence and to seek a place for it in the depth of the divine life. The doctrine of God as *actus purus* prevented Thomism from solving the problem, but Protestant mysticism, using motifs of Duns Scotus and Luther, tried to introduce a dynamic element into the vision of the divine life. Late Romanticism as well as the philosophies of life and of process have followed this line, though always in danger of losing the divinity of the divine in their attempts to transform the static God of the *actus purus* into the living God. It is obvious, however, that any ontology which suppresses the dynamic element in the structure of being is unable to explain the nature of a life-process and to speak meaningfully of the divine life.

The polarity of dynamics and form appears in man's immediate experience as the polar structure of vitality and intentionality. Both terms need justification and explanation. Vitality is the power which keeps a living being alive and growing. *Élan vital* is the creative drive of the living substance in everything that lives toward new forms. However, a narrower use of the term is more frequent. Ordinarily one speaks of the vitality of men, not of the vitality of animals or plants. The meaning of the word is colored by its polar contrast. Vitality, in the full sense of the word, is human because man has intentionality. The dynamic element in man is open in all directions; it is bound by no a priori limiting structure. Man is able to create a world beyond the given world; he creates the technical and the spiritual realms. The dynamics of subhuman life remain within the limits of natural necessity, notwithstanding the infinite variations it produces and notwithstanding the new forms created by the evolutionary process. Dynamics reaches out beyond nature only in man. This is his vitality, and therefore man alone has vitality in the full sense of the word.

Man's vitality lives in contrast with his intentionality and is conditioned by it. On the human level form is the rational structure of subjective reason actualized in a life-process. One could call this pole "rationality", but rationality means having reason, not actualizing reason. One could call it "spirituality", but spirituality means the unity of dynamics and form in man's moral and cultural acts. Therefore, we recommend the use of the term "intentionality", which means being related to meaningful structures, living in universals, grasping and shaping reality. In this context "intention" does not mean the will to act for a purpose; it means living in tension with (and toward) something objectively valid. Man's dynamics, his creative vitality, is not undirected, chaotic, self-contained activity. It is directed, formed; it transcends itself toward meaningful contents. There is no vitality as such and no intentionality as such. They are interdependent, like the other polar elements.

The dynamic character of being implies the tendency of everything to transcend itself and to create new forms. At the same time everything tends to conserve its own form as the basis of its self-transcendence. It tends to unite identity and difference, rest and movement, conservation and change. Therefore, it is impossible to speak of being without also speaking of becoming. Becoming is just as genuine in the structure of being as is that which remains unchanged in the process of becoming. And, vice versa, becoming would be impossible if nothing were preserved in it as the measure of change. A process philosophy which sacrifices the persisting identity of that which is in process sacrifices the process itself, its continuity, the relation of what is conditioned to its conditions, the inner aim (*telos*) which makes a process a whole. Bergson was right when he combined the *élan vital*, the universal tendency toward self-transcendence, with duration, with continuity and self-conservation in the temporal flux.

The growth of the individual is the most obvious example of self-transcendence based on self-conservation. It shows very clearly the simultaneous interdependence of the two poles. Inhibition of growth ultimately destroys the being which does not grow. Misguided growth destroys itself and that which transcends itself without self-conservation. An example of wider scope is biological evolution from lower or less complex forms of life to higher and more complex forms. It is this example, more than anything else, which has inspired the philosophy of process and of creative evolution.

Self-transcendence and self-conservation are experienced immediately by man in man himself. Just as the self on the subhuman level is imperfect and in correlation with an environment, while on the human level the self is perfect and in correlation with a world, so self-transcendence on the subhuman level is limited by a constellation of conditions, while self-transcendence on the human level is limited only by the structure which makes man what he is — a complete self which has a world. On the basis of achieving self-conservation (the preservation of his humanity), man can transcend any given situation. He can transcend himself without limits in all directions just because of this basis. His creativity breaks through the biological realm to which he belongs and establishes new realms never attainable on a nonhuman level. Man is able to create a new world of technical tools and a world of cultural forms. In both cases something new comes into being through man's grasping and shaping activity. Man uses the material given by nature to create technical forms which transcend nature, and he creates cultural forms which have validity and meaning. Living in these forms, he transforms himself, while originating them. He is not only a tool for their creation; he is at the same time their bearer and the result of their transforming effect upon him. His self-transcendence in this direction is indefinite, while the biological self-transcendence has reached its limits in him. Any step beyond that biological structure which makes intentionality and historicity possible would be a relapse, a false growth, and a destruction of man's power of indefinite cultural self-transcendence. "Super-man", in a biological sense, would be less than man, for man has freedom, and freedom cannot be trespassed biologically.

### c. Freedom and destiny

The third ontological polarity is that of freedom and destiny, in which the description of the basic ontological structure and its elements reaches both its fulfillment and its turning point. Freedom in polarity with destiny is the structural element which makes existence possible because it transcends the essential necessity of being without destroying it. In view of the immense role the problem of freedom has played in the history of theology, it is surprising to see how little ontological inquiry into the meaning and nature of freedom is carried on by modern theologians, or even how little the results of previous inquiry are used by them, for a concept of freedom is just as important for theology as a concept of reason. Revelation cannot be understood without a concept of freedom.

Man is man because he has freedom, but he has freedom only in polar interdependence with destiny. The term "destiny" is unusual in this context. Ordinarily one speaks of freedom and necessity. However, necessity is a category and not an element. Its contrast is possibility, not freedom. Whenever freedom and necessity are set over against each other, necessity is understood in terms of mechanistic determinacy and freedom is thought of in terms of indeterministic contingency. Neither of these interpretations grasps the structure of being as it is experienced immediately in the one being who has the possibility of experiencing it because he is free, that is, in man. Man experiences the structure of the individual as the bearer of freedom within the larger structures to which the individual structure belongs. Destiny points to this situation in which man finds himself, facing the world to which, at the same time, he belongs.

The methodological perversion of much ontological inquiry is more obvious in the doctrine of freedom than at any other point. The traditional discussion of determinism and indeterminism necessarily is inconclusive because it moves on a level which is secondary to the level on which the polarity of freedom and destiny lies. Both conflicting parties presuppose that there is a *thing* among other things called "will", which may or may not have the quality of freedom. But by definition a *thing* as a completely determined object lacks freedom. The *freedom* of a *thing* is a contradiction in terms. Therefore, determinism always is right in this kind of discussion; but it is right because, in the last analysis, it expresses the tautology that a thing is a thing. Indeterminism protests against the deterministic thesis, pointing to the fact that the moral and the cognitive consciousness presupposes the power of responsible decision. However, when it draws the consequences and attributes freedom to an object or a function called "will", indeterminism falls into a contradiction in terms and inescapaby succumbs to the deterministic tautology. Indeterministic freedom is the negation of deterministic necessity. But the negation of necessity never constitutes experienced freedom. It asserts something absolutely contingent, a decision without motivation, an unintelligible accident which is in no way able to do justice to the moral and the cognitive consciousness for the sake of which it is invented. Both determinism and indeterminism are theoretically impossible because by implication they deny their claim to express truth. Truth presupposes a decision for the true against the false. Both determinism and indeterminism make such a decision unintelligible.

Freedom is not the freedom of a function (the "will") but of man, that is, of that being who is not a thing but a complete self and a rational person. It is possible, of course, to call the "will" the personal center and to substitute it for the totality of the self. Voluntaristic psychologies would support such a procedure. But it has proved to be very misleading, as the deadlock in the traditional controversy about freedom indicates. One should speak of the freedom of *man*, indicating that every part and every function which constitutes man a personal self participates in his freedom. This includes even the cells of his body, in so far as they participate in the constitution of his personal center. That which is not centered, that which is isolated from the total process of the self, either by natural or by artificial separation (disease or laboratory situations, for instance), is determined by the mechanism of stimulus and response or by the dynamism of the relation between the unconscious and the conscious. However, it is impossible to derive the determinacy of the whole, including its nonseparated parts, from the determinacy of isolated parts. Ontologically the whole precedes the parts and gives them their character as parts of this special whole. It is possible to understand the determinacy of isolated parts in the light of the freedom of the whole — namely, as a partial disintegration of the whole — but the converse is not possible.

Freedom is experienced as deliberation, decision, and responsibility. The etymology of each of these words is revealing. Deliberation points to an act of weighing (*librare*) arguments and motives. The person who does the weighing is above the motives; as long as he weighs them, he is not identical with any of the motives but is free from all of them. To say that the stronger motive always prevails is an empty tautology, since the test by which a motive is proved stronger is simply that it prevails. The self-centered person does the weighing and reacts as a whole, through his personal center, to the struggle of the motives. This reaction is called "decision". The word "decision", like the word "incision", involves the image of cutting. A decision cuts off possibilities, and these were real possibilities; otherwise no cutting would have been necessary.* The person who does the "cutting" or the "excluding" must be beyond what he cuts off or excludes. His personal center has possibilities, but it is not identical with any of them. The word "responsibility" points to the obligation of the person who has freedom to respond if he is questioned about his decisions. He cannot ask anyone else to answer for him. He alone must respond, for his acts are determined neither by something outside him nor by any part of him but by the centered totality of his being. Each of us is responsible for what has happened through the center of his self, the seat and organ of his freedom.

In the light of this analysis of freedom the meaning of destiny becomes understandable. Our destiny is that out of which our decisions arise; it is the indefinitely broad basis of our centered selfhood; it is the concreteness of our being which makes all our decisions *our* decisions.

---

* In the German word *Ent-scheidung* the image of *scheiden* ("to separate") is implied, pointing to the fact that in every decision several possibilities are excluded — *ausgescheiden*.

When I make a decision, it is the concrete totality of everything that constitutes my being which decides, not an epistemological subject. This refers to body structure, psychic strivings, spiritual character. It includes the communities to which I belong, the past unremembered and remembered, the environment which has shaped me, the world which has made an impact on me. It refers to all my former decisions. Destiny is not a strange power which determines what shall happen to me. It is myself as given, formed by nature, history, and myself. My destiny is the basis of my freedom; my freedom participates in shaping my destiny.

Only he who has freedom has a destiny. Things have no destiny because they have no freedom. God has no destiny because he *is* freedom. The word "destiny" points to something which is going to happen to someone; it has an eschatological connotation. This makes it qualified to stand in polarity with freedom. It points not to the opposite of freedom but rather to its conditions and limits. *Fatum* ("that which is foreseen") or *Schicksal* ("that which is sent"), and their English correlate "fate", designate a simple contradiction to freedom rather than a polar correlation, and therefore they hardly can be used in connection with the ontological polarity under discussion. But even the deterministic use of these words usually leaves a place for freedom; one has the possibility of accepting his fate or of revolting against it. Strictly speaking, this means that only he who has this alternative has a fate. And to have this alternative means to be free.

Since freedom and destiny constitute an ontological polarity, everything that participates in being must participate in this polarity. But man, who has a complete self and a world, is the only being who is free in the sense of deliberation, decision, and responsibility. Therefore, freedom and destiny can be applied to subhuman nature only by way of analogy; this parallels the situation with respect to the basic ontological structure and the other ontological polarities. . . .

## 3. BEING AND FINITUDE

### a. Being and nonbeing

The question of being is produced by the "shock of nonbeing". Only man can ask the ontological question because he alone is able to look beyond the limits of his own being and of every other being. Looked at from the standpoint of possible nonbeing, being is a mystery. Man is able to take this standpoint because he is free to transcend every given reality. He is not bound to "beingness"; he can envisage nothingness; he can ask the ontological question. In doing so, however, he also must ask a question about that which creates the mystery of being; he must consider the mystery of nonbeing. Both questions have been joined together since the beginning of human thought, first in mythological, then in cosmogonic, and finally in philosophical terms. The way in which the early Greek philosophers, above all, Parmenides, wrestled with the question of nonbeing is most impressive. Parmenides realized that in speaking of nonbeing one gives it some kind of being which contradicts its character as the negation of being. Therefore, he excluded it from rational thought. But in doing so he rendered the realm of becoming unintelligible and evoked the atomistic solution which identifies nonbeing with empty space, thus giving it some kind of being. What kind of being must we attribute to nonbeing? This question never has ceased to fascinate and to exasperate the philosophical mind.

There are two possible ways of trying to avoid the question of nonbeing, the one logical and the other ontological. One can ask whether nonbeing is anything more than the content of a logical judgment — a judgment in which a possible or real assertion is denied. One can assert that nonbeing is a negative judgment devoid of ontological significance. To this we must reply that every logical structure which is more than merely a play with a possible relations is rooted in an ontological structure. The very fact of logical denial presupposes a type of being which can transcend the immediately given situation by means of expectations which may be disappointed. An anticipated event does not occur. This means that the judgment concerning the situation has been mistaken, the necessary conditions for the occurrence of the expected event have been nonexistent. Thus disappointed, expectation creates the distinction between being and nonbeing. But how is such an expectation possible in the first place? What is the structure of this being which is able to transcend the given situation and to fall into error? The answer is that man, who is this being, must be separated from his being in a way which enables him to look at it as something strange and questionable. And such a separation is actual because man participates not only in being but also in nonbeing. Therefore, the very structure which makes negative judgments possible proves the ontological character of nonbeing. Unless man participates in nonbeing, no negative judgments are possible; in fact, no judgments of any kind are possible. The mystery of nonbeing cannot be solved by transforming it into a type of logical judgment. The ontological attempt to avoid the mystery of nonbeing follows the strategy of trying to deprive it of its dialectical character. If being and nothingness are placed in absolute contrast, nonbeing is excluded from being in every respect; everything is excluded except being itself (i.e., the whole world is excluded). There can be no world unless there is a dialectical participation of nonbeing in being. It is not by chance that historically the recent rediscovery of the ontological question has been guided by pre-Socratic philosophy and that systematically there has been an overwhelming emphasis on the problem of nonbeing.

The mystery of nonbeing demands a dialectical approach. The genius of the Greek language has provided a possibility of distinguishing the dialectical concept of nonbeing from the nondialectical by calling the first *me on* and the second *ouk on*. *Ouk on* is the "nothing" which has no relation at all to being; *me on* is the "nothing" which has a dialectical relation to being. The Platonic school identified *me on* with that which does not yet have being but which can become being if it is united with essences or ideas. The mystery of nonbeing was not, however, removed, for in spite of its "nothingness" nonbeing was credited with having the power of resisting a complete union with the ideas. The *meontic* matter of Platonism represents the dualistic element which underlies all paganism and which is the ultimate ground of the tragic interpretation of life.

Christianity has rejected the concept of *me-ontic* matter on the basis of the doctrine of *creatio ex nihilo*. Matter is not a second principle in addition to God. The *nihil* out of which God creates is *ouk on*, the undialectical negation of being. Yet Christian theologians have had to face the dialectical problem of nonbeing at several points. When Augustine and many theologians and mystics who followed him called sin "nonbeing", they were perpetuating a remnant of the Platonic tradition. They did not mean by this assertion that sin has no reality or that it is a lack of perfect realization, as critics often have misrepresented their view. They meant that sin has no positive ontological standing, while at the same time they interpreted nonbeing in terms of resistance against being and perversion of being. The doctrine of man's creatureliness is another point in the doctrine of man where nonbeing has a dialectical character. Being created out of nothing means having to return to nothing. The stigma of having originated out of nothing is impressed on every creature. This is the reason why Christianity has to reject Arius' doctrine of the Logos as the highest of the creatures. As such he could not have brought eternal life. And this also is the reason why Christianity must reject the doctrine of natural immortality and must affirm instead the doctrine of eternal life given by God as the power of being-itself.

A third point at which theologians have had to face the dialectical problem of nonbeing is the doctrine of God. Here it must be stated immediately that historically it was not the theology of the *via negativa* which drove Christian thinkers to the question of God and nonbeing. The nonbeing of negative theology means "not being anything special", being beyond every concrete predicate. This nonbeing embraces everything; it means being everything; it is being-itself. The dialectical question of nonbeing was and is a problem of affirmative theology. If God is called the living God, if he is the ground of the creative processes of life, if history has significance for him, if there is no negative principle in addition to him which could account for evil and sin, how can one avoid positing a dialectical negativity in God himself? Such questions have forced theologians to relate nonbeing dialectically to being-itself and consequently to God. Böhme's *Ungrund*, Schelling's "first potency", Hegel's "antithesis", the "contingent" and the "given" in God in recent theism, Berdyaev's "meonic freedom", — all are examples of the problem of dialectical nonbeing exerting influence on the Christian doctrine of God.

Recent existentialism has "encountered nothingness" (Kuhn) in a profound and radical way. Somehow it has replaced being-itself by nonbeing, giving to nonbeing a positivity and a power which contradict the immediate meaning of the word. Heidegger's "annihilating nothingness" describes man's situation of being threatened by nonbeing in an ultimately inescapable way, that is, by death. The anticipation of nothingness at death gives human existence its existential character. Sartre includes in nonbeing not only the threat of nothingness but also the threat of meaningfulness (i.e., the destruction of the structure of being). In existentialism there is no way of conquering this threat. The only way of dealing with it lies in the courage of taking it upon one's self: courage! As this survey shows, the dialectical problem of nonbeing is inescapable. It is the problem of finitude. Finitude unites being with dialectical nonbeing. Man's finitude, or creatureliness, is unintelligible without the concept of dialectical nonbeing.

## b. The finite and the infinite

Being, limited by nonbeing, is finitude. Nonbeing appears as the "not yet" of being and as the "no more" of being. It confronts that which is with a definite end (*finis*). This is true of everything except being-itself — which is not a "thing". As the power of being, being-itself cannot have a beginning and an end. Otherwise it would have arisen out of nonbeing. But nonbeing is literally nothing except in relation to being. Being precedes nonbeing in ontological validity, as the word "nonbeing" itself indicates. Being is the beginning without a beginning, the end without an end. It is its own beginning and end, the initial power of everything that is. However, everything which participates in the power of being is "mixed" with nonbeing. It is being in process of coming from and going toward nonbeing. It is finite.

Both the basic ontological structure and the ontological elements imply finitude. Selfhood, individuality, dynamics, and freedom all include manifoldness, definiteness, differentiation, and limitation. To be something is not to be something else. To be here and now in the process of becoming is not to be there and then. All categories of thought and reality express this situation. To be something is to be finite.

Finitude is experienced on the human level; nonbeing is experienced as the threat to being. The end is anticipated. The process of self-transcendence carries a double meaning in each of its moments. At one and the same time it is an increase and a decrease in the power of being. In order to experience his finitude, man must look at himself from the point of view of a potential infinity. In order to be aware of moving toward death, man must look out over his finite being as a whole; he must in some way be beyond it. He must also be able to imagine infinity; and he is able to do so, although not in concrete terms, but only as an abstract possibility. The finite self faces a world; the finite individual has the power of universal participation; man's vitality is united with an essentially unlimited intentionality; as finite freedom he is involved in an embracing destiny. All the structures of finitude force finite being to transcend itself and, just for this reason, to become aware of itself as finite.

According to this analysis, infinity is related to finitude in a different way than the other polar elements are related to one another. As the negative character of the word indicates, it is defined by the dynamic and free self-transcendence of finite being. Infinity is a directing concept, not a constituting concept. It directs the mind to experience its own unlimited potentialities, but it does not establish the existence of an infinite being. On this basis it is possible to understand the classical antinomies regarding the finite and the infinite character of the world. Even a physical doctrine of the finitude of space cannot keep the mind from asking what lies behind finite space. This is a self-contradictory question; yet it is inescapable. On the other hand, it is impossible to say that the world is infinite because infinity never is given as an object. Infinity is a demand, not a thing. This is the stringency of Kant's solution of the antinomies between the finite and the infinite character of time and space. Since neither time nor space is a thing, but both are forms of things, it is possible to transcend every finite time and every finite space without exception. But this does not establish an infinite thing in an infinite time and space. The human mind can keep going endlessly by transcending finite realities in the macrocosmic or in the microcosmic direction. But the mind itself remains bound to the finitude of its individual bearer. Infinitude is finitude transcending itself without any a priori limit.

The power of infinite self-transcendence is an expression of man's belonging to that which is beyond nonbeing, namely, to being-itself. The potential presence of the infinite (as unlimited self-transcendence) is the negation of the negative element in finitude. It is the negation of nonbeing. The fact that man never is satisfied with any stage of his finite development, the fact that nothing finite can hold him, although finitude is his destiny, indicates the indissoluble relation of everything finite to being-itself. Being-itself is not infinity; it is that which lies beyond the polarity of finitude and infinite self-transcendence. Being-itself manifests itself to finite beings in the infinite drive of the finite beyond itself. But being-itself cannot be identified with infinity, that is, with the negation of finitude. It precedes the finite, and it precedes the infinite negation of the finite.

Finitude in awareness is anxiety. Like finitude, anxiety is an ontological quality. It cannot be derived; it can only be seen and described. Occasions in which anxiety is aroused must be distinguished from anxiety itself. As an ontological quality, anxiety is as omnipresent as is finitude. Anxiety is independent of any special object which might produce it; it is dependent only on the threat of nonbeing — which is identical with finitude. In this sense it has been said rightly that the object of anxiety is "nothingness" — and nothingness is not an "object". Objects are feared. A danger, a pain, an enemy, may be feared, but fear can be conquered by action. Anxiety cannot, for no finite being can conquer its finitude. Anxiety is always present, although often it is latent. Therefore, it can become manifest at any and every moment, even in situations where nothing is to be feared.*

The recovery of the meaning of anxiety through the combined endeavors of existential philosophy, depth psychology, neurology, and the arts is one of the achievements of the twentieth century. It has become clear that fear as related to a definite object and anxiety as the awareness of finitude are two radically different concepts. Anxiety is ontological; fear, psychological.† Anxiety is an ontological concept because it expresses finitude from "inside". Here it must be said that there is no reason for preferring concepts taken from "outside" to those taken from "inside". According to the self-world structure, both types are equally valid. The self being aware of itself and the self looking at its world (including itself) are equally significant for the description of the ontological structure. Anxiety is the self-awareness of the finite self as finite. The fact that it has a strongly emotional character does not remove its revealing power. The emotional element simply indicates that the totality of the finite being participates in finitude and faces the threat of nothingness. . . .

### c. Finitude and the ontological elements

Finitude is actual not only in the categories‡ but also in the ontological elements. Their polar character opens them to the threat of nonbeing. In every polarity each pole is limited as well as sustained by the other one. A complete balance between them presupposes a balanced whole. But such a whole is not given. There are special structures in which,

* Psychotherapy cannot remove ontological anxiety, because it cannot change the structure of finitude. But it can remove compulsive forms of anxiety and can reduce the frequency and intensity of fears. It can put anxiety "in its proper place".

† The English word "anxiety" has received the connotation of *Angst* only during the past decade. Both *Angst* and anxiety are derived from the Latin word *angustiae*, which means "narrows". Anxiety is experienced in the narrows of threatening nothingness. Therefore, anxiety should not be replaced by the word "dread", which points to a sudden reaction to a danger but not to the ontological situation of facing nonbeing.

‡ Tillich's discussion of the "categories" (time, space, causality, substance) has not been included in this volume. The four categories are four aspects of finitude, each expressing the union of being and nonbeing in everything finite. The threat of nonbeing causes anxiety in each category just as it does in each of the ontological polarities discussed in this section. (M.K.T.)

under the impact of finitude, polarity becomes tension. Tension refers to the tendency of elements within a unity to draw away from one another, to attempt to move in opposite directions. For Heraclitus everything is in inner tension like a bent bow, for in everything there is a tendency downward (earth) balanced by a tendency upward (fire). In his view nothing whatever is produced by a process which moves in one direction only; everything is an embracing but transitory unity of two opposite processes. Things are hypostasized tensions.

Our own ontological tension comes to awareness in the anxiety of losing our ontological structure through losing one or another polar element and, consequently, the polarity to which it belongs. This anxiety is ... anxiety about disintegrating and falling into nonbeing through existential disruption. It is anxiety about the breaking of the ontological tensions and the consequent destruction of the ontological structure.

This can be seen in terms of each of the polar elements. Finite individualization produces a dynamic tension with finite participation; the break of their unity is a possibility. Self-relatedness produces the threat of a loneliness in which world and communion are lost. On the other hand, being in the world and participating in it produces the threat of a complete collectivization, a loss of individuality and subjectivity whereby the self loses its self-relatedness and is transformed into a mere part of an embracing whole. Man as finite is anxiously aware of this two-fold threat. Anxiously he experiences the trend from the possible loneliness to collectivity and from possible collectivity to loneliness. He oscillates anxiously between individualization and participation, aware of the fact that he ceases to be if one of the poles is lost, for the loss of either pole means the loss of both.

The tension between finite individualization and finite participation is the basis of many psychological and sociological problems, and for this reason it is a very important subject of research for depth psychology and depth sociology. Philosophy often has overlooked the question of essential solitude and its relation to existential loneliness and self-seclusion. It also has overlooked the question of essential belongingness and its relation to existential self-surrender to the collective. The merit of existential thinking in all centuries, but especially since Pascal, is that it has rediscovered the ontological basis of the tension between loneliness and belongingness.

Finitude also transforms the polarity of dynamics and form into a tension which produces the threat of a possible break and anxiety about this threat. Dynamics drives toward form, in which being is actual and has the power of resisting nonbeing. But at the same time dynamics is threatened because it may lose itself in rigid forms, and, if it tries to break through them, the result may be chaos, which is the loss of both dynamics and form. Human vitality tends to embody itself in cultural creations, forms, and institutions through the exercise of creative intentionality. But every embodiment endangers the vital power precisely by giving it actual being. Man is anxious about the threat of a final form in which his vitality will be lost, and he is anxious about the threat of a chaotic formlessness in which both vitality and intentionality will be lost.

There is abundant witness to this tension in literature from Greek tragedy to the present day, but it has not been given sufficient attention in philosophy except in the "philosophy of life" or in theology except by some Protestant mystics. Philosophy has emphasized the rational structure of things but has neglected the creative process through which things and events come into being. Theology has emphasized the divine "law" and has confused creative vitality with the destructive separation of vitality from intentionality. Philosophical rationalism and theological legalism have prevented a full recognition of the tension between dynamics and form.

Finally, finitude transforms the polarity of freedom and destiny into a tension which produces the threat of a possible break and its consequent anxiety. Man is threatened with the loss of freedom by the necessities implied in his destiny, and he is equally threatened with the loss of his destiny by the contingencies implied in his freedom. He is continuously in danger of trying to preserve his freedom by arbitrarily defying his destiny and of trying to save his destiny by surrendering his freedom. He is embarrassed by the demand that he make decisions implied in his freedom, because he realizes that he lacks the complete cognitive and active unity with his destiny which should be the foundation of his decisions. And he is afraid of accepting his destiny without reservations, because he realizes that his decision will be partial, that he will accept only a part of the destiny, and that he will fall under a special determination which is not identical with his real destiny. So he tries to save his freedom by arbitrariness, and then he is in danger of losing both his freedom and his destiny.

The traditional discussion between determinism and indeterminism concerning "freedom of the will" is an "objectified" form of the ontological tension between freedom and destiny. Both partners in this discussion defend an ontological element without which being could not be conceived. Therefore, they are right in what they affirm but wrong in what they negate. The determinist does not see that the very affirmation of determinism as true presupposes the freedom of decision between true and false, and the indeterminist does not see that the very potentiality of making decisions presupposes a personality structure which includes destiny. Speaking pragmatically, people always act as if they consider one another to be free and to be destined simultaneously. No one ever treats a man either as a mere locus of a series of contingent actions or as a mechanism in which calculable effects follow from calculated causes. Man always considers man — including himself — in terms of a unity of freedom and destiny. The fact that finite man is threatened with the loss of one side of the polarity — and consequently with the loss of the other, since loss of either side destroys the polarity as a whole — only confirms the essential character of the ontological structure.

To lose one's destiny is to lose the meaning of one's being. Destiny is not a meaningless fate. It is necessity united with meaning. The threat of possible meaninglessness is a social as well as an individual reality. There are periods in social life, as well as in personal life, during which this threat is especially acute. Our present situation is characterized by a profound and desperate feeling of meaninglessness. Individuals and groups have lost any faith they may have had in their destiny as well as any love of it. The question, "What for?" is cynically dismissed. Man's essential anxiety about the possible loss of his destiny has been transformed into an existential despair about destiny as such. Accordingly, freedom has been declared an absolute, separate from destiny (Sartre). But absolute freedom in a finite being becomes arbitrariness and falls under biological and psychological necessities. The loss of a meaningful destiny involves the loss of freedom also.

Finitude is the possibility of losing one's ontological structure and, with it, one's self. But this is possibility, not a necessity. To be finite is to be threatened. But a threat is possibility, not actuality. The anxiety of finitude is not the despair of self-destruction. Christianity sees in the picture of Jesus as the Christ a human life in which all forms of anxiety are present but in which all forms of despair are absent. In the light of this picture it is possible to distinguish "essential" finitude from "existential" disruption, ontological anxiety from the anxiety of guilt which is despair.*

---

* The material discussed in this chapter is by no means complete. Poetic,

# GOD AS BEING AND AS LIVING

*In a sermon, after acknowledging that the word "God" might not have much meaning for his hearers, Tillich suggested to them: "translate it and speak of the depth of your life and the source of your ultimate concern and of what you take seriously without reservation" (Tillich,* The Shaking of the Foundations, *p. 57). In one's ultimate concern God is "the name of this infinite and inexhaustible depth and ground of all being". The following selections from the* Systematic Theology *(1, pp. 235-49 passim) show how Tillich correlates the term God with his previously delineated ontological structure and elements, i.e. with the depths of personal and communal life. Here God is rendered as being-itself, grounding and unifying the elemental polarities in the divine life and so preserving being in the face of nonbeing, thereby nurturing human courage in the face of anxiety.*

## 1. GOD AS BEING

### a. *God as being and finite being*

The being of God is being-itself. The being of God cannot be understood as the existence of a being alongside others or above others. If God is *a* being, he is subject to the categories of finitude, especially to space and substance. Even if he is called the "highest being" in the sense of the "most perfect" and the "most powerful" being, this situation is not changed. When applied to God, superlatives become diminutives. They place him on the level of other beings while elevating him above all of them. Many theologians who have used the term "highest being" have known better. Actually they have described the highest as the absolute, as that which is on a level qualitatively different from the level of any being — even the highest being. Whenever infinite or unconditional power and meaning are attributed to the highest being, it has ceased to be *a* being and has become being-itself. Many confusions in the doctrine of God and many apologetic weaknesses could be avoided if God were understood first of all as being-itself or as the ground of being. The power of being is another way of expressing the same thing in a circumscribing phrase. Ever since the time of Plato it has been known — although it often has been disregarded, especially by the nom-

---

scientific, and religious psychology have made available an almost unmanageable amount of material concerning finitude and anxiety. The purpose of this analysis is to give only an ontological description of the structures underlying all these facts and to point to some outstanding confirmations of the analysis.

inalists and their modern followers — that the concept of being as being, or being-itself, points to the power inherent in everything, the power of resisting nonbeing. Therefore, instead of saying that God is first of all being-itself, it is possible to say that he is the power of being in everything and above everything, the infinite power of being. A theology which does not dare to identify God and the power of being as the first step toward a doctrine of God relapses into monarchic monotheism, for if God is not being-itself, he is subordinate to it, just as Zeus is subordinate to fate in Greek religion. The structure of being-itself is his fate, as it is the fate of all other beings. But God is his own fate; he is "by himself"; he possesses "aseity". This can be said of him only if he is the power of being, if he is being-itself.

As being-itself God is beyond the contrast of essential and existential being. We have spoken of the transition of being into existence, which involves the possibility that being will contradict and lose itself. This transition is excluded from being-itself (except in terms of christological paradox), for being-itself does not participate in nonbeing. In this it stands in contrast to every being. As classical theology has emphasized, God is beyond essence and existence. Logically, being-itself is "before", "prior to", the split which characterizes finite being. . . . God is being-itself, not *a* being. On this basis a first step can be taken toward the solution of the problem which usually is discussed as the immanence and the transcendence of God. As the power of being, God transcends every being and also the totality of beings — the world. Being-itself is beyond finitude and infinity; otherwise it would be conditioned by something other than itself, and the real power of being would lie beyond both it and that which conditioned it. Being-itself infinitely transcends every finite being. There is no proportion or gradation between the finite and the infinite. There is an absolute break, as infinite "jump". On the other hand, everything finite participates in being-itself and in its infinity. Otherwise it would not have the power of being. It would be swallowed by nonbeing, or it never would have emerged out of nonbeing. This double relation of all beings to being-itself gives being-itself a double characteristic. In calling it creative, we point to the fact that everything participates in the infinite power of being. In calling it abysmal, we point to the fact that everything participates in the power of being in a finite way, that all beings are infinitely transcended by their creative ground.

Man is bound to the categories of finitude. He uses the two categories of relation — causality and substance — to express the relation of being-itself to finite beings. The "ground" can be interpreted in both ways, as the cause of finite beings and as their substance. The former has been elaborated by Leibniz in the line of the Thomistic tradition, and the latter has been elaborated by Spinoza in the line of the mystical tradition. Both ways are impossible. Spinoza establishes a naturalistic pantheism, in contrast to the idealistic type which identifies God with the universal essence of being, which denies finite freedom and in so doing denies the freedom of God. By necessity God is merged into the finite beings, and their being is his being. Here again it must be emphasized that pantheism does not say that God is everything. It says that God is the substance of everything and that there is no substantial independence and freedom in anything finite.

Therefore, Christianity, which asserts finite freedom in man and spontaneity in the nonhuman realm, has rejected the category of substance in favor of the category of causality in attempting to express the relation of the power of being to the beings who participate in it. Causality seems to make the world dependent on God, and, at the same time, to separate God from the world in the way a cause is separated from its effect. But the category of causality cannot "fill the bill", for cause and effect are not separate; they include each other and form a series which is endless in both directions. What is cause at one point in this series is effect at another point and conversely. God as cause is drawn into this series, which drives even him beyond himself. In order to disengage the divine cause from the series of causes and effects, it is called the first cause, the absolute beginning. What this means is that the category of causality is being denied while it is being used. In other words, causality is being used not as a category but as a symbol. And if this is done and is understood, the difference between substance and causality disappears, for if God is the cause of the entire series of causes and effects, he is the substance underlying the whole process of becoming. But this "underlying" does not have the character of a substance which underlies its accidents and which is completely expressed by them. It is an underlying in which substance and accidents preserve their freedom. In other words, it is substance not as a category but as a symbol. And, if taken symbolically, there is no difference between *prima causa* and *ultima substantia*. Both mean, what can be called a more directly symbolic term, "the creative and abysmal ground of being". In this term both naturalistic pantheism, based on the category of substance, and rationalistic theism, based on the category of causality, are overcome.

Since God is the ground of being, he is the ground of the structure of being. He is not subject to this structure; the structure is grounded in him. He *is* this structure, and it is impossible to speak about him except in terms of this structure. God must be approached cognitively through the structural elements of being-itself. These elements make him a living God, a God who can be man's concrete concern. They enable us to use symbols which we are certain point to the ground of reality.

### b.  God as being and the knowledge of God

The statement that God is being-itself is a nonsymbolic statement. It does not point beyond itself. It means what it says directly and properly; if we speak of the actuality of God, we first assert that he is not God if he is not being-itself. Other assertions about God can be made theologically only on this basis. Of course, religious assertions do not require such a foundation for what they say about God; the foundation is implicit in every religious thought concerning God. Theologians must make explicit what is implicit in religious thought and expression; and, in order to do this, they must begin with the most abstract and completely unsymbolic statement which is possible, namely, that God is being-itself or the absolute.

However, after this has been said, nothing else can be said about God as God which is not symbolic. As we already have seen, God as being-itself is the ground of the ontological structure of being without being subject to this structure himself. He *is* the structure; that is, he has the power of determining the structure of everything that has being. Therefore, if anything beyond this bare assertion is said about God, it no longer is a direct and proper statement, no longer a concept. It is indirect, and it points to something beyond itself. In a word, it is symbolic.

The general character of the symbol has been described. Special emphasis must be laid on the insight that symbol and sign are different; that, while the sign bears no necessary relation to that to which it points, the symbol participates in the reality of that for which it stands. The sign can be changed arbitrarily according to the demands of expediency, but the symbol grows and dies according to the correlation between that which is symbolized and the persons who receive it as a symbol. Therefore, the religious symbol, the symbol which points to the divine, can be a true symbol only if it participates in the power of the divine to which it points.

There can be no doubt that any concrete assertion about God must be symbolic, for a concrete assertion is one which uses a segment of finite experience in order to say something about him. It transcends the content of this segment, although it also includes it. The segment of finite reality which becomes the vehicle of a concrete assertion about God is affirmed and negated at the same time. It becomes a symbol, for a symbolic expression is one whose proper meaning is negated by that to which it points. And yet it also is affirmed by it, and this affirmation gives the symbolic expression an adequate basis for pointing beyond itself.

The crucial question must now be faced. Can a segment of finite reality become the basis for an assertion about that which is infinite? The answer is that it can, because that which is infinite is being-itself and because everything participates in being-itself. The *analogia entis* is not the property of a questionable natural theology which attempts to gain knowledge of God by drawing conclusions about the infinite from the finite. The *analogia entis* gives us our only justification of speaking at all about God. It is based on the fact that God must be understood as being-itself.

The truth of a religious symbol has nothing to do with the truth of the empirical assertions involved in it, be they physical, psychological, or historical. A religious symbol possesses some truth if it adequately expresses the correlation of revelation in which some person stands. A religious symbol *is* true if it adequately expresses the correlation of some person with final revelation. A religious symbol can die only if the correlation of which it is an adequate expression dies. This occurs whenever the revelatory situation changes and former symbols become obsolete. The history of religion, right up to our own time, is full of dead symbols which have been killed not by a scientific criticism of assumed superstitions but by a religious criticism of religion. The judgment that a religious symbol *is* true is identical with the judgment that the revelation of which it is the adequate expression is true. This double meaning of the truth of a symbol must be kept in mind. A symbol *has* truth: it is adequate to the revelation it expresses. A symbol *is* true: it is the expression of a true revelation.

Theology as such has neither the duty nor the power to confirm or to negate religious symbols. Its task is to interpret them according to theological principles and methods. In the process of interpretation, however, two things may happen: theology may discover contradictions between symbols within the theological circle and theology may speak not only as theology but also as religion. In the first case, theology can point out the religious dangers and the theological errors which follow from the use of certain symbols; in the second case, theology can become prophecy, and in this role it may contribute to a change in the revelatory situation.

Religious symbols are double-edged. They are directed toward the infinite which they symbolize *and* toward the finite through which they symbolize it. They force the infinite down to finitude and the finite up to infinity. They open the divine for the human and the human for the divine. For instance, if God is symbolized as "Father", he is brought down to the human relationship of father and child. But at the same time this human relationship is consecrated into a pattern of the divine-human relationship. If "Father" is employed as a symbol for God, fatherhood is seen in its theonomous, sacramental depth. One cannot arbitrarily "make" a religious symbol out of a segment of secular reality. Not even the collective unconscious, the great symbol-creating source, can do this. If a segment of reality is used as a symbol for God, the realm of reality from which it is taken is, so to speak, elevated into the realm of the holy. It no longer is secular. It is theonomous. If God is called the "king", something is said not only about God but also about the holy character of kinghood. If God's work is called "making whole" or "healing", this not only says something about God but also emphasizes the theonomous character of all healing. If God's self-manifestation is called "the word", this not only symbolizes God's relation to man but also emphasizes the holiness of all words as an expression of the spirit. The list could be continued. Therefore, it is not surprising that in a secular culture both the symbols for God and the theonomous character of the material for which the symbols are taken disappear.

A final word of warning must be added in view of the fact that for many people the very term "symbolic" carries the connotation of non-real. This is partially the result of confusion between sign and symbol and partially due to the identification of reality with empirical reality, with the entire realm of objective things and events. Both reasons have been undercut explicitly and implicitly in the foregoing chapters. But one reason remains, namely, the fact that some theological movements, such as Protestant Hegelianism and Catholic modernism, have interpreted religious language symbolically in order to dissolve its realistic meaning and to weaken its seriousness, its power, and its spiritual impact. This was not the purpose of the classical essays on the "divine names", in which the symbolic character of all affirmations about God was strongly emphasized and explained in religious terms, nor was it a consequence of these essays. Their intention and their result was to give to God and to all his relations to man more reality and power than a nonsymbolic and therefore easily superstitious interpretation could give them. In this sense symbolic interpretation is proper and necessary; it enhances rather than diminishes the reality and power of religious language, and in so doing it performs an important function.

## 2. GOD AS LIVING

### a. *God as being and God as living*

Life is the process in which potential being becomes actual being. It is the actualization of the structural elements of being in their unity and in their tension. These elements move divergently and convergently in every life-process; they separate and reunite simultaneously. Life ceases in the moment of separation without union or of union without separation. Both complete identity and complete separation negate life. If we call God the "living God", we deny that he is a pure identity of being as being; and we also deny that there is a definite separation of being from being in him. We assert that he is the eternal process in which separation is posited and is overcome by reunion. In this sense, God lives. Few things about God are more emphasized in the Bible, especially in the Old Testament, than the truth that God is a living God. Most of the so-called anthropomorphisms of the biblical picture of God are expressions of his character as living. His actions, his passions, his remembrances and anticipations, his suffering and joy, his personal relations and his plans — all these make him a living God and distinguish him from the pure absolute, from being-itself.

Life is the actuality of being, or, more exactly, it is the process in which potential being becomes actual being. But in God as God there is no distinction between potentiality and actuality. Therefore, we cannot speak of God as living in the proper or nonsymbolic sense of the word "life". We must speak of God as living in symbolic terms. Yet every true symbol participates in the reality which it symbolizes. God lives in so far as he is the ground of life.* Anthropomorphic symbols are adequate for speaking of God religiously. Only in this way can he be the living God for man. But even in the most primitive intuition of the divine a feeling should be, and usually is, present that there is a mystery about divine names which makes them improper, self-transcending, symbolic. Religious instruction should deepen this feeling without depriving the divine names of their reality and power. One of the most surprising

* "He that formed the eye, shall he not see?" (Ps. 94:9).

qualities of the prophetic utterances in the Old Testament is that, on the one hand, they always appear concrete and anthropomorphic and that, on the other hand, they preserve the mystery of the divine ground. They never deal with being as being or with the absolute as the absolute; nevertheless, they never make God a being alongside others, into something conditioned by something else which also is conditioned. Nothing is more inadequate and disgusting than the attempt to translate the concrete symbols of the Bible into less concrete and less powerful symbols. Theology should not weaken the concrete symbols, but it must analyze them and interpret them in abstract ontological terms. Nothing is more inadequate and confusing than the attempt to restrict theological work to half-abstract, half-concrete terms which do justice neither to existential intuition nor to cognitive analysis.

The ontological structure of being supplies the material for the symbols which point to the divine life. However, this does not mean that a doctrine of God can be derived from an ontological system. The character of the divine life is made manifest in revelation. Theology can only explain and systematize the existential knowledge of revelation in theoretical terms, interpreting the symbolic significance of the ontological elements and categories.

While the symbolic power of the categories appears in the relation of God to the creature, the elements give symbolic expression to the nature of the divine life itself. The polar character of the ontological elements is rooted in the divine life, but the divine life is not subject to this polarity. Within the divine life, every ontological element includes its polar element completely, without tension and without the threat of dissolution, for God is being-itself. However, there is a difference between the first and the second elements in each polarity with regard to their power of symbolizing the divine life. The elements of individualization, dynamics, and freedom represent the self or subject side of the basic ontological structure within the polarity to which they belong. The elements of participation, form, and destiny represent the world or object side of the basic ontological structure within the polarity to which they belong. Both sides are rooted in the divine life. But the first side determines the existential relationship between God and man, which is the source of all symbolization. Man is a self who has a world. As a self he is an individual person who participates universally, he is a dynamic self-transcending agent within a special and a general form, and he is freedom which has a special destiny and which participates in a general destiny. Therefore, man symbolizes that which is his ultimate concern in terms taken from his own being. From the subjective side of the polarities he takes — or more exactly, receives — the material with which he symbolizes the divine life. He sees the divine life as personal, dynamic, and free. He cannot see it in any other way, for God is man's ultimate concern, and therefore he stands in analogy to that which man himself is. But the religious mind — theologically speaking, man in the correlation of revelation — always realizes implicitly, if not explicitly, that the other side of the polarities also is completely present in the side he uses as symbolic material. God is called a person, but he is a person not in finite separation but in an absolute and unconditional participation in everything. God is called dynamic, but he is dynamic not in tension with form but in an absolute and unconditional unity with form, so that his self-transcendence never is in tension with his self-preservation, so that he always remains God. God is called "free", but he is free not in arbitrariness but in an absolute and unconditional identity with his destiny, so that he himself is his destiny, so that the essential structures of being are not strange to his freedom but are the actuality of his freedom. In this way, although the symbols used for the divine life are taken from the concrete situation of man's relationship to God, they imply God's ultimacy, the ultimacy in which the polarities of being disappear in the ground of being, in being-itself.

The basic ontological structure of self and world is transcended in the divine life without providing symbolic material. God cannot be called a self, because the concept "self" implies separation from and contrast to everything which is not self. God cannot be called the world even by implication. Both self and world are rooted in the divine life, but they cannot become symbols for it. But the elements which constitute the basic ontological structure can become symbols because they do not speak of kinds of being (self and world) but of qualities of being which are valid in their proper sense when applied to all beings and which are valid in their symbolic sense when applied to being-itself.

### b. The divine life and the ontological elements

The symbols provided by the ontological elements present a great number of problems for the doctrine of God. In every special case it is necessary to distinguish between the proper sense of the concepts and their symbolic sense. And it is equally necessary to balance one side of the ontological polarity against the other without reducing the symbolic power of either of them. The history of theological thought is a continuous proof of the difficulty, the creativeness, and the danger of this situation. This is obvious if we consider the symbolic power of the polarity of individualization and participation. The symbol "personal God" is absolutely fundamental because an existential relation is a person-to-person relation. Man cannot be ultimately concerned about anything that is less than personal, but since personality (*persona, prosopon*) includes individuality, the question arises in what sense God can be called an individual. Is it meaningful to call him the "absolute individual"? The answer must be that it is meaningful only in the sense that he can be called the "absolute participant". The one term cannot be applied without the other. This can only mean that both individualization and participation are rooted in the ground of the divine life and that God is equally "near" to each of them while transcending them both.

The solution of the difficulties of the phrase "personal God" follows from this. "Personal God" does not mean that God is *a* person. It means that God is the ground of everything personal and that he carries within himself the ontological power of personality. He is not a person, but he is not less than personal. It should not be forgotten that classical theology employed the term *persona* for the trinitarian hypostases but not for God himself. God became "a person" only in the nineteenth century, in connection with the Kantian separation of nature ruled by physical law from personality ruled by moral law. Ordinary theism has made God a heavenly, completely perfect person who resides above the world and mankind. The protest of atheism against such a highest person is correct. There is no evidence for his existence, nor is he a matter of ultimate concern. God is not God without universal participation. "Personal God" is a confusing symbol.

God is the principle of participation as well as the principle of individualization. The divine life participates in every life as its ground and aim. God participates in everything that is; he has community with it; he shares in its destiny. Certainly such statements are highly symbolic. They can have the unfortunate logical implication that there is something alongside God in which he participates from the outside. But the divine participation creates that in which it participates. Plato uses the word *parousia* for the presence of the essences in temporal existence. This word later becomes the name for the preliminary and final presence of the transcendent Christ in the church and in the world. *Par-ousia* means "being by", "being with" — but on the basis of being absent, of being separated. In the same way God's participation is not a spatial or temporal presence. It is meant not categorically but symbolically. It is the parousia, the "being with" of that which is neither here nor there. If applied to God, participation and community are not less symbolic than individualization and personality. While active religious communication between God and man depends on the symbol of the personal God, the symbol of universal participation expresses the passive experience of the divine parousia in terms of the divine omnipresence.

The polarity of dynamics and form supplies the material basis for a group of symbols which are central for any present-day doctrine of God. Potentiality, vitality, and self-transcendence are indicated in the term "dynamics", while the term "form" embraces actuality, intentionality, and self-preservation.

Potentiality and actuality appear in classical theology in the famous formula that God is *actus purus,* the pure form in which everything potential is actual, and which is the eternal self-intuition of the divine fullness (*pleroma*). In this formula the dynamic side in the dynamics-form polarity is swallowed by the form side. Pure actuality, that is, actuality free from any element of potentiality, is a fixed result; it is not alive. Life includes the separation of potentiality and actuality. The nature of life is actualization, not actuality. The God who is *actus purus* is not the living God. It is interesting that even those theologians who have used the concept of *actus purus* normally speak of God in the dynamic symbols of the Old Testament and of Christian experience. This situation has induced some thinkers — partly under the influence of Luther's dynamic conception of God and partly under the impact of the problem of evil — to emphasize the dynamics in God and to depreciate the stabilization of dynamics in pure actuality. They try to distinguish between two elements in God, and they assert that, in so far as God is a living God, these two elements must remain in tension. Whether the first element is called the *Ungrund* or the "nature in God" (Böhme) or the first potency (Schelling), or the will (Schopenhauer), or the "given" in God (Brightman), or *me-onic* freedom (Berdyaev), or the contingent (Hartshorne) — in all these cases it is an expression of what we have called "dynamics", and it is an attempt to prevent the dynamics in God from being transformed into pure actuality.

Theological criticism of these attempts is easy if the concepts are taken in their proper sense, for then they make God finite, dependent on a fate or an accident which is not himself. The finite God, if taken literally, is a finite god, a polytheistic god. But this is not the way in which these concepts should be interpreted. They point symbolically to a quality of the divine life which is analogous to what appears as dynamics in the ontological structure. The divine creativity, God's participation in history, his outgoing character, are based on this dynamic element. It includes a "not yet" which is, however, always balanced by an "already" within the divine life. It is not an absolute "not yet", which would make it a divine-demonic power, nor is the "already" an absolute already. It also can be expressed as the negative element in the ground of being which is overcome as negative in the process of being-itself. As such it is the basis of the negative element in the creature, in which it is not overcome but is effective as a threat and a potential disruption.

These assertions include a rejection of a nonsymbolic, ontological doctrine of God as becoming. If we say that being is actual as life, the element of self-transcendence is obviously and emphatically included. But it is included as a symbolic element in balance with form. Being is not in balance with becoming. Being comprises becoming and rest, becoming as an implication of dynamics and rest as an implication of form. If we say that God is being-itself, this includes both rest and becoming, both the static and the dynamic elements. However, to speak of a "becoming" God disrupts the balance between dynamics and form and subjects God to a process which has the character of a fate or which is completely open to the future and has the character of an absolute accident. In both cases the divinity of God is undercut. The basic error of these doctrines is their metaphysical-constructive character. They apply the ontological elements to God in a nonsymbolic manner and are driven to religiously offensive and theologically untenable consequences.

If the element of form in the dynamics-form polarity is applied symbolically to the divine life, it expresses the actualization of its potentialities. The divine life inescapably unites possibility with fulfillment. Neither side threatens the other, nor is there a threat of disruption. In terms of self-preservation one could say that God cannot cease to be God. His going-out from himself does not diminish or destroy his divinity. It is united with the eternal "resting in himself".

The divine form must be conceived in analogy with what we have called "intentionality" on the human level. It is balanced with vitality, the dynamic side on the human level. The polarity in this formulation appears in classical theology as the polarity of will and intellect in God. It is consistent that Thomas Aquinas had to subordinate the will in God to the intellect when he accepted the Aristotelian *actus purus* as the basic character of God. And it must be remembered that the line of theological thought which tries to preserve the element of dynamics in God actually begins with Duns Scotus, who elevated the will in God over the intellect. Of course, both will and intellect in their application to God expresss infinitely more than the mental acts of willing and understanding as these appear in human experience. They are symbols for dynamics in all its ramifications and for form as the meaningful structure of being-itself. Therefore, it is not a question of metaphysical psychology, whether Aquinas or Duns Scotus is right. It is a question of the way in which psychological concepts should be employed as symbols for the divine life. And with respect to this question it is obvious that for more than a century a decision has been made in favor of the dynamic element. The philosophy of life, existential philosophy, and process philosophy agree on this point. Protestantism has contributed strong motives for this decision, but theology must balance the new with the old (predominantly Catholic) emphasis on the form character of the divine life.

If we consider the polarity of freedom and destiny in its symbolic value, we find that there hardly is a word said about God in the Bible which does not point directly or indirectly to his freedom. In freedom he creates, in freedom he deals with the world and man, in freedom he saves and fulfills. His freedom is freedom from anything prior to him or alongside him. Chaos cannot prevent him from speaking the word which makes light out of darkness; the evil deeds of men cannot prevent him from carrying through his plans; the good deeds of men cannot force him to reward them; the structure of being cannot prevent him from revealing himself; etc. Classical theology has spoken in more abstract terms of the aseity of God, of his being *a se*, self-derived. There is no ground prior to him which could condition his freedom; neither chaos nor nonbeing has power to limit or resist him. But aseity also means that there is nothing given in God which is not at the same time affirmed by his freedom. If taken nonsymbolically, this naturally leads to an unanswerable question, whether the structure of freedom, because it constitutes his freedom, is not itself something given in relation to which God has no freedom. The answer can only be that freedom, like the other ontological concepts, must be understood symbolically and in terms of the existential correlation of man and God. If taken in this way, freedom means that that which is man's ultimate concern is in no way dependent on man or on any finite being or on any finite concern. Only that which is unconditional can be the expression of unconditional concern. A conditioned God is no God.

Can the term "destiny" be applied symbolically to the divine life? The

175

gods of polytheism have a destiny — or, more correctly, a fate — because they are not ultimate. But can one say that he who is unconditional and absolute has a destiny in the same manner in which he has freedom? Is it possible to attribute destiny to being-itself? It is possible, provided the connotation of a destiny-determining power above God is avoided and provided one adds that God is his own destiny and that in God freedom and destiny are one. It may be argued that this truth is more adequately expressed if destiny is replaced by necessity, not mechanical necessity, but structural necessity, of course, or if God is spoken of as being his own law. Such phrases are important as interpretations, but they lack two elements of meaning which are present in the word "destiny". They lack the mystery of that which precedes any structure and law, being-itself; and they lack the relation to history which is included in the term "destiny". If we say that God is his own destiny, we point both to the infinite mystery of being and to the participation of God in becoming and in history.

*

## THE COURAGE TO BE

*In 1952, Tillich followed the appearance of volume I of* Systematic Theology *(1951) with* The Courage to Be *(New Haven: Yale University Press). His writing on courage in relation to post-World War II existential anguish reflects the increasing influence of Sigmund Freud on his work. Some termed him, "the therapeutic theologian". The influence of Karl Marx, while not wholly absent, is not as strong as during his earlier Religious Socialist period.* The Courage to Be *soon was a bestseller, its striking title drawing many to purchase the book, even if they lacked the stamina for moving beyond the book's first chapter on the etymology of the word courage. The book joined into one text both theology and depth psychology and spoke of the relation of "God" to the courage to stand alone (to be herself or himself). But the courage to be was not for an individualistic psychology, it was also about the courage to be a part of larger wholes (society) and therefore also about love, power and justice. In the following selection, taken from the last chapter of* The Courage to Be, *Tillich describes the kind of faith he sees as characteristic of this courage and points his readers beyond traditional theisms to "the god beyond God", the creative power of being in which all creatures participate. (Reprinted from* The Courage to Be, *pp. 155-90.)*

Courage is the self-affirmation of being in spite of the fact of nonbeing. It is the act of the individual self in taking the anxiety of nonbeing upon itself by affirming itself either as part of an embracing whole or in its individual selfhood. Courage always includes a risk, it is always threatened by nonbeing, whether the risk of losing oneself and becoming a thing within the whole of things or of losing one's world in an empty self-relatedness. Courage needs the power of being, a power transcending the nonbeing which is experienced in the anxiety of fate and death, which is present in the anxiety of emptiness and meaninglessness, which is effective in the anxiety of guilt and condemnation. The courage which takes this threefold anxiety into itself must be rooted in a power of being that is greater than the power of oneself and the power of one's world. Neither self-affirmation as a part nor self-affirmation as oneself is beyond the manifold threat of nonbeing. Those who are mentioned as representatives of these forms of courage try to transcend themselves and the world in which they participate in order to find the power of being-itself and a courage to be which is beyond the threat of nonbeing. There are no exceptions to this rule; and this means that every courage to be has an open or hidden religious root. For religion is the state of being grasped by the power of being-itself. In some cases the religious root is carefully covered, in others it is passionately denied; in some it is deeply hidden and in others superficially. But it is never completely absent. For everything that is participates in being-itself, and everybody has some awareness of this participation, especially in the moments in which he experiences the threat of nonbeing. . . .

### 1. ABSOLUTE FAITH AND THE COURAGE TO BE

How is the courage to be possible if all the ways to create it are barred by the experience of their ultimate insufficiency? If life is as meaningless as death, if guilt is as questionable as perfection, if being is no more meaningful than nonbeing, on what can one base the courage to be?

There is an inclination in some Existentialists to answer these questions by a leap from doubt to dogmatic certitude, from meaninglessness to a set of symbols in which the meaning of a special ecclesiastical or political group is embodied. This leap can be interpreted in different ways. It may be the expression of a desire for safety; it may be as arbitrary as, according to Existentialist principles, every decision is; it may be the feeling that the Christian message is the answer to the questions raised by an analysis of human existence; it may be a genuine conversion, independent of the theoretical situation. In any case it is not a solution of the problem of radical doubt. It gives the courage to be to those who are converted but it does not answer the question as to how such a courage is possible in itself. The answer must accept, as its precondition, the state of meaninglessness. It is not an answer if it demands the removal of this state; for that is just what cannot be done. He who is in the grip of doubt and meaninglessness cannot liberate himself from this grip; but he asks for an answer which is valid within and not outside the situation of his despair. He asks for the ultimate foundation of what we have called the "courage of despair". There is only one possible answer, if one does not try to escape the question; namely that the acceptance of despair is in itself faith and on the boundary line of the courage to be. In this situation the meaning of life is reduced to despair about the meaning of life. But as long as this despair is an act of life it is positive in its negativity. Cynically speaking, one could say that it is true to life to be cynical about it. Religiously speaking, one would say that one accepts oneself as accepted in spite of one's despair about the meaning of this acceptance. The paradox of every radical negativity, as long as it is an active negativity, is that it must affirm itself in order to be able to negate itself. No actual negation can be without an implicit affirmation. The hidden pleasure produced by despair witnesses to the paradoxical character of self-negation. The negative lives from the positive it negates.

The faith which makes the courage of despair possible is the acceptance of the power of being, even in the grip of nonbeing. Even in the despair about meaning being affirms itself through us. The act of accepting meaninglessness is in itself a meaningful act. It is an act of faith. We have seen that he who has the courage to affirm his being in spite of fate and guilt has not removed them. He remains threatened and hit by them. But he accepts his acceptance by the power of being-itself in which he participates and which gives him the courage to take the anxieties of fate and guilt upon himself. The same is true of doubt and meaninglessness. The faith which creates the courage to take them into itself has no special content. It is simply faith, undirected, absolute. It is undefinable, since everything defined is dissolved by doubt and meaninglessness. Nevertheless, even absolute faith is not an eruption of subjective emotions or a mood without objective foundation. . . .

## 2. THE COURAGE TO BE AS THE KEY TO BEING-ITSELF

### a. *Nonbeing opening up being*

The courage to be in all its forms has, by itself, revelatory character. It shows the nature of being, it shows that the self-affirmation of being is an affirmation that overcomes negation. In a metaphorical statement (and every assertion about being-itself is either metaphorical or symbolic) one could say that being includes nonbeing but nonbeing does not prevail against it. "Including" is a spatial metaphor which indicates that being embraces itself and that which is opposed to it, nonbeing. Nonbeing belongs to being, it cannot be separated from it. We could not even think "being" without a double negation: being must be thought as the negation of the negation of being. This is why we describe being best by the metaphor "power of being". Power is the possibility a being has to actualize itself against the resistance of other beings. If we speak of the power of being-itself we indicate that being affirms itself against nonbeing. In our discussion of courage and life we have mentioned the dynamic understanding of reality by the philosophers of life. Such an understanding is possible only if one accepts the view that nonbeing belongs to being, that being could not be the ground of life without nonbeing. The self-affirmation of being without nonbeing would not even be self-affirmation but an immovable self-identity. Nothing would be manifest, nothing expressed, nothing revealed. But nonbeing drives being out of its seclusion, it forces it to affirm itself dynamically. Philosophy has dealt with the dynamic self-affirmation of being-itself wherever it spoke dialectically, notably in Neoplatonism, Hegel, and the philosophers of life and process. Theology has done the same whenever it took the idea of the living God seriously, most obviously in the trinitarian symbolization of the inner life of God. Spinoza, in spite of his static definition of substance (which is his name for the ultimate power of being), unites philosophical and mystical tendencies when he speaks of the love and knowledge with which God loves and knows himself through the love and knowledge of finite beings. Nonbeing (that in God which makes his self-affirmation dynamic) opens up the divine self-seclusion and reveals him as power and love. Nonbeing makes God a living God. Without the No he has to overcome in himself and in his creature, the divine Yes to himself would be lifeless. There would be no revelation of the ground of being, there would be no life.

But where there is nonbeing there is finitude and anxiety. If we say that nonbeing belongs to being-itself, we say that finitude and anxiety belong to being-itself. Wherever philosophers or theologians have spoken of the divine blessedness they have implicitly (and sometimes explicitly) spoken of the anxiety of finitude which is eternally taken into the blessedness of the divine infinity. The infinite embraces itself and the finite, the Yes includes itself and the No which it takes into itself, blessedness comprises itself and the anxiety of which it is the conquest. All this is implied if one says that being includes nonbeing and that through nonbeing it reveals itself. It is a highly symbolic language which must be used at this point. But its symbolic character does not diminish its truth; on the contrary, it is a condition of its truth. To speak unsymbolically about being-itself is untrue.

The divine self-affirmation is the power that makes the self-affirmation of the finite being, the courage to be, possible. Only because being-itself has the character of self-affirmation inspite of nonbeing is courage possible. Courage participates in the self-affirmation of being-itself, it participates in the power of being which prevails against nonbeing. He who receives this power in an act of mystical or personal or absolute faith is aware of the source of his courage to be.

Man is not necessarily aware of this source. In situations of cynicism and indifference he is not aware of it. But it works in him as long as he maintains the courage to take his anxiety upon himself. In the act of the courage to be the power of being is effective in us, whether we recognize it or not. Every act of courage is a manifestation of the ground of being, however questionable the content of the act may be. The content may hide or distort true being, the courage in it reveals true being. Not arguments but the courage to be reveals the true nature of being-itself. By affirming our being we participate in the self-affirmation of being-itself. There are no valid arguments for the "existence" of God, but there are acts of courage in which we affirm the power of being, whether we know it or not. If we know it, we accept acceptance consciously. If we do not know it, we nevertheless accept it and participate in it. And in our acceptance of that which we do not know the power of being is manifest to us. Courage has revealing power, the courage to be is the key to being-itself.

### b. *Theism transcended*

The courage to take meaninglessness into itself presupposes a relation to the ground of being which we have called "absolute faith". It is without a *special* content, yet it is not without content. The content of absolute faith is the "God above God". Absolute faith and its consequence, the courage that takes the radical doubt, the doubt about God, into itself, transcends the theistic idea of God.

Theism can mean the unspecified affirmation of God. Theism in this sense does not say what it means if it uses the name of God. Because of the traditional and psychological connotations of the word God such an empty theism can produce a reverent mood if it speaks of God. Politicians, dictators, and other people who wish to use rhetoric to make an impression on their audience like to use the word God in this sense. It produces the feeling in their listeners that the speaker is serious and morally trustworthy. This is especially successful if they can brand their foes as atheistic. On a higher level people without a definite religious commitment like to call themselves theistic, not for special purposes but because they cannot stand a world without God, whatever this God may be. They need some of the connotations of the word God and they are afraid of what they call atheism. On the highest level of this kind of theism the name of God is used as a poetic or practical symbol, expressing a profound emotional state or the highest ethical idea. It is a theism which stands on the boundary line between the second type of theism and what we call "theism transcended". But it is still too indefinite to cross this boundary line. The atheistic negation of this whole type of theism is as vague as the theism itself. It may produce an irreverent mood and angry reaction of those who take their theistic affirmation seriously. It may even be felt as justified against the rhetorical-political abuse of the name God, but it is ultimately as irrelevant as the theism which it negates. It cannot reach the state of despair any more than the theism against which it fights can reach the state of faith.

Theism can have another meaning, quite contrary to the first one: it can be the name of what we have called the divine-human encounter. In this case it points to those elements in the Jewish-Christian tradition which emphasize the person-to-person relationship with God. Theism in this sense emphasizes the personalistic passages in the Bible and the Protestant creeds, the personalistic image of God, the word as the tool of creation and revelation, the ethical and social character of the kingdom of God, the personal nature of human faith and divine forgiveness, the historical vision of the universe, the idea of a divine purpose, the infinite distance between creator and creature, the absolute separation between God and the world, the conflict between holy God and sinful man, the person-to-person character of prayer and practical devotion. Theism in this sense is the nonmystical side of biblical religion and historical Christianity. Atheism from the point of view of this theism is the human attempt to escape the divine-human encounter. It is an existential — not a theological — problem.

Theism has a third meaning, a strictly theological one. Theological theism is, like every theology, dependent on the religious substance which it conceptualizes. It is dependent on theism in the first sense insofar as it tries to prove the necessity of affirming God in some way; it usually develops the so-called arguments for the "existence" of God. But it is more dependent on theism in the second sense insofar as it tries to establish a doctrine of God which transforms the person-to-person encounter with God into a doctrine about two persons who may or may not meet but who have a reality independent of each other.

Now theism in the first sense must be transcended because it is irrelevant, and theism in the second sense must be transcended because it is one-sided. But theism in the third sense must be transcended because it is wrong. It is bad theology. This can be shown by a more penetrating analysis. The God of theological theism is a being beside others and as such a part of the whole of reality. He certainly is considered its most important part, but as a part and therefore as subjected to the structure of the whole. He is supposed to be beyond the ontological elements and categories which constitute reality. But every statement subjects him to them. He is seen as a self which has a world, as an ego which is related to a thou, as a cause which is separated from its effect, as having a definite space and an endless time. He is a being, not being-itself. As such he is bound to the subject-object structure of reality, he is an object for us as subjects. At the same time we are objects for him as a subject. And this is decisive for the necessity of transcending theological theism. For God as a subject makes me into an object which is nothing more than an object. He deprives me of my subjectivity because he is all-powerful and all-knowing. I revolt and try to make *him* into an object, but the revolt fails and becomes desperate. God appears as the invincible tyrant, the being in contrast with whom all other beings are without freedom and subjectivity. He is equated with the recent tyrants who with the help of terror try to transform everything into a mere object, a thing among things, a cog in the machine they control. He becomes the model of everything against which Existentialism revolted. This is the God Nietzsche said had to be killed because nobody can tolerate being made into a mere object of absolute knowledge and absolute control. This is the deepest root of atheism. It is an atheism which is justified as the reaction against theological theism and its disturbing implications. It is also the deepest root of the Existentialist despair and the widespread anxiety of meaninglessness in our period.

Theism in all its forms is transcended in the experience we have called absolute faith. It is the accepting of the acceptance without somebody or something that accepts. It is the power of being-itself that accepts and gives the courage to be. This is the highest point to which our analysis has brought us. It cannot be described in the way the God of all forms of theism can be described. It cannot be described in mystical terms either. It transcends both mysticism and personal encounter, as it transcends both the courage to be as a part and the courage to be as oneself.

### c.  The God above God and the courage to be

The ultimate source of the courage to be is the "God above God"; this is the result of our demand to transcend theism. Only if the God of theism is transcended can the anxiety of doubt and meaninglessness be taken into the courage to be. The God above God is the object of all mystical longing, but mysticism also must be transcended in order to reach him. Mysticism does not take seriously the concrete and the doubt concerning the concrete. It plunges directly into the ground of being and meaning, and leaves the concrete, the world of finite values and meanings, behind. Therefore it does not solve the problem of meaninglessness. In terms of the present religious situation this means that Eastern mysticism is not the solution of the problems of Western Existentialism, although many people attempt this solution. The God above the God of theism is not the devaluation of the meanings which doubt has thrown into the abyss of meaninglessness; he is their potential restitution. Nevertheless absolute faith agrees with the faith implied in mysticism in that both transcend the theistic objectivation of a God who is a being. For mysticism such a God is not more real than any finite being, for the courage to be such a God has disappeared in the abyss of meaninglessness with every other value and meaning.

The God above the God of theism is present, although hidden, in every divine-human encounter. Biblical religion as well as Protestant theology are aware of the paradoxical character of this encounter. They are aware that if God encounters man God is neither object nor subject and is therefore above the scheme into which theism has forced him. They are aware that personalism with respect to God is balanced by a

183

transpersonal presence of the divine. They are aware that forgiveness can be accepted only if the power of acceptance is effective in man — biblically speaking, if the power of grace is effective in man. They are aware of the paradoxical character of every prayer, of speaking to somebody to whom you cannot speak because he is not "somebody", of asking somebody of whom you cannot ask anything because he gives or gives not before you ask, of saying "thou" to somebody who is nearer to the I than the I is to itself. Each of these paradoxes drives the religious consciousness toward a God above the God of theism.

The courage to be which is rooted in the experience of the God above the God of theism unites and transcends the courage to be as a part and the courage to be as oneself. It avoids both the loss of oneself by participation and the loss of one's world by individualization. The acceptance of the God above the God of theism makes us a part of that which is not also a part but is the ground of the whole. Therefore our self is not lost in a larger whole, which submerges it in the life of a limited group. If the self participates in the power of being-itself it receives itself back. For the power of being acts through the power of the individual selves. It does not swallow them as every limited whole, every collectivism, and every conformism does. This is why the Church, which stands for the power of being-itself or for the God who transcends the God of the religions, claims to be the mediator of the courage to be. A church which is based on the authority of the God of theism cannot make such a claim. It inescapably develops into a collectivist or semicollectivist system itself.

But a church which raises itself in its message and its devotion to the God above the God of theism without sacrificing its concrete symbols can mediate a courage which takes doubt and meaninglessness into itself. It is the Church under the Cross which alone can do this, the Church which preaches the Crucified who cried to God who remained his God after the God of confidence had left him in the darkness of doubt and meaninglessness. To be as a part in such a church is to receive a courage to be in which one cannot lose one's self and in which one receives one's world.

Absolute faith, or the state of being grasped by the God beyond God, is not a state which appears beside other states of the mind. It never is something separated and definite, an event which could be isolated and described. It is always a movement in, with, and under other states of the mind. It is the situation on the boundary of man's possibilities. It *is* this boundary. Therefore it is both the courage of despair and the courage in and above every courage. It is not a place where one can live, it is without the safety of words and concepts, it is without a name, a church, a cult, a theology. But it is moving in the depth of all of them. It is the power of being, in which they participate and of which they are fragmentary expressions.

One can become aware of it in the anxiety of fate and death when the traditional symbols, which enable men to stand the vicissitudes of fate and the horror of death have lost their power. When "providence" has become a superstition and "immortality" something imaginary that which once was the power in these symbols can still be present and create the courage to be in spite of the experience of a chaotic world and a finite existence. The Stoic courage returns but not as the faith in universal reason. It returns as the absolute faith which says Yes to being without seeing anything concrete which could conquer the nonbeing in fate and death.

And one can become aware of the God above the God of theism in the anxiety of guilt and condemnation when the traditional symbols that enable men to withstand the anxiety of guilt and condemnation have lost their power. When "divine judgment" is interpreted as a psychological complex and forgiveness as a remnant of the "father-image", what once was the power in those symbols can still be present and create the courage to be in spite of the experience of an infinite gap between what we are and what we ought to be. The Lutheran courage returns but not supported by the faith in a judging and forgiving God. It returns in terms of the absolute faith which says Yes although there is no special power that conquers guilt. The courage to take the anxiety of meaninglessness upon oneself is the boundary line up to which the courage to be can go. Beyond it is mere nonbeing. Within it all forms of courage are re-established in the power of the God above the God of theism. *The courage to be is rooted in the God who appears when God has disappeared in the anxiety of doubt.*

# 4

## AMID STRUCTURES OF DESTRUCTION
## CHRIST AS NEW BEING*

### EXISTENTIALISM AND CHRISTIAN THEOLOGY

*At the outset of the second volume of Systematic Theology Tillich injects a strong dose of existentialist analysis into the theology which, in volume 1, was predominantly an essentialist vision of human life grounded in the divine life. In the short sections that follow, Tillich insists that theologians learn from Søren Kierkegaard, Karl Marx, Arthur Schopenhauer, Friedrich Nietzsche and others who question the essentialist or idealist visions of human being. Sympathetic though he was with the idealism of Hegel, Tillich also resonated with a post-World War II sensibility that everywhere highlighted the estrangement and despair frequently found in the mid-twentieth century. Volume 2 on estranged existence and the Christ, however, provides no more the whole story about the human life to which the theologian responds, than did volume 1 on Being and God. Volumes 1 and 2 are both abstractions from the complexities and ambiguities of life in which humans experience elements of both essential being and also existential estrangement. This selection is from Systematic Theology, vol. 2 (Chicago: The University of Chicago Press, 1957, pp. 24-8).*

### 1. EXISTENTIALISM AGAINST ESSENTIALISM

It was in protest to Hegel's perfect essentialism that the existentialism of the nineteenth and twentieth centuries arose. It was not a special trait of his thought which was criticized by the existentialists, some of whom were his pupils. They were not interested in correcting him. They attacked the essentialist idea as such, and with it the whole modern development of man's attitude toward himself and his world. Their attack was and is a revolt against the self-interpretation of man in modern industrial society.

The immediate attack on Hegel came from several sides. In systematic theology we cannot deal with the individual rebels, such as Schelling, Schopenhauer, Kierkegaard, or Marx. Suffice it to state that

---

* See also pp. 24-28 above.

in these decades (1830-50) was prepared the historical destiny and the cultural self-expression of the Western world in the twentieth century. In systematic theology we must show the character of the existentialist revolt and confront the meaning of existence which has developed in it with the religious symbols pointing to the human predicament.

The common point in all existentialist attacks is that man's existential situation is a state of estrangement from his essential nature. Hegel is aware of this estrangement, but he believes that it has been overcome and that man has been reconciled with his true being. According to all the existentialists, this belief is Hegel's basic error. Reconciliation is a matter of anticipation and expectation, but not of reality. The world is not reconciled, either in the individual — as Kierkegaard shows — or in society — as Marx shows — or in life as such — as Schopenhauer and Nietzsche show. Existence is estrangement and not reconciliation; it is dehumanization and not the expression of essential humanity. It is the process in which man becomes a thing and ceases to be a person. History is not the divine self-manifestation but a series of unreconciled conflicts, threatening man with self-destruction. The existence of the individual is filled with anxiety and threatened by meaninglessness. With this description of man's predicament all existentialists agree and are therefore opposed to Hegel's essentialism. They feel that it is an attempt to hide the truth about man's actual state.

The distinction has been made between atheistic and theistic existentialism. Certainly there are existentialists who could be called "atheistic", at least according to their intention; and there are others who can be called "theistic". But, in reality, there is no atheistic or theistic existentialism. Existentialism gives an analysis of what it means to exist. It shows the contrast between an essentialist description and an existentialist analysis. It develops the question implied in existence, but it does not try to give the answer, either in atheistic or in theistic terms. Whenever existentialists give answers, they do so in terms of religious or quasi-religious traditions which are not derived from their existentialist analysis. Pascal derives his answers from the Augustinian tradition, Kierkegaard from the Lutheran, Marcel from the Thomist, Dostoevski from the Greek Orthodox. Or the answers are derived from humanistic traditions, as with Marx, Sartre, Nietzsche, Heidegger, and Jaspers. None of these men was able to develop answers out of his questions. The answers of the humanists come from hidden religious sources. They are matters of ultimate concern or faith, although garbed in a secular gown. Hence the distinction between atheistic and theistic existentialism fails. Existentialism is an anaylsis of the human predicament. And the answers to the questions implied in man's predicament are religious, whether open or hidden. . . .

## 2. EXISTENTIALISM AND CHRISTIAN THEOLOGY

Christianity asserts that Jesus is the Christ. The term "the Christ" points by marked contrast to man's existential situation. For the Christ, the Messiah, is he who is supposed to bring the "new eon", the universal regeneration, the new reality. New reality presupposes an old reality; and this old reality, according to prophetic and apocalyptic descriptions, is the state of the estrangement of man and his world from God. This estranged world is ruled by structures of evil, symbolized as demonic powers. They rule individual souls, nations, and even nature. They produce anxiety in all its forms. It is the task of the Messiah to conquer them and to establish a new reality from which the demonic powers or the structures of destruction are excluded.

Existentialism has analyzed the "old eon", namely, the predicament of man and his world in the state of estrangement. In doing so, existentialism is a natural ally of Christianity. Immanuel Kant once said that mathematics is the good luck of human reason. In the same way, one could say that existentialism is the good luck of Christian theology. It has helped to rediscover the classical Christian interpretation of human existence. Any theological attempt to do this would not have had the same effect. This positive use refers not only to existentialist philosophy but also to analytic psychology, literature, poetry, drama, and art. In all these realms there is an immense amount of material which the theologian can use and organize in the attempt to present Christ as the answer to the questions implied within existence. In earlier centuries a similar task was undertaken mainly by monastic theologians, who analyzed themselves and the members of their small community so penetratingly that there are few present-day insights into the human predicament which they did not anticipate. The penitential and devotional literature impressively shows this. But this tradition was lost under the impact of the philosophies and theologies of pure consciousness, represented, above all, by Cartesianism and Calvinism. Notwithstanding differences, they were allies in helping to repress the unconscious and half-conscious sides of human nature, thus preventing a full understanding of man's existential predicament (in spite of Calvin's doctrine of man's total depravity and the Augustinianism of the Cartesian school). In recovering the elements of man's nature which were suppressed by the psychology of consciousness, existentialism and contemporary theology should become allies and analyze the character of existence in all its manifestations, the unconscious as well as the conscious.

The systematic theologian cannot do this alone; he needs the help of creative representatives of existentialism in all realms of culture. He needs the support of the practical explorers of man's predicament, such as ministers, educators, psychoanalysts, and counselors. The theologian must reinterpret the traditional religious symbols and theological concepts in the light of the material he receives from these people. He must be aware of the fact that terms like "sin" and "judgment" have lost not their truth but rather an expressive power which can be regained only if they are filled with the insights into human nature which existentialism (including depth psychology) has given to us. Now the biblicistic theologian is right in maintaining that all these insights can be found in the Bible. And the Roman Catholic is equally right in pointing to these insights in the Church Fathers. The question is not whether something can be found somewhere — almost everything can — but whether a period is ripe for rediscovering a lost truth. For example, he who reads Ecclesiastes or Job with eyes opened by existentialist analyses will see more in either than he was able to see before. The same is true of many other passages of the Old and New Testaments.

Existentialism has been criticized as being too "pessimistic". Terms like "non-being", "finitude", "anxiety", "guilt", "meaninglessness", and "despair" seem to justify such criticism. Criticism also has been directed against much biblical writing, as, for instance, Paul's description of the human predicament in Romans, chapters 1 and 7. But Paul is pessimistic (in the sense of hopeless) in these passages only if they are read in isolation and without the answer to the question implied in them.

Certainly this is not the case within a theological system. The word "pessimism" should be avoided in connection with descriptions of human nature, for it is a mood, not a concept or description. From the point of view of systematic structure, it must be added that the existential elements are only one part of the human predicament. They are always combined ambiguously with essential elements; otherwise they would have no being at all. Essential as well as existential elements are always abstractions from the concrete actuality of being, namely, "Life". This is the subject of the fourth part of *Systematic Theology*. For the sake of analysis, however, abstractions are necessary, even if they have a strongly negative sound. And no existentialist analysis of the human predicament can escape this, even if it is hard to bear — as the doctrine of sin always has been in traditional theology.

*

## FROM ESSENCE TO EXISTENCE (THE FALL)

*To Tillich, taking the existentialist analysis seriously meant taking radical sin and evil seriously — so much so, in fact, that evil is interpreted as a universal quality of finite being. This is the "tragic element" in the transition from essence to estranged existence. Tillich also argues, as Christian tradition has typically argued, that there is also a "moral element", i.e. that the Fall involves human responsibility for a historical Fall away from God and from the state of grace. But Tillich continually stresses the tragic element, how human fallenness is not simply one of a series of choices by people in history. It is a universal dimension of our existence. Precisely at this point, Reinhold Niebuhr declared Tillich to have made the biblical account captive to "ontological speculation", thus becoming "the Origen of our period" (R. Niebuhr, "Biblical Thought and Ontological Speculation in Tillich's Theology", in Kegley, p. 253). Tillich held firm, arguing that the tragic element is not merely speculative and has the support of biblical precedent, of the Christian tradition as well as of contemporary reflection — indeed, of all who would take radical evil seriously. Since Tillich's death, the following section of his* Systematic Theology, *vol. 2 (Chicago: The University of Chicago Press, 1957, pp. 31-9) has drawn other kinds of commentary and critique; two recent examples being those by feminists (Judith Plaskow,* Sex, Sin and Grace, *pp. 95-148) and by the German theologian Wolfhart Pannenberg,* Anthropology in Theological Persepctive *(Philadelphia: Westminster Press, 1985, pp. 281-4).*

### 1. FINITE FREEDOM AS THE POSSIBILITY OF THE TRANSITION FROM ESSENCE TO EXISTENCE

The story of Genesis, chapters 1-3, if taken as a myth, can guide our description of the transition from essential to existential being. It is the profoundest and richest expression of man's awareness of his existential estrangement and provides the scheme in which the transition from essence to existence can be treated.

In the part entitled "Being and God", the polarity of freedom and destiny was discussed in relation to being as such, as well as in relation to human beings. On the basis of the solution given there, we can answer the question of how the transition from essence to existence is possible in terms of "freedom", which is always in polar unity with destiny. But this is only a first step to the answer. In the same section of the first volume, we described man's awareness of his finitude and of finitude universally, and we analyzed the situation of being related to and excluded from infinity. This provides the second step toward an answer. It is not freedom as such, but finite freedom. Man has freedom in contrast to all other creatures. They have analogies to freedom but not freedom itself. But man is finite, excluded from the infinity to which he belongs. One can say that nature is finite necessity, God is infinite freedom, man is finite freedom. It is finite freedom which makes possible the transition from essence to existence.

Man is free, in so far as he has language. With his language, he has universals which liberate him from bondage to the concrete situation to which even the highest animals are subjected. Man is free, in so far as he is able to ask questions about the world he encounters, including himself, and to penetrate into deeper and deeper levels of reality. Man is free, in so far as he can receive unconditional moral and logical imperatives which indicate that he can transcend the conditions which determine every finite being. Man is free, in so far as he has the power of deliberating and deciding, thus cutting through the mechanisms of stimulus and response. Man is free, in so far as he can play and build imaginary structures above the real structures to which he, like all beings, is bound. Man is free, in so far as he has the faculty of creating worlds above the given world, of creating the world of technical tools and products, the world of artistic expressions, the world of theoretical structures and practical organizations. Finally, man is free, in so far as he has the power of contradicting himself and his essential nature. Man is free even from his freedom; that is, he can surrender his humanity. This final quality of his freedom provides the third step toward the answer to the question of how the transition from essence to existence is possible.

Man's freedom is finite freedom. All the potentialities which constitute his freedom are limited by the opposite pole, his destiny. In nature, destiny has the character of necessity. In spite of analogies to human destiny, God is his own destiny. This means that he transcends the polarity of freedom and destiny. In man freedom and destiny limit each other, for he has finite freedom. This is true of every act of human freedom; it is true also of the final quality of human freedom, namely, the power of surrendering his freedom. Even the freedom of self-contradiction is limited by destiny. As finite freedom, it is possible only within the context of the universal transition from essence to existence. There is no individual Fall. In the Genesis story the two sexes and nature, represented by the serpent, work together. The transition from essence to existence is possible because finite freedom works within the frame of a universal destiny; this is the fourth step toward the answer.

Traditional theology discussed the possibility of the Fall in terms of Adam's *potuit peccare* — his freedom to sin. This freedom was not seen in unity with the total structure of his freedom and therefore was considered as a questionable divine gift. Calvin thought the freedom to fall to be a weakness of man, regrettable from the point of view of man's happiness, since it meant eternal condemnation for most human beings (e.g., all pagans). This gift is understandable only from the point of view of the divine glory, in that God decided to reveal his majesty not only through salvation but also through the condemnation of men. But the freedom of turning away from God is a quality of the structure of freedom as such. The possibility of the Fall is dependent on all the qualities of human freedom taken in their unity. Symbolically speaking, it is the image of God in man which gives the possibility of the Fall. Only he who is the image of God has the power of separating himself from God. His greatness and his weakness are identical. Even God could not remove the one without removing the other. And if man had not received this possibility, he would have been a thing among things, unable to serve the divine glory, either in salvation or in condemnation. Therefore, the doctrine of the Fall has always been treated as the doctrine of the Fall of man, although it was also seen as a cosmic event.

## 2. "DREAMING INNOCENCE" AND TEMPTATION

Having discussed how the transition from essence to existence is possible, we now come to the question of the motifs driving to the transition. In order to answer this, we must have an image of the state of essential being in which the motifs are working. The difficulty is that the state of essential being is not an actual stage of human development which can be known directly or indirectly. The essential nature of man is present in all stages of his development, although in existential distortion. In myth and dogma man's essential nature has been projected into the past as a history before history, symbolized as a golden age or paradise. In psychological terms one can interpret this state as that of "dreaming innocence". Both words point to something that precedes actual existence. It has potentiality, not actuality. It has no place, it is *ou topos* (utopia). It has no time; it precedes temporality, and it is suprahistorical. Dreaming is a state of mind which is real and non-real at the same time — just as is potentiality. Dreaming anticipates the actual, just as everything actual is somehow present in the potential. In the moment of awakening, the images of the dream disappear as images and return as encountered realities. Certainly, reality is different from the images of the dream, but not totally different. For the actual is present in the potential in terms of anticipation. For these reasons the metaphor "dreaming" is adequate in describing the state of essential being.

The word "innocence" also points to non-actualized potentiality. One is innocent only with respect to something which, if actualized, would end the state of innocence. The word has three connotations. It can mean lack of actual experience, lack of personal responsibility, and lack of moral guilt. In the metaphorical use suggested here, it is meant in all three senses. It designates the state before actuality, existence, and history. If the metaphor "dreaming innocence" is used, concrete connotations appear, taken from human experience. One is reminded of the early stages of a child's development. The most striking example is the growth of his sexual consciousness. Up to a certain point, the child is unconscious of his sexual potentialities. In the difficult steps of transition from potentiality to actuality, an awakening takes place. Experience, responsibility, and guilt are acquired, and the state of dreaming innocence is lost. This example is evident in the biblical story, where sexual consciousness is the first consequence of the loss of innocence. One should not confuse this metaphorical use of the term "innocence" with the false assertion that the newborn human being is in a state of sinlessness. Every life always stands under the conditions of existence. The word "innocence", like the word "dreaming", is used not in its proper but in its analogical sense. But, if used in this way, it can provide a psychological approach to the state of essential or potential being.

The state of dreaming innocence drives beyond itself. The possibility of the transition to existence is experienced as temptation. Temptation is unavoidable because the state of dreaming innocence is uncontested and undecided. It is not perfection. Orthodox theologians have heaped perfection after perfection upon Adam before the Fall, making him equal with the picture of the Christ. This procedure is not only absurd; it makes the Fall completely unintelligible. Mere potentiality or dreaming innocence is not perfection. Only the conscious union of existence and essence is perfection, as God is perfect because he transcends essence and existence. The symbol "Adam before the Fall" must be understood as the dreaming innocence of undecided potentialites.

193

If we ask what it is that drives dreaming innocence beyond itself, we must continue our analysis of the concept "finite freedom". Man is not only finite, as is every creature; he is also aware of his finitude. And this awareness is "anxiety". In the last decade the term "anxiety" has become associated with the German and Danish word *Angst*, which itself is derived from the Latin *angustiae*, "narrows". Through Søren Kierkegaard the word *Angst* has become a central concept of existentialism. It expresses the awareness of being finite, of being a mixture of being and nonbeing, or of being threatened by nonbeing. All creatures are driven by anxiety; for finitude and anxiety are the same. But in man freedom is united with anxiety. One could call man's freedom "freedom in anxiety" or "anxious freedom" (in German, *sich ängstigende Freiheit*). This anxiety is one of the driving forces toward the transition from essence to existence. Kierkegaard particularly has used the concept of anxiety to describe (not to explain) the transition from essence to existence.

Using this idea and analyzing the structure of finite freedom, one may show in two interrelated ways the motifs of the transition from essence to existence. There is an element in the Genesis story which has often been overlooked — the divine prohibition not to eat from the tree of knowledge. Any command presupposes that what is commanded is not yet fulfilled. The divine prohibition presupposes a kind of split between creator and creature, a split which makes a command necessary, even if it is given only in order to test the obedience of the creature. This cleavage is the most important point in the interpretation of the Fall. For it presupposes a sin which is not yet sin but which is also no longer innocence. It is the desire to sin. I suggest calling the state of this desire "aroused freedom". In the state of dreaming innocence, freedom and destiny are in harmony, but neither of them is actualized. Their unity is essential or potential; it is finite and therefore open to tension and disruption — just like uncontested innocence. The tension occurs in the moment in which finite freedom becomes conscious of itself and tends to become actual. This is what could be called the moment of aroused freedom. But in the same moment a reaction starts, coming from the essential unity of freedom and destiny. Dreaming innocence wants to preserve itself. This reaction is symbolized in the biblical story as the divine prohibition against actualizing one's potential freedom and against acquiring knowledge and power. Man is caught between the desire to actualize his freedom and the demand to preserve his dreaming innocence. In the power of his finite freedom, he decides for actualization.

The same analysis can be made, so to speak, from the inside, namely, from man's anxious awareness of his finite freedom. At the moment when man becomes conscious of his freedom, the awareness of his dangerous situation gets hold of him. He experiences a double threat, which is rooted in his finite freedom and expressed in anxiety. Man experiences the anxiety of losing himself by not actualizing himself and his potentialities and the anxiety of losing himself by actualizing himself and his potentialities. He stands between the preservation of his dreaming innocence without experiencing the actuality of being and the loss of his innocence through knowledge, power, and guilt. The anxiety of this situation is the state of temptation. Man decides for self-actualization, thus producing the end of dreaming innocence.

Again it is sexual innocence which psychologically gives the most adequate analogy to the preceding. The typical adolescent is driven by the anxiety of losing himself, either in the actualization of himself sexually or in his nonactualization sexually. On the one hand, the taboos imposed on him by society have power over him in confirming his own anxiety about losing his innocence and becoming guilty by actualizing his potentiality. On the other hand, he is afraid of not actualizing himself sexually and of sacrificing his potentialities by preserving his innocence. He usually decides for actualization, as men universally do. Exceptions (e.g., for the sake of conscious asceticism) limit the analogy to the human situation generally, but they do not remove the analogy.

The analysis of temptation, as given here, makes no reference to a conflict between the bodily and the spiritual side of man as a possible cause. The doctrine of man indicated here implies a "monistic" understanding of man's nature in contrast to a dualistic one. Man is a whole man, whose essential being has the character of dreaming innocence, whose finite freedom makes possible the transition from essence to existence, whose aroused freedom puts him between two anxieties which threaten the loss of self, whose decision is against the preservation of dreaming innocence and for self-actualization. Mythologically speaking, the fruit of the tree of temptation is both sensuous and spiritual.

### 3. THE MORAL AND THE TRAGIC ELEMENT IN THE TRANSITION FROM ESSENTIAL TO EXISTENTIAL BEING

The transition from essence to existence is the original fact. It is not the first fact in a temporal sense or a fact beside or before others, but it is that which gives validity to every fact. It is the actual in every fact. We do exist and our world with us. This is the original fact. It means that the transition from essence to existence is a universal quality of finite being. It is not an event of the past; for it ontologically precedes everything that happens in time and space. It sets the conditions of spatial and temporal existence. It is manifest in every individual person in the transition from dreaming innocence to actualization and guilt.

If the transition from essence to existence is expressed mythologically — as it must be in the language of religion — it is seen as an event of the past, although it happens in all three modes of time. The event of the past to which traditional theology refers is the story of the Fall as told in the Book of Genesis. Perhaps no text in literature has received so many interpretations as the third chapter of Genesis. This is partly due to its uniqueness — even in biblical literature — partly to its psychological profundity, and partly to its religious power. In mythological language it describes the transition from essence to existence as a unique event which happened long ago in a special place to individual persons — first to Eve, then to Adam. God himself appears as an individual person in time and space as a typical "father figure". The whole description has a psychological-ethical character and is derived from the daily experiences of people under special cultural and social conditions. Nevertheless, it has a claim to universal validity. The predominance of psychological and ethical aspects does not exclude other factors in the biblical story. The serpent represents the dynamic trends of nature; there is the magical character of the two trees, the rise of sexual consciousness, the curse over the heredity of Adam, the body of the woman, the animals and the land.

These traits show that a cosmic myth is hidden behind the psychological-ethical form of the story and that the prophetic "demythologization" of this myth has not removed, but rather subordinated, the mythical elements to the ethical point of view. The cosmic myth reappears in the Bible in the form of the struggle of the divine with demonic powers and the powers of chaos and darkness. It reappears also in the myth of the Fall of the angels and in the interpretation of the serpent of Eden as the embodiment of a fallen angel. These examples all point to the cosmic presuppositions and implications of the Fall of Adam. But the most consistent emphasis on the cosmic character of the Fall is given in the myth of the transcendent Fall of the souls. While it probably has Orphic roots, it is first told by Plato when he contests essence and existence. It received a Christian form by Origen, a humanistic one by Kant, and is present in many other philosophies and theologies of the Christian Era.

All have recognized that existence cannot be derived from within existence, that it cannot be derived from an individual event in time and space. They have recognized that existence has a universal dimension.

The myth of the transcendent Fall is not directly biblical, but neither does it contradict the Bible. It affirms the ethical-psychological element in the Fall and carries through the cosmic dimensions which we find in biblical literature. The motif of the myth of the transcendent Fall is the tragic-universal character of existence. The meaning of the myth is that the very constitution of existence implies the transition from essence to existence. The individual act of existential estrangement is not the isolated act of an isolated individual; it is an act of freedom which is imbedded, nevertheless, in the universal destiny of existence. In every individual act the estranged or fallen character of being actualizes itself. Every ethical decision is an act both of individual freedom and of universal destiny. This justifies both forms of the myth of the Fall. Obviously, both are myths and are absurd if taken literally instead of symbolically. Existence is rooted both in ethical freedom and in tragic destiny. If the one or the other side is denied, the human situation becomes incomprehensible. Their unity is the great problem of the doctrine of man. Of all the aspects of the cosmic myth of Genesis, the doctrine of "original sin" has been most violently attacked since the early eighteenth century. This concept was the first point criticized by the Enlightenment, and its rejection is one of the last points defended by contemporary humanism. Two reasons explain the violence with which the modern mind has fought against the idea of original sin. First, its mythological form was taken literally by attackers and defenders and therefore was unacceptable to an awakening, historical-critical way of thinking. Second, the doctrine of original sin seemed to imply a negative evaluation of man, and this radically contradicted the new feeling for life and world as it had developed in industrial society. It was feared that the pessimism about man would inhibit the tremendous impulse of modern man, technically, politically, and educationally to transform world and society. There was and still is the apprehension that authoritarian and totalitarian consequences could follow from a negative valuation of man's moral and intellectual power. Theology must join — and in most cases has done so — the historical-critical attitude toward the biblical and ecclesiastical myth. Theology further must emphasize the positive valuation of man in his essential nature. It must join classical humanism in protecting man's created goodness against naturalistic and existentialistic denials of his greatness and dignity. At the same time, theology should reinterpret the doctrine of original sin by showing man's existential self-estrangement and by using the helpful existentialist analyses of the human predicament. In doing so, it must develop a realistic doctrine of man, in which the ethical and the tragic element in his self-estrangement are balanced. It may well be that such a task demands the definite removal from the theological vocabulary of terms like "original sin" or "hereditary sin" and their replacement by a description of the interpenetration of the moral and the tragic elements in the human situation.

The empirical basis for such a description has become quite extensive in our period. Analytic psychology, as well as analytic sociology, has shown how destiny and freedom, tragedy and responsibility, are interwoven in every human being from early childhood on and in all social and political groups in the history of mankind. The Christian church has maintained a stable balance of both sides in its description of the human situation, although frequently in inadequate language and always in conflicting directions. Augustine fought for a way between Manichaeism and Pelagianism; Luther rejected Erasmus but was interpreted by Flacius Illyricus in a half-Manichaean way; the Jansenists were accused by the Jesuits of destroying man's rationality; liberal theology is criticized by neo-orthodoxy as well as by a kind of existentialism (e.g., Sartre, Kafka) which has some Manichaean traits. Christianity cannot escape these tensions. It must simultaneously acknowledge the tragic universality of estrangement and man's personal responsibility for it.

*

## ESTRANGEMENT AND SIN

*"Sin", commented Tillich in his sermon entitled "You Are Accepted" (see Tillich, The New Being, pp. 153-4), is one of those words which, along with "grace", is strange to most contemporaries. Tillich insisted on keeping the traditional term, while at the same time arguing that the term needs rediscovery with the aid of the term "estrangement". Through commentary on estrangement, Tillich reinterpreted three traditional understandings of sin as "unbelief", as "concupiscence", and as "hubris". In this brief, but significant selection (Systematic Theology, vol. 2, Chicago: The University of Chicago Press 1957, pp. 44-9, 58-9), Tillich sets out the relationship between estrangement and sin, discusses just the first mark of estrangement ("unbelief"), and then reflects on the individual and collective forms of estrangement.*

## 1. ESTRANGEMENT AND SIN

The state of existence is the state of estrangement. Man is estranged from the ground of his being, from other beings, and from himself. The transition from essence to existence results in personal guilt and universal tragedy. It is now necessary to give a description of existential estrangement and its self-destructive implications. But, before doing so, we must answer the question which has already arisen: What is the relation of the concept of estrangement to the traditional concept of sin? . . . Man as he exists is not what he essentially is and ought to be. He is estranged from his true being. The profundity of the term "estrangement" lies in the implication that one belongs essentially to that from which one is estranged. Man is not a stranger to his true being, for he belongs to it. He is judged by it but cannot be completely separated, even if he is hostile to it. Man's hostility to God proves indisputably that he belongs to him. Where there is the possibility of hate, there and there alone is the possibility of love.

Estrangement is not a biblical term but is implied in most of the biblical descriptions of man's predicament. It is implied in the symbols of the expulsion from paradise, in the hostility between man and nature, in the deadly hostility of brother against brother, in the estrangement of nation from nation through the confusion of language, and in the continuous complaints of the prophets against their kings and people who turn to alien gods. Estrangement is implied in Paul's statement that man perverted the image of God into that of idols, in his classical description of "man against himself", in his vision of man's hostility against man as combined with his distorted desires. In all these interpretations of man's predicament, estrangement is implicitly asserted. Therefore, it is certainly not unbiblical to use the term "estrangement" in describing man's existential situation.

Nevertheless, "estrangement" cannot replace "sin". Yet the reasons for attempts to replace the word "sin" with another word are obvious. The term has been used in a way which has little to do with its genuine biblical meaning. Paul often spoke of "Sin" in the singular and without an article. He saw it as a quasi-personal power which ruled this world. But in the Christian churches, both Catholic and Protestant, sin has been used predominantly in the plural, and "sins" are deviations from moral laws. This has little to do with "sin" as the state of estrangement from that to which one belongs — God, one's self, one's world. Therefore, the characteristics of sin are here considered under the heading of "estrangement". And the word "estrangement" itself implies a reinterpretation of sin from a religious point of view.

Nevertheless, the word "sin" cannot be overlooked. It expresses what is not implied in the term "estrangement", namely, the personal act of turning away from that to which one belongs. Sin expresses most sharply the personal character of estrangement over against its tragic side. It expresses personal freedom and guilt in contrast to tragic guilt and the universal destiny of estrangement. The word "sin" can and must be saved, not only because classical literature and liturgy continuously employ it but more particularly because the word has a sharpness which accusingly points to the element of personal responsibility in one's estrangement. Man's predicament is estrangement, but his estrangement is sin. It is not a state of things, like the laws of nature, but a matter of both personal freedom and universal destiny. For this reason the term "sin" must be used after it has been reinterpreted religiously. An important tool for this reinterpretation is the term "estrangement".

Reinterpretation is also needed for the terms "original" or "hereditary" with respect to sin. But in this case reinterpretation may demand the rejection of the terms. Both point to the universal character of estrangement, expressing the element of destiny in estrangement. But both words are so much burdened with literalistic absurdities that it is practically impossible to use them any longer.

If one speaks of "sins" and refers to special acts which are considered as sinful, one should always be conscious of the fact that "sins" are the expressions of "sin". It is not the disobedience to a law which makes an act sinful but the fact that it is an expression of man's estrangement from God, from men, from himself. Therefore, Paul calls everything sin which does not result from faith, from the unity with God. And in another context (following Jesus) all laws are summed up in the law of love by which estrangement is conquered. Love as the striving for the reunion of the separated is the opposite of estrangement. In faith and love, sin is conquered because estrangement is overcome by reunion.

## 2. ESTRANGEMENT AS "UNBELIEF"

The Augsburg Confession defines sin as the state of man in which he is "without faith in God and with concupiscence" (*sine fide erga deum et cum concupiscentia*). One could add to these two expressions of estrangement a third one, namely *hubris* ($\nu\beta\rho\iota\varsigma$), the so-called spiritual sin of pride or self-elevation, which, according to Augustine and Luther, precedes the so-called sensual sin. This gives the three concepts of "unbelief", "concupiscence", and *hubris* as the marks of man's estrangement. Each of them needs reinterpretation in order to mediate insights into man's existential predicament.

Unbelief, in the view of the Reformers, is not the unwillingness or inability to believe the doctrines of the church, but, like faith, it is an act of the total personality, including practical, theoretical, and emotional elements. If there were such a word as "un-faith", it should be used instead of the word "unbelief". The latter has an unavoidable connotation associated with the term "belief", which came to mean the acceptance of statements without evidence. "Unbelief" for Protestant Christianity means the act or state in which man in the totality of his being turns away from God. In his existential self-realization he turns toward himself and his world and loses his essential unity with the ground of his being and his world. This happens both through individual responsibility and through tragic universality. It is freedom and destiny in one and the same act. Man, in actualizing himself, turns to himself and away from God in knowledge, will, and emotion. Unbelief is the disruption of man's cognitive participation in God. It should not be called the "denial" of God. Questions and answers, whether positive or negative, already presuppose the loss of a cognitive union with God. He who asks for God is already estranged from God, though not cut off from him. Unbelief is the separation of man's will from the will of God. It should not be called "disobedience"; for command, obedience, and disobedience already presuppose the separation of will from will. He who needs a law which tells him how to act or how not to act is already estranged from the source of the law which demands obedience. Unbelief is also the empirical shift from the blessedness of the divine life to the pleasures of a separated life. It should not be called "self-love". In order to have a self which not only can be loved but can love God, one's center must already have left the divine center to which it belongs and in which self-love and love to God are united.

All this is implied in the term "unbelief". It is the first mark of estrangement, and its character justifies the term "estrangement". Man's unbelief is his estrangement from God in the center of his being. This is the religious understanding of sin as rediscovered by the Reformers and as lost again in most Protestant life and thought.

If unbelief is understood as man's estrangement from God in the center of his self, then the Augustinian interpretation of sin as love turned away from God to self can be accepted by Protestant theology. Un-faith is ultimately identical with un-love; both point to man's estrangement from God. For Augustine, sin is the love which desires finite goods for their own sake and not for the sake of the ultimate good. Love of one's self and one's world can be justified if it affirms everything finite as a manifestation of the infinite and wants to be united with it for this reason. Love of one's self and one's world is distorted if it does not penetrate through the finite to its infinite ground. If it turns away from the infinite ground to its finite manifestations, then it is unbelief. The disruption of the essential unity with God is the innermost character of sin. It is estrangement in terms of faith as well as in terms of love.

There is, however, a difference between the two definitions of sin. In the concept of faith an element of "in spite of" is implied, the courage to accept that one is accepted in spite of sin, estrangement, and despair. If this question is asked — and asked as passionately and desperately as the Reformers did — the primacy of faith is established. This reunion of the estranged with God is "reconciliation". It has the character of "in spite of", since it is God who wants us to be reconciled with him. For this reason Protestantism holds to the primacy of faith, both in the doctrine of sin and in the doctrine of salvation.

For Augustine the union between God and man is re-established by the mystical power of grace through the mediation of the church and its sacraments. Grace, as the infusion of love, is the power which over-comes estrangement. Therefore, for Augustine and the Roman Catholic church, love has primacy in the doctrine of sin as well as in the doctrine of salvation. For the Reformers, estrangement is overcome by personal reconciliation with God and by the love which follows this reconciliation. For Augustine, estrangement is overcome by the infused love of God and the faith which is doctrinally expressed by the Roman Catholic church. But in spite of this profound difference, there is a point at which the two doctrines converge. Both emphasize the religious character of sin, as indicated in the term "estrangement". The first mark of estrangement — unbelief — includes un-love. Sin is a matter of our relation to God and not to ecclesiastical, moral, or social authorities. Sin is a religious concept, not in the sense that it is used in religious contexts, but in the sense that it points to man's relation to God in terms of estrangement and possible reunion.

## 3. ESTRANGEMENT INDIVIDUALLY AND COLLECTIVELY

The description of estrangement given thus far deals exclusively with the individual person, his freedom and destiny, his guilt and possible reconciliation. In connection with recent events, as in the case of nations, the question of collective guilt has become urgent. It was never completely absent from human consciousness, for there were always ruling individuals, classes, and movements which committed acts against man's essential nature and brought destruction upon the group to which they belonged. Judaism and Christianity placed emphasis on the personal guilt of the individual, but they could not overlook issues such as the suffering of children due to the sins of the parents. Social condemnation of personally innocent descendants of morally condemned parents was not unknown in the Christian Era. And lately whole nations have been morally condemned for the atrocities of their rulers and of many individuals who were coerced into crime through their rulers. A confession of guilt was demanded of the whole nation, including those who resisted the ruling group and suffered because of their resistance.

The latter point shows that there is a fundamental difference between a person and a social group. In contrast to the centered individual whom we call a "person", the social group has no natural, deciding center. A social group is a power structure, and in every power structure certain individuals determine the actions of all individuals who are parts of the group. There is, therefore, always a potential or real conflict within the group, even if the outcome is the united action of the group as a whole. As such, a social group is not estranged, and, as such, a social group is not reconciled. There is no collective guilt. But there is the universal destiny of mankind, which, in a special group, becomes special destiny without ceasing to be universal. Every individual participates in this destiny and cannot extricate himself.

And destiny is inseparably united with freedom. Therefore, individual guilt participates in the creation of the universal destiny of mankind and in the creation of the special destiny of the social group to which a person belongs. The individual is not guilty of the crimes performed by members of his group if he himself did not commit them. The citizens of a city are not guilty of the crimes committed in their city; but they are guilty as participants in the destiny of man as a whole and in the destiny of their city in particular; for their acts in which freedom was united with destiny have contributed to the destiny in which they participate. They are guilty, not of committing the crimes of which their group is accused, but of contributing to the destiny in which these crimes happened. In this indirect sense, even the victims of tyranny in a nation are guilty of this tyranny. But so are the subjects of other nations and of mankind as a whole. For the destiny of falling under the power of a tyranny, even a criminal tyranny, is a part of the universal destiny of man to be estranged from what he essentially is.

If accepted, such considerations would restrain victorious nations from exploiting their victory in the name of the assumed "collective guilt" of the conquered nation. And they would constrain every individual within the conquered nation, even if he suffered in consequence of his resistance against the crimes committed by her, to accept part of the responsibility for the destiny of his nation. He himself, perhaps unwittingly and unwillingly but nevertheless responsibly, helped to prepare, or to retain, or to aggravate the conditions out of which the actual crime developed.

*

## SELF-DESTRUCTION AND EVIL

*That estrangement is experienced both individually and collectively becomes especially clear in this selection from the* Systematic Theology, *vol. 2 (pp. 59-68). Here, Tillich draws on his ontology to describe self-destruction and world evil. Note especially that, under the conditions of existence, the basic ontological structure, in which self and world mutually co-inhere, is disrupted. Further, each of the ontological polarities now no longer displays unity. Now there is separation. The tension and anxiety that characterized the polarities in essential union are now dissolved into destruction and despair. Separating from one another, each element in its polarity undergoes distortion into a particular destructive force: freedom into arbitrariness, destiny into mechanical necessity; dynamics into chaos, form into rigid formalism; individualization into loneliness or subjectivism, participation into collectivization.*

### 1. SELF-LOSS AND WORLD-LOSS IN THE STATE OF ESTRANGEMENT

Man finds himself, together with his world, in existential estrangement, unbelief, *hubris*, and concupiscence. Each expression of the estranged state contradicts man's essential being, his potency for goodness. It contradicts the created structure of himself and his world and their interdependence. And self-contradiction drives toward self-destruction. The elements of essential being which move against each other tend to annihilate each other and the whole to which they belong. Destruction under the conditions of existential estrangement is not caused by some external force. It is not the work of special divine or demonic interferences, but it is the consequence of the structure of estrangement itself. One can describe this structure with a seemingly paradoxical term, "structure of destruction" — pointing to the fact that destruction has no independent standing in the whole of reality but that it is dependent on the structure of that in and upon which it acts destructively. Here, as everywhere in the whole of being, nonbeing is dependent on being, the negative on the positive, death on life. Therefore, even destruction has structures. It "aims" at chaos; but, as long as chaos is not attained, destruction must follow the structures of wholeness; and if chaos is attained, both structure and destruction have vanished.

As previously shown, the basic structure of finite being is the polarity of self and world. Only in man is this polarity fulfilled. Only man has a completely centered self and a structured universe to which he belongs and at which he is able to look at the same time. All other beings within our experience are only partly centered and consequently bound to their environment. Man also has environment, but he has it as a part of his world. He can and does transcend it with every word he speaks. He is free to make his world into an object which he beholds, and he is free to make himself into an object upon which he looks. In this situation of finite freedom he can lose himself and his world, and the loss of one necessarily includes the loss of the other. This is the basic "structure of destruction", and it includes all others. The analysis of this structure is the first step to the understanding of what is often described as "evil". . . .

Self-loss as the first and basic mark of evil is the loss of one's determining center; it is the disintegration of the centered self by disruptive drives which cannot be brought into unity. So long as they are centered, these drives constitute the person as a whole. If they move against one another, they split from the person. The further the disruption goes, the more the being of man as man is threatened. Man's centered self may break up, and, with the loss of self, man loses his world.

Self-loss is the loss of one's determining center, the disintegration of the unity of the person. This is manifest in moral conflicts and in psychopathological disruptions, independently or interdependently. The horrifying experience of "falling to pieces" gets hold of the person. To the degree in which this happens, one's world also falls to pieces. It ceases to be a world, in the sense of a meaningful whole. Things no longer speak to man; they lose their power to enter into a meaningful encounter with man, because man himself has lost this power. In extreme cases the complete unreality of one's world is felt; nothing is left except the awareness of one's own empty self. Such experiences are extreme, but extreme situations reveal possibilities in the ordinary situation. Possibilities of disruption are always present in man as a fully centered being. He cannot take his centeredness for granted. It is a form but not an empty one. It is actual only in unity with its content. The form of centeredness gives to the self the center which it needs to be what it is. There is no empty self, no pure subjectivity. Under the control of *hubris* and concupiscence, the self can approach the state of disintegration. The attempt of the finite self to be the center of everything gradually has the effect of its ceasing to be the center of anything. Both self and world are threatened. Man becomes a limited self, in dependence on a limited environment. He has lost his world; he has only his environment.

This fact includes the basic criticism of the environmental theories of man. They assert a view of man's essential nature which actually describes man's existential estrangement *from* his essential nature. Man essentially has a world because he has a fully centered self. He is able to transcend every given environment in the direction of his world. Only the loss of his world subjects him to the bondage of an environment which is not really *his* environment, namely, the result of a creative encounter with his world represented by a part of it. Man's true environment is the universe, and every special environment is qualified as a section of the universe. Only in estrangement can man be described as a mere object of environmental impact.

### 2. THE CONFLICTS IN THE ONTOLOGICAL POLARITIES IN THE STATE OF ESTRANGEMENT

#### a. *The separation of freedom from destiny*

The interdependence of self-loss and world-loss in the state of estrangement is manifest in the interdependent loss of the polar elements of being. The first of these are freedom and destiny. In essential being, i.e., the state of dreaming innocence, freedom and destiny lie within each other, distinct but not separated, in tension but not in conflict. They are rooted in the ground of being, i.e., the source of both of them and the ground of their polar unity. In the moment of aroused freedom a process starts in which freedom separates itself from the destiny to which it belongs. It becomes arbitrariness. Willful acts are acts in which freedom moves toward the separation from destiny. Under the control of *hubris* and concupiscence, freedom ceases to relate itself to the objects provided by destiny. It relates itself to an indefinite number of contents. When man makes himself the center of the universe, freedom loses its definiteness. Indefinitely and arbitrarily, freedom turns to objects, persons, and things which are completely contingent upon the choosing subject and which therefore can be replaced by others of equal contingency and ultimate unrelatedness. Existentialism, supported by depth psychology, described the dialectics of this situation in terms of the restlessness, emptiness, and meaninglessness connected with it. If no essential relation between a free agent and his objects exists, no choice is objectively preferable to any other; no commitment to a cause or a person is meaningful; no dominant purpose can be established. The indications coming from one's destiny remain unnoticed or are disregarded. This certainly is the description of an extreme situation; but in its radicalism it can reveal a basic trend in the state of universal estrangement.

To the degree to which freedom is distorted into arbitrariness, destiny is distorted into mechanical necessity. If man's freedom is not directed by destiny or if it is a series of contingent acts of arbitrariness, it falls under the control of forces which move against one another without a deciding center. What seems to be free proves to be conditioned by internal compulsions and external causes. Parts of the self overtake the center and determine it without being united with the other parts. A contingent motive replaces the center which is supposed to unite the motives in a centered decision; but it is unable to do so. This is the ontological character of the state described in classical theology as the "bondage of the will". In view of this "structure of destruction", one could say: Man has used his freedom to waste his freedom; and it is his destiny to lose his destiny.

The distortion of freedom into arbitrariness and of destiny into mechanical necessity is mirrored in the traditional controversy between interdeterminism and determinism. Like the environmental theory of man, indeterminism as well as determinism is a theory of man's essential nature in terms which are descriptions of man's estranged nature. Indeterminism makes man's freedom a matter of contingency. In doing so, it removes the very responsibility which it tried to preserve against determinism. And determinism surrenders man's freedom to mechanical necessity, transforming him into a completely conditioned thing which, as such, has no destiny — not even the destiny of having a *true* theory of determinism; for under the control of mechanical necessity there is neither truth nor destiny. Indeterminism, as well as determinism, is a mirror of man's state of estrangement (with respect to freedom and destiny!).

### b. *The separation of dynamics from form*

Every living being (and, in terms of analogy, every being) drives beyond itself and beyond the given form through which it has being. In man's essential nature, dynamics and form are united. Even if a given form is transcended, this happens in terms of form. In essential being there are forms of the self-transcendence of form. Their unity with the dynamics of being is never disrupted. One can see this unity fragmentarily in personalities in whom grace is effective, in the secular as well as the religious realm. In contrast to such "symbols of reunion", the existential disruption of dynamics and form is obvious. Under the control of *hubris* and concupiscence, man is driven in all directions without any definite aim and content. His dynamics are distorted into a formless urge for self-transcendence. It is not the new form which attracts the self-transcendence of the person; the dynamics has become an aim in itself. One can speak of the "temptation of the new", which in itself is a necessary element in all creative self-actualization but which in distortion sacrifices the creative for the new. Nothing real is created if the form is lacking, for nothing is real without form.

Yet form without dynamics is equally destructive. If a form is abstracted from the dynamics in which it is created and is imposed on the dynamics to which it does not belong, it becomes external law. It is oppressive and produces either legalism without creativity or the rebellious outbreaks of dynamic forces leading to chaos and often, in reaction, to stronger ways of suppression. Such experiences belong to man's predicament in individual as well as in social life, in religion as well as in culture. There is a continuous flight from law to chaos and from chaos to law. There is a continuous breaking of vitality by form and of form by vitality. But, if the one side disappears, the other does also. Dynamics, vitality, and the drive to form-breaking end in chaos and emptiness. They lose themselves in their separation from form. And form, structure, and law end in rigidity and emptiness. They lose themselves in their separation from dynamics.

This includes the basic criticism of all doctrines of man which describe man's essential nature either in terms of mere dynamics or in terms of mere form. . . . If man is understood as essentially unlimited libido or unlimited will to power, the basis for such understanding is not man's essential nature but his state of existential estrangement. The inability to reach a form in which the dynamics of man's nature are preliminary or lastingly satisfied is an expression of man's estrangement from himself and the essential unity of dynamics and form. The same criticism must be applied to interpretations of human nature which deprive him of the dynamics in his being by reducing his true being to a system of logical, moral, and aesthetic forms to which he must conform. Common-sense philosophies, as well as some rationalistic and idealistic doctrines of man, eliminate the dynamics in man's self-realization. Creativity is replaced by subjection to law — a characteristic of man in estrangement.

Both types of the doctrine of man — the dynamic and the formal — describe man's existential predicament. This is their truth and the limit of their truth.

### c. The separation of individualization from participation

Life individualizes in all its forms; at the same time, mutual participation of being in "being" maintains the unity of being. The two poles are interdependent. The more individualized a being is, the more it is able to participate. Man as the completely individualized being participates in the world in its totality through perception, imagination, and action. In principle, there are no limits to his participation, since he is a completely centered self. In the state of estrangement man is shut within himself and cut off from participation. At the same time, he falls under the power of objects which tend to make him a mere object without a self. If subjectivity separates itself from objectivity, the objects swallow the empty shell of subjectivity.

This situation has been described sociologically and psychologically. These descriptions have shown the interdependence of the loneliness of the individual and his submergence in the collective in a convincing way. However, they are directed toward a particular historical situation, predominantly our own. They give the impression that the situation to which they point is historically and sociologically conditioned and would change basically with a change in conditions. Theology must join existentialism in showing the universally human character of loneliness in interdependence with submergence in the collective. It is true that special situations reveal more sharply special elements in man's existential situation. They reveal them, but they do not create them. The danger of depersonalization of "objectivization" (becoming a thing) is most outspoken in Western industrial society. But there are dangers of the same character in all societies; for the separation of individualization from participation is a mark of estrangement generally. These dangers belong to the structures of destruction and are grounded in the level of evil in all history.

This situation is also mirrored in those doctrines of man which claim to describe man's essential nature but which give a true account only about man's estrangement. Isolated subjectivity appears in idealistic epistemologies which reduce man to a cognitive subject (*ens cogitans*), who perceives, analyzes, and controls reality. The act of knowing is deprived of any participation of the total subject in the total object. There is no *eros* in the way in which the subject approaches the object and in which the object gives itself to the subject. On some levels of abstraction this is necessary; but if it determines the cognitive approach as a whole, it is a symptom of estrangement. And, since man is a part of his world, he himself becomes a mere object among objects. He becomes a part of the physically calculable whole, thus becoming a thoroughly calculable object himself. This is the case whether the psychological level is explained physiologically and chemically or whether it is described in terms of independent psychological mechanisms. In both cases a theoretical objectivation is carried through which can be and is being used for the practical dealing with men as though they were mere objects. The situation of estrangement is mirrored in both the theoretical and the practical encounter with man as a mere object. Both are "structures of self-destruction", i.e., basic sources of evil.

### 3. FINITUDE AND ESTRANGEMENT

#### a. *Death, finitude, and guilt*

Estranged from the ultimate power of being, man is determined by his finitude. He is given over to his natural fate. He came from nothing, and he returns to nothing. He is under the domination of death and is driven by the anxiety of having to die. This, in fact, is the first answer to the question about the relation of sin and death. In conformity with biblical religion, it asserts that man is naturally mortal. Immortality as a natural quality of man is not a Christian doctrine, though it is possibly a Platonic doctrine. But even Plato has Socrates put a question mark on the very arguments for the immortality of the soul which Socrates develops in the discussions prior to his death. Certainly, the nature of the eternal life which he attributes to the soul has little resemblance to the popular beliefs of many Christians about the "hereafter". Plato speaks of the participation of the soul in the eternal realm of essences (ideas), of its fall from and possible return to this realm — though not a realm in any spatial or temporal sense. In the biblical story of paradise a quite different interpretation of the relation of the Fall and death is given. The biblical symbols are even farther removed from the popular image of immortality. According to the Genesis account, man comes from dust and returns to dust. He has immortality only as long as he is allowed to eat from the tree of life, the tree which carries the divine food or the food of eternal life. The symbolism is obvious. Participation in the eternal makes man eternal; separation from the eternal leaves man in his natural finitude. It was therefore in line with these ideas that the early Church Fathers called the sacramental food of the Lord's Supper the "medicine of immortality", and that the Eastern church let the message of the Christ focus on his resurrection as the moment in which eternal life is provided for those who are otherwise left to their natural mortality. In estrangement man is left to his finite nature of having to die. Sin does not produce death but gives to death the power which is conquered only in participation in the eternal. The idea that the "Fall" has physically changed the cellular or psychological structure of man (and nature?) is absurd and unbiblical.

If man is left to his "having to die", the essential anxiety about nonbeing is transformed into the horror of death. Anxiety about nonbeing is present in everything finite. It is consciously or unconsciously effective in the whole process of living. Like the beating of the heart, it is always present, although one is not always aware of it. It belongs to the potential state of dreaming innocence, as well as to the contested and decided unity with God as expressed in the picture of Jesus as the Christ. The dramatic description of the anxiety of Jesus in having to die confirms the universal character of the relation of finitude and anxiety.

Under the conditions of estrangement, anxiety has a different character, brought on by the element of guilt. The loss of one's potential eternity is experienced as something for which one is responsible in spite of its universal tragic actuality. Sin is the sting of death, not its physical cause. It transforms the anxious awareness of one's having to die into the painful realizaton of a lost eternity. For this reason the anxiety about having to die can be connected with the desire to get rid of one's self. One desires annihilation in order to escape death in its nature, not only as end, but also as guilt. Under the condition of estrangement, anxiety about death is more than anxiety about annihilation. It makes death an evil, a structure of destruction.

The transformation of essential finitude into existential evil is a general characteristic of the state of estrangement. It has been depicted most recently in both Christian and non-Christian analyses of the human situation, recently and very powerfully in existentialist literature. Such descriptions are acceptable — and extremely important — for theology, if the sharp distinction between finitude and estrangement, as illustrated in the analysis of death, is maintained. If this is not done, the description, no matter how much valuable material it provides, must be revised in the light of the doctrine of creation and the distinction between essential and existential being.

*

## JESUS AS THE CHRIST

*Essential to Tillich's basic christological approach is his insistence that the very name "Jesus Christ" is an intersubjective event, occurring when followers are impelled to say of Jesus, "Thou art the Christ." Christology, for Tillich, lives from an event that is both a "fact" occurring in history, but also one that never occurs apart from a "reception" by believing subjects. Here, Tillich also indicates why he viewed the biblical witness to Jesus Christ neither as just a historical record of the fact of Jesus' life, nor as only a confessional testimony of Christians who believe without or in spite of fact. Rather, he interpreted the biblical witness as a particular kind of "picture", an "expressionist portrait", enabling its viewers to participate in the most profound meaning of Jesus Christ. This "expressionist Christology" is guided by an artistic sensibility that seeks to steer between the naturalistic and "photographic" drives for reality in the "life of Jesus" quests of the nineteenth century, on the one hand; and the subjective, idealizing tendencies to make christological assertions divorced from history, on the other. At the heart of Tillich's christological approach, then, is a notion of the biblical picture of Jesus the Christ that plays out his preference for the expressionist art and the "historical realism" affirmed earlier in his writing (see "Realism and Faith," above pp. 66ff.). The following selections are from Systematic Theology, vol. 2 (pp. 97-118, passim).*

## 1. THE NAME "JESUS CHRIST"

Christianity is what it is through the affirmation that Jesus of Nazareth, who has been called "the Christ", is actually the Christ, namely, he who brings the new state of things, the New Being. Wherever the assertion that Jesus is the Christ is maintained, there is the Christian message; wherever this assertion is denied, the Christian message is not affirmed. Christianity was born, not with the birth of the man who is called "Jesus," but in the moment in which one of his followers was driven to say to him, "Thou art the Christ." And Christianity will live as long as there are people who repeat this assertion. For the event on which Christianity is based has two sides: the fact which is called "Jesus of Nazareth" and the reception of this fact by those who received him as the Christ. The first of those who received him as the Christ in the early tradition was named Simon Peter. This event is reported in a story in the center of the Gospel of Mark; it takes place near Caesarea Philippi and marks the turning point in the narrative. The moment of the disciples' acceptance of Jesus as the Christ is also the moment of his rejection by the powers of history. This gives the story its tremendous symbolic power. He who is the Christ has to die for his acceptance of the title "Christ". And those who continue to call him the Christ must assert the paradox that he who is supposed to overcome existential estrangement must participate in it and its self-destructive consequences. This is the central story of the Gospel. Reduced to its simplest form, it is the statement that the man Jesus of Nazareth is the Christ.

The first step demanded of christological thought is an interpretation of the name "Jesus Christ", preferably in the light of the Caesarea Philippi story. One must clearly see that Jesus Christ is not an individual name, consisting of a first and a second name, but that it is the combination of an individual name — the name of a certain man who lived in Nazareth between the years 1 and 30 — with the title "the Christ", expressing in the mythological tradition a special figure with a special function. The Messiah — in Greek, *Christos* — is the "anointed one" who has received an unction from God enabling him to establish the reign of God in Israel and in the world. Therefore, the name Jesus Christ must be understood as "Jesus who is called the Christ", or "Jesus who is the Christ", or "Jesus as the Christ", or "Jesus the Christ". The context determines which of these interpretative phrases should be used; but one of them should be used in order to keep the original meaning of the name "Jesus Christ" alive, not only in theological thought but also in

213

ecclesiastical practice. Christian preaching and teaching must continually re-emphasize the paradox that the man Jesus is called the Christ — a paradox which is often drowned in the liturgical and homiletic use of "Jesus Christ" as a proper name. "Jesus Christ" means — originally, essentially, and permanently — "Jesus who is the Christ".

## 2. EVENT, FACT AND RECEPTION

Jesus as the Christ is both a historical fact and a subject of believing reception. One cannot speak the truth about the event on which Christianity is based without asserting both sides. Many theological mistakes could have been avoided if these two sides of the "Christian event" had been emphasized with equal strength. And Christian theology as a whole is undercut if one of them is completely ignored. If theology ignores the fact to which the name of Jesus of Nazareth points, it ignores the basic Christian assertion that Essential God-Manhood has appeared within existence and subjected itself to the conditions of existence without being conquered by them. If there were no personal life in which existential estrangement had been overcome, the New Being would have remained a quest and an expectation and would not be a reality in time and space. Only if the existence is conquered in *one* point — a personal life, representing existence as a whole — is it conquered in principle, which means "in beginning and in power". This is the reason that Christian theology must insist on the actual fact to which the name Jesus of Nazareth refers. It is why the church prevailed against competing groups in the religious movements of the first centuries. This is the reason that the church had to fight a vehement struggle with the gnostic-docetic elements within itself — elements which entered Christianity as early as the New Testament. And this is the reason that anyone who takes seriously the historical approach to the New Testament and its critical methods becomes suspect of docetic ideas, however strongly he may emphasize the factual side of the message of Jesus the Christ.

Nevertheless, the other side, the believing reception of Jesus *as* the Christ, calls for equal emphasis. Without this reception the Christ would not have been the Christ, namely, the manifestation of the New Being in time and space. If Jesus had not impressed himself as the Christ on his disciples and through them upon all following generations, the man who is called Jesus of Nazareth would perhaps be remembered as a historically and religiously important person. As

such, he would belong to the preliminary revelation, perhaps to the preparatory segment of the history of revelation. He could then have been a
prophetic anticipation of the New Being, but not the final manifestation
of the New Being itself. He would not have been the Christ even if he
had claimed to be the Christ. The receptive side of the Christian event is
as important as the factual side. And only their unity creates the event
upon which Christianity is based. According to later symbolism, the
Christ is the head of the church, which is his body. As such, they are
necessarily interdependent. *Vol. 2, pp. 97-9*

\*

### 3. HISTORY AND THE CHRIST

There was an urgent desire to discover the reality of this man, Jesus of
Nazareth, behind the coloring and covering traditions which are almost
as old as the reality itself. So the research for the so-called "historical
Jesus" started. Its motives were religious and scientific at the same time.
The attempt was courageous, noble, and extremely significant in many
respects. Its theological consequences are numerous and rather
important. But, seen in the light of its basic intention, the attempt of historical criticism to find the empirical truth about Jesus of Nazareth was
a failure. The historical Jesus, namely, the Jesus behind the symbols of
his reception as the Christ, not only did not appear but receded farther
and farther with every new step. The history of the attempts to write a
"life of Jesus", elaborated by Albert Schweitzer in his early work, *The
Quest of the Historical Jesus,* is still valid. His own constructive attempt has
been corrected. Scholars, whether conservative or radical, have
become more cautious, but the methodological situation has not
changed. This became manifest when R. Bultmann's bold program of a
"demythologization of the New Testament" aroused a storm in all
theological camps and the slumber of Barthianism with respect to the
historical problem was followed by an astonished awakening. But
the result of the new (and very old) questioning is not a picture of the
so-called historical Jesus but the insight that there is no picture behind
the biblical one which could be made scientifically probable.

   This situation is not a matter of a preliminary shortcoming of historical research which will some day be overcome. It is caused by the nature
of the sources itself. The reports about Jesus of Nazareth are those of
Jesus as the Christ, given by persons who had received him as the
Christ. Therefore, if one tries to find the real Jesus behind the picture of

Jesus as the Christ, it is necessary critically to separate the elements which belong to the factual side of the event from the elements which belong to the receiving side. In doing so, one sketches a "Life of Jesus"; and innumerable such sketches have been made. In many of them scientific honesty, loving devotion, and theological interest have worked together. In others critical detachment and even malevolent rejection are visible. But none can claim to be a probable picture which is the result of the tremendous scientific toil dedicated to this task for two hundred years. At best, they are more or less probable results, able to be the basis neither of an acceptance nor of a rejection of the Christian faith.

In view of this situation, there have been attempts to reduce the picture of the historical Jesus to the "essentials", to elaborate a *Gestalt* while leaving the particulars open to doubt. But this is not a way out. Historical research cannot paint an essential picture after all the particular traits have been eliminated because they are questionable. It remains dependent on the particulars. Consequently, the pictures of the historical Jesus in which the form of a "Life of Jesus" is wisely avoided still differ from one another as much as those in which such self-restriction is not applied. . . .

The search for the historical Jesus was an attempt to discover a minimum of reliable facts about the man Jesus of Nazareth, in order to provide a safe foundation for the Christian faith. This attempt was a failure. Historical research provided probabilities about Jesus of a higher or lower degree. On the basis of these probabilities, it sketched "Lives of Jesus". But they were more like novels than biographies; they certainly could not provide a safe foundation for the Christian faith. Christianity is not based on the acceptance of a historical novel; it is based on the witness to the messianic character of Jesus by people who were not interested at all in a biography of the Messiah. . . .   *Vol. 2, pp. 102-3, 105*

\*

## 4. FAITH AND HISTORICAL SKEPTICISM

It is necessary systematically to raise once more a question which is continuously being asked with considerable religious anxiety. Does not the acceptance of the historical method for dealing with the source documents of the Christian faith introduce a dangerous insecurity into the thought and life of the church and of every individual Christian? Could not historical research lead to a complete skepticism about the biblical records? Is it not imaginable that historical criticism could come to the judgment that the man Jesus of Nazareth never lived? Did not some scholars, though only a few and not very important ones, make just this statement? And even if such a statement can never be made with certainty, is it not destructive for the Christian faith if the nonexistence of Jesus can somehow be made probable, no matter how low the degree of probability? In reply, let us first reject some insufficient and misleading answers. It is inadequate to point out that historical research has not yet given any evidence to support such skepticism. Certainly, it has not yet! But the anxious question remains of whether it could not do so sometime in the future! Faith cannot rest on such unsure ground. The answer, taken from the "not-yet" of skeptical evidence, is insufficient. There is another possible answer, which, though not false, is misleading. This is to say that the historical foundation of Christianity is an essential element of the Christian faith itself and that this faith, through its own power, can overrule skeptical possibilities within historical criticism. It can, it is maintained, guarantee the existence of Jesus of Nazareth and at least the essentials in the biblical picture. But we must analyze this answer carefully, for it is ambiguous. The problem is: Exactly what can faith guarantee? And the inevitable answer is that faith can guarantee only its own foundation, namely, the appearance of that reality which has created the faith. This reality is the New Being, who conquers existential estrangement and thereby makes faith possible. This alone faith is able to guarantee — and that because its own existence is identical with the presence of the New Being. Faith itself is the immediate (not mediated by conclusions) evidence of the New Being within and under the conditions of existence. Precisely that is guaranteed by the very nature of the Christian faith. No historical criticism can question the immediate awareness of those who find themselves transformed into the state of faith. One is reminded of the Augustinian-Cartesian refutation of radical skepticism. That tradition pointed to the immediacy of a self-consciousness which guaranteed itself by its participation in being. By analogy, one must say that participation, not historical argument, guarantees the reality of the event upon which Christianity is based. It guarantees a personal life in which the New Being has conquered the old being. But it does not guarantee his name to be Jesus of Nazareth. Historical doubt concerning the existence and the life of someone with this name cannot be overruled. He might have had another name. (This is a historically absurd, but logically necessary, consequence of the historical method.) Whatever his name, the New Being was and is actual in this man.

217

But here a very important question arises. How can the New Being who is called "the Christ" transform reality if no concrete trait of his nature is left? Kierkegaard exaggerates when he says that it is sufficient for the Christian faith nakedly to assert that in the years 1-30 God sent his son. Without the concreteness of the New Being, its newness would be empty. Only if existence is conquered concretely and in its manifold aspects, is it actually conquered. The power which has created and preserved the community of the New Being is not an abstract statement about its appearance; it is the picture of him in whom it has appeared. No special trait of this picture can be verified with certainty. But it can be definitely asserted that through this picture the New Being has power to transform those who are transformed by it. This implies that there is an *analogia imaginis,* namely, an analogy between the picture and the actual personal life from which it has arisen. It was this reality, when encountered by the disciples, which created the picture. And it was, and still is, this picture which mediates the transforming power of the New Being. One can compare the *analogia imaginis* suggested here with the *analogia entis* — not as a method of knowing God but as a way (actually the only way) of speaking of God. In both cases it is impossible to push behind the analogy and to the state directly what can be stated only indirectly, that is, symbolically in the knowledge of God and mediated through faith in the knowledge of Jesus. But this indirect, symbolic, and mediated character of our knowledge does not diminish its truth-value. For in both cases what is given to us as material for our indirect knowledge is dependent on the object of our knowledge. The symbolic material through which we speak about God is an expression of the divine self-manifestation, and the mediated material which is given to us in the biblical picture of the Christ is the result of the reception of the New Being and its transforming power on the part of the first witness. The concrete biblical material is not guaranteed by faith in respect to empirical factuality; but it is guaranteed as an adequate expression of the transforming power of the New Being in Jesus as the Christ. Only in this sense does faith guarantee the biblical picture of Jesus. And it can be shown that, in all periods of the history of the church, it was this picture which created both the church and the Christian, and not a hypothetical description of what may lie behind the biblical picture. But the picture has this creative power, because the power of the New Being is expressed in and through it. This consideration leads to the distinction between an imaginary picture and a real picture. A picture imagined by the same contemporaries of Jesus would have expressed their untransformed existence and their quest for a New Being. But it would not have been the New Being itself. That is tested by its transforming power.

The word "picture" may lead to another analogy. Those who try to push behind the biblical picture to discover the "historical Jesus" with the help of the critical method try to provide a photograph (corroborated by a phonograph and, if possible, a psychograph). A good photograph is not without subjective elements, and no one would deny that every empirical description of a historical figure has such elements. The opposite attitude would be to interpret the New Testament picture as the painted projection of the experiences and ideals of the most religiously profound minds in the period of the Emperor Augustus. The idealistic style of art is analogous to this attitude. The third way is that of an "expressionist" portrait ("expressionist" used in the sense of the predominant artistic style in most periods of history — rediscovered in our period). In this approach a painter would try to enter into the deepest levels of the person with whom he deals. And he could do so only by a profound participation in the reality and the meaning of his subject matter. Only then could he paint this person in such a way that his surface traits are neither reproduced as in photography (or naturalistically imitated) nor idealized according to the painter's ideal of beauty but are used to express what the painter has experienced through his participation in the being of his subject. This third way is meant when we use the term "real picture" with reference to the Gospel records of Jesus as the Christ. With Adolf Schlatter we can say that we know nobody as well as Jesus. In contrast to all other persons, the participation in him takes place not in the realm of contingent human individuality (which can never be approached completely by any other individual) but in the realm of his own participation in God, a participation which, in spite of the mystery of every person's relation to God, has a universality in which everyone can participate. Of course, in terms of historical documentation we do know many people better than Jesus. But in terms of personal participation in his being, we do not know anyone better because his being is the New Being which is universally valid for every human being.

A very interesting argument against the position taken here must be mentioned. It is based on the common assumption that faith, by its very nature, includes an element of risk and on the question asked by this argument: Why not take the risk of historical uncertainty as well? The affirmation that Jesus is the Christ is an act of faith and consequently of daring courage. It is not an arbitrary leap into darkness but a decision in which elements of immediate participation and therefore certitude are mixed with elements of strangeness and therefore incertitude and doubt. But doubt is not the opposite of faith; it is an element of faith. Therefore, there is no faith without risk. The risk of faith is that it could affirm a wrong symbol of ultimate concern, a symbol which does not really express ultimacy (as, e.g., Dionysus or one's nation). But this risk lies in quite a different dimension from the risk of accepting uncertain historical facts. It is wrong, therefore, to consider the risk concerning uncertain historical facts as part of the risk of faith. The risk of faith is existential; it concerns the totality of our being, while the risk of historical judgments is theoretical and open to permanent scientific correction. Here are two different dimensions which should never be confused. A wrong faith can destroy the meaning of one's life; a wrong historical judgment cannot. It is misleading, therefore, to use the word "risk" for both dimensions in the same sense.

## 5. THE BIBLICAL WITNESS TO JESUS AS THE CHRIST

In all aspects the New Testament is the document wherein there appears the picture of Jesus as the Christ in its original and basic form. All other documents, from the Apostolic Fathers to the writings of the present-day theologians, are dependent upon this original document. In itself the New Testament is an integral part of the event which it documents. The New Testament represents the receptive side of that event and provides, as such, a witness to its factual side. If this is true, one can say that the New Testament as a whole is the basic document of the event upon which the Christian faith rests. In this respect the several parts of the New Testament agree. In other respects there is much difference. All New Testament books are united, however, in the assertion that Jesus is the Christ. It was the desire of so-called *liberal theology* to go behind the biblical records of Jesus as the Christ. In such an attempt the first three Gospels emerge as by far the most important part of the New Testament, and this is what they become in the estimation of many modern theologians. But the moment when one realizes that the Christian faith cannot be built on such a foundation, the Fourth Gospel and the Epistles become equally important with the Synoptics. One then sees that there is no conflict between them in their one decisive point of pronouncing Jesus as the Christ. The difference between the Synoptic Gospels and the other literature of the New Testament — including the Fourth Gospel — is that the former give the picture on which the assertion that Jesus is the Christ is based, while the latter give the elaboration of this assertion and its implications for Christian thought and life. This distinction is not exclusive, for it is a difference in emphasis, not in substance. Harnack was wrong, therefore, when he contrasted the message given by Jesus with the message about Jesus. There is no substantial difference between the message given by the Synoptic Jesus and the message about Jesus given in Paul's Epistles. This statement is independent of the attempts of liberal theology to deprive the first three Gospels of all Paulinian elements. Historical criticism can do that with a certain degree of probability. But the more successfully this is done, the less remains of the Synoptic picture of Jesus as the Christ. This picture and Paul's message of the Christ do not contradict each other. The New Testament witness is unanimous in its witness to Jesus as the Christ. This witness is the foundation of the Christian church.　*Vol. 2, pp. 113-8*

\*

# THE NEW BEING IN JESUS AS THE CHRIST

*The power of the New Being in Jesus Christ is not for Tillich, as for earlier metaphysical traditions of the incarnation, the power of one who is a God-man, i.e. one who is "truly God and truly man". (See McKelway,* The Systematic Theology of Paul Tillich, *p. 168.) It is, for Tillich, more the power of a biblical* picture, *which by means of all the lines and shades of color that depict Jesus' concrete personal life, allows a divinely grounded, essential humanness to shine forth under the conditions of estranged existence. For a further study of the many aspects of this picture — its central symbols of cross and resurrection, its expression of New Being in Jesus' words, deeds and sufferings — readers must attend to the entire christology presented in vol. 2* (Systematic Theology, *pp. 97-180). Tillich summarized the power of the New Being, again drawing from a language of expressionist portraiture: "It shines through as the power of the New Being in a three-fold color: first and decisively, as the undisrupted unity of [Jesus'] being with God; second, as the serenity and majesty of him who preserves this unity against all the attacks coming from estranged existence; and third, as the self-surrendering love which represents and actualizes the divine love in taking the existential self-destruction upon himself." (*Systematic Theology, *vol. 2, p. 138.) In volume 2, Tillich does not comment on the ontological polarities when describing how Jesus Christ as New Being heals the estrangement characterized by the separation of those polarities. That description must await volume 3, in which Tillich further develops the*

*historical dimension of the New Being. The selections below are from*
Systematic Theology, *vol. 2 (pp. 118-36).*

## 1. THE NEW BEING AND THE NEW EON

According to eschatological symbolism, the Christ is the one who brings the new eon. When Peter called Jesus "the Christ", he expected the coming of a new state of things through him. This expectation is implicit in the title "Christ". But it was not fulfilled in accordance with the expectations of the disciples. The state of things, of nature as well as of history, remained unchanged, and he who was supposed to bring the new eon was destroyed by the powers of the old eon. This meant that the disciples either had to accept the breakdown of their hope or radically transform its content. They were able to choose the second way by identifying the New Being with the being of Jesus, the sacrificed. In the Synoptic records Jesus himself reconciled the messianic claim with the acceptance of a violent death. The same records show that the disciples resisted this combination. Only the experiences which are described as Easter and Pentecost created their faith in the paradoxical character of the messianic claim. It was Paul who gave the theological frame in which the paradox could be understood and justified. One approach to the solution of the problem was to state the distinction between the first and the second coming of the Christ. The new state of things will be created with the second coming, the return of the Christ in glory. In the period between the first and the second coming the New Being is present in him. He *is* the Kingdom of God. In him the eschatological expectation is fulfilled in principle. Those who participate in him participate in the New Being, though under the condition of man's existential predicament and, therefore, only fragmentarily and by anticipation.

New Being is essential being under the conditions of existence, conquering the gap between essence and existence. For the same idea Paul uses the term "new creature", calling those who are "in" Christ "new creatures". "In" is the preposition of participation; he who participates in the newness of being which is in Christ has become a new creature. It is a creative act by which this happens. Inasmuch as Jesus as the Christ is a creation of the divine Spirit, according to Synoptic theology, so is he who participates in the Christ made into a new creature by the Spirit. The estrangement of his existential from his essential being is conquered in principle, i.e., in power and as a beginning. The term "New Being", as used here, points directly to the cleavage between essential and existential being — and is the restorative principle of the whole of this theological system. The New Being is new in so far as it is the undistorted manifestation of essential being within and under the conditions of existence. It is new in two respects: it is new in contrast to the merely potential character of essential being; and it is new over against the estranged character of existential being. It is actual, conquering the estrangement of actual existence.

There are other ways of expressing the same idea. The New Being is new in so far as it is the conquest of the situation under the law — which is the old situation. The law is man's essential being standing against his existence, commanding and judging it. In so far as his essential being is taken into his existence and actualized in it, the law has ceased to be law for him. Where there is New Being, there is no commandment and no judgment. If, therefore, we call Jesus as the Christ the New Being, we say with Paul that the Christ is the end of the law.

In terms of the eschatological symbolism it can also be said that Christ is the end of existence. He is the end of existence lived in estrangement, conflicts, and self-destruction. The biblical idea that the hope of mankind for a new reality is fulfilled in Jesus as the Christ is an immediate consequence of the assertion that in him the New Being is present. His appearance is "realized eschatology" (Dodd). Of course, it is fulfillment "in principle", it is the manifestation of the power and the beginning of fulfillment. But it is realized eschatology in so far as no other principle of fulfillment can be expected. In him has appeared what fulfillment qualitatively means.

With the same qualification, one can say that in him history has come to an end, namely, that its preparatory period has reached its aim. Nothing qualitatively new in the dimension of the ultimate can be produced by history which is not implicitly present in the New Being in Jesus as the Christ. The assertion that the Christ is the "end" of history seems to be absurd in the light of the history of the last two thousand years. But it is not absurd if one understands the double sense of "end", namely, "finish" and "aim". In the sense of "finish", history has not yet come to an end. It goes on and shows all the characteristics of existential estrangement. It is the place in which finite freedom is at work, producing existential distortion and the great ambiguities of life. In the sense of "aim", history has come to an intrinsic end qualitatively, namely, in the appearance of the New Being as a historical reality. But, quantitatively considered, the actualization of the New Being within history is drawn into the distortions and ambiguities of man's historical predicament.

This oscillation between "already" and "not yet" is the experience which is symbolized in the tension between the first and second comings of the Christ; it belongs inseparably to the Christian existence.

## 2. THE NEW BEING APPEARING IN A PERSONAL LIFE

The New Being has appeared in a personal life, and for humanity it could not have appeared in any other way; for the potentialities of being are completely actual in personal life alone. Only a person, within our experience, is a fully developed self, confronting a world to which it belongs at the same time. Only in a person are the polarities of being complete. Only a person is completely individualized, and for just this reason he is able to participate without limits in his world. Only a person has an unlimited power of self-transcendence, and for just this reason he has the complete structure, the structure of rationality. Only a person has freedom, including all its characteristics, and for just this reason he alone has destiny. Only the person is finite freedom, which gives him the power of contradicting himself and returning to himself. Of no other being can all this be said. And only in such a being can the New Being appear. Only where existence is most radically existence — in him who is finite freedom — can existence be conquered.

But what happens to man happens implicitly to all realms of life, for in man all levels of being are present. He belongs to physical, biological, and psychological realms and is subject to their manifold degrees and the various relations between them. For this reason the philosophers of the Renaissance called man the "microcosmos". He is a universe in himself. What happens in him happens, therefore, by mutual universal participation. This, of course, is said in qualitative, not quantitative terms. Quantitatively speaking, the universe is largely indifferent to what happens in man. Qualitatively speaking, nothing happens in man that does not have a bearing on the elements which constitute the universe. This gives cosmic significance to the person and confirms the insight that only in a personal life can the New Being manifest itself.

*Vol. 2, pp. 118-21*

## 3. THE NEW BEING IN JESUS AS THE CHRIST AS THE CONQUEST OF ESTRANGEMENT

### a. *The New Being in the Christ and the marks of estrangement*

In all its concrete details the biblical picture of Jesus as the Christ confirms his character as the bearer of the New Being or as the one in whom the conflict between the essential unity of God and man and man's existential estrangement is overcome. Point by point, not only in the Gospel records but also in the Epistles, this picture of Jesus as the Christ contradicts the marks of estrangement which we have elaborated in the analysis of man's existential predicament. This is not surprising, since the analysis was partly dependent on the confrontation of man's existential predicament with the image of the New Being in the Christ.

According to the biblical picture of Jesus as the Christ, there are, in spite of all tensions, no traces of estrangement between him and God and consequently between him and himself and between him and his world (in its essential nature). The paradoxical character of his being consists in the fact that, although he has only finite freedom under the conditions of time and space, he is not estranged from the ground of his being. There are no traces of unbelief, namely, the removal of his personal center from the divine center which is the subject of his infinite concern. Even in the extreme situation of despair about his messianic work, he cries to his God who has forsaken him. In the same way the biblical picture shows no trace of *hubris* or self-elevation in spite of his awareness of his messianic vocation. In the critical moment in which Peter first calls him the Christ, he combines the acceptance of this title with the acceptance of his violent death, including the warning to his disciples not to make his messianic function public. This is equally emphasized in Paul's christological hymn, Philippians, chapter 2, where he combines the divine form of the transcendent Christ with the acceptance of the form of a servant. The Fourth Gospel provides the theological foundation for this in the passage ascribed to Jesus: "He who believes in me does not believe in me, but in Him who has sent me." Nor is there any trace of concupiscence in the picture. This point is stressed in the story of the temptation in the desert. Here the desires for food, acknowledgment, and unlimited power are used by Satan as the possible weak spots in the Christ. As the Messiah, he could fulfill these desires. But then he would have been demonic and would have ceased to be the Christ.

The conquest of estrangement by the New Being in Jesus as the

Christ should not be described in the term "the sinlessness of Jesus". This is a negative term and is used in the New Testament merely to show his victory over the messianic temptation (Letter to the Hebrews) to set forth the dignity of him who is the Christ in refusing to sacrifice himself by subjection to the destructive consequences of estrangement. There is, in fact, no enumeration of special sins which he did not commit, nor is there a day-by-day description of the ambiguities of life in which he proved to be unambiguously good. He rejects the term "good" as applicable to himself in isolation from God and puts the problem in the right place, namely, the uniqueness of his relation to God. His goodness is goodness only in so far as he participates in the goodness of God. Jesus, like every man, is finite freedom. Without that, he would not be equal with mankind and could not be the Christ. God alone is above freedom and destiny. In him alone the tensions of this and all other polarities are eternally conquered; in Jesus they are actual. The term "sinlessness" is a rationalization of the biblical picture of him who has conquered the forces of existential estrangement within existence. As early as in the New Testament, such rationalizations appear in several places, as, for example, in some miracle stories — the story of the empty tomb, the virgin birth, the bodily ascendance, etc. Whether it appears in stories or concepts, their character is always the same. Something positive is affirmed concerning the Christ (and, later on, of other biblical figures) and is interpreted in terms of negations which, in principle, are open to empirical verification. In this way a religious statement of existential-symbolic character is transformed into a theoretical statement of rational-objectifying character.

The biblical picture is thoroughly positive in showing a threefold emphasis: first, the complete finitude of the Christ; second, the reality of the temptations growing out of it; third, the victory over these temptations in so far as the defeat in them would have disrupted his relation to God and ruined his messianic vocation. Beyond these three points, which are based on the actual experience of the disciples, no inquiry is possible and meaningful, and especially not if sin is used in the singular, as it should be.                                        *Vol. 2, pp. 125-7*

*

### b.  The marks of his finitude

The seriousness of the temptation of the Christ is based on the fact that he is finite freedom. The degree to which the biblical picture of Jesus as the Christ stresses his finitude is remarkable. As a finite being, he is subject to the contingency of everything that is not by itself but is "thrown" into existence. He has to die, and he experiences the anxiety of having to die. This anxiety is described by the evangelists in the most vivid way. It is not relieved by the expectation of resurrection "after three days", or by the ecstasy of a substitutional self-sacrifice, or even by the ideal of the heroism of wise men such as Socrates. Like every man, he experiences the threat of the victory of nonbeing over being, as, for instance, in the limits of the span of life given to him. As in the case of all finite beings, he experiences the lack of a definite place. From his birth on, he appears strange and homeless in his world. He has bodily, social, and mental insecurity, is subject to want, and is expelled by his nation. In relation to other persons, his finitude is manifest in his loneliness, both in respect to the masses and in respect to his relatives and disciples. He struggles to make them understand, but during his life he never succeeds. His frequent desire for solitude shows that many hours of his daily life were filled with various finite concerns produced by his encounter with the world. At the same time, he is deeply affected by the misery of the masses and of everyone who turns to him. He accepts them, even though he will be rejected by them. He experiences all the tensions which follow from the self-relatedness of every finite person and proves the impossibility of penetrating into the center of anyone else.

In relation to reality as such, including things and persons, he is subject to uncertainty in judgment, risks of error, the limits of power, and the vicissitudes of life. The Fourth Gospel says of him that he *is* truth, but this does not mean that he *has* omniscience or absolute certainty. He *is* the truth in so far as his being — the New Being in him — conquers the untruth of existential estrangement. But being the truth is not the same as knowing the truth about all finite objects and situations. Finitude implies openness to error, and error belongs to the participation of the Christ in man's existential predicament. Error is evident in his ancient conception of the universe, his judgments about men, his interpretation of the historical moment, his eschatological imagination. If we finally look at his relation to himself, we can refer again to what was said about the seriousness of his temptations. They presuppose want and desire. We can also refer to his doubt about his own work, as in his hesitation to accept the messianic title, and, above all, his feeling of having been left alone by God without God's expected interference on the Cross.

All this belongs to the description of the finitude of Jesus as the Christ and has its place within the totality of his picture. It is *one* element along with others; but it must be emphasized against those who attribute to him a hidden omnipotence, omniscience, omnipresence, and eternity. The latter take away the seriousness of his finitude and with it the reality of his participation in existence.

### c. His participation in the tragic element of existence

Every encounter with reality, whether with situations, groups, or individuals, is burdened with practical and theoretical uncertainty. This uncertainty is caused not only by the finitude of the individual but also by the ambiguity of that which a person encounters. Life is marked by ambiguity, and one of the ambiguities is that of greatness and tragedy (which I shall deal with in Vol. 3). This raises the question of how the bearer of the New Being is involved in the tragic element of life. What is his relation to the ambiguity of tragic guilt? What is his relation to the tragic consequences of his being, including his actions and decisions, for those who are with him or who are against him and for those who are neither one nor the other?

The first and historically most important example in this area is the conflict of Jesus with the leaders of his nation. The ordinary Christian view is that their hostility toward him is unambiguously their religious and moral guilt. They decided against him, although they could have decided for him. But this "could" is just the problem. It removes the tragic element which universally belongs to existence. It places the leaders out of the context of humanity and makes them into representatives of unambiguous evil. But there is no unambiguous evil. This is acknowledged by Jesus when he refers to the traditions and when he expresses that he belongs to the "house of Israel". Although continuously persecuted by the Jews, Paul witnesses to their zeal to fulfill the law of God. The Pharisees were the pious ones of their time, and they represented the law of God, the preparatory revelation, without which the final revelation could not have happened. If Christians deny the tragic element in the encounter between Jesus and the Jews (and analogously between Paul and the Jews), they are guilty of a profound injustice. And this injustice early produced a Christian anti-Judaism which is one of the permanent sources of modern anti-Semitism. It is regrettable that even today much Christian instruction is consciously or unconsciously responsible for this kind of anti-Jewish feeling. This can be changed only if we frankly admit that the conflict between Jesus and his enemies was a tragic one. This means that Jesus was involved in the tragic element of guilt, in so far as he made his enemies inescapably guilty. This element of guilt did not touch his personal relation to God. It did not produce estrangement. It did not split his personal center. But it is an expression of his participation in existential estrangement, and its implication, namely, the ambiguity of creation and destruction. It was a profound insight into the tragic element of guilt when Kierkegaard questioned the right of anyone to let himself be killed for the truth. He who does so must know that he becomes tragically responsible for the guilt of those who kill him.

Many embarrassing questions have been asked about the relation of Jesus and Judas — from the New Testiment period on. One of the problems in the stories of the betrayal of Judas is indicated by Jesus himself. On the one hand, he asserts the providential necessity — the fulfillment of the prophecies — of the deed of Judas, and, on the other hand, he emphasizes the immensity of the personal guilt of Judas. The tragic and the moral elements in the guilt of Judas are equally stated. But, besides this more universal element of tragedy in the guilt of Judas, there is a special one. The betrayal presupposes that Judas belonged to the intimate group of disciples. And this could not have been the case without the will of Jesus. Implicitly, we have already referred to this point when we spoke of the errors in judgment which cannot be separated from finite existence. Explicitly, we must say that, as the story stands in the records (and this is the only question we are dealing with here), the innocent one becomes tragically guilty in respect to the very one who contributes to his own death. One should not try to escape these consequences, if one takes seriously the participation in the ambiguities of life, on the part of him who is the bearer of the New Being. If Jesus as the Christ were seen as a God walking on earth, he would be neither finite nor involved in tragedy. His judgment would be ultimate, and that means an unambiguous judgment. But, according to biblical symbolism, this is a matter of his "second coming" and is therefore connected with the transformation of reality as a whole. The Christ of the biblical picture takes upon himself the consequences of his tragic involvement in existence. The New Being in him has eternal significance also for those who caused his death, including Judas.

### d. His permanent unity with God

The conquest of existential estrangement in the New Being, which is the being of the Christ, does not remove finitude and anxiety, ambiguity and tragedy; but it does have the character of taking the negativities of existence into unbroken unity with God. The anxiety about having to die is not removed; it is taken into participation in the "will of God", i.e., in his directing creativity. His homelessness and insecurity with respect to a physical, social, and mental place are not diminished but rather increased to the last moment. Yet they are accepted in the power of a participation in a "transcendent place", which in actuality is no place but the eternal ground of every place and of every moment of time. His loneliness and his frustrated attempts in trying to be received by those to whom he came do not suddenly end in a final success; they are taken into the divine acceptance of that which rejects God, into the vertical line of the uniting love which is effective where the horizontal line from being to being is barred. Out of his unity with God he has unity with those who are separated from him and from one another by finite self-relatedness and existential self-seclusion. Both error and doubt equally are not removed but are taken into the participation in the divine life and thus indirectly into the divine omniscience. Both error and truth are taken into the transcendent truth. Therefore, we do not find symptoms of repression of doubt in the picture of Jesus as the Christ. Those who are not able to elevate their doubts into the truth which transcends every finite truth must repress them. They perforce become fanatical. Yet no traces of fanaticism are present in the biblical picture. Jesus does not claim absolute certitude for a finite conviction. He rejects the fanatical attitude of the disciples toward those who do not follow him. In the power of a certitude which transcends certitude and incertitude in matters of religion as well as secular life, he accepts incertitude as an element of finiteness. This also refers to the doubt about his own work — a doubt which breaks through most intensively on the Cross but still does not destroy his unity with God.

This is the picture of the New Being in Jesus as the Christ. It is not the picture of a divine-human automaton without serious temptation, real struggle, or tragic involvement in the ambiguities of life. Instead of that, it is the picture of a personal life which is subjected to all the consequences of existential estrangement but wherein estrangement is conquered in himself and a permanent unity is kept with God. Into this unity he accepts the negativities of existence without removing them. This is done by transcending them in the power of this unity. This is the New Being as it appears in the biblical picture of Jesus as the Christ.

## 4. THE HISTORICAL DIMENSION OF THE NEW BEING

There is no personal life without the encounter with other persons within a community, and there is no community without the historical dimension of past and future. This is clearly indicated in the biblical picture of Jesus as the Christ. Although his personal life is considered as the criterion by which past and future are judged, it is not an isolated life, and the New Being, which is the quality of his own being, is not restricted to his being. This refers to the community out of which he comes and to the preparatory manifestations of the New Being within it; it refers to the community which he creates and to the received manifestations of the New Being in it. The New Testament records take very seriously the descent of Jesus from the life of bearers of the preparatory revelation. The otherwise questionable and contradictory lists of the ancestors of Jesus have this symbolic value, as do the symbol "Son of David" and the interest in the figure of his mother. These are all symbols of the historical dimension of the past. In the selection of the Twelve Apostles, the past of the twelve tribes of Israel is symbolically connected with the future of the church. And, without the reception of Jesus as the Christ by the church, he could not have become the Christ, because he would not have brought the New Being to anyone. While the Synoptic picture is especially interested in the direction of the past, the Fourth Gospel is predominantly interested in the direction toward the future. Clearly, however, the biblical picture is not responsible for a theology which, in the name of the "uniqueness" of Jesus as the Christ, cuts him off from everything before the year 1 and after the year 30. In this way the continuity of the divine self-manifestation through history is denied not only for the pre-Christian past but also for the Christian present and future. This tends to cut off the contemporary Christian of today from direct connection with the New Being in Christ. He is asked to jump over the millennia to the years "1 through 30" and to subject himself to the event upon which Christianity is based. But this jump is an illusion because the very fact that he is a Christian and that he calls Jesus the Christ is based on the continuity through history of the power of the New Being. No anti-Catholic bias should prevent Protestant theologians from acknowledging this fact.

Although appearing in a personal life, the New Being has a spatial breadth in the community of the New Being and a temporal dimension in the history of the New Being. The appearance of the Christ in an individual person presupposes the community out of which he came and the community which he creates. Of course, the criterion of both is the picture of Jesus as the Christ; but, without them, this criterion never could have appeared. . . .

The question now must be asked whether, in fact, there is such a unified picture in the New Testament or whether the conflicting views of the different writers of the New Testament make the painting of such a picture impossible. The question first demands a historical, then a systematic, answer. The historical answer has been partly given by the earlier statement that all parts of the New Testament agree in their assertion that Jesus is the Christ. This is necessarily so because the New Testament is the book of the community whose foundation is the acceptance of Jesus as the Christ. But the question is not fully answered by this statement; for there are different, and somehow contrasting, ways of interpreting the assertion that Jesus is the Christ. One can emphasize the participation of the New Being in the conditions of existence or the victory of the New Being over the conditions of existence. Obviously, the first is the Synoptic, the second the Johannine, emphasis. The question here is not whether one can produce a harmonious historical picture by a combination of both pictures. Historical research has answered this question almost unanimously in the negative. *Vol. 2, pp. 131-6*

# 5

## AMONG THE AMBIGUITIES OF LIFE: SPIRIT AND THE CHURCHES*

### THE DIVINE SPIRIT IN THE FUNCTIONS OF LIFE

*At the outset of his third volume, from which the following sections are taken, Tillich referred to his system as "the incompleted of the completed". As he described human life generally in volume 3, so his own project is "fragmentary and often inadequate and questionable" (Systematic Theology, vol. 3, p.v.). The Paucks report that many readers found the third volume, especially sections on "Life and the Spirit", to be "tedious because of its repetitiveness" (see Wilhelm & Marion Pauck, p. 236). Because of this tendency of the text, I have here reorganized the themes in volume 3 in order to introduce them as they relate to the structure presented in the first two volumes. The selection appearing under this heading (Systematic Theology, vol. 3, pp. 30-118, passim) provides Tillich's basic view that "life" is an ambiguous play of "essential" and "existential" elements. Within this basic ambiguity, he identifies many other ambiguities and groups them in terms of three "functions of life": self-integration (morality), self-creativity (culture) and self-transcendence (religion). Note that each of these functions corresponds, respectively, to the ontological polarities of individualization and participation, dynamics and form, and freedom and destiny. The third volume may be read as Tillich's own systematic fulfillment of the "self-transcending realist" attitude that he sketched earlier in his life, and of the task of a "theology of culture" to articulate a "theonomous" life for humanity and the world. Tillich seeks this through a doctrine of the Spirit and of the Kingdom of God that presents the Divine Spirit as working in and with the structures of all life functions, while also enabling their self-transcendence toward fulfillment in unambiguous life.*

#### 1. THE QUEST FOR UNAMBIGUOUS LIFE AND THE SYMBOLS OF ITS ANTICIPATION

In all life processes an essential and an existential element, created goodness and estrangement, are merged in such a way that neither one nor the other is exclusively effective. Life always includes essential and

* See also pp. 28-31 above.

233

existential elements; this is the root of its ambiguity.

The ambiguities of life are manifest under all dimensions, in all processes and all realms of life. The question of unambiguous life is latent everywhere. All creatures long for an unambiguous fulfillment of their essential possibilities; but only in man as the bearer of the spirit do the ambiguities of life and the quest for unambiguous life become conscious. He experiences the ambiguity of life under all dimensions since he participates in all of them, and he experiences them immediately within himself as the ambiguity of the functions of the spirit: of morality, culture, and religion. The quest for unambiguous life arises out of these experiences; this quest is for a life which has reached that toward which it transcends itself.

Since religion is the self-transcendence of life in the realm of the spirit, it is in religion that man starts the quest for unambiguous life and it is in religion that he receives the answer. But the answer is not identical with religion, since religion itself is ambiguous. The fulfillment of the quest for unambiguous life transcends any religious form or symbol in which it is expressed. The self-transcendence of life never unambiguously reaches that toward which it transcends, although life can receive its self-manifestation in the ambiguous form of religion.

Religious symbolism has produced three main symbols for unambiguous life: Spirit of God, Kingdom of God, and Eternal Life. Each of them and their relation to each other require a short preliminary consideration. The Spirit of God is the presence of the Divine Life within creaturely life. The Divine Spirit is "God present". The spirit of God is not a separated being. Therefore one can speak of "Spiritual Presence" in order to give the symbol its full meaning.

The word "presence" has an archaic connotation, pointing to the place where a sovereign or a group of high dignitaries is. In capitalizing it, we indicate that it is supposed to express the divine presence in creaturely life. "Spiritual Presence", then, is the first symbol expressing unambiguous life. It is directly correlated to the ambiguities of life under the dimension of spirit although, because of the multidimensional unity of life, it refers indirectly to all realms. In it both "Spiritual" and "Presence" are capitalized, and the word "Spiritual" is used for the first time in this part of *Systematic Theology*. It has *not* been used as an adjective from spirit with a small "s", designating a dimension of life. . . .

The second symbol of unambiguous life is the "Kingdom of God". Its symbolic material is taken from the historical dimension of life and the dynamics of historical self-transcendence. Kingdom of God is the answer to the ambiguities of man's historical existence but, because of the multidimensional unity of life, the symbol includes the answer to the ambiguity under the historical dimension in all realms of life. The dimension of history is actualized, on the one hand, in historical events which reach out of the past and determine the present, and on the other hand, in the historical tension which is experienced in the present, but runs irreversibly into the future. Therefore, the symbol of the Kingdom of God covers both the struggle of unambiguous life with the forces which make for ambiguity, and the ultimate fulfillment toward which history runs.

This leads to the third symbol: unambiguous life is Eternal Life. Here the symbolic material is taken from the temporal and spatial finitude of all life. Unambiguous life conquers the servitude to the categorical limits of existence. It does not mean an endless continuation of categorical existence but the conquest of its ambiguities. . . .

The relation of the three symbols, "Spiritual Presence", "Kingdom of God", and "Eternal Life" can be described in the following way: all three are symbolic expressions of the answer revelation give to the quest for unambiguous life. Unambiguous life can be described as life under the Spiritual Presence, or as life in the Kingdom of God, or as Eternal Life. But as shown before, the three symbols use different symbolic material and in doing so express different directons of meaning within the same idea of unambiguous life. The symbol "Spiritual Presence" uses the dimension of spirit, the bearer of which is man, but in order to be present in the human spirit, the Divine Spirit must be present in all the dimensions which are actual in man, and this means, in the universe.

The symbol Kingdom of God is a social symbol, taken from the historical dimension in so far as it is actualized in man's historical life. But the historical dimension is present in all life. Therefore, the symbol "Kingdom of God" embraces the destiny of the life of the universe, just as does the symbol "Spiritual Presence". But history's quality of running irreversibly toward a goal introduces another element into its symbolic meaning, and that is the "eschatological" expectation, the expectation of the fulfillment toward which self-transcendence strives and toward which history runs. Like Spiritual Presence, the Kingdom of God is working and struggling in history; but as eternal fulfillment of life, the Kingdom of God is above history.

The symbolic material of the third symbol of unambiguous life, Eternal Life, is taken from the categorical structure of finitude. Unambiguous life is Eternal Life. As with Spiritual Presence and Kingdom of

God, Eternal Life is also a universal symbol, referring to all dimensions of life and including the two other symbols. Spiritual Presence creates Eternal Life in those who are grasped by it. And the Kingdom of God is the fulfillment of temporal life in Eternal Life.

The three symbols for unambiguous life mutually include each other, but because of the different symbolic material they use, it is preferable to apply them in different directions of meaning: Spiritual Presence for the conquest of the ambiguities of life under the dimension of the spirit, Kingdom of God for the conquest of the ambiguities of life under the dimension of history, and Eternal Life for the conquest of the ambiguities of life beyond history. Yet in all three of them we find a mutual immanence of all. Where there is Spiritual Presence, there is Kingdom of God and Eternal Life, and where there is Kingdom of God there is Eternal Life and Spiritual Presence, and where there is Eternal Life there is Spiritual Presence and Kingdom of God. The emphasis is different, the substance is the same — life unambiguous.

The quest for such unambiguous life is possible because life has the character of self-transcendence. Under all dimensions life moves beyond itself in the vertical direction. But under no dimension does it reach that toward which it moves, the unconditional. It does not reach it, but the quest remains. Under the dimension of the spirit it is the quest for an unambiguous morality and an unambiguous culture reunited with an unambiguous religion. The answer to this quest is the experience of revelation and salvation; they constitute religion above religion, although they become religion when they are received. In religious symbolism they are the work of the Spiritual Presence or of the Kingdom of God or of Eternal Life. This quest is effective in all religions and the answer received underlies all religions, giving them their greatness and dignity. But both quest and answer become matters of ambiguity if expressed in the terms of a concrete religion. It is an age-old experience of all religions that the quest for something transcending them is answered in the shaking and transforming experiences of revelation and salvation; but that under the conditions of existence even the absolutely great — the divine self-manifestation — becomes not only great but also small, not only divine but also demonic.

*Vol. 3, pp. 107-10*

\*

## 2. THE BASIC FUNCTIONS OF LIFE

Life was defined as the actualization of potential being. In every life process such actualization takes place. The terms "act", "action", "actual", denote a centrally intended movement ahead, a going-out from a center of action. But this going-out takes place in such a way that the center is not lost in the outgoing movement. The self-identity remains in the self-alteration. The other (*alterum*) in the process of alteration is turned both away from the center and back toward it. So we can distinguish three elements in the process of life: self-identity, self-alteration, and return to one's self. Potentiality becomes actuality only through these three elements in the process which we call life.

This character of the structure of life processes leads to the recognition of *the first function of life: self-integration.* In it the center of self-identity is established, drawn into self-alteration and re-established with the contents of that into which it has been altered. There is centeredness in all life, both as reality and as task. The movement in which centeredness is actualized shall be called the self-integration of life. The syllable "self" indicates that it is life itself which drives toward centeredness in every process of self-integration. There is nothing outside life which could cause its movement from centeredness through alteration back to centeredness. The nature of life itself expresses itself in the function of self-integration in every particular life process.

But the process of actualization does not imply only the function of self-integration, the circular movement of life from a center and back to this center; it also implies the function of producing new centers, *the function of self-creation.* In it the movement of actualization of the potential, the movement of life, goes forward in the horizontal direction. In it also self-identity and self-alteration are effective, but under the predominance of self-alteration. Life drives toward the new. It cannot do this without centeredness, but it does it by transcending every individual center. It is the principle of growth which determines the function of self-creation, growth within the circular movement of a self-centered being and grwoth in the creation of new centers beyond this circle.

The word "creation" is one of the great symbol-words describing the relation of God to the universe. Contemporary language has applied the words "creative", "creativity", and even "creation" to human (and pre-human) beings, actions, and products. And it is consistent with this fashion to speak of the self-creative function of life. Of course, life is not self-creative in an absolute sense. It presupposes the creative ground out of which it comes. Nevertheless, as we can speak of Spirit only because we have spirit, so we can speak of Creation only because creative power is given to us.

The third direction in which the actualization of the potential goes is in contrast to the circular and the horizontal — the vertical direction. This metaphor stands for the function of life which we suggest calling *the self-transcending function*. In itself the term "self-transcendence" could also be used for the two other functions: self-integration, going from identity through alteration back to identity, is a kind of intrinsic self-transcendence within a centered being, and in every process of growth a later stage transcends a former one in the horizontal direction. But in both cases the self-transcendence remains within the limits of finite life. One finite situation is transcended by another; but finite life is not transcended. Therefore, it seems appropriate to reserve the term "self-transcendence" for that function of life in which this does occur — in which life drives beyond itself as finite life. It is *self*-transcendence because life is not transcended by something that is not life. Life, by its very nature as life, is both *in* itself and *above* itself, and this situation is manifest in the function of self-transcendence. For the way in which this elevation of life beyond itself becomes apparent, I suggest using the phrase "driving toward the sublime". The words "sublime", "sublimation", "sublimity" point to a "going beyond limits" toward the great, the solemn, the high.

Thus, within the process of actualization of the potential, which is called life, we distinguish the three functions of life: self-integration under the principle of centeredness, self-creation under the principle of growth, and self-transcendence under the principle of sublimity. The basic structure of self-identity and self-alteration is effective in each, and each is dependent on the basic polarities of being: self-integration on the polarity of individualization and participation, self-creation on the polarity of dynamics and form, self-transcendence on the polarity of freedom and destiny. And the structure of self-identity and self-alteration is rooted in the basic ontological self-world correlation. (The relation of the structure and the functions of life to the ontological polarities will receive a fuller treatment in the discussion of the particular functions.)

The three functions of life unite elements of self-identity with elements of self-alteration. But this unity is threatened by existential estrangement, which drives life in one or the other direction, thus disrupting the unity. To the degree in which this disruption is real, self-integration is countered by disintegration, self-creation is countered by destruction, self-transcendence is countered by profanization. Every life process has the ambiguity that the positive and negative elements are mixed in such a way that a definite separation of the negative from the positive is impossible: life at every moment is ambiguous. It is my intention to discuss the particular functions of life, not in their essential nature, separate from their existential distortion, but in the way they appear within the ambiguities of their actualization, for life is neither essential nor existential but ambiguous. *Vol. 3, pp. 30-2*

\*

### 3. STRUCTURE, ECSTASY AND SPIRIT

The Spiritual Presence does not destroy the structure of the centered self which bears the dimension of spirit. Ecstasy does not negate structure. . . . A dualism of levels logically leads to the destruction of the finite, for example, the human spirit for the sake of the divine Spirit. But, religiously speaking, God does not need to destroy his created world, which is good in its essential nature, in order to manifest himself in it. . . .

However, should we give a "phenomenology" of the Spiritual Presence, we should find in the history of religion a large number of reports and descriptions which indicate that ecstasy as the work of the Spirit disrupts created structure. The Spiritual Presence's manifestations since the earliest times, as well as in biblical literature, have a miraculous character. The Spirit has bodily effects: the transference of a person from one place to another, changes within the body, such as generation of new life in it, penetration of rigid bodies, and so on. The Spirit also has psychological effects of an extraordinary character which endow the intellect or will with powers not within the scope of a person's natural capacity, such as knowledge of strange tongues, penetration into the innermost thoughts of another person, and healing influences even at a distance. However questionable their historical reliability may be, these reports point to two important qualities of Spiritual Presence: its universal and extraordinary character. The universal impact of the Spiritual Presence on all realms of life is expressed in these reports of miracles in all dimensions; in supra-naturalistic language they point to the truth of the unity of life. Spiritual presence answers questions implied in the ambiguities of all life's dimensions: spatial and temporal separation and bodily and psychological disorders and limitations are overcome. . . .

The two terms "inspiration" and "infusion" express the way in which man's spirit receives the impact of Spiritual Presence. Both terms are spatial metaphors and involve, respectively, "breathing" and "pouring" into the human spirit. In the discussion of revelation, we sharply rejected the distortion which occurs when the experience of inspiration is turned into an informative lesson about God and divine matters. The Spiritual Presence is not that of a teacher but of a meaning-bearing power which grasps the human spirit in an ecstatic experience. After the experience, the teacher can analyze and formulate the element of meaning in the ecstasy of inspiration (as the systematic theologian does), but when the analysis of the teacher begins, the inspirational experience has already passed.

The other term which describes the impact of the Spiritual Presence in a spatial metaphor is "infusion". This concept is central in the early church and later in the Catholic church, where it describes the relation of the divine Spirit to the human spirit. Such terms as *infusio fidei* or *infusio amoris* derive faith and love from *infusio Spiritus Sancti* ("the infusion of the Holy Spirit"). Protestantism was and remains suspicious of this terminology because of the magic-materialistic perversion to which the idea was subjected in the later Roman church. The Spirit became a substance the reality of which was not necessarily noticed by the centered self-awareness of the person. It became a kind of "matter" which was transmitted by the priest in the performance of the sacraments, provided that the receiving subject did not resist. This a-personalistic understanding of the Spiritual Presence resulted in an objectivation of the religious life which culminated in the business practice of selling indulgence. For Protestant thinking, the Spirit is always personal. Faith and love are impacts of the Spiritual Presence on the centered self, and the vehicle of this impact is the "word", even within the administration of the sacraments. This is why Protestantism is reluctant to use the term "infusion" for the impact of the Spiritual Presence.

But this reluctance is not wholly justified, and Protestantism is not wholly consistent about it. When reading and interpreting the story of Pentecost and similar stories in the New Testament, especially in the book of Acts and in passages of the Epistles (particularly Paul's), the Protestant also uses the metaphor of the "outpouring" of the Holy Spirit. And he does so rightly, because even if we prefer "in-spiration", we do not escape a substantial metaphor, for "breath" is also a substance entering him who receives the Spirit. But there is another reason for using the term "infusion" as well as "inspiration", and that is contemporary psychology's rediscovery of the significance of the unconscious and the consequent re-evaluation of symbols and sacraments that has taken place in contrast to the traditional Protestant emphasis on the doctrinal and moral word as the medium of the Spirit.

But as the ecstatic reception of the Spiritual Presence is described as "inspiration" or "infusion" or as both, we must observe the basic rule that the Spiritual Presence's reception can only be described in such a way that ecstasy does not disrupt structure. The unity of ecstasy and structure is classically expressed in Paul's doctrine of the Spirit. Paul is primarily the theologian of the Spirit. His Christology and his eschatology are both dependent on this central point in this thinking. His doctrine of justification through faith by grace is a matter of support and defense of his main assertion that with the appearance of the Christ a new state of things came into being, created by the Spirit. Paul strongly emphasizes the ecstatic element in the experience of the Spiritual Presence, and he does so in accordance with all the New Testament stories in which it is described. These experiences, which he acknowledges in others, he claims also for himself. He knows that every successful prayer, i.e., every prayer which reunites with God, has ecstatic character. Such a prayer is impossible for the human spirit, because man does not know how to pray; but it is possible for the divine Spirit to pray through man, even should man not use words ("unspeakable sighs" — Paul). The formula — being in Christ — which Paul often uses, does not suggest a psychological empathy with Jesus Christ; rather it involves an ecstatic participation in the Christ who "is the Spirit", whereby one lives in the sphere of this Spiritual power.

At the same time, Paul resists any tendency that would permit ecstasy to disrupt structure. The classical expression of this is given in the first letter to the Corinthians where Paul speaks of the gifts of the Spirit and rejects ecstatic speaking in tongues if it produces chaos and disrupts the community, the emphasis on personal ecstatic experiences if they produce *hubris*, and the other charismata (gifts of the Spirit) if they are not subjected to *agape*. He then discusses the greatest creation of the Spiritual Presence, *agape* itself. In the hymn to *agape* in 1 Corinthians, chapter 13, the structure of the moral imperative and the ecstasy of the Spiritual Presence are completely united. Similarly, the first three chapters of the same letter indicate a way to unite the structure of cognition with the ecstasy of the Spiritual Presence. The relation to the divine ground of being through the divine Spirit is not agnostic (as it is not amoral); rather it includes the knowledge of the "depth" of the

241

divine. However, as Paul shows in these chapters, this knowledge is not the fruit of *theoria*, the receiving function of the human spirit, but has an ecstatic character, as indicated by the language Paul uses in these chapters as well as in the chapter on *agape*. In ecstatic language Paul points to *agape* and *gnosis* — forms of morality and knowledge in which ecstasy and structure are united.

The church had and continues to have a problem in actualizing Paul's ideas, because of concrete ecstatic movements. The church must prevent the confusion of ecstasy with chaos, and it must fight for structure. On the other hand, it must avoid the institutional profanization of the Spirit which took place in the early Catholic church as a result of its replacement of *charisma* with office. Above all, it must avoid the secular profanization of contemporary Protestantism which occurs when it replaces ecstasy with doctrinal or moral structure. The Pauline criterion of the unity of structure and ecstasy stands against both kinds of profanization. The use of this criterion is an ever present duty and an ever present risk for the churches. It is a duty, because a church which lives in its institutional forms and disregards the Spiritual Presence's ecstatic side opens the door to the chaotic or disrupting forms of ecstasy and is even responsible for the growth of secularized reactions against the Spiritual Presence. On the other hand, a church which takes ecstatic movements seriously risks confusing the Spiritual Presence's impact with that of a psychologically determined overexcitement.

This danger can be reduced by investigating ecstasy's relation to the different dimensions of life. . . . This whole part of the present system is a defense of the ecstatic manifestations of the Spiritual Presence against its ecclesiastical critics; in this defense, the whole New Testament is the most powerful weapon.                    *Vol. 3, pp. 14-18*

*

## THE SPIRIT IN SELF-INTEGRATION (MORALITY)

*The selections presented here (Systematic Theology, vol. 3, pp. 32-271 passim) enable readers in the third volume to follow Tillich's reflections on just the first function, "self-integration", the function that expresses the polarity of individualization and participation. In the human dimension of life (in contrast to "inorganic" or "organic" dimensions) this function is at work in the task of personal self-integration, which Tillich terms "morality". Below, Tillich discusses the ambiguities attending personal self-integration and indicates how the Spiritual Presence "conquers" the anxiety arising from these ambiguities and makes possible a fulfillment in theonomous morality. Elsewhere in the third volume, Tillich identifies "ambiguities in the moral law" as also bearing on the task of personal self-integration. (See* Systematic Theology, *vol. 3, 44-50, 271-5). Several of Tillich's other reflections on morality were published in Paul Tillich,* Morality and Beyond *(New York: Harper & Row, 1963). These should be compared with his posthumously published "The Absolute and the Relative Element in Moral Decisions", in Paul Tillich,* My Search for Absolutes, *pp. 92-112.*

## 1. INDIVIDUALIZATION AND CENTEREDNESS

The first of the polarities in the structure of being is that of individualization and participation. It is expressed in the function of self-integration through the principle of centeredness. Centeredness is a quality of individualization, in so far as the indivisible thing is the centered thing. To continue the metaphor, the center is a point, and a point cannot be divided. A centered being can develop another being out of itself, or it can be deprived of some parts which belong to the whole; but the center as such cannot be divided — it can only be destroyed. A fully individualized being, therefore, is at the same time a fully centered being. Within the limits of human experience only man has these qualities fully; in all other beings, both centeredness and individualization are limited. But they are qualities of everything that is, whether limited or fully developed.

The term "centeredness" is derived from the geometrical circle and metaphorically applied to the structure of a being in which an effect exercised on one part has consequences for all other parts, directly or indirectly. The words "whole" or *Gestalt* have been used for things with such structure; and these terms have sometimes been applied to all dimensions except the inorganic ones. Occasionally, the inorganic dimensions have also been included. The line of thought we have followed leads to the more inclusive interpretation. Since individualization is an ontological pole, it has universal significance, and so has centeredness, which is the condition of the actualization of the individual in life. However, this makes the term "centeredness" preferable to wholeness or *Gestalt*. It does not imply an integrated *Gestalt*, or "whole", but only processes going out from and returning to a point which cannot be localized in a special place in the whole but which is the point of direction of the two basic movements of all life processes. In this sense, centeredness exists under the control of all dimensions of being, but as a process of outgoing and returning. For where there is a center, there is a periphery which includes an amount of space or, in non-metamorphical terms, which unites a manifoldness of elements. This corresponds to participation, with which individualization forms a polarity. Individualization separates. The most individualized being is the most unapproachable and the most lonely one. But, at the same time, he has the greatest potentiality of universal participation. He can have communion with his world and *eros* toward it. This *eros* can be theoretical as well as practical. He can participate in the universe in all its dimensions and draw elements of it into himself. Therefore the process of self-integration moves between the center and the manifoldness which is taken into the center.

This description of integration implies the possibility of disintegration. Disintegration means failure to reach or to preserve self-integration. This failure can occur in one of two directions. Either it is the inability to overcome a limited, stabilized, and immovable centeredness, in which case there is a center, but a center which does not have a life process whose content is changed and increased; thus it approaches the death of mere self-identity. Or it is the inability to return because of the dispersing power of the manifoldness, in which case there is life, but it is dispersed and weak in centeredness, and it faces the danger of losing its center altogether — the death of mere self-alteration. The function of self-integration ambiguously mixed with disintegration works between these two extremes in every life process. . . .

In man complete centeredness is essentially given, but it is not actually given until man actualizes it in freedom and through destiny. The act in which man actualizes his essential centeredness is the moral act. Morality is the function of life by which the realm of the spirit comes into being. Morality is the constitutive function of spirit. A moral act, therefore, is not an act in which some divine or human law is obeyed but an act in which life integrates itself in the dimension of spirit, and this means as personality within a community. Morality is the function of life in which the centered self constitutes itself as a person; it is the totality of those acts in which a potentially personal life process becomes an actual person. Such acts happen continuously in a personal life; the constitution of the person as a person never comes to an end during his whole life process.           *Vol. 3, pp. 32-4, 38*

*

## 2. THE AMBIGUITIES OF PERSONAL SELF-INTEGRATION: THE POSSIBLE, THE REAL, AND THE AMBIGUITY OF SACRIFICE

As does any other form of self-integration, the personal moves between the poles of self-identity and self-alteration. Integration is the state of balance between them, disintegration the disruption of this balance. Both trends are always effective in actual life processes under the conditions of existential estrangement. Personal life is ambiguously pulled between forces of essential centeredness and of existential disruption. There is no moment in a personal life process in which one or the other force is exclusively dominant.

As in the organic and the psychological realms, the ambiguity of life in the function of self-integration is rooted in the necessity for a being to take the encountered content of reality into its centered unity without being disrupted by its quantity or quality. Personal life is always the life of somebody — as in all dimensions, life is the life of some individual being, according to the principle of centeredness. I speak of my life, of your life, of our lives. Everything is included in my life which belongs to me: my body, my self-awareness, my memories and anticipations, my perceptions and thoughts, my will, and my emotions. All this belongs to the centered unity which I am. I try to increase this content by going out and try to preserve it by returning to the centered unity which I am. In this process I encounter innumerable possibilities, each of which, if accepted, means a self-alteration and consequently a danger of disruption. For the sake of my present reality, I must keep many possibilities outside of my centered self, or I must give up something of what I now am for the sake of something possible which may enlarge and strengthen my centered self. So my life process oscillates between the possible and the real and requires the surrender of the one for the other — the sacrificial character of all life.

Every individual has essential potentialities which he tends to actualize, according to the general movement of being from the potential to the actual. Some of these potentialities never reach the stage of concrete possibilities; historical, social, and individual conditions reduce the possibilities drastically. From the point of view of human potentialities, a Central American rural Indian may have the same human potentialities as a North American college student, but he does not have the same possibilities of actualizing them. His choices are much more limited, although he also has to sacrifice possibilities for realities and vice versa.

Examples illustrating this situation are abundant. We must sacrifice

245

possible interests for those which are or could become real. We must surrender possible work and possible vocations for the one we have chosen. We must sacrifice possible human relations for the sake of real ones or real ones for the sake of possible ones. We must choose between a consistent but self-limiting building-up of our life and a breaking-through of as many limits as possible with a loss of consistency and direction. We must continuously decide between abundance and poverty and between special kinds of abundance and special kinds of poverty. There is the abundance of life into which one is driven by the anxiety of remaining poor in some respect, or in many respects; but this abundance may surpass our power of doing justice to it and to us, and then the abundance becomes an empty repetition. If thereupon the opposite anxiety, that of losing oneself in life, leads to a partial resignation or complete withdrawal from abundance, the poverty becomes empty self-relatedness — the centered unity of the personal self comprises many different trends, each of which tends to dominate the center. . . .

The self-integration of life includes the sacrifice of the possible for the real, or of the real for the possible, as an inescapable process in all dimensions other than that of the spirit and as an inescapable decision within the dimension of the spirit. In the common judgment, sacrifice is unambiguously good. In Christianity, in which God himself makes the sacrifice according to Christian symbolism, the act of sacrifice seems to transcend any ambiguity. But this is not true, as theological thoughts and penitential practice well know. They know that every sacrifice is a moral risk and that hidden motives may even make a seemingly heroic sacrifice questionable. This does not mean that there should not be sacrifice; the moral life demands it continuously. But the risk must be taken with awareness that it is a risk and not something unambiguously good on which an easy conscience can rely. One of the risks is the decision whether to sacrifice the real for the possible or the possible for the real. The "anxious conscience" tends to prefer the real to the possible, because the real is at least familiar, whereas the possible is unknown. But the moral risk in sacrificing an important possibility can be equally as great as the risk in sacrificing an important reality. The ambiguity of sacrifice also becomes visible when the question is asked, What is to be sacrificed? Self-sacrifice may be worthless if there is no self worthy of being sacrificed. The other one, or the cause, for which it is sacrificed may receive nothing from it, nor does he who makes the sacrifice achieve moral self-integration by it. He may merely gain the power which weakness gives over the strong one for whom the sacrifice is made. If, however, the self which is sacrificed is worthy, the question arises whether that for which it is sacrificed is worthy to receive it. The cause which receives it may be evil, or the person for whom it is offered may use it for selfish exploitation. Thus the ambiguity of sacrifice is a decisive and all-permeating expression of the ambiguity of life in the function of self-integration. It shows the human situation in the mixture of essential and existential elements and the impossibility of separating them as good and evil in an unambiguous way.         *Vol. 3, pp. 41-4*

\*

### 3. THE SPIRITUAL PRESENCE AND THE AMBIGUITIES OF PERSONAL SELF-INTEGRATION

In our description of the ambiguities of the integration of the moral personality, we pointed to the polarity of self-identity and self-alteration and the loss of a centered self either in an empty self-identity or in a chaotic self-alteration. The problems implied in this polarity led us to the concept of sacrifice and its ambiguities. The continual alternative — to sacrifice either the actual for the possible or the possible for the actual — appeared as an outstanding example of the ambiguities of self-integration. The ever returning questions are: How many contents of the encountered world *can* I take into the unity of my personal center without disrupting it? And, How many contents of the encountered world *must* I take into the unity of my personal center in order to avoid an empty self-identity? Into how many directions *can* I push beyond a given state of my being without losing all directedness of the life process? And, Into how many directions *must* I try to encounter reality in order to avoid a narrowing-down of my life process to monolithic poverty? And the basic question is: How many potentialities, given to me by virtue of my being man and, further, by being this particular man, *can* I actualize without losing the power to actualize anything seriously? And, How many of my potentialities *must* I actualize in order to avoid the state of mutilated humanity? These sets of questions, of course, are not asked *in abstracto* but always in the concrete form: Shall I sacrifice this that I have for this that I could have?

The alternative is resolved, though fragmentarily, under the impact of the Spiritual Presence. The Spirit takes the personal center into the universal center, the transcendent unity which makes faith and love possible. When taken into the transcendent unity, the personal center is superior to encounters with reality on the temporal plane, because the transcendent unity embraces the content of all possible encounters. It embraces them beyond potentiality and actuality, because the transcendent unity is the unity of the divine life. In the "communion of the Holy Spirit", the essential being of the person is liberated from the contingencies of freedom and destiny under the conditions of existence. The acceptance of this liberation is the all-inclusive sacrifice which, at the same time, is the all-inclusive fulfillment. This is the only unambiguous sacrifice a human being can make. But since it is made within the processes of life, it remains fragmentary and open to distortion by the ambiguities of life.

The consequences of this consideration for the three double questions asked above can be described as follows: In so far as the personal center is established in relation to the universal center, the encountered contents of finite reality are judged for their significance in expressing the essential being of the person before they are allowed to enter, or are barred from entering, the unity of the centered self. The element of Wisdom in the Spirit makes such judgment possible (compare, for example, the judging function of the Spirit in 1 Corinthians, chapter 3). It is a judgment directed toward what we have distinguished as the two poles in the self-integration of the moral self, self-identity and self-alteration. The Spiritual Presence maintains the identity of the self without impoverishing the self, and it drives toward the alteration of the self without disrupting it. In this way the Spirit conquers the double anxiety which logically (but not temporally) precedes the transition from essence to existence, the anxiety of not actualizing one's essential being and the anxiety of losing oneself within one's self-actualization. Where there is Spirit, the actual manifests the potential and the potential determines the actual. In the Spiritual Presence, man's essential being appears under the conditions of existence, conquering the distortions of existence in the reality of the New Being. This statement is derived from the basic christological assertion that in the Christ the eternal unity of God and man becomes actual under the conditions of existence without being conquered by them. Those who participate in the New Being are in an analogous way beyond the conflict of essence and existential predicament. The Spiritual Presence actualizes the essential within the existential in an unambiguous way.

The question of the amount of strange content which can be taken into the unity of the centered self has led to an answer which refers to all three questions asked above and especially to the question of the sacrifice of the potential for the actual. But more concrete answers are necessary. The ambiguity of the life process with respect to their directions and aims must be conquered by an unambiguous determination of the life processes. Where Spiritual Presence is effective, life is turned into the direction which is more than one direction among others — the direction toward the ultimate within all directions. This direction does not replace the others but appears within them as their ultimate end and therefore as the criterion of the choice between them. The "saint" (he who is determined by the Spiritual Presence) knows *where* to go and where *not* to go. He knows the way between impoverished asceticism and disrupting libertinism. In the life of most people the question of where to go, in which directions to spread and which direction to make predominant, is a continuous concern. They do not know where to go, and therefore many cease to go at all and permit their life processes to fall into the poverty of anxious self-restriction; others start off in so many directions that they cannot follow up any of them. The Spirit conquers restriction as well as disruption by preserving the unity in divergent directions, both the unity of the centered self who takes the divergent directions and the unity of the directions which reconverge after they have diverged. They reconverge in the direction of the ultimate.

With respect to the double question of how many potentialities — in general human and in particular individual — one *can* actualize and how many one *must* actualize, the answer is the following: Finitude demands the sacrifice of potentialities which can be actualized only by the sum of all individuals, and even the power of these potentialities to be actualized is restricted by the external conditions of the human race and its finitude. Potentialities remain unactualized in every moment of history because their actualization has never become a possibility. In the same way, in every moment of every individual life potentialities remain unactualized because they have never reached the state of possibility. However, there are potentialities that are also possibilities that, nevertheless, must be sacrificed because of human finitude. Not all the creative possibilities of a person, or all the creative possibilities of the human race, have been or will be actualized. The Spiritual Presence does not change that situation — for although the finite can participate in the infinite, it cannot become infinite — but the Spirit can create an acceptance of man's and mankind's finitude, and in so doing can give a new meaning to the sacrifice of potentialities. It can remove the ambiguous and tragic character of the sacrifice of life possibilities and restore the genuine meaning of sacrifice, namely, the acknowledgment of one's finitude. In every religious sacrifice, finite man deprives himself of a power of being which seems to be his but which is not his in an absolute sense, as he acknowledges by the sacrifice; it is his only because it is given to him and, therefore, not ultimately his, and the acknowledgment of this situation is the sacrifice. Such an understanding of the sacrifice excludes the humanistic ideal of the all-round personality in which every human potentiality is actualized. It is a God-man idea, which is quite different from the God-man image created by the divine Spirit as the essence of the man Jesus of Nazareth. This image shows the sacrifice of all human potentialities for the sake of the one which man himself cannot actualize, the uninterrupted unity with God. But the image also shows that this sacrifice is indirectly creative in all directions of truth, expressiveness, humanity, justice — in the picture of the Christ as well as in the life of the churches. In contrast to the humanist idea of man which actualizes what man can be directly and without sacrifice, the Spirit-determined fulfillment of man sacrifices all human potentialities, to the extent that they lie on the horizontal plane, to the vertical direction and receives them back into the limits of man's finitude from the vertical direction, the direction of the ultimate. This is the contrast between autonomous and theonomous personal fulfillment.

*Vol. 3, pp. 268-71*

\*

## THE SPIRIT IN SELF-CREATIVITY (CULTURE)

*The second function of life, "self-creativity", concerns a whole host of ambiguities that arise from tensions spawned by the polarity of dynamics and form. The ambiguities of self-creativity in human life are discussed by Tillich under the term, "culture". But human cultural self-creativity itself occurs in many ways: in the general activities of language and technology, in the theoretical self-creativity of cognition and aesthetics, and in the practical self-creativity of personal formation and communal transformation. In all of these areas Tillich identifies special ambiguities, and then suggests that the Spiritual Presence drives through them all toward forms of theonomous culture. In the selection immediately below (Systematic Theology, vol. 3, pp. 50-265 passim), we only track Tillich's discussion of the ambiguities of human self-creativity (culture) in the area of "communal transformation", and as self-creativity in communal forms is then nurtured toward fulfillment by the Spiritual Presence. Many other cultural ambiguities of self-creativity, other than those pertaining to communal trans-*

*formation, may be studied in* Systematic Theology *(cf. vol. 3, pp. 55-77, 253-62). For an earlier statement of Tillich's views of the relationship of the Divine Spirit to communal transformation, see Tillich's* Love, Power and Justice, *especially pp. 54-125.*

## 1. DYNAMICS AND GROWTH

The second polarity in the structure of being is that of dynamics and form. It is effective in the function of life which we have called self-creativity, and it is effective in the principle of growth. Growth is dependent on the polar element of dynamics in so far as growth is the process by which a formed reality goes beyond itself to another form which both preserves and transforms the original reality. This process is the way in which life creates itself. It does not create itself in terms of original creation. It is given to itself by the divine creativity which transcends and underlies all processes of life. But on this basis, life creates itself through the dynamics of growth. The phenomenon of growth is fundamental under all dimensions of life. It is frequently used as the ultimate norm by philosophers who openly reject all ultimate norms (for example, pragmatists). It is used for processes under the dimension of the spirit and for the work of the divine Spirit. It is a main category in individual as well as social life, and in the "philosophies of process" it is the hidden reason for their preference of "becoming" to "being".

But dynamics is held in a polar interdependence with form. Self-creation of life is always creation of form. Nothing that grows is without form. The form makes a thing what it is, and the form makes a creation of man's culture into what it is: a poem or a building or a law, and so on. However, a continuous series of forms alone is not growth. Another element, coming from the pole of dynamics, makes itself felt. Every new form is made possible only by breaking through the limits of an old form. In other words, there is a moment of "chaos" between the old and the new form, a moment of no-longer-form and not-yet-form. This chaos is never absolute; it cannot be absolute because, according to the structure of the ontological polarities, being implies form. Even relative chaos has a relative form. But relative chaos with relative form is transitional, and as such it is a danger to the self-creative function of life. At this crisis life may fall back to its starting point and resist creation, or it may destroy itself in the attempt to reach a new form. Here one thinks of the destructive implications of every birth, whether of individuals or species, of the psychological phenomenon of repression, and of the

251

creation of a new social entity or a new artistic style. The chaotic element which appears here is already manifest in the creation myths, even in the creation stories of the Old Testament. Creation and chaos belong to each other, and even the exclusive monotheism of biblical religion confirms this structure of life. It is echoed in the symbolic descriptions of the divine life, of its abysmal depth, of its character as burning fire, of its suffering over and with the creatures, of its destructive wrath. But in the divine life the element of chaos does not endanger its eternal fulfillment, whereas in the life of the creature, under the conditions of estrangement, it leads to the ambiguity of self-creativity and destructiveness. Destruction can then be described as the prevalence of the elements of chaos over against the pole of form in the dynamics of life.

But there is no pure destruction in any life process. The merely negative has no being. In every process of life structures of creation are mixed with powers of destruction in such a way that they cannot be unambiguously separated. And in the actual processes of life, one never can establish with certainty which process is dominated by one or the other of these forces.

One could consider integration as an element of creation and disintegration as a form of destruction. And one could ask why integration and disintegration should be understood as a special function of life. However, they must be distinguished — as must the two polarities on which they are dependent. Self-integration constitutes the individual being in its centeredness; self-creation gives the dynamic impulse which drives life from one centered state to another under the principle of growth. Centeredness does not imply growth, but growth does presuppose coming from and going to a state of centeredness. Likewise, disintegration is possibly, but not necessarily, destruction. Disintegration takes place within a centered unity; destruction can occur only in the encounter of centered unity with centered unity. Disintegration is represented by disease, destruction by death.　　　　　　　　　　　　　　*Vol. 3, pp. 50-1*

*

## 2. THE AMBIGUITIES OF COMMUNAL TRANSFORMATION

The frame in which cultural self-creation occurs is the life and growth of the social group under the dimension of spirit. Discussion of this framework has been deferred to this point because of the difference in structure between the personal self and the community.

Whereas the centered self is the knowing, deliberating, deciding, and acting subject in every personal act, a social group has no such center. One can only call the seat of authority and power the "center" of a group by analogy, for in many cases authority and power are split, although the cohesion of the group persists, being rooted in life processes that may reach back into the past or that may be determined by unconscious forces which are stronger than any political or social authority. A person's free act makes him responsible for the consequences of the act. An act of the representative of authority in a group may be highly responsible, or completely irresponsible, with the whole group's having to bear the consequences. But the group is not a personal unity which becomes responsible for acts which, for example, are forced upon it against the will of the majority or through the preliminary superiority of one part in a situation where power is split. The life of a social group belongs under the historical dimension, which unites the other dimensions, adding to them the direction toward the future. . . . At this point we must deal with the ambiguities which follow from the principle of justice as such, without entering upon a discussion of justice in the historical dimension.

Under the dimension of spirit and in the function of culture, life creates itself in human groups whose nature and development is the subject matter of sociology and historiography. Here we ask the normative question: What are social groups intended to be by their essential nature, and what ambiguities appear in the actual processes of their self-creation? . . .

One may distinguish between social organisms and the organizational forms which special human activities take to enable them to grow toward justice. Families, friendship groups, local and vocational communities, tribal and national groups, have grown naturally within the cultural self-creation of life. But as parts of cultural creativity they are, at the same time, objects of organizing activity; in fact, they are never the one without the other. This distinguishes them from flocks in the organic-psychological dimension. The justice of a flock or a grove of trees is the natural power of the more powerful ones to force their potentialities into actualization against the natural resistance of the others. In a human group the relation of the members is ordered under traditional rules, conventionally or legally fixed. The natural differences in the power of being are not excluded in the organizational structure, but they are ordered according to the principles implied in the idea of justice. The interpretation of these principles is endlessly varied, but justice itself is the point of identity in all interpretations. The relations of man and wife, parents and children, relatives and strangers, members of the same local group, citizens of the same nation, and so on, are ordered by rules which, consciously or unconsciously, seek to express some form of justice. This is true even in the relation of the conquering group to the conquered within the same social context. The justice given to the slave is still justice, however unjust slavery may be from a higher point of view. According to the polarity of dynamics and form, a social group could not have being without form. And the social group's form is determined by the understanding of justice effective in the group.

The ambiguities of justice appear wherever justice is demanded and actualized. The growth of life in social groups is full of ambiguities which — if not understood — lead either to an attitude of despairing resignation of all belief in the possibility of justice or to an attitude of utopian expectation of a complete justice, which is later frustrated.

The first ambiguity in the actualization of justice is that of "*inclusiveness and exclusion*". A social group is a group because it includes a particular kind of people and excludes all others. Social cohesion is impossible without such exclusion. . . . It is inherent in the essential justice of a group to preserve its centeredness, and the group tries to establish a center in all acts in which it actualizes itself. . . . The ambiguity of cohesion implies that in every act by which social cohesion is strengthened individuals or groups on the boundary line are expelled or rejected and, conversely, that every act in which such individuals or groups are retained or accepted weakens the cohesion of the group. Those on the boundary line include individuals from a different social class, individuals who enter closed family and friendship groups, national or racial strangers, minority groups, dissenters, or newcomers simply because they are newcomers. In all these cases, justice does not demand unambiguous acceptance of those who would possibly disturb or destroy group cohesion, but it certainly does not permit their unambiguous rejection.

The second ambiguity of justice is that of "*competition and equality*". Inequality in the power of being between individuals and groups is not a matter of static differences but of continuous dynamic decisions. This happens in every encounter of being with being, in every glimpse of each other, in every conversation, in every demand, question, or appeal. It happens in the competitive life in family, school, work, business, intellectual creation, social relations, and the struggle for political power. There is a pushing ahead in all these encounters, a trying, a withdrawing into an existing unity, a pushing out of it, a coalescing, a splitting, a continuous alteration between victory and defeat. These dynamic inequalities are actual under all dimensions from the beginning of each life process to its end. Under the dimension of the spirit, they are judged by the principle of justice and the element of equality in it. The question is, In what respect does justice include equality?

There is *one* unambiguous answer: every person is equal to every other, in so far as he is a person. In this respect there is no difference between an actually developed personality and a mentally diseased one who is merely a potential personality. By the principle of justice incarnate in them, they both demand to be acknowledged as persons. The equality is unambiguous up to this point, and the implications are also logically unambiguous: equality before the law in all those respects in which the law determines the distribution of rights and duties, chances and limitations, goods and burdens, and in just returns for obedience to or defiance of the law, for merit and demerit, for competence and incompetence.

However, although the logical implications of the principle of equality are unambiguous, every concrete application is ambiguous. Past and present history incontestably documents this fact. In the past not even the recognition of a mentally diseased individual of the human genus as a potential person has been acknowledged, and there are still limits to this recognition in the present. In addition, there are the terrifying relapses which have occurred in the demonic destruction of justice in our century. However, even if this situation should change in the future, it could not change the ambiguities of competition, which work continuously for inequality in the encounters of people in daily life, in the stratification of society, and in the political self-creation of life. The very attempt to apply the principle of equality, as contained unambiguously in the acknowledgment of the person as person, can have destructive consequences for the realization of justice. It may deny the right embodied in a particular power of being and give it to individuals or groups whose power of being does not warrant it. Or it may keep individuals or groups under conditions which make growth of their potentialities technically impossible. Or it may prevent one kind of competition and foster another kind, thus removing one source of unjust inequality only to produce another. Or it may apply unjust power in order to crush unjust power. These examples make it clear that a state of unambiguous justice is a figment of the utopian imagination.

The third ambiguity in the self-actualization of a social group is "*the ambiguity of leadership*". It runs through all human relations from the parent-child to the ruler-subject relationship. And in its many forms it shows the ambiguity of creativity and destruction which characterizes all life processes. "Leadership" is a structure which starts rather early in the organic realm and which is effective under the dimensions of inner awareness, of the spirit, and of history. It is very poorly interpreted if it is derived from the existence of different degrees of strength and the drive of the stronger to enslave the weaker. This is a permanent abuse of the principle of leadership and not its essence. Leadership is the social analogy to centeredness. As we have seen, it is only an analogy, but it is a valid one. For without the centeredness given by leadership, no self-integration and self-creation of a group would be possible. This function of leadership can be derived from the very fact that would seem to be its refutation — the personal centeredness of the individual member of the group. Without a leader or leading group, a group could be united only through a psychological power, directing all individuals in a way similar to mass shock reactions, by which spontaneity and freedom would be lost in the movement of a mass in which the particles had no independent decision. Propagandists of all kinds try to produce such behavior. They do not want to be leaders but managers of a casually determined mass movement. But just this possibility of using the power of leadership for transforming leadership into mass-management shows that this is not the intrinsic nature of leadership, which presupposes and preserves the centered person whom it leads. The possibility just mentioned shows the ambiguity of leadership. The leader represents not only the power and justice of the group but also himself, his power of being, and the justice implied in it. This applies not only to him as an individual but to the particular social stratum in which he stands and which, willingly or unwillingly, he also represents. This situation is the permanent source of the ambiguity of every ruling power, whether it is a dictator, an aristocracy, or a parliament. And this is true also of voluntary groups whose chosen leaders manifest the same ambiguous motives as do political rulers. The ambiguity of rationalization or ideology production is present in every leadership structure. But the attempt to remove such a structure, for example, in a state of anarchy, is self-defeating because chaos breeds dictatorship and the ambiguities of life cannot be conquered by producing a vacuum.

Leaders in special functions have been called "authorities", but this is a misleading application of a term which has a more fundamental meaning than leadership and, consequently, more conspicuous ambiguities. "Authority", first of all, denotes the ability to start and to augment (*augere, auctor*) something. In this sense, there are authorities in all realms of cultural life. They result from the "division of experience" and are necessary because of every individual's finite range of knowledge and ability. There is nothing ambiguous in this situation, but the ambiguity of leadership in the sense of authority starts the moment that actual authority, which is based on the division of experience, is frozen into an authority bound to a particular social position, for example, to scholars as scholars, kings as kings, priests as priests, or parents as parents. In these cases, persons with less knowledge and ability come to exert authority over some who have more, and thus the genuine meaning of authority is distorted. This, however, is not only a regrettable fact which could and should be prevented but also an inevitable ambiguity, because of the unavoidable transformation of actual into established authority. This is most obvious in the case of parental authority but is also true of the relations of age-classes in general, of the professions to those whom they serve, and of representatives of power to those whom they direct or rule. All institutional hierarchy is based on this transformation of actual into established authority. But authority is authority over persons and therefore open to rejection in the name of justice. Established authority tries to prevent such rejection, and here an ambiguity appears: a successful rejection of authority would undercut the social structure of life, whereas a surrender to authority would destroy the basis of authority — the personal self and its claim for justice.

The fourth ambiguity of justice is the *"ambiguity of legal form"*. . . . The ambiguities of the legal form as expressed in the laws of states, for example, in civil and criminal law, are . . . supposed to establish justice but instead give rise to both justice and injustice. The ambiguity of the legal form has two causes, one external, the other internal. The external cause is the relation between the legal form and the legalizing, interpreting, and executing powers. There the ambiguities of leadership exert their influence on the character of the legal form. It claims to be the form of justice, but it is the legal expression of a particular — individual or social — power of being. Thus in itself is not only unavoidable; it is also true to the essential nature of being, that is, the multidimensional unity of life.

Every creation under the dimension of spirit unites expression with validity. It expresses an individual or social situation, which is indicated by the particular style. The legal style of a law-establishing group in a special period tells us not only about logical solutions of legal problems but also about the nature of the economic and social stratification existing at the time and about the character of the ruling classes or groups. Nevertheless, the logic of the law is not replaced by the will to power and the pressure of ideologies which serve the preservation of or the attack on the existing power structure. The legal form is not used simply for other purposes; it retains its own structural necessities and can serve those other purposes only because it retains its own structure, for power without valid legal form destroys itself.

The internal ambiguity of the legal form is independent of the law-giving, interpreting, and executing authorities. Like the moral law, it is abstract and, consequently, inadequate to any unique situation, for according to the principle of individualization every situation is unique — even if very similar to others in some respects. Many legal systems are aware of this fact and have built-in safety measures against the abstract equality of everyone before the law, but they can only partly remedy the injustice which is based on the abstract character of the law and the uniqueness of every concrete situation. *Vol. 3, pp. 77-84*

\*

### 3. SPIRITUAL PRESENCE AND THE AMBIGUITIES OF COMMUNAL TRANSFORMATION

The Spiritual Presence drives toward the conquest of the ambiguities of culture by creating theonomous forms in the different realms of the cultural self-creation of life. In order to present these forms it is necessary to refer to the enumeration of cultural ambiguities given before and to indicate what happens to them under the impact of the Spiritual Presence. But this must be preceded by a discussion of the basic ambiguity which has appeared, more or less obviously, in all cultural functions, the cleavage of subject and object, and of the way in which it is conquered under the impact of the Spiritual Presence. Is there a general theono-mous answer to the question of subject against object? Philosophers, mystics, lovers, seekers of intoxication — even of death — have tried to conquer this cleavage. In some of these attempts the Spiritual Presence is manifest; in others the desperate and often demonic desire to escape the cleavage by escaping reality is visible. Psychology has become aware of this problem; the unconscious desire to return to the mother's womb or to the devouring womb of nature or to the protective womb of contemporary society is an expression of the will to dissolve one's subjectivity into something transsubjective, which is not objective (otherwise it would reinstate the subject) but lies beyond subjectivity and objectivity. The most pertinent answers have been given by two phenomena that are related in this respect — mysticism and *eros*. Mysticism answers with the description of a state of mind in which the "universe of discourse" has disappeared but the experiencing self is still aware of this disappearance. Only in eternal fulfillment does the subject (and consequently the object) disappear completely. Historical man can only anticipate in a fragmentary way the ultimate fulfillment in which subject ceases to be subject and object ceases to be object.

A similar phenomenon is human love. The separation of the lover and the beloved is the most conspicuous and painful expression of the subject-object cleavage of finitude. The subject of love is never able to penetrate fully into the object of love, and love remains unfulfilled, and necessarily so, for if it were ever fulfilled it would eliminate the lover as well as the loved; this paradox shows the human situation and with it the question to which theonomy, as the creation of the Spiritual Presence gives the answer. . . .

In the communal realm, too, the gap between subject and object leads to a great number of ambiguities. We have referred to some of them, and we must now show what happens to them under the impact of the Spiritual Presence. Where there is Spirit, they are conquered, though fragmentarily.

The first problem following from the establishment of any kind of community is the exclusiveness which corresponds to the limitation of its inclusiveness. As every friendship excludes the innumerable others with whom there is no friendship, so every tribe, class, town, nation, and civilization excludes all those who do not belong to it. The justice of social cohesion implies the injustice of social rejection. Under the impact of the Spiritual Presence, two things happen in which the injustice within communal justice is conquered. The churches, in so far as they represent the Spiritual Community, are transformed from religious communities with demonic exclusiveness into a holy community with universal inclusiveness, without losing their identity. The indirect effect this has on the secular communities is one side of the impact of the Spiritual Presence in the communal realm. The other is the direct effect the Spirit has on the understanding and actualizing of the idea of justice. The ambiguity of cohesion and rejection is conquered by the creation of more embracing unities through which those who are rejected by the unavoidable exclusiveness of any concrete group are included in a larger group — finally in mankind. On this basis family-exclusiveness is fragmentarily overcome by friendship-inclusiveness, friendship-rejection by acceptance in local communities, class-exclusiveness by national-inclusiveness, and so on. Of course, this is a continuous struggle of the Spiritual Presence, not only against exclusiveness, but also against an inclusiveness which disintegrates a genuine community and deprives it of its identity (as in some expressions of mass society).

This example leads directly to another of the ambiguities of justice, that of inequality. Justice implies equality; but equality of what is essentially unequal is as unjust as inequality of what is essentially equal. Under the impact of the Spiritual Presence (which is the same as saying, determined by faith and love), the ultimate equality of everyone who is called to the Spiritual Community is united with the preliminary inequality that is rooted in the self-actualizaton of the individual as individual. Everyone has his own destiny, based partly on the given conditions of his existence and partly on his freedom to react in a centered way to the situation and the different elements in it, as provided by his destiny. The ultimate equality, however, cannot be separated from the existential inequality; the latter is under a continuous Spiritual judgment, because it tends to produce social situations in which ultimate equality becomes invisible and ineffective. Although it was the influence of Stoic philosophy more than that of the Christian churches that reduced the injustice of slavery in its dehumanizing power, it was (and is) the Spiritual Presence which acted through the philosophers of Stoic provenience. But here also the struggle of the Spirit against the ambiguities of *praxis* is directed not only toward communal inequality but also toward forms of communal equality in which essential inequality is disregarded, for example, in the principle of equal education in a mass society. Such education is an injustice to those whose charisma is their ability to transcend the conformity of an equalizing culture. With the affirmation of the ultimate equality of all men, the Spiritual Presence affirms the polarity of relative equality and relative inequality in the actual communal life. The theonomous solution of the ambiguities of equality produces a genuine theonomy.

Among the most conspicuous ambiguities of community is that of leadership and power. It also most obviously shows the subject-object split as the source of the ambiguities. Because of the lack of a physiological centeredness such as we find in the individual person, the community must create centeredness, as far as it is possible at all, by a ruling group which itself is represented by an individual (king, president, and so on). In such an individual, communal centeredness is embodied in psychosomatic centeredness. He represents the center, but he *is* not the center in the way in which his own self is the center of his whole being. The ambiguities of justice which follow from this character of communal centeredness are rooted in the unavoidable fact that the ruler and the ruling group actualize their own power of being when they actualize the power of being of the whole community they represent. The tyranny which pervades all systems of power, even the most liberal, is one consequence of this highly dialectical structure of social power. The other consequence, resulting from opposition to the implications of power, is a powerless liberalism or anarchism, which is usually soon succeeded by a conscious and unrestricted tyranny. Under the impact of the Spiritual Presence, the members of the ruling group (including the ruler) are able to sacrifice their subjectivity in part by becoming objects of their own rule along with all other objects and by transferring the sacrificed part of their subjectivity to the ruled. This partial sacrifice of the subjectivity of the rulers and this partial elevation of the ruled to subjectivity is the meaning of the "democratic" idea. It is not identical with any particular democratic constitution which attempts to actualize the democratic principle. This principle is an element in the Spiritual Community and its justice. It is present even in aristocratic and monarchic constitutions — and it may be greatly distorted in historical democracies. Wherever it is fragmentarily actual the Spiritual Presence is at work — through or in opposition to the churches or outside the overtly religious life.

Justice in communal life is, above all, justice of the law, law in the sense of a power-supported legal system. Its ambiguities are twofold: the ambiguity of the establishment of the law and the ambiguity of its execution. The first is partly identical with the ambiguity of leadership. Legal power, exercised by the ruling group (and the individual who represents the group), is first of all legislative power. The justice of a system of laws is inseparably tied to justice as conceived by the ruling group, and this justice expresses both principles of right and wrong and principles by which the ruling group affirms and sustains and defends its own power. The spirit of a law inseparably unites the spirit of justice and the spirit of the powers in control, and this means that its justice implies injustice. Under the impact of the Spiritual Presence, the law can receive a theonomous quality to the extent that the Spirit is effective. It can represent justice unambiguously though fragmentarily; in symbolic language, it can become "the justice of the Kingdom of God". This does not mean that it can become a rational system of justice above the life of any communal group, such as some Neo-Kantian philosophers of law have tried to develop. There is no such thing, because the multidimensional unity of life does not admit a function of the spirit in which the preceding dimensions are not effectively present. The spirit of the law is necessarily not only the spirit of justice but also the spirit of a communal group. There is no justice that is not someone's justice — not the justice of an individual but of a society. The Spiritual Presence does not suppress the vital basis of the law but removes its injustices by fighting against the ideologies which justify them. This fight has sometimes been waged through the voice of the churches as images of the Spiritual Community and sometimes in a direct way by the creation of the prophetic movements within the secular realm itself. Theonomous legislation is the work of the Spiritual Presence through the medium of prophetic self-criticism in those who are responsible for it. Such a statement is not "idealistic" in the negative sense of the word as long as we maintain the "realistic" statement that the Spirit works indirectly through all dimensions of life, though directly only through the dimensions of man's spirit.

The other ambiguity of the legal form of communal life is the ambiguity of the execution of the law. Here two considerations are needed. One is related to the fact that the execution of the law is dependent on the power of those who render judgments and who are, in so doing, dependent, like the lawgivers, upon their own total being in all its dimensions. Each of their judgments expresses not only the meaing of the law, not only its spirit, but also the spirit of the judge, including all the dimensions which belong to him as a person. One of the most important functions of the Old Testament prophet was to exhort the judges to exercise justice against their class interest and against their changing moods. The dignity with which the office and functions of the judge are vested is a reminder of the theonomous origins of, and theonomous ideal in, the execution of the law.

However, there is another ambiguity of the legal form of communal life, one which is rooted in the very nature of the law — its abstraction and inability to fit precisely any concrete case in which it is applied. History has shown that the situation is not improved, but rather worsened, when new, more specific laws are added to the more general ones. They are equally inadequate to any concrete situation. The wisdom of the judge lies between the abstract law and the concrete situation, and this wisdom can be theonomously inspired. In so far as this is the case, the demand of the particular case is perceived and obeyed. The law in its abstract majesty does not overrule individual differences, nor does it deprive itself of its general validity in acknowledging differences.

*Vol. 3, pp. 252-3, 262-5*

\*

# THE SPIRIT IN SELF-TRANSCENDENCE (RELIGION)

*This section enables readers to follow Tillich's commentary on the third function of life, "self-transcendence", which in humans he terms "religion". This function also has its own distinctive ambiguities. There is a unique and more complex move in this segment of his* Systematic Theology, *however, since the Spiritual Presence that "conquers" the ambiguities of religion involves the specific activity of the Christian churches with their own ambiguities and paradox. Tillich's discussion of the Spiritual Presence's role in healing the ambiguities of religion, therefore, turns specifically to the role of the churches, and here his pneumatology is joined by an ecclesiology in order to fulfill the christology begun in volume 2. That is to say, only in ecclesial communities, which occasion the Spirit's healing of the estrangement and ambiguity attending each of the ontological polarities, does the New Being in Jesus as the Christ begin to have its full effect. This healing begins when the churches, or other groups ("latent" Spiritual Community) conquer the ambiguities of religion, and then also enable the fulfillment of culture and morality. The following selections (from* Systematic Theology, *vol. 3, pp. 86-245 passim) have been carefully crafted together in order to display Tillich's most influential views concerning the self-transcending religious function, its distinctive ambiguities, and the way the churches mediate (or may often inhibit!) the Spiritual Presence in life and history.*

## 1. FINITE FREEDOM AS GREAT AND TRAGIC

### *a. Freedom and finitude*

The polarity of freedom and destiny (and its analogies in the realms of being which precede the dimension of the spirit) creates the possibility and reality of life's transcending itself. Life, in degrees, is free from itself, from a total bondage to its own finitude. It is striving in the vertical direction toward ultimate and infinite being. The vertical transcends both the circular line of centeredness and the horizontal line of growth. In the words of Paul (Romans 8:19-22), the longing of all creation for the liberation from the "subjection to futility" (RSV) and "the shackles of morality" (NEB) is described with a profound poetic empathy. These words are a classical expression of the self-transcendence of life under all dimensions. One can also think of Aristotle's doctrine that the movements of all things are caused by their *eros* toward the "unmoved mover".

The question as to how the self-transcendence of life manifests itself cannot be answered in empirical terms, as is possible in the case of self-integration and self-creativity. One can speak about it only in terms which describe the reflection of the inner self-transcendence of things in man's consciousness. Man is the mirror in which the relation of everything finite to the infinite becomes conscious. No empirical observation of this relation is possible, because all empirical knowledge refers to finite interdependences, not to the relation of the finite to the infinite.

The self-transcendence of life is contradicted by the profanization of life, a tendency which, like self-transcendence, cannot be described empirically but only through the mirror of man's consciousness. But profanization appears in man's consciousness, like self-transcendence, as an experience which has been expressed and was extremely effective in all epochs of man's history. Man has witnessed to the conflict between the affirmation and the denial of the holiness of life wherever he has reached full humanity. And even in such ideologies as communism, the attempt toward a total profanization of life has resulted in the unexpected consequence that the profane itself received the glory of holiness. The term "profane" in its genuine meaning expresses exactly what we call "resisting self-transcendence", that is, remaining before the door of the temple, standing outside the holy, although in English "profane" has received the connotation of attacking the holy in vulgar or blasphemous terms and consequently has come to mean vulgar language in general. In religious terminology (though not in German and the Romance languages), "profane" has been replaced by "secular", derived from *saeculum* in the sense of the "world". But this does not express the contrast to the holy as graphically as "profane" does, and therefore I wish to keep the word for the important function of expressing the resistance against self-transcendence under all dimensions of life.

The general assertion may be made that in every act of the self-transcendence of life profanization is present or, in other words, that life transcends itself ambiguously. Although this ambiguity is most conspicuous in the religious realm, it is manifest under all dimensions.

*Vol. 3, pp. 86-7*

### b. The great and the tragic

The self-transcendence of life, which reveals itself to man as the greatness of life, leads under the conditions of existence to the tragic character of life, to the ambiguity of the great and the tragic. Only the great is able to have tragedy. In Greece the heroes, the bearers of highest value and power, and the great families are the subjects of tragedy in myths as well as in plays. The small ones, or those who are ugly or evil, are below the level at which tragedy starts. But there is a limit to this aristocratic feeling: every Athenian citizen was asked by the government to participate in the performance of the tragedies, thus implying that no human being is without some greatness, that is, the greatness of being of divine nature. The performance of the tragedy, appealing to every citizen, is an act of democratic valuation of man as man, as a potential subject of tragedy, and therefore as a bearer of greatness. . . .

The tragic, though first formulated in the context of the Dionysian religion, is, like the Apollonian logos, a universally valid concept. It describes the universality of man's estrangement and its inescapable character, which nevertheless is a matter of responsibility. We have used the term *hubris* to describe one element in man's estrangement; the other element is "concupiscence". In the description of existence, *hubris* and concupiscence appear merely as negative elements. In the present part, dealing with life processes, they appear in their ambiguity — *hubris* ambiguously united with greatness and concupiscence with *eros*. *Hubris* in this sense is not pride — the compulsive overcompensation of actual smallness — but the self-elevation of the great beyond the limits of its finitude. The result is both the destruction of others and self-destruction.

If greatness is inescapably connected with tragedy, it is natural that people should try to avoid tragedy by avoiding greatness. This, of course, is an unconscious process, but it is the most widespread of all life processes under the dimension of the spirit. In many respects it is possible to avoid tragedy by avoiding greatness, although not ultimately, for every man has the greatness of being partially responsible for his destiny. And if he avoids the amount of greatness that is possible for him he becomes a tragic figure. This anxiety of avoiding tragedy throws him into the tragic loss of himself and of the greatness to be a self.

It belongs to the ambiguity of greatness and tragedy that the subjects of tragedy are not aware of their situation. Several great tragedies are tragedies of the revelation of the human predicament (as in the case of Oedipus, who blinds himself after his eyes have seen himself in the mirror held before him by the messengers); and there have been entire civilizations, such as the later ancient and the modern Western, whose tragic *hubris* has been revealed by prophetic messengers at the moment that its catastrophe was approaching (for example, the pagan and Christian seers of the end of the empire in late ancient Rome and the existentialist prophets of the arrival of Western nihilism in the nineteenth and early twentieth centuries). If one asks what the guilt of the tragic hero is, the answer must be that he perverts the function of self-transcendence by identifying himself with that to which self-transcendence is directed — the great itself. He does not resist self-transcendence, but he resists the demand to transcend his own greatness. He is caught by his own power of representing the self-transcendence of life.

It is impossible to speak meaningfully of tragedy without understanding the ambiguity of greatness. Sad events are not tragic events. The tragic can be understood only on the basis of the understanding of greatness. It expresses the ambiguity of life in the function of self-transcendence, including all dimensions of life but becoming conscious only under the dominance of the dimension of spirit.

But under the dimension of the spirit something else happens. The great reveals its dependence on its relation to the ultimate, and with this awareness the great becomes the holy. The holy is beyond tragedy, although those who represent the holy stand with all other beings under the law of greatness and its consequence, tragedy (compare the section on the tragic involvement of the Christ, Vol. 2, pp. 132-4).

*Vol. 3, pp. 92-4*

\*

## 2. THE AMBIGUITIES OF RELIGION

### a. *The holy and the secular (profane)*

In contrast to all other realms in which the ambiguities of life appear, the self-transcendence of life in religion shows a double ambiguity. The first has already been mentioned as one which is a universal characteristic of life, the ambiguity of the great and the profane. We have seen how in the process of profanization life, in all cultural acts of self-creativity and in the moral act of self-integration, loses its greatness and dignity. And . . . in order to maintain itself as self-transcendent, life under the dimension of spirit expresses itself in a function which is defined by self-transcendence, that is, religion.

But this character of religion leads to a reduplication of ambiguities. Religion, as the self-transcending function of life, claims to be the answer to the ambiguities of life in all other dimensions; it transcends their finite tensions and conflicts. But in doing so, it falls into even profounder tensions, conflicts, and ambiguities. Religion is the highest expression of the greatness and dignity of life; in it the greatness of life becomes holiness. Yet religion is also the most radical refutation of the greatness and dignity of life; in it the great becomes most profanized, the holy most desecrated. These ambiguities are the central subject of any honest understanding of religion, and they are the background with which church and theology must work. They are the decisive motive for the expectation of a reality which transcends the religious function.

The first ambiguity of religion is that of self-transcendence and profanization in the religious function itself. The second ambiguity of religion is the demonic elevation of something conditional to unconditional validity. One can say that religion always moves between the danger points of profanization and demonization, and that in every genuine act of the religious life both are present, openly or covertly.

The profanization of religion has the character of transforming it into a finite object among finite objects. In religion as a particular function of the spirit, it is the process of the profanization of the holy to which we refer. If in religion the great is called the holy, this indicates that religion is based on the manifestation of the holy itself, the divine ground of being. Every religion is the receptive answer to revelatory experiences. This is its greatness and its dignity; this makes religion and its expressions holy in *theoria* as well as in *praxis*. In this sense one can speak of Holy Scriptures, holy communities, holy acts, holy offices, holy persons. These predicates mean that all these realities are more than they are in their immediate finite appearance. They are self-transcendent, or, seen from the side of that to which they transcend — the holy — they are translucent toward it. This holiness is not their moral or cognitive or even religious quality but their power of pointing beyond themselves. If the predicate "holiness" refers to persons, the actual participation of the person in it is possible in many degrees, from the lowest to the highest. It is not the personal quality that decides the degree of participation but the power of self-transcendence. Augustine's great insight in the Donatist struggle was that it is not the quality of the priest that makes a sacrament effective but the transparency of his office and the function he performs. Otherwise the religious function would be impossible, and the predicate of the holy could not be applied at all. . . . The first ambiguity of religion is the presence of profanized elements in every religious act. There are two opposite ways in which this is true, the one institutional, the other reductive. *The institutional way* is not restricted to so-called institutionalized relgion, for, as psychology has shown, there are institutions in the inner life of the individual, "ritual activities" as Freud has called them, which produce and preserve methods of action and reaction. The relentless attacks on "organized religion" are mostly based on a deeply rooted confusion, for life is organized in all its self-actualizations; without form it could not even have dynamics, and this is true of the personal as well as the communal life. But the real object of honest attacks on organized religion is the ambiguity of religion in the context of its institutional form. Instead of transcending the finite in the direction of the infinite, institutionalized religion actually becomes a finite reality itself — a set of prescribed activities to be performed, a set of stated doctrines to be accepted, a social pressure group along with others, a political power with all the implications of power politics. The critics cannot see the self-transcendent, great, and holy character of religion in this structure, which is subject to the sociological laws which govern all secular groups. But even if all this is internalized and performed by individuals in their personal religious life, the institutional character is not removed. The content of the personal religious life is always taken from the religious life of a social group. Even the silent language of prayer is formed by tradition. The critics of such profanized religion are justified in their criticism and often serve religion better than those whom they attack. It would, however, be a utopian fallacy to attempt to use these criticisms to remove the profanizing tendencies in the religious life and to retain pure self-transcendence of holiness. Insight into the inescapable ambiguity of life prevents such a fallacy. In all forms of communal and personal religion, profanizing elements are effective; and conversely, most profanized forms of religion draw their power to continue from the elements of greatness and holiness within them. The pettiness of average daily-life religion is no argument against its greatness, and the way in which it is drawn down to the level of undignified mechanization is no argument against its dignity. Life, transcending itself, at the same time remains within itself, and the first ambiguity of religion follows from this tension.

The preceding description deals with only one way in which religion shows its ambiguity, the "institutional" way. There is another, *the "reductive" way,* based on the fact that culture is the form of religion and that morality is the expression of its seriousness. This fact can lead to the reduction of religion to culture and morality, whereby its symbols are interpreted as results merely of cultural creativity, whether as veiled concepts or as images. If one takes away the veil of self-transcendence, one finds cognitive insight and aesthetic expression. In this view the myths are a combination of primitive science and primitive poetry; they are creations of *theoria* and as such have lasting significance, but their claim to express transcendence must be discarded. The same kind of interpretation is given of the manifestations of religion in *praxis*: the holy personality and the holy community are developments of personality and community which must be judged by the principles of humanity and justice, but their claim to transcend these principles must be rejected.

As it appears in such ideas, the reduction of religion is not radical. Religion is given a place in the whole of man's cultural creativity, and its usefulness for moral self-actualization is not denied. But this is a preliminary state in the process of a reductionist profanization of religion. It soon becomes clear either that the claim of religion must be accepted or that it has no claim to a place among the functions of cultural creativity and morality has no need of it. Religion, which in principle has a home in every function of the spirit, has become homeless in all of them. The benevolent treatment it has received from those who reject its claim to self-transcendence does not help it, and its benevolent critics soon become much more radical. Religion is explained away in the cognitive realm as being derived from psychological or sociological sources and is considered as illusion or ideology, while in the aesthetic realm, religious symbols are replaced by finite objects in the different naturalistic styles, especially in critical naturalism and some types of nonobjective art. Education does not initiate into the mystery of being to which religion points, but introduces people only into the needs of a society whose needs and ends remain finite in spite of their endlessness. All communities become agents for the actualization of such a society, rejecting any kind of self-transcending symbols and trying to dissolve the churches into the organizations of secular life. Within large sections of contemporary mankind, this reductive way of profanizing religion, reduction by annihilation, is tremendously successful — not only in the communist East, but also in the democratic West. In the world-historical view, one must say that in our period this way is much more successful than the institutional way of profanizing religion.

Nevertheless, here also the ambiguity of life resists an unambiguous solution. First of all, we must remind ourselves of the fact that the profanizing forces are not simply the negation of religion as a function of the spirit but that they are present in its very nature: actual religion lives in the cognitive forms, from language to ontology, which are the results of cultural creativity. In using language, historical research, psychological descriptions of human nature, existentialist analyses of man's predicament, prephilosophical and philosophical concepts, it uses the secular material which becomes independent in the processes of reductive profanization. Religion can be secularized and finally dissolved into secular forms only because it has the ambiguity of self-transcendence.

But when this is attempted, the ambiguity of religion shows its effect on these processes of reductive profanization, just as it shows its effect in the center of religious self-transcendence. The way in which this happens suggests the larger concept of religion as experience of the unconditional, both in the moral imperative and in the depth of culture. The ambiguity of radical secularism is that it cannot escape the element of self-transcendence which appears in these two experiences. Often these experiences are rather hidden and any expression of them is carefully avoided; but if the radically secular philosopher is asked by a tyrannical power — dictatorial or conformist — to give up his secularism, he resists such a demand, experiencing the unconditional imperative of honesty up to total self-sacrifice. In the same way, if the radically secular writer whose novel has been written with the totality of his being sees that it is being used as a mere piece of entertainment, he feels this as an abuse and as profanization. Reductive profanization may succeed in abolishing religion as a special function, but it is not able to remove religion as a quality that is found in all functions of the spirit — the quality of ultimate concern.

### b. The divine and the demonic

In religion the ambiguity of self-transcendence appears as the ambiguity of the divine and the demonic. The symbol of the demonic does not need justification as it did thirty years ago, when it was reintroduced into theological language. It has become a much-used and much-abused term to designate antidivine forces in individual and social life. In this way it has frequently lost the ambiguous character implied in the word itself. Demons in mythological vision are divine-antidivine beings. They are not simply negations of the divine but participate in a distorted way in the power and holiness of the divine. The term must be understood against this mythological background. The demonic does not resist self-transcendence as does the profane, but it distorts self-transcendence by identifying a particular bearer of holiness with the holy itself. In this sense all polytheistic gods are demonic, because the basis of being and meaning on which they stand is finite, no matter how sublime, great, or dignified it may be. And the claim of something finite to infinity or to divine greatness is the characteristic of the demonic. Demonization of the holy occurs in all religions day by day, even in the religion which is based on the self-negation of the finite in the Cross of the Christ. The quest for unambiguous life is, therefore, most radically directed against the ambiguity of the holy and the demonic in the religious realm.

The tragic is the inner ambiguity of human greatness. But the subject of tragedy does not *aspire* to divine greatness. He does not intend "to be like God." He touches, so to speak, the divine sphere, and he is rejected by it into self-destruction, but he does not claim divinity for himself. Wherever *this* is done, the demonic appears. A main characteristic of the tragic is the state of being blind; a main characteristic of the demonic is the state of being split.

This is easily understandable on the basis of the demonic's claim to divinity on a finite basis: the elevation of one element of finitude to infinite power and meaning necessarily produces the reaction from other elements of finitude, which deny such a claim or make it for themselves. The demonic self-elevation of one nation over against all the others in the name of her God or system of values produces the reaction from other nations in the name of *their* God. The demonic self-elevation of particular forces in the centered personality and the claim of their absolute superiority leads to the reaction of other forces and to a split consciousness. The claim of *one* value, represented by *one* God, to be the criterion of all others leads to the splits in polytheistic religion.

A consequence of these splits, connected with the nature of the demonic, is the state of being "possessed" by the power which produces the split. The demoniacs are the possessed ones. The freedom of centeredness is removed by the demonic split. Demonic structures in the personal and communal life cannot be broken by acts of freedom and good will. They are strengthened by such acts — except when the changing power is a divine structure, that is, a structure of grace.

Wherever the demonic appears, it shows religious traits, even if the appearance is moral or cultural. This is a logical consequence of the mutual immanence of the three functions of life in the dimension of spirit and of the dual concept of religion as unconditional concern and as a realm of concrete symbols that express concrete concerns. Here also examples are abundant: the unconditional demands of commitment by states which vest themselves with religious dignity, by cultural functions which control all others (as in scientific absolutism), by individuals who seek idolization of themselves, by particular drives in the person which take over the personal center — in all these cases, distorted self-transcendence takes place.

A revealing example of the ambiguity of the demonic in the cultural realm is the Roman empire, whose greatness, dignity, and sublime character was universally acknowledged, but which became demonically possessed when it vested itself with divine holiness and produced the split which led to the antidemonic struggle of Christianity and the demonic persecution of the Christians.

This historical reminder furnishes a transition to the discussion of religion in the narrower sense of the word and its demonization. The basic ambiguity of religion has a deeper root than any of the other ambiguities of life, for religion is the point at which the answer to the quest for the unambiguous is received. Religion in this respect (that is, in the respect of man's possibility of receiving this answer) is unambiguous; the actual reception, however, is profoundly ambiguous, for it occurs in the changing forms of man's moral and cultural existence. These forms participate in the holy to which they point, but they are not the holy itself. The claim to be the holy itself makes them demonic.

This is the reason why theologians have protested against applying the term "religion" to Christianity. They have contrasted religion with revelation and have described religion as man's attempt to glorify himself. This is, indeed, a correct description of demonized religion, but it ignores the fact that every religion is based on revelation and that every revelation expresses itself in a religion. In so far as religion is based on revelation it is unambiguous; in so far as it receives revelation it is ambiguous. This is true of all religions, even those which their followers call revealed religion. But no religion is revealed; religion is the creation and the distortion of revelation.

The concept of religion cannot be avoided in any theology, although the criticism of religion is an element in the history of all religions. The revelatory impact behind the religions awakens people everywhere to an awareness of the contrast between the unambiguous life toward which the self-transcendence of life is directed and the often terrifying ambiguities of actual religions. One can read the history of religion, especially of the great religions, as a continuous inner religious struggle against religion for the sake of the holy itself. Christianity claims that in the Cross of the Christ the final victory in this struggle has been reached, but even in claiming this, the form of the claim itself shows demonic traits; that which is rightly said about the Cross of the Christ is wrongly transferred to the life of the church, whose ambiguities are denied, although they have become increasingly powerful throughout its history.

But at this point it is the demonization of religion in general of which we want to give some examples. Religion as a historical reality uses cultural creations both in *theoria* and *praxis*. It uses some and rejects others, and in doing so it establishes a realm of religious culture which lies alongside the other cultural creations. But religion as the self-transcendence of life in all realms claims a superiority over them which is justified in so far as religion points to that which transcends all of them, but the claim to superiority becomes demonic when religion as a social and personal reality makes this claim for itself and the finite forms by which it points to the infinite.

We can show this in the four functions of man's cultural creativity . . . : the communal, the personal, the aesthetic, the cognitive. Religion is actual in social groups which are united with or separated from political groups. In both cases they constitute a social, legal, and political reality which is consecrated by the holy embodied in them. In the power of this consecration they consecrate the other communal structures and in this way try to control them. In case of their resistance, they try to destroy them. The power of the bearers of the holy is the unconditional character of the holy, in whose name they break the resistance of all those who do not accept the symbols of self-transcendence under which the religious community lives. This is the source of the power of those who represent a religious community, as it is the source of the solidarity of the holy institutions, sacred customs, divinely ordered systems of law, hierarchical orders, myths and symbols, and so on. But this very solidity betrays its divine-demonic ambiguity; it is able to reject all criticisms which are raised in the name of justice. It overrules them in the name of the holy, which has the principle of justice within itself, breaking the minds and bodies of those who try to resist. No examples need be given for this ambiguity of religion, for they fill the pages of world history. It is enough to show why the quest for unambiguous life must transcend religion, even though the answer is given in religion.

In the realm of the personal life, the divine-demonic ambiguity of religion appears in the idea of the saint. Here is reflected the conflict between humanity and holiness and the divine support and demonic suppression of personal development toward humanity. These conflicts with their integrating, disintegrating, creative, and destructive consequences go on first of all within the individual person. One of the ways religion uses its own consecrated idea of personality to suppress the idea of humanity within the individual is by engendering an uneasy conscience in him who does not accept the absolute claim of religion. The psychologist knows the devastation in personal development which is caused by this conflict. Very often in the history of religion it is the negative, ascetic principle which receives religious consecration and which stands as a condemning judge against the positive implications of the idea of humanity. But the power contained in the religious image of personal holiness would not exist if there were not the other side — the impact on the development of the person coming from the divine, antidemonic (and antiprofane) character of the holy to which religion points. But again one must say that the answer to the quest for unambiguous life is not in the idea of the saint, although the answer can be received only in the depth of the self-transcending personality — religiously speaking, in the act of faith.

The discussion about the divine-demonic ambiguity in the relation of religion to *theoria* naturally focuses on the problem of religious doctrine, particularly when it appears in the form of an established dogma. The conflict arising here is one between the consecrated truth of the dogma and the truth which unites dynamic change and creative form. But it is not the theoretical conflict as such in which the divine-demonic ambiguity appears but in its significance for the holy community and holy personality. The demonic suppression of honest obedience to the structures of truth is at stake here. What is happening in this respect to the cognitive function happens equally to the aesthetic function; the suppression of authentic expressiveness in art and literature is equal to the suppression of honest cognition. It is done in the name of a religiously consecrated truth and a religiously consecrated style. There is no doubt that self-transcendence opens the eyes to cognitive truth and aesthetic authenticity. Divine power lies behind religious doctrines and religious art. But the demonic distortion begins when new insight presses toward the surface and is trodden down in the name of the dogma, the consecrated truth, or when new styles seek to express the drives of a period and are prevented from doing so in the name of religiously approved forms of expression. In all these cases the resisting community and the resisting personalities are victims of the demonic destruction of truth and expressiveness in the name of the holy. As in relation to justice and to humanity directly, so in relation to truth and to expressiveness indirectly — religion is *not* the answer to the quest for unambiguous life, although the answer can only be received through religion.

*Vol. 3, pp. 98-106*

*

### 3. SPIRITUAL PRESENCE AND THE AMBIGUITIES OF RELIGION

#### a. *The ontological character of the Spiritual Community*

The term "Spiritual Community" has been used to characterize sharply that element in the concept of the church which is called the "body of Christ" by the New Testament and the "church invisible or Spiritual" by the Reformation. In the previous discussion this element has sometimes been called the "invisible essence of the religious communities". Such a statement implies that the Spiritual Community is not a group existing beside other groups but rather a power and a structure inherent and effective in such groups, that is, in religious communities. If they are consciously based on the appearance of the New Being in Jesus as the Christ, these groups are called churches. If they have other foundations, they are called synagogues, temple congregations, mystery groups, monastic groups, cult groups, movements. In so far as they are determined by an ultimate concern, the Spiritual Community is effective in its hidden power and structure in all such groups. In the language of the New Testament, the manifestation of the Spiritual Community in the Christian church is described in the following way: The church in New Testament Greek is *ecclesia*, the assembly of those who are called out of all nations by the *apostoloi*, the messengers of the Christ, to the congregation of the *eleutheroi*, those who have become free citizens of the "Kingdom of the Heavens". There is a "church", an "assembly of God" (or the Christ), in every town in which the message has been successful and a Christian *koinonia*, or communion, has come into being. But there is also the over-all unity of these local assemblies in the Church universal, by virtue of which the particular groups become churches (local, provincial, national, or after the split of the Church universal, denominational). The Church universal, as well as the particular churches included in it, is seen in a double aspect as the "body of Christ", on the one hand — a Spiritual reality — and as a social group of individual Christians on the other. In the first sense, they show all the characteristics which we have attributed to the Spiritual Community in the preceding chapters: in the second sense, all the ambiguities of religion, culture, and morality that were already discussed in connection with the ambiguties of life in general are present.

For the sake of semantic clarification, we have used the term "Spiritual Community" as an equivalent of "the church" (as the body of Christ), avoiding the term "the Church" (with a capital "C") completely. Of course, this term cannot be removed from liturgical language; but systematic theology has the right to use nonbiblical and nonecclesiastical terms, if such use serves to free the genuine meanings of the traditional terms from confusing connotations which obscure their meaning. When the reformers distinguished sharply between the invisible and the visible church they did the same thing. They also had to resist dangerous and even demonic distortions of the true meaning of "church" and "churches".

It cannot be denied, however, that a new terminology, though helpful in one respect, may produce new confusions in another. This has certainly been the case in the distinction between the church visible and invisible, and it might happen to the distinction between the Spiritual Community and the churches. In the first case, the confusion is that the "church invisible" is understood as a reality beside the Church visible or, more precisely, beside the visible churches. But in the thought of the reformers, there was no invisible church alongside the historicial churches. The invisible church is the Spiritual essence of the visible church; like everything Spiritual, it is hidden, but it determines the nature of the visible church. In the same way the Spiritual Community does not exist as an entity beside the churches, but it is their Spiritual essence, effective in them through its power, its structure, and its fight against their ambiguities.

To the question of the logical-ontological character of the Spiritual Community, one can answer that it is essentially determining existence and being resisted by existence. Two mistakes must be avoided here. One is the interpretation of the Spiritual Community as an ideal — as against the reality of the churches — that is, as constructed from the positive elements in the ambiguities of religion and projected onto the screen of transcendence. This image creates the expectation that the actual churches will progress toward an approximation of this ideal picture of the Spiritual Community. But this raises the question: What justifies such an expectation? Or more concretely, Where do the churches get the power of establishing and actualizing such an ideal? The familiar answer is that they get it from the divine Spirit, working in the church. But this answer leads to the further question as to the way in which the divine Spirit is present. How does the Spirit use the word and the sacrament as media of his creative work? How can faith be created, except by the power of faith; and love, except by the power of love? Essential power must precede actualization. In biblical terms one would say that the church as the Body of Christ, or as the Spiritual Temple, is the New Creation into which the individual Christian and the particular church is taken. This kind of thinking is more strange to our time than it was to most periods in the history of the church, including the Reformation. But it is certainly biblical thinking, and as long as the churches affirm that Jesus is the Christ, the mediator of the New Being, it is theologically necessary.

However, there is another danger to be avoided, and that is a kind of Platonism or mythological literalism which interprets the Spiritual Community as an assembly of so-called Spiritual beings, angelic hierarchies, saints and the saved from all periods and countries, represented on earth by ecclesiastical hierarches and sacraments. This idea is in the line of Greek Orthodox thinking. Whatever its symbolic truth may be, it is not what we have called the Spiritual Community. The "heavenly assembly of God" is a supranaturalistic counterpart to the earthly assembly of God, the church, but it is not this quality in the churches which makes them churches — it is their invisible, essential Spirituality.

This calls for a category to be used in interpreting reality which is neither realistic nor idealistic nor supranaturalistic but essentialistic — a category pointing to the power of the essential behind and within the existential. This analysis holds true of every life process: everywhere, the essential is one of the determining powers. Its power is not causal but directive. One could call it teleological, but his word has been misused in the sense of a further causality, which certainly must be rejected by both science and philosophy. And yet, it would be possible to say that the Spiritual Community is the inner *telos* of the churches and that as such it is the source of everything which makes them churches.

*Vol. 3, pp. 162-5*

### b. *The New Being in Jesus as the Christ and in the Spiritual Community*

As we have emphasized in the christological part of the system, the Christ would not be the Christ without those who receive him as the Christ. He could not have brought the new reality without those who have accepted the new reality in him and from him. Therefore, the creativity of the Spiritual Presence in mankind must be seen as a threefold one: in mankind as a whole in preparation for the central manifestation of the divine Spirit, in the divine Spirit's central manifestation itself, and in the manifestation of the Spiritual Community under the creative impact of the central event. We do not use the word "church" for the Spiritual Community, because this word has been used, of necessity, in the frame of the ambiguities of religion. At this point we speak instead of that which is able to conquer the ambiguities of religion — the New Being — in anticipation, in central appearance, and in reception. Such words as "body of Christ", "assembly (*ecclesia*) of God" or "of Christ", express the unambiguous life created by the divine Presence, in a sense similar to that of the term "Spiritual Community". Its relation to what is called "Church" or "church" in a rather equivocal terminology will be discussed later.

The Spiritual Community is unambiguous; it is New Being, created by the Spiritual Presence. But, although it is a manifestation of unambiguous life, it is nonetheless fragmentary, as was the manifestation of unambiguous life in the Christ and in those who expected the Christ. The Spiritual Community is an unambiguous, though fragmentary, creation of the divine Spirit. In this context, "fragmentary" means appearing under the conditions of finitude but conquering both estrangement and ambiguity.

The Spiritual Community is also Spiritual in the sense in which Luther often uses the word, that is, "invisible", "hidden", "open to faith alone", but nevertheless real, unconquerably real. This is analogous to the New Being's hidden presence in Jesus and in those who were vehicles of preparation for him. From the Spiritual Community's hiddenness, its "dialectical" relation (of identity and nonidentity) to the churches follows, just as the dialectical relation of Jesus and the Christ and, to take a similar case, of the history of religion and revelation also follows from the same hiddenness. In all three cases only the "eyes of faith" see what is hidden or Spiritual, and the "eyes of faith" are the Spirit's creation: only Spirit can discern Spirit.

The relation of the New Being in Christ to the New Being in the

Spiritual Community is symbolized in several central stories of the New Testament. The first one, which is most significant for the meaning of "Christ", is also most significant for the relation of Christ to the Spiritual Community. It is the story of Peter's confession to Jesus that he is the Christ at Caesarea Philippi and Jesus' answer that the recognition of him as the Christ is a work of God; this recognition is the result not of an ordinary experience but of the impact of the Spiritual Presence. It is the Spirit grasping Peter that enables his spirit to recognize the Spirit in Jesus which makes him the Christ. This recognition is the basis of the Spiritual Community against which the demonic powers are powerless and which Peter and the other disciples represent. Therefore we can say: As the Christ is not the Christ without those who receive him as the Christ, so the Spiritual Community is not Spiritual unless it is founded on the New Being as it has appeared in the Christ.

The story of Pentecost powerfully emphasizes the Spiritual Community's character. The story, of course, combines historical, legendary, and mythological elements, the distinction between which, in the light of probability, is a task for historical research. But the symbolic meaning of the story in all its elements is of first importance for our purposes. We may distinguish five such elements. The first is the ecstatic character of the creation of Spiritual Community. It confirms what has been said about the Spiritual Presence's character, that is, the unity of ecstasy and structure. The story of Pentecost is an example of this unity. It is ecstasy, with all the characteristics of ecstasy; but it is an ecstasy united with faith, love, unity, and universality, as the story's other elements show. In light of the element of ecstasy in the Pentecost story, we must say that without ecstasy there is no Spiritual Community.

The second element in the story of Pentecost is the creation of a faith which was threatened and almost destroyed by the crucifixion of him who was supposed to be the bearer of the New Being. If we compare the Pentecost story with the Pauline report of the appearances of the resurrected Christ, we find that in both cases an ecstatic experience reassured the disciples and released them from a state of total incertitude. The fugitives who had dispersed in Galilee were not a manifestation of the Spiritual Community. They became its manifestation only after the Spiritual Presence grasped them and re-established their faith. In light of the certainty which overcomes doubt in the story of Pentecost, we must say that without the certainty of faith there is no Spiritual Community.

The third element in the story of Pentecost is the creation of a love which expresses itself immediately in mutual service, especially toward those who are in need, including strangers who have joined the original group. In the light of the service created by love in the story of Pentecost, we must say that there is no Spiritual Community without self-surrendering love.

The fourth element in the story of Pentecost is the creation of unity. The Spiritual Presence had the effect of uniting different individuals, nationalities, and traditions and gathering them together for the sacramental meal. The disciples' ecstatic speaking with tongues was interpreted as the conquest of the disruption of mankind as symbolized in the story of the Tower of Babel. In light of the unity apparent in the story of Pentecost, we must say that there is no Spiritual Community without the ultimate reunion of all the estranged members of mankind.

The fifth element in the story of Pentecost is the creation of universality, expressed in the missionary drive of those who were grasped by the Spiritual Presence. It was impossible that they should not give the message of what had happened to them to everybody, because the New Being would not be the New Being were not mankind as a whole and even the universe itself included in it. In the light of the element of universality in the story of Pentecost we must say that there is no Spiritual Community without openness to all individuals, groups, and things and the drive to take them into itself.

All these elements which will reappear in our discussion as the marks of the Spiritual Community are derived from the image of Jesus as the Christ and the New Being manifest in him. This is expressed symbolically in the image of him as the head and the Spiritual Community as his body. In a more psychological symbolism, it is expressed in the image of him as the bridegroom and the Spiritual Community as the bride. In a more ethical symbolism, it is expressed in the image of him as the Lord of the Spiritual Community. This imagery points to the fact, to which we have already referred, that the divine Spirit is the Spirit of Jesus as the Christ and that the Christ is the criterion to which every Spiritual claim must submit. . . .

### c. The Spiritual Community in its latent and in its manifest stages

The Spiritual Community is determined by the appearance of Jesus as the Christ, but it is not identical with the Christian churches. The question then arises: What is the Spiritual Community's relation to the manifold religious communities in the history of religion? This question reformulates our discussion of the problem of universal and final revelation and of the Spiritual Presence in the period antecedent to the central manifestation of the New Being. In the present context, however, we are seeking the appearance of the Spiritual Community in the preparatory period and are thereby implying that where there is the impact of the Spiritual Presence and therefore revelation (and salvation) there must also be the Spiritual Community. If, on the other hand, the appearance of the Christ is the central manifestation of the divine Spirit, the Spiritual Community's appearance in the period of preparation must differ from its appearance in the period of reception. I propose to describe this difference as that between the Spiritual Community in its latency and in its manifestation.

The terms "latent" and "manifest" church have been used by me for many years, and they have been both accepted and rejected quite frequently. Sometimes they were confused with the classical distinction between the invisible and the visible church. But the two distinctions overlap. The qualities invisible and visible must be applied to the church both in its latency and in its manifestation. The distinction between the Spiritual Community and the churches suggested here may be helpful in avoiding possible confusions between latency and invisibility. It is the Spiritual Community that is latent before an encounter with the central revelation and manifest after such an encounter. This "before" and "after" has a double meaning. It points to the world-historical event, the "basic *kairos*", which has established the center of history once and for all, and it refers to the continually recurring and derivative *kairoi* in which a religious cultural group has an existential encounter with the central event. "Before" and "after" in connection with the Spiritual Community's latency and manifestation refer directly to the second sense of the words and only indirectly to the first.

The concrete occasion for the distinction between the latent and the manifest church comes with the encounter of groups outside the organized churches who show the power of the New Being in an impressive way. There are youth alliances, friendship groups, educational, artistic, and political movements, and, even more obviously, individuals without any visible relation to each other in whom the Spiritual Presence's impact is felt, although they are indifferent or hostile to all overt expressions of religion. They do not belong to a church, but they are not excluded from the Spiritual Community. It is impossible to deny this if one looks at the manifold instances of profanization and demonization of the Spiritual Presence in those groups — the churches — which claim to be the Spiritual Community. Certainly the churches are not excluded from the Spiritual Community, but neither are their secular opponents. The churches represent the Spiritual Community in a manifest religious self-expression, whereas the others represent the Spiritual Community in secular latency. The term "latent" comprises a negative and a positive element. Latency is the state of being partly actual, partly potential; one cannot attribute latency to that which is merely potential, for example, the reception of Jesus as the Christ by those who have not yet encountered him. In the state of latency, there must be actualized elements and elements not actualized. And this is just what characterizes the latent Spiritual Community. There is the Spiritual Presence's impact in faith and love; but the ultimate criterion of both faith and love, the transcendent union of unambiguous life as it is manifest in the faith and the love of the Christ, is lacking. Therefore the Spiritual Community in its latency is open to profanization and demonization without an ultimate principle of resistance, whereas the Spiritual Community organized as a church has the principle of resistance in itself and is able to apply it self-critically, as in the movements of prophetism and Reformation.

It was the latency of the Spiritual Community under the veil of Christian humanism which led to the concept of latency, but the concept proved to possess a wider relevance. It could be applied to the whole history of religion (which is in most cases identical with the history of culture).

There is a latent Spiritual Community in the assembly of the people of Israel, in the schools of the prophets, in the community of the temple, in the synagogues in Palestine and the Diaspora, and in the medieval and modern synagogues. There is a latent Spiritual Community in the Islamic devotional communities, in the mosques and theological schools, and in the mystical movements of Islam. There is a latent Spiritual Community in the communities worshiping the great mythological gods, in esoteric priestly groups, in the mystery cults of the later ancient world, and in the half-scientific, half-ritual communities of the Greek philosophical schools. There is a latent Spiritual Community in classical mysticism in Asia and Europe and in the monastic and half-monastic groups to which the mystical religions gave rise. The impact of the Spiritual Presence, and therefore of the Spiritual Community, is in all of these and many others. There are elements of faith in the sense of being grasped by an ultimate concern, and there are elements of love in the sense of a transcendent reunion of the separated. The Spiritual Community, however, is still latent. The ultimate criterion, the faith and love of the Christ, has not yet appeared to these groups — whether they existed before or after the years 1 to 30. As a consequence of their lack of this criterion, such groups are unable to actualize a radical self-negation and self-transformation as it is present as reality and symbol in the Cross of Christ. This means that they are teleologically related to the Spiritual Community in its manifestation; they are unconsciously driven toward the Christ, even though they reject him when he is brought to them through the preaching and actions of the Christian churches. In their opposition to this form of his appearance, they may represent the Spiritual Community better than the churches, at least in some respects. They may become critics of the churches in the name of the Spiritual Community, and this is true even of such antireligious and anti-Christian movements as world communism. Not even communism could live if it were devoid of all elements of the Spiritual Community. Even world communism is teleologically related to the Spiritual Community.

It is most important for the practice of the Christian ministry, especially in its missionary activities toward those both within and without the Christian culture, to consider pagans, humanists, and Jews as members of the latent Spiritual Community and not as complete strangers who are invited into the Spiritual Community from outside. This insight serves as a powerful weapon against ecclesiastical and hierarchical arrogance.                                        *Vol. 3, pp. 148-55*

*

#### d. The paradox of the churches

The paradox of the churches is the fact that they participate, on the one hand, in the ambiguities of life in general and of the religious life in particular and, on the other hand, in the unambiguous life of the Spiritual Community. The first consequence of this is that whenever they are interpreted and judged the churches must be seen under two aspects. The awareness of this necessity has been expressed in the distinction between the church invisible and visible, to which we have already referred. As long as one who uses these terms is aware that he does not speak of two churches but of two aspects of one church in time and space, this terminology is possible and even unavoidable, for it is necessary to emphasize the invisible character of the Spiritual Community, which is the essential power in every actual church. If, however, these terms are so abused as to suggest two distinct churches, the result is either a devaluation of the empirical church here and now or an ignoring of the invisible church as an irrelevant idea. Both consequences have characterized many phases of Protestantism's history. The first consequence has appeared in certain types of Spirit-movements, the second in liberal Protestantism.

Therefore, it might be useful to speak in an epistemological language of the sociological and the theological aspects of the church (meaning every particular church in time and space). Every church is a sociological reality. As such it is subject to the laws which determine the life of social groups with all their ambiguities. The sociologists of religion are justified in conducting these inquiries in the same way as the sociologists of law, of the arts, and of the sciences. They rightly point to the social stratification within the churches, to the rise and fall of elites, to power struggles and the destructive weapons used in them, to the conflict between freedom and organization, to aristocratic esotericism in contrast to democratic exotericism, and so forth. Seen in this light, the history of the churches is a secular history with all the disintegrating, destructive, and tragic-demonic elements which make historical life as ambiguous as all other life processes. If this aspect is looked at to the exclusion of the other, one can deal with the churches polemically or apologetically. If the intention is polemical (often born of undiscerning expectations and the disappointments which inevitably ensue), the rather miserable reality of concrete churches is emphasized and this reality is compared with their claim to embody the Spiritual Community. The church at the street corner hides the church Spiritual from view.

If, conversely, the churches as sociological realities are cited for apologetic purposes, they are valued because of their social significance. They are praised as the largest and most effective social agencies dedicated to the enhancement of the good life. People are asked to join the churches at least for a try, for the sake of psychological security, for example, and to participate in the work of helping others toward the same goal. In light of this view, the history of the churches is told as the history of humanity's progress. Of course, on this basis the churches' critics can point to the reactionary, superstitious, and inhuman impact of the churches on Western civilization, and this they have done with tremendous success. This contrast shows that judging the churches from the point of view of their sociological functions and their social influence, past or present, is utterly inadequate. A church which is nothing more than a benevolent, socially useful group can be replaced by other groups not claiming to be churches; such a church has no justification for its existence.

The other view of the churches is the theological. It does not refuse to recognize the sociological aspect, but it does deny its exclusive validity. The theological view points, within the ambiguities of the social reality of the churches, to the presence of the unambiguous Spiritual Community.

However, a danger, similar to that found with respect to the sociological view, threatens and distorts the theological: exclusiveness. Of course the theological view cannot be exclusive in the sense that it simply denies the existence of the sociological characteristics of the churches and their ambiguities. But it can deny their significance for the Spiritual nature of the church. This is the offical Roman Catholic doctrine, according to which the Roman church is a sacred reality above the sociological ambiguities of past and present. Church history, from this point of view, becomes sacred history, elevated above all other history in spite of the fact that the disintegrating, destructive, and demonic features of life are shown in it as strongly, and often even more strongly, than in secular history. This makes it impossible to criticize the Roman church in essentials — in doctrine, ethics, hierarchical organization, and so forth. Since the Roman church identifies its historical existence with the Spiritual Community, every attack on it (often even on nonessentials) is felt as an attack on the Spiritual Community and consequently on the Spirit itself. This is one of the main roots both of hierarchical arrogance and, in opposition to it, of anti-ecclesiastical and antihierarchical movements. The Roman church tries to ignore the ambiguities of its life and to submerge the church's sociological character in its theological character, but the relation of the two is paradoxical and cannot be understood either by eliminating the one or by subjecting the one to the other. *Vol. 3, pp. 165-7*

\*

### e. The relating functions of the churches

The churches, in paradoxical unity with their Spiritual essence, are sociological realities, showing all the ambiguities of the social self-creation of life. Therefore they have continuous encounters with other sociological groups, acting upon them and receiving from them. Systematic theology cannot deal with the practical problems following from these relations, but it must try to formulate the ways and principles by which the churches as churches relate themselves to other social groups.

There are three ways in which this happens: the way of silent inter-penetration, the way of critical judgment, and the way of political estab-lishment. The first can be described as the continuous radiation of the Spiritual essence of the churches into all groups of the society in which they live. Their very existence changes the whole of social existence. One could call it the pouring of priestly substance into the social struc-ture of which the churches are a part. In view of the rapid secularization of life in the last centuries, one is inclined to overlook this influence, but if in imagination one removes the churches, the empty space left in all realms of man's personal and communal life shows the significance of their silent influence. Even if the educational possibilities of the churches are officially limited, their very existence has an educational impact on the culture of a period, whether it is directly, by communi-cating Spiritual reality, or indirectly, by provoking a protest against what they represent.

Moreover, the influence is mutual; the churches receive the silent influx of the developing and changing cultural forms of the society, con-sciously or unconsciously. The most obvious of these influences is felt in the continuous transformation of the ways of understanding and expressing experiences in a living culture. The churches silently give Spiritual substance to the society in which they live, and the churches silently receive Spiritual forms from the same society. This mutual exchange, silently exercised at every moment, is the first relating function of the church.

The second is the way of critical judgment, exercised mutually by the church and the other social groups. This relation between churches and society is most manifest in the modern period of Western history, but it has existed in all periods, even under the theocratic systems of the East-ern and Western churches. The early church's criticism of the imperial Roman society was directed against its pagan ways of life and thought, and it finally transformed the pagan society into a Christian one. If the silent penetration of a society by the Spiritual Presence can be called "priestly", the open attack on this society in the name of the Spiritual Presence can be called "prophetic". Its success may be rather limited, but the fact that the society is put under judgment and must react posi-tively or negatively to the judgment is in itself a success. A society which rejects or persecutes the bearers of the prophetic criticism against itself does not remain the same as it was before. It may be weakened or it may be hardened in its demonic and profane traits; in either case it is transformed. Therefore the churches should not only fight for the preservation and strengthening of their priestly influence (for example, in the realm of education), but they should encourage prophetic criticism of the negatives in their society up to the point of martyrdom and in spite of their awareness that the result of a prophetic criticism of society is not the Spiritual Community but, perhaps, a state of society which approaches theonomy — the relatedness of all cultural forms to the ultimate.

But again the relation is mutual. There is, on the part of society, a criticism directed toward the churches, a criticism which is as justified as the churches' prophetic criticism of society. It is the criticism of "holy injustice" and "saintly inhumanity" within the churches and in their relation to the society in which they live. The world-historical significance of this criticism in the nineteenth and twentieth centuries is obvious. Its first consequence was to produce an almost unbridgeable gap between the churches and large groups of society, in particular the labor movements; but beyond this it had the effect of inducing the Christian churches to revise their interpretations of justice and humanity. It was a kind of reverse prophetism, an unconsciously prophetic criticism directed toward the churches from outside, just as a reverse priestly impact occurred in the effect of the changing cultural forms on the churches, an unconsciously priestly influence directed toward the churches from outside. This mutual criticism exercised and received by the churches is their second relating function.

The third is the way of political establishment. While the priestly and the prophetic ways remain within the religious sphere, the third way seems to fall completely outside this sphere. But religious symbolism has always added the royal to the priestly and the prophetic religious functions. Christology attributes the royal office to the Christ. Every church has a political function, from the local up to the international level. One task of the church leaders on all levels is to influence the leaders of the other social groups in such a way that the right of the church to exercise its priestly and prophetic function is acknowledged by them. There are many ways in which this can be done, dependent on the constitutional structure of the society and the legal position of the churches within it; but in any case, if the churches act politically, they must do it in the name of the Spiritual Community, i.e., Spiritually. This excludes the use of means which contradict its character as Spiritual Community, such as the use of military force, intoxicating propaganda, and diplomatic ruses, the arousing of religious fanaticism, and so on. The more sharply a church rejects such methods, the more power it will ultimately exercise, for its real power lies in its being a creation of the Spiritual Presence. The fact that the Roman church has disregarded these principles has contributed to the scepticism in Protestantism with regard to the royal function of the church. But such scepticism is not justified. The Protestant churches cannot escape their political responsibility and they have always exercised it, though with uneasy conscience, having forgotten that there is a royal function of the Christ. Certainly, as the royal function belongs to the Christ Crucified, so the royal function must be exercised by the church under the Cross, the humble church.

In doing so, it acknowledges that there is also a justified political impact on the churches from the side of society. One need only think of the influence of the late ancient and medieval forms of society on the structure of the churches. Political establishment is the result of a deal between different political forces inside and outside the larger groups. Even the churches are subject to the law of political compromise. They must be ready not only to direct but also to be directed. There is only one limit in the political establishment of the churches: the character of the church as expression of the Spiritual Community must remain manifest. This is first endangered if the symbol of the royal office of the Christ, and through him of the church, is understood as a theocratic-political system of totalitarian control over all realms of life. On the other hand, if the church is forced to assume the role of an obedient servant of the state, as if it were another deparment or agency, this means the end of its royal office altogether and a humiliation of the church which is not the humility of the Crucified but the weakness of the disciples who fled the Cross.

If we turn now to the principles under which the churches as actualizations of the Spiritual Community relate themselves to other social groups, we find a polarity between the principle of belonging to them according to the ambiguities of life and the principle of opposing them according to the fight against the ambiguities of life. Each of these principles has far-reaching consequences. The first implies that the relation of the churches to other groups has the character of mutuality, as we have seen with respect to the three ways in which the churches are related to them. The reason for this mutuality is the equality of predicament. This principle is the antidemonic criterion of the holiness of the churches, because it prevents the arrogance of finite holiness, which is the basic temptation of all churches. If they interpret their paradoxical holiness as absolute holiness, they fall into a demonic *hubris*, and their priestly, prophetic, and royal functions toward the "world" become tools of a pseudo-Spiritual will to power. It was the experience of the demonization of the Roman church in the later Middle Ages which produced the protest of both the Reformation and Renaissance. These protests liberated Christianity in large sections from bondage to the demonically distorted power of the church by making the people aware of the ambiguities of actual religion.

But in achieving this they also frequently brought about, not only in the secular world but also in the sphere of Protestantism, the loss of the other side of the relation, the opposition of the churches to the other social groups. The danger in this respect was obvious from the beginning of the two great movements. Both propagated a nationalism of which culture as well as religion became victims. The church's opposition to nationalistic ideology, with its unjust claims and untrue assertions, became weaker with every decade of modern history. The church's prophetic voice was silenced by nationalistic fanaticism. Its priestly function was distorted by the introduction of national sacraments and rites into education at all levels, especially the lowest ones. Its royal function was not taken seriously and was made impotent either by the subjection of the churches to the national states or by the liberal ideal of separation of church and state, which pushed the churches into a narrow corner of the social fabric. The power of opposition was lost in all these cases, and when the church loses its radical otherness, it loses itself and becomes a benevolent social club. Such phrases as "the church against the world" point to the one principle which essentially determines the relation of the churches to society as a whole and which should determine it actually. Yet if such phrases are used without being balanced by other phrases, such as "the church within the world," they have an arrogant ring and miss the ambiguity of the religious life.

It is part and parcel of this ambiguity that the world which is opposed by the church is not simply not-church but has in itself elements of the Spiritual Community in its latency which work toward a theonomous culture.

*Vol. 3, pp. 212-6*

\*

### f. Four principles determining the New Being as process

The exclusiveness of the different types of interpreting the process of sanctification is diminishing under the impact of secular criticism which questions the significance of all of them. Therefore we must ask whether we can find criteria for a future doctrine of life under the Spiritual Presence. One may give the following principles: first, increasing awareness; second, increasing freedom; third, increasing relatedness; fourth, increasing transcendence. How these principles will unite in a new type of life under the Spiritual Presence cannot be described before it happens, but elements of such a life can be seen in individuals and groups who anticipated what may possibly lie in the future. The principles themselves unite religious as well as secular traditions and can, in their totality, create an indefinite but distinguishable image of the "Christian life".

The principle of *awareness* is related to contemporary depth psychology, but it is as old as religion itself and is sharply expressed in the New Testament. It is the principle according to which man in the process of sanctification becomes increasingly aware of his actual situation and of the forces struggling around him and his humanity but also becomes aware of the answers to the questions implied in this situation. Sanctification includes awareness of the demonic as well as of the divine. Such awareness, which increases in the process of sanctification, does not lead to the Stoic "wise man", who is superior to the ambiguities of life because he has conquered his passions and desires, but rather to an awareness of these ambiguities in himself, as in everyone, and to the power of affirming life and its vital dynamics in spite of its ambiguities. Such awareness includes sensitivity toward the demands of one's own growth, toward the hidden hopes and disappointments within others, toward the voiceless voice of a concrete situation, toward the grades of authenticity in the life of the spirit in others and oneself. All this is not a matter of cultural education or sophistication but of growth under the impact of the Spiritual power and it is therefore noticeable in every human being who is open to this impact. The aristocracy of the spirit and the aristocracy of the Spirit are not identical, although they overlap in part.

The second principle of the process of sanctification is the principle of *increasing freedom*. The emphasis on it is especially conspicuous in Paul's and Luther's descriptions of life in the Spirit. In contemporary literature the oracles of Nietzsche and the existentialist struggle for the freedom of man's personal self from slavery to the objects he has produced are most important. Here also depth psychology contributes by its claim to liberate men from particular compulsions which are impediments to growth in Spiritual freedom. Growth in Spiritual freedom is first of all growth in freedom from the law. This follows immediately from the interpretation of the law as man's essential being confronting him in the state of estrangement. The more one is reunited with his true being under the impact of the Spirit, the more one is free from the commandments of the law. This process is most difficult, and maturity in it is very rare. The fact that reunion is fragmentary implies that freedom from the law is always fragmentary. In so far as we are estranged, prohibitions and commandments appear and produce an uneasy conscience. In so far as we are reunited, we actualize what we essentially are in freedom, without command. Freedom from the law in the process of sanctification is the increasing freedom from the commanding form of the law. But it is also freedom from its particular content. Specific laws, expressing the experience and wisdom of the past, are not only helpful, they are also oppressive, because they cannot meet the ever concrete, ever new, ever unique situation. Freedom from the law is the power to judge the given situation in the light of the Spiritual Presence and to decide upon adequate action, which is often in seeming contradiction to the law. This is what is meant when the spirit of the law is contrasted with its letter (Paul) or when the Spirit-determined self is empowered to write a new and better law than Moses (Luther) or — in a secularized form — when the bearer of freedom revaluates all values (Nietzsche) or when the existing subject resolves the impasse of existence by resoluteness (Heidegger). The mature freedom to give new laws or to apply the old ones in a new way is an aim of the process of sanctification. The danger that such freedom may turn out to be willfulness is overcome wherever the reuniting power of the Spiritual Presence is effective. Willfulness is a symptom of estrangement and a surrender to enslaving conditions and compulsions. Mature freedom from the law implies the power of resisting the forces which try to destroy such freedom from inside the personal self and from its social surroundings; and, of course, the enslaving powers from outside can succeed only because there are inside trends toward servitude. Resistance against both may include ascetic decisions and readiness for martyrdom, but the significance of these actions lies in the demand upon them to help preserve freedom in the concrete situation and not in their providing a higher degree of sanctity itself. They are tools under special conditions but are not themselves aims in the process of sanctification.

The third priniciple is that of *increasing relatedness*. It balances, so to speak, the principle of increasing freedom which, through the necessity of resisting enslaving influences, may isolate the maturing person. Both freedom and relatedness, as well as awareness and self-transcendence, are rooted in the Spiritual creations of faith and love. They are present whenever the Spiritual Presence is manifest. They are the conditions of participation in regeneration and acceptance of justification, and they determine the process of sanctification. But the way in which they do so is characterized by the four principles which qualify the New Being as process. For example, the principle of increasing freedom cannot be imagined without the courage to risk a wrong decision on the basis of faith, and the principle of increasing relatedness cannot be imagined without the reuniting power of *agape* to overcome *self-seclusion* fragmentarily. But in both cases the principles of sanctification make the basic manifestation of the Spiritual Presence concrete for the progress toward maturity.

Relatedness implies the awareness of the other one and the freedom to relate to him by overcoming self-seclusion within oneself and within the other one. There are innumerable barriers to this process as may be learned from the large body of literature (with analogies in the visual arts) in which the self-seclusion of the individual from others is described. The analyses of introversion and hostility given in these works are interdependent with the psychotherapeutic analyses of the same structures. And the biblical accounts of relatedness within the Spiritual Community presuppose the same unrelatedness in the pagan world out of which its members came, an unrelatedness still ambiguously present in actual congregations.

The New Being as process drives toward a mature relatedness. The divine Spirit has rightly been described as the power of breaking through the walls of self-seclusion. There is no way of overcoming self-seclusion lastingly other than the impact of the power which elevates the individual person above himself ecstatically and enables him to find the other person — if the other person is also ready to be elevated above himself. All other relations are transitory and ambiguous. They certainly exist and fill the daily life, but they are symptoms of estrangement as much as of reunion. All human relations have this character. Alone, they cannot conquer loneliness, self-seclusion, and hostility. Only a relation which is inherent in all other relations, and which can even exist without them, is able to do so. Sanctification, or the process toward Spiritual maturity, conquers loneliness by providing for solitude and communion in interdependence. A decisive symptom of Spiritual maturity is the power to sustain solitude. Sanctification conquers introversion by turning the personal center not outward, in extroversion, but toward the dimension of its depth and its height. Relatedness needs the vertical dimension in order to actualize itself in the horizontal dimension.

This is also true of self-relatedness. The state of loneliness, introversion, and hostility is just as contrary to self-relatedness as it is to relatedness to others. The species of terms having self as the first syllable is dangerously ambiguous. The term "self-centeredness" can be used to describe the greatness of man as a fully centered self or an ethically negative attitude of bondage to one's self; the terms "self-love" and "self-hate" are difficult to understand because it is impossible to separate the self as subject of love or hate from the self as object. But there is no real love or real hate without such separation. The same ambiguity damages the term "self-relatedness". Nevertheless we must use such terms, conscious of the fact that they are used analogically and not properly.

In the analogical sense, one can speak of the process of sanctification as creating a mature self-relatedness in which self-acceptance conquers both self-elevation and self-contempt in a process of reunion with one's self. Such a reunion is created by transcending both the self as subject, which tries to impose itself in terms of self-control and self-discipline on the self as object, and the self as object, which resists such imposition in terms of self-pity and flight from one's self. A mature self-relatedness is the state of reconciliation between the self as subject and the self as object and the spontaneous affirmation of one's essential being beyond subject and object. As the process of sanctification approaches a more mature self-relatedness, the individual is more spontaneous, more self-affirming, without self-elevation or self-humiliation.

The "search for identity" is the search for what has here been called "self-relatedness". Properly understood, this search is not the desire to preserve an accidental state of the existential self, the self in estrangement but rather the drive toward a self which transcends every contingent state of its development and which remains unaltered in its essence through such changes. The process of sanctification runs toward a state in which the "search for identity" reaches its goal, which is the identity of the essential self shining through the contingencies of the existing self.

The fourth principle determining the process of sanctification is the principle of *self-transcendence*. The aim of maturity under the impact of the Spiritual Presence comprises awareness, freedom, and relatedness, but in each case we have found that the aim cannot be reached without an act of self-transcendence. This implies that sanctification is not possible without a continuous transcendence of oneself in the direction of the ultimate — in other words, without participation in the holy.

This participation is usually described as the devotional life under the Spiritual Presence. This description is justified if the term "devotion" is understood in such a way that the holy embraces both itself and the secular. If it is used exclusively in the ordinary sense of the devotional life — a life centered in prayer as a particular act — it does not exhaust the possibilities of self-transcendence. In the mature life, determined by the Spiritual Presence, participation in the devotional life of the congregation may be restricted or refused, prayer may be subordinated to meditation, religion in the narrower sense of the word may be denied in the name of religion in the larger sense of the word; but all this does not contradict the principle of self-transcendence. It may even happen that an increased experience of transcendence leads to an increase in criticism of religion as a special function. But in spite of these qualifying statements, "self-transcendence" is identical with the attitude of devotion toward that which is ultimate.

In discussion of the devotional life the distinction is often made between organized or formalized and private devotion. This distinction has a very limited significance. He who prays in solitude prays in the words of the religious tradition which has given him the language, and he who contemplates without words also participates in a long tradition which is represented by religious men inside and outside the churches. The distinction is meaningful only in so far as it affirms that there is no law which requires participation in the religious services in the name of the Spiritual Presence. Luther reacted violently against such a law, but at the same time he created a liturgy for Protestant services and one can say in general that withdrawal from communal devotion is dangerous because it easily produces a vacuum in which the devotional life disappears altogether.

The self-transcendence which belongs to the principles of sanctification is actual in every act in which the impact of the Spiritual Presence is experienced. This can be in prayer or meditation in total privacy, in the exchange of Spiritual experiences with others, in communications on a secular basis, in the experience of creative works of man's spirit, in the midst of labor or rest, in private counseling, in church services. It is like the breathing-in of another air, an elevation above average existence. It is the most important thing in the process of Spiritual maturity. Perhaps one can say that with increasing maturity in the process of sanctification the transcendence becomes more definite and its expressions more indefinite. Participation in communal devotion may decrease and the religious symbols connected with it may become less important, while the state of being ultimately concerned may become more manifest and the devotion to the ground and aim of our being more intensive.

This element in the reality of the New Being as process has caused the so-called resurgence of religion in the decades following the Second World War. People have felt that the experience of transcendence is necessary for a life in which a New Being becomes actual. The awareness of such a demand is widespread, the freedom from prejudice against religion as the mediator of transcendence increasing. In the present situation what one wants is concrete symbols of self-transcendence.

In light of the four principles which determine the New Being as process we can say: The Christian life never reaches the state of perfection — it always remains an up-and-down course — but in spite of its mutable character it contains a movement toward maturity, however fragmentary the mature state may be. It is manifest in the religious as well as the secular life, and it transcends both of them in the power of the Spiritual Presence.                                *Vol. 3, pp. 231-7*

\*

### e. The conquest of religion by the Spiritual Presence and the Protestant principle

In so far as the Spiritual Presence is effective in the churches and their individual members, it conquers religion as a particular function of the human spirit. When contemporary theology rejects the name "religion" for Christianity, it is in the line of New Testament thought. The coming of the Christ is not the foundation of a new religion but the transformation of the old state of things. Consequently, the church is not a religious community but the anticipatory representation of a new reality, the New Being as community. In the same way, the individual member of the church is not a religious personality but the anticipatory representation of a new reality, the New Being as personality.

Everything said heretofore about the churches and the life of their members points in the direction of a conquest of religion. Conquest of religion does not mean secularization but rather the closing of the gap between the religious and the secular by removing both through the Spiritual Presence. This is the meaning of faith as the state of being grasped by that which concerns us ultimately and not as a set of beliefs, even if the object of belief is a divine being. This is the meaning of love as reunion of the separated in all dimensions, including that of the spirit, and not as an act of negation of all dimensions for the sake of a transcendence without dimensions.

In so far as religion is conquered by the Spiritual Presence, profanization and demonization are conquered. The inner-religious profanization of religion, its transformation into a sacred mechanism of hierarchical structure, doctrine, and ritual, is resisted by the participation of church members in the Spiritual Community, which is the dynamic essence of the churches and of which the churches are both the existential representation and the existential distortion. The freedom of the Spirit breaks through mechanizing profanization — as it did in the creative moments of the Reformation. In doing so it also resists the secular form of profanization, for the secular as secular lives from the protest against the profanization of religion within itself. If this protest becomes meaningless, the functions of morality and culture are opened again for the ultimate, the aim of the self-transcendence of life.

Demonization is also conquered in so far as religion is conquered by the Spiritual Presence. We have distinguished between the demonic that is hidden — the affirmation of a greatness which leads to the tragic conflict with the "great itself" — and the openly demonic — the affirmation of a finite as infinite in the name of the holy. Both the tragic and the demonic are conquered in principle by the Spiritual Presence. Christianity has always claimed that neither the death of the Christ nor the suffering of Christians is tragic, because neither is rooted in the affirmation of its greatness but in the participation in the predicament of estranged man to which each belongs and does not belong. If Christianity teaches that the Christ and the martyrs suffered "innocently", this means that their suffering is not based on the tragic guilt of self-affirmed greatness but on their willingness to participate in the tragic consequences of human estrangement.

Self-affirmed greatness in the realm of the holy is demonic. This is true of the claim of a church to represent in its structure the Spiritual Community unambiguously. The consequent will to unlimited power over all things holy and secular is in itself the judgment against a church which makes this claim. The same is true of individuals who, as adherents of a group making such a claim, become self-assured, fanatical, and destructive of life in others and the meaning of life within themselves. But in so far as the divine Spirit conquers religion, it prevents the claim to absoluteness by both the churches and their members. Where the divine Spirit is effective, the claim of a church to represent God to the exclusion of all other churches is rejected. The freedom of the Spirit resists it. And when the divine Spirit is effective, a church member's claim to an exclusive possession of the truth is undercut by the witness of the divine Spirit to his fragmentary as well as ambiguous participation in the truth. The Spiritual Presence excludes fanaticism, because in the presence of God no man can boast about his grasp of God. No one can grasp that by which he is grasped — the Spiritual Presence.

In other connections I have called this truth the "Protestant principle". It is here that the Protestant principle has its place in the theological system. The Protestant principle is an expression of the conquest of religion by the Spiritual Presence and consequently an expression of the victory over the ambiguities of religion, its profanization, and its demonization. It is Protestant, because it protests against the tragic-demonic self-elevation of religion and liberates religion from itself for the other functions of the human spirit, at the same time liberating these functions from their self-seclusion against the manifestations of the ultimate. The Protestant principle (which is a manifestation of the prophetic Spirit) is not restricted to the churches of the Reformation or to any other church; it transcends every particular church, being an expression of the Spiritual Community. It has been betrayed by every church, including the churches of the Reformation, but it is also effective in every church as the power which prevents profanization and demonization from destroying the Christian churches completely. It alone is not enough; it needs the "Catholic substance", the concrete embodiment of the Spiritual Presence; but it is the criterion of the demonization (and profanization) of such embodiment. It is the expression of the victory of the Spirit over religion.     *Vol. 3, pp. 243-5*

*

## h. *Religion in relation to morality and culture*

.... In accordance with their essential nature, morality, culture, and religion interpenetrate one another. They constitute the unity of the spirit, wherein the elements are distinguishable but not separable. Morality, or the constitution of the person as person in the encounter with other persons, is essentially related to culture and religion. Culture provides the contents of morality — the concrete ideals of personality and community and the changing laws of ethical wisdom. Religion gives to morality the unconditional character of the moral imperative, the ultimate moral aim, the reunion of the separated in *agape*, and the motivating power of grace. Culture, or the creation of a universe of meaning in *theoria* and *praxis*, is essentially related to morality and religion. The validity of cultural creativity in all its functions is based on the person-to-person encounter in which the limits to arbitrariness are established. Without the force of the moral imperative, no demand coming from the logical, aesthetic, personal, and communal forms could be felt. The religious element in culture is the inexhaustible depth of a genuine creation. One may call it substance or the ground from which culture lives. It is the element of ultimacy which culture lacks in itself but to which it points. Religion, or the self-transcendence of life under the dimension of spirit, is essentially related to morality and culture. There is no self-transcendence under the dimension of the spirit without the constitution of the moral self by the unconditional imperative, and this self-transcendence cannot take form except within the universe of meaning created in the cultural act.

This picture of the essential relation of the three functions of the spirit is both "transhistorical remembrance" and "utopian anticipation". As such, it judges their actual relations under the conditions of existence. But it is more than an external judge. It is actual in so far as essential and existential elements are mixed in life and since the unity of the three functions is as effective as their separation. It is just this that is the root of all ambiguities under the dimension of the spirit. And only because the essential element is effective in life — though ambiguously — can its image be drawn as the criterion of life.

The three functions of life under the dimension of spirit separate in order to become actual. In their essential unity there is no moral act which is not at the same time an act both of cultural self-creation and of religious self-transcendence. There is no independent morality in "dreaming innocence". And in the essential unity of the three functions, there is no cultural act which is not at the same time an act of moral self-integration and religious self-transcendence. There is no independent culture in dreaming innocence. And in the essential unity of the three functions, there is no religious act which is not at the same time an act of moral self-integration and cultural self-creation. There is no independent religion in dreaming innocence.

But life is based on the loss of dreaming innocence, on the self-estrangement of essential being and the ambiguous mixture of essential and existential elements. In the actuality of life, there is separated morality with the ambiguities it implies; there is separated culture with its ambiguities; and there is separated religion with its most profound ambiguities. We must now turn to these.

Religion was defined as the self-transcendence of life under the dimension of spirit. This definition makes the image of the essential unity of religion with morality and culture possible, and it also explains the ambiguities of the three functions in their separation. The self-transcendence of life is effective in the unconditional character of the moral act and in the inexhaustible depth of meaning in all meanings created by culture. Life is sublime in every realm dominated by the dimenisions of the spirit. The self-integration of life in the moral act and self-creativity of life in the cultural act are sublime. Within them, life transcends itself in the vertical direction, the direction of the ultimate. But because of the ambiguity of life, they are also profane; they resist self-transcendence. And this is inevitable because they are separated from their essential unity with religion and are actualized independently.

The definition of religion as self-transcendence of life in the dimension of the spirit has the decisive implication that religion must first of all be considered as a quality of the two other functions of the spirit and not as an independent function. Such a consideration is logically necessary, for self-transcendence of life cannot become a function of life beside others, because if it did it would have to be itself transcended, and so on in endless repetition. Life cannot genuinely transcend itself in one of its own functions. This is the argument against religion as a function of the spirit, and one cannot deny that theologians who advance this argument have a strong point. Therefore, if religion is defined as a function of the human mind, they are consistent in rejecting the concept of religion altogether in a theology which is supposed to be based on revelation.

But these assertions make incomprehensible the fact that there is religion in life under the dimension of the spirit, not only as a quality in morality and culture, but also as an independent reality beside them. This fact of the existence of religion in the ordinary sense of the word is one of the great stumbling blocks in life under the dimension of the spirit. According to the definition of religion as the self-transcendence of life, there should be no religion, individual or organized, as a particular function of the spirit. Every act of life should in itself point beyond itself, and no realm of particular acts should be necessary. But, as in all realms of life, self-transcendence is resisted by profanization in the realm of the spirit. Morality and culture in existential separation from religion become what is usually called "secular". Their greatness is contradicted by their profanity. Under the pressure of profanization the moral imperative becomes conditional, dependent on fears and hopes, a result of psychological and sociological compulsion; an ultimate moral aim is replaced by utilitarian calculations, and the fulfillment of the law is a matter of futile attempts at self-determination. The self-transcendence of the moral act is denied; morality is activity between finite possibilities. In the sense of our basic definition it is profanized — even if, in conflict with the meaning of grace, it is as restrictive as some forms of religious morality. It is unavoidable that such morality should fall under the ambiguities of the law. Under the analogous pressure of profanization, the cultural creation of a universe of meanings loses the substance which is received in self-transcendence — an ultimate and inexhaustible meaning. This phenomenon is well known and has been widely discussed by the analysts of our present civilization, usually under the heading of the secularization of culture. They have often rightly referred to the analogous phenomenon in ancient civilization and derived a general rule about the relation of religion and culture from these two examples of Western intellectual history. With the loss of its religious substance, culture is left with an increasingly empty form. Meaning cannot live without the inexhaustible source of meaning to which religion points.

Out of this situation religion arises as a special function of the spirit. The self-transcendence of life under the dimension of spirit cannot become alive without finite realities which are transcended. Thus there is a dialectical problem in self-transcendence in that something is transcended and at the same time not transcended. It must have concrete existence, otherwise nothing would be there to be transcended; yet it should not "be there" anymore but should be negated in the act of being transcended. This is exactly the situation of all religions in history. Religion as the self-transcendence of life needs the religions and needs to deny them. *Vol. 3, pp. 94-8*

\*

# THE KINGDOM OF GOD AND WORLD HISTORY

*It is true that Tillich's later writings did not directly address concrete affairs of his day to the degree we observe in his early Religious Socialist writings. But as the selection below displays, Tillich seeks to bring his system to bear on such concrete historical dynamics as empire-building, revolution and reaction, pacifism and militarism. Now, the polarities he introduced and discussed in volumes 1 and 2 spawn distinctive ambiguities on the world-historical scale. The churches, which for Tillich should lead the way in the quest for unambiguous life in the Kingdom of God, struggle to find their way among the ambiguities of* historical *self-integration, self-creativity, and self-transcendence. The following selection is from* Systematic Theology, *vol. 3, pp. 382-93.*

## 1. CHURCH HISTORY AND WORLD HISTORY

The meaning of the term "world" in the context of this and the preceding chapters is determined by its contrast to the terms "church" and "the churches". It does not imply the belief that there is a world history which is a coherent and continuous history of the all-embracing historical group "mankind". As discussed before, there is no history of mankind in this sense. Mankind is the place on which historical developments occur. These developments are partly unconnected and partly interdependent, but they never have a united center of action. Even today, when a technical unity of mankind has been achieved, no centered action by mankind as such is being performed. And if, in an unforeseeable future, mankind as such were to perform centered actions particular histories would still be the main content of world history. Therefore we must look at these particular histories in our consideration of the relation of the Kingdom of God to world history. Whether they are connected or disconnected, the phenomena under discussion takes place in each of them.

The first problem concerns the relation between church history and world history. The difficulty of this question stems from the fact that church history, as the representation of the Kingdom of God, is a part both of world history and of that which transcends world history and from the other fact that world history is both opposed to and dependent on church history (including the activities of the latent church which prepare for church history proper). This obviously is a highly dialectical relationship, including several mutual affirmations and negations. The following points must be considered.

The history of the churches shows all the characteristics of the history of the world, that is, all the ambiguities of social self-integration, self-creativity, and self-transcendence. The churches in these respects are the world. They would not exist without structures of power, of growth, of sublimation, and the ambiguities implied in these structures. Seen from this point of view the churches are nothing but a special section of world history. But in spite of its truth, this point of view cannot claim exclusive validity. In the churches there is also unconquered resistance against the ambiguities of world history and fragmentary victories over them. World history is judged by the churches in their capacity as the embodiment of the Spiritual Community. The churches as representatives of the Kingdom of God judge that without which they themselves could not exist. But they do not merely judge it theoretically while accepting it practically. Their judgment consists not only in prophetic words but also in prophetic withdrawals from the ambiguous situations in which world history moves. Churches which resign from political power are more entitled to judge the ambiguities of political power than those which never saw the questionable character of their own power politics. The Catholic judgment against communism, however justified it may be in itself, necessarily evokes the suspicion that it is done as a struggle between two competing power groups, each making ultimate claims for its particular validity. Protestant criticism is not free of this deception but instead is open to the question whether the criticism is done in the name of man's ultimate concern or in the name of a particular political group which uses the religious judgment for its political-economical purposes (as in the alliance of fundamentalism and ultra-conservativism in America). The judgment of a Protestant group against communism may be equally as justified and equally as questionable as that of the Catholic group. But it can have undergone the test of its honesty, this test being that it has first brought judgment against the churches themselves, even in their basic structure; and this is a test which the Roman church would never be able to undergo. For her church history is sacred history without any restriction in principle, although, of course, restrictions may be invoked with respect to individual members and particular events.

Church history judges world history while judging itself because it is a part of world history. Church history has an impact on world history. The last two thousand years of world history in the Western part of mankind move under the transforming influence of the churches. For example, the climate of social relations is changed by the existence of the churches. This is a fact as well as a problem. It is a fact that Christianity has changed person-to-person relations in a fundamental way, wherever it has been accepted. This does not mean that the consequences of this change have been practiced by a majority of people or even by many people. But it does mean that whoever does not practice the new way of human relations, although aware of them, is stricken by an uneasy conscience. Perhaps one can say that the main impact of church history on world history is that it produces an uneasy conscience in those who have received the impact of the New Being but follow the ways of the old being. Christian civilization is not the Kingdom of God, but it is a continuous reminder of it. Therefore one should never use changes in the state of the world as a basis for proving the validity of the Christian message. Such arguments do not convince because they miss the paradox of the churches and the ambiguities of every stage of world history. Often historical providence works through demonizations and profanizations of the churches toward the actualization of the Kingdom of God in history. Such providential developments do not excuse the churches in their distortion, but they show the independence of the Kingdom of God from its representatives in history.

Writing church history under these conditions requires a double viewpoint in the description of every particular development. First, church history must show facts and their relations with the best methods of historical research and must do so without bringing in divine providence as a particular cause in the general chain of causes and effects. The church historian is not supposed to write a history of divine interferences in world history when he writes the history of the Christian churches. Secondly, the church historian, as a theologian, must remain aware of the fact that he speaks about a historical reality in which the Spiritual Community is effective and by which the Kingdom of God is represented. The section of world history with which he deals has a providential vocation for all world history. Therefore he must not only look at world history as the large matrix within which church history moves but also from a threefold point of view: first, as that reality in which church history as the representation of the Kingdom of God has been and is being prepared; second, as that reality which is the object of the transforming activities of the Spiritual Community; and third, as that reality by which church history is judged while judging it. Church history, written in this manner, is a part of the history of the Kingdom of God, actualized in historical time. But there is another part to this history, and that is world history itself.

## 2. THE KINGDOM OF GOD AND THE AMBIGUITIES OF HISTORICAL SELF-INTEGRATION

We have described the ambiguities of history as consequences of the ambiguities of life processes in general. The self-integration of life under the dimension of history shows the ambiguities implied in the drive toward centeredness: the ambiguities of "empire" and of "control", the first appearing in the drive of expansion toward a universal historical unity, and the second, in the drive toward a centered unity in the particular history-bearing group. In each case the ambiguity of power lies behind the ambiguities of historical integration. So the question arises: What is the relation of the Kingdom of God to the ambiguities of power? The answer to this question is also the answer to the question of the relation of the churches to power.

The basic theological answer must be that, since God as *the* power of being is the source of all particular powers of being, power is divine in its essential nature. The symbols of power for God or the Christ or the church in biblical literature are abundant. And Spirit is the dynamic unity of power and meaning. The depreciation of power in most pacifist pronouncements is unbiblical as well as unrealistic. Power is the eternal possibility of resisting nonbeing. God and the Kingdom of God "exercise" this power eternally. But in the divine life — of which the divine kingdom is the creative self-manifestation — the ambiguities of power, empire, and control are conquered by unambiguous life.

*Within historical existence this means that every victory of the Kingdom of God in history is a victory over the disintegrating consequences of the ambiguity of power.* Since this ambiguity is based on the existential split between subject and object, its conquest involves a fragmentary reunion of subject and object. For the internal power structure of a history-bearing group, this means that the struggle of the Kingdom of God in history is actually victorious in institutions and attitudes and conquers, even if only fragmentarily, that compulsion which usually goes with power and transforms the objects of centered control into mere objects. In so far as democratization of political attitudes and institutions serves to resist the destructive implications of power, it is a manifestation of the Kingdom of God in history. But it would be completely wrong to identify democratic institutions with the Kingdom of God in history. This confusion, in the minds of many people, has elevated the idea of democracy to the place of a direct religious symbol and has simply substituted it for the symbol "Kingdom of God". Those who argue against this confusion are right when they point to the fact that aristocratic hierarchical systems of power have for long periods prevented the total transformation of men into objects by the tyranny of the strongest. And beyond this they also correctly point out that by their community and personality-creating effects aristocratic systems have developed the democratic potential of leaders and masses. However, this consideration does not justify the glorification of authoritarian systems of power as expressions of the will of God. In so far as the centering and liberating elements in a structure of political power are balanced, the Kingdom of God in history has conquered fragmentarily the ambiguities of control. This is, at the same time, the criterion according to which churches must judge political actions and theories. Their judgment against power politics should not be a rejection of power but an affirmation of power and even of its compulsory element in cases where justice is violated ("justice" is used here in the sense of protection of the individual as a potential personality in a community). Therefore, although the fight against "objectivation" of the personal subject is a permanent task of the churches, to be carried out by prophetic witness and priestly initiation, it is not their function to control the political powers and force upon them particular solutions in the name of the Kingdom of God. The way in which the Kingdom of God works in history is not identical with the way the churches want to direct the course of history.

The ambiguity of self-integration of life under the historical dimensions is also effective in the trend toward the reunion of all human groups in an empire. Again it must be stated that the Kingdom of God in history does not imply the denial of power in the encounter of centered political groups, for example, nations. As in every encounter of living beings, including individual men, power of being meets power of being and decisions are made about the higher or lower degree of such power — so it is in the encounter of political power groups. And as it is in the particular group and its structure of control, so it is in the relations of particular groups to each other that decisions are made in every moment in which the significance of the particular group for the unity of the Kingdom of God in history is actualized. In these struggles it might happen that a complete political defeat becomes the condition for the greatest significance a group gets in the manifestation of the Kingdom of God in history — as in Jewish history and, somehow analogously, in Indian and Greek history. But it also may be that a military defeat is the way in which the Kingdom of God, fighting in history, deprives national groups of a falsely claimed ultimate significance — as in the case of Hitler's Germany. Although this was done through the conquerors of naziism, their victory did not give them an unambiguous claim that they themselves were the bearers of the reunion of mankind. If they raised such a claim they would, by this very fact, show their inability to fulfill it. (See, for example, some hate propaganda in the United States and the absolutism of Communist Russia.)

For the Christian churches this means that they must try to find a way between a pacifism which overlooks or denies the necessity of power (including compulsion) in the relation of history-bearing groups and a militarism which believes in the possibility of achieving the unity of mankind through the conquest of the world by a particular historical group. The ambiguity of empire-building is fragmentarily conquered when higher political unities are created which, although they are not without the compulsory element of power, are nonetheless brought about in such a way that community between the united groups can develop and none of them is transformed into a mere object of centered control.

This basic solution of the problem of power in expansion toward larger unities should determine the attitude of the churches to empire-building and war. War is the name for the compulsory element in the creation of higher imperial unities. A "just" war is either a war in which arbitrary resistance against a higher unity has to be broken (for example, the American Civil War) or a war in which the attempt to create or maintain a higher unity by mere suppression is resisted (for example, the American Revolutionary War). There is no way of saying with more than daring faith whether a war was or is a just war in this sense. This incertitude, however, does not justify the cynical type of realism which surrenders all criteria and judgments, nor does it justify utopian idealism which believes in the possibility of removing the compulsory element of power from history. But the churches as representatives of the Kingdom of God can and must condemn a war which has only the appearance of a war but is in reality universal suicide. One never can start an atomic war with the claim that it is a just war, because it cannot serve the unity which belongs to the Kingdom of God. But one must be ready to answer in kind, even with atomic weapons, if the other side uses them first. The threat itself could be a deterrent.

All this implies that the pacifist way is not the way of the Kingdom of God in history. But certainly it is the way of the churches as representatives of the Spiritual Community. They would lose their representative character if they used military or economic weapons as tools for spreading the message of the Christ. The church's valuation of pacifist movements, groups, and individuals follows from this situation. The churches must reject political pacifism but support groups and individuals who try symbolically to represent the "Peace of the Kingdom of God" by refusing to participate in the compulsory element of power struggles and who are willing to bear the unavoidable reactions by the political powers to which they belong and by which they are protected. This refers to such groups as the Quakers and to such individuals as conscientious objectors. They represent within the political group the resignation of power which is essential for the churches but cannot be made by them into a law to be imposed on the body politic.

## 3. THE KINGDOM OF GOD AND THE AMBIGUITIES OF HISTORICAL SELF-CREATIVITY

While the ambiguities of historical self-integration lead to problems of political power, the ambiguities of historical self-creativity lead to problems of social growth. It is the relation of the new to the old in history which gives rise to conflicts between revolution and tradition. The relations of the generations to each other is the typical example for the unavoidable element of unfairness on both sides in the process of growth. *A victory of the Kingdom of God creates a unity of tradition and revolution in which the unfairness of social growth and its destructive consequences, "lies and murder", are overcome.*

They are not overcome by rejecton of revolution or tradition in the name of the transcendent side of the Kingdom of God. The principal antirevolutionary attitude of many Christian groups is fundamentally wrong, whether unbloody cultural or unbloody and bloody political revolutions are concerned. The chaos which follows any kind of revolution can be a creative chaos. If history-bearing groups are unwilling to take this risk and are successful in avoiding any revolution, even an unbloody one, the dynamics of history will leave them behind. And certainly they cannot claim that their historical obsolescence is a victory of the Kingdom of God. But neither can this be said of the attempt of revolutionary groups to destroy the given structures of the cultural and political life by revolutions which are intended to force the fulfillment of the Kingdom of God and its justice "on earth". It was against such ideas of a Christian revolution to end all revolutions that Paul wrote his words in Romans, chapter 13, about the duty of obedience to the authorities in power. One of the many politico-theological abuses of biblical statements is the understanding of Paul's words as justifying the antirevolutionary bias of some churches, particularly the Lutheran. But neither these words nor any other New Testament statement deals with the methods of gaining political power. In Romans, Paul is addressing eschatological enthusiasts, not a revolutionary political movement.

The Kingdom of God is victorious over the ambiguities of historical growth only where it can be discerned that revolution is being built into tradition in such a way that, in spite of the tensions in every concrete situation and in relation to every particular problem, a creative solution in the direction of the ultimate aim of history is found.

It is the nature of democratic institutions, in relation to questions of political centeredness and of political growth, that they try to unite the truth of the two conflicting sides. The two sides here are the new and the old, represented by revolution and tradition. The possibility of removing a government by legal means is such an attempted union; and in so far as it succeeds it represents a victory of the Kingdom of God in history, because it overcomes the split. But this fact does not remove the ambiguities inherent in democratic institutions themselves. There have been other ways of uniting tradition and revolution within a political system, as is seen in federal, pre-absolutistic organizations of society. And we must not forget that democracy can produce a mass conformity which is more dangerous for the dynamic element in history and its revolutionary expression than is an openly working absolutism. The Kingdom of God is as hostile to established conformism as it is to negativistic nonconformism.

If we look at the history of the churches we find that religion, including Christianity, has stood overwhelmingly on the conservative-traditionalistic side. The great moments in the history of religion when the prophetic spirit challenged priestly doctrinal and ritual traditions are exceptions. These moments are comparatively rare (the Jewish prophets, Jesus and the apostles, the reformers) — according to the general law that the normal growth of life is organic, slow, and without catastrophic interruptions. This law of growth is most effective in realms in which the given is vested with the taboo of sacredness and in which, consequently, every attack on the given is felt as a violation of a taboo. The history of Christianity up to the present is full of examples of this feeling and consequently of the traditionalist solution. But whenever the spiritual power produced a spiritual revolution, one stage of Christianity (and religion in general) was transformed into another. Much tradition-bound accumulation is needed before a prophetic attack on it is meaningful. This accounts for the quantitative predominance of religious tradition over religious revolution. But every revolution in the power of the Spirit creates a new basis for priestly conservation and the growth of lasting traditions. This rhythm of the dynamics of history (which has analogies in the biological and psychological realms) is the way in which the Kingdom of God works in history.

## 4. THE KINGDOM OF GOD AND THE AMBIGUITIES OF HISTORICAL SELF-TRANSCENDENCE

The ambiguities of self-transcendence are caused by the tension between the Kingdom of God realized in history and the Kingdom as expected. Demonic consequences result from absolutizing the fragmentary fulfillment of the aim of history within history. On the other hand if the consciousness of realization is completely absent, utopianism alternates with the inescapable disappointments that are the seedbed of cynicism.

*Therefore no victory of the Kingdom of God is given if either the consciousness of realized fulfillment or the expectation of fulfillment is denied.* As we have seen, the symbol of the "third stage" can be used in both ways. But it also can be used in such a way as to unite the consciousness of the presence and the not-yet-presence of the Kingdom of God in history. This was the problem of the early church, and it remained a problem for all church history, as well as for the secularized forms of the self-transcending character of history. While it is comparatively easy to see the theoretical necessity of the union of the presence and not-yet-presence of the Kingdom of God, it is very difficult to keep the union in a state of living tension without letting it deteriorate into a shallow "middle way" of ecclesiastical or secular satisfaction. In the case of either ecclesiastical or secular satisfaction, it is the influence of those social groups which are interested in the preservation of the status quo that is largely, though not exclusively, responsible for such a situation. And the reaction of the critics of the status quo leads in each case to a restatement of the "principle of hope" (Ernst Bloch) in utopian terms. In such movements of expectation, however unrealistic they may be, the fighting Kingdom of God scores a victory against the power of complacency in its different sociological and psychological forms. But of course, it is a precarious and fragmentary victory because the bearers of it tend to ignore the given, but fragmentary, presence of the Kingdom.

The implication of this for the churches as representatives of the

Kingdom of God in history is that it is their task to keep alive the tension between the consciousness of presence and the expectation of the coming. The danger for the receptive (sacramental) churches is that they will emphasize the presence and neglect the expectation; and the danger for the activistic (prophetic) churches is that they will emphasize the expectation and neglect the consciousness of the presence. The most important expression of this difference is the contrast between the emphasis on individual salvation in the one group and on social transformation in the other. Therefore it is a victory of the Kingdom of God in history if a sacramental church takes the principle of social transformation into its aim or if an activistic church pronounces the Spiritual Presence under all social conditions, emphasizing the vertical line of salvation over against the horizontal line of historical activity. And since the vertical line is primarily the line from the individual to the ultimate, the question arises as to how the Kingdom of God, in its fight within history, conquers the ambiguities of the individual in his historical existence.

## 5. THE KINGDOM OF GOD AND THE AMBIGUITIES OF THE INDIVIDUAL IN HISTORY

The phrase "individual in history" in this context means the individual in so far as he actively participates in the dynamics of history. Not only he who acts politically participates in history but so does everybody who in some realm of creativity contributes to the universal movement of history. And this is so in spite of the predominance of the political in historical existence. Therefore everybody is subject to the ambiguities of this participation, the basic character of which is the ambiguity of historical sacrifice.

It is not a victory of the Kingdom of God in history if the individual tries to take himself out of participation in history in the name of the transcendent Kingdom of God. Not only is it impossible, but the attempt itself deprives the individual of full humanity by separating him from the historical group and its creative self-realization. One cannot reach the transcendent Kingdom of God without participating in the struggle of the inner-historical Kingdom of God. For the transcendent is actual within the inner-historical. Every individual is thrown into the tragic destiny of historical existence. He cannot escape it, whether he dies as an infant or as a great historical leader. Nobody's destiny is uninfluenced by historical conditions. But the more one's destiny is directly determined by one's active participation, the more historical sacrifice is demanded. Where such sacrifice is maturely accepted a victory of the Kingdom of God has occurred.

However, if there were no other answer to the question of the individual in history, man's historical existence would be meaningless and the symbol "Kingdom of God" would have no justification. This is obvious as soon as we ask the question: Sacrifice for what? A sacrifice the purpose of which bears no relation to him of whom it is demanded is not sacrifice but enforced self-annihilation. Genuine sacrifice fulfills rather than annihilates him who makes the sacrifice. Therefore historical sacrifice must be surrender to an aim in which more is achieved than just the power of a political structure or the life of a group or a progress in historical movement or the highest state of human history. Rather, it must be an aim the sacrifice for which produces also the personal fulfillment of him who surrenders himself. The personal aim, the *telos*, may be "glory", as in classical Greece; or it may be "honor", as in feudal cultures; or it may be a mystical identification with the nation, as in the era of nationalism, or with the party, as in the era of neo-collectivism; or it may be the establishment of truth, as in scientism; or the attainment of a new stage of human self-actualization, as in progressivism. It may be the glory of God, as in ethical types of religion; or union with the Ultimate One, as in mystical types of religious experience; or Eternal Life in the divine ground and aim of being, as in classical Christianity. *Wherever historical sacrifice and the certainty of personal fulfillment are united in this way, a victory of the Kingdom of God has taken place.* The participation of the individual in historical existence has received an ultimate meaning.

If we now compare the manifold expressions of the ultimate meaning of the individual's participation in the dynamics of history, we may transcend them all — by the symbol of the Kingdom of God. For this symbol unites the cosmic, social, and personal elements. It unites the glory of God with the love of God and sees in the divine transcendence inexhaustible manifoldness of creative potentialities.

# 6

## IN THE END:
## REVISIONING AND HOPE*

### THE SIGNIFICANCE OF THE HISTORY OF
### RELIGIONS FOR THE SYSTEMATIC THEOLOGIAN

*The following selection is Tillich's last public lecture, given at the Divinity School at the University of Chicago on October 12, 1965. Tillich had served as "the distinguished theologian in residence" at Chicago since 1962. In his final year there, he conducted a seminar on the History of Religions with historian and phenomenologist of religion Mircea Eliade. Eliade and other participants in the seminar recount observing Tillich's reawakened love of the great non-Christian religions, his appreciation of their strangeness, and his conviction that his now completed* Systematic Theology, *more attuned to the demands of Western science and theology, could and should undergo revision. Tillich's long-standing interest in History of Religions was renewed by his travel to Japan (1960) and his encounter there with Buddhist and Shinto priests and scholars. The essay below seems to envision a renewed systematic theological effort — one much more appreciative of religious symbols' roots in local surroundings than his own systematic effort had been, and even more focused on symbols' political and economic ramifications. In many ways, this effort would be only an intensification of Tillich's long-standing interests, but the field of History of Religions and increased interreligious encounters opened him toward a genuinely new phase of theology, seeking a theological discourse that focused the human situation with a still more powerful lens and a greater sense of location. This essay is reprinted from Jerald C. Brauer, ed.,* The Future of Religions, *New York: Harper & Row, Pubs., 1966, pp. 80-94.*

In this lecture, I wish to deal with three basic considerations. I call the first one "two basic decisions". A theologian who accepts the subject, "The Significance of the History of Religions for the Systematic Theologian", and takes this subject seriously, has already made, explicitly or implicitly, two basic decisions. On the one hand, he has separated himself from a theology which rejects all religions other than that of which he is a theologian. On the other hand, if he accepts the subject affirma-

* See also pp. 31-34 above.

312

tively and seriously, he has rejected the paradox of a religion of nonreligion, or a theology without theos (also called a theology of the secular).

Both of these attitudes have a long history. The former has been renewed in our century by Karl Barth. The latter is now most sharply expressed in the so-called theology-without-God language. For the former attitude, either the one religion is *vera religio*, true religion, against all others, which are *religiones falsâe*, false religions, or as it is expressed in modern terms, one's own religion is revelation, but any other religion is only a futile human attempt to reach God. This becomes the definition of all religion — a futile human attempt to reach God.

Therefore, from this point of view it is not worthwhile to go into the concrete differences of the religions. I remember the half-hearted way in which, for instance, Emil Brunner did it. I recall the theological isolation of historians of religion like my very highly esteemed friend, the late Rudolf Otto, and even today the similar situation of a man like Friedrich Heiler. One also recalls the bitter attacks on Schleiermacher for his use of the concept of religion for Christianity. I remember the attacks on my views when for the first time (forty years ago) I gave a seminar on Schleiermacher at Marburg. Such an approach was considered a crime at that time.

In order to reject both this old and new orthodox attitude, one must accept the following systematic presuppositions. First, one must say that revelatory experiences are universally human. Religions are based on something that is given to a man wherever he lives. He is given a revelation, a particular kind of experience which always implies saving powers. One can never separate revelation and salvation. There are revealing and saving powers in all religions. God has not left himself unwitnessed. This is the first presupposition.

The second presupposition is that revelation is received by man in terms of his finite human situation. Man is biologically, psychologically, and sociologically limited. Revelation is received under the conditions of man's estranged character. It is always received in a distorted form, especially if religion is used as a means to an end and not as an end in itself.

There is a third presupposition that one must accept. When systematic theologians assume the significance of the history of religions, they must also believe not only that there are particular revelatory experiences throughout human history but there is a revelatory process in which the limits of adaptation and the failures of distortion are subjected to criticism. Such criticism takes three forms: the mystical, the prophetic, and the secular.

A fourth presupposition is that there may be — and I stress this, there *may* be — a central event in the history of religions which unites the positive results of those critical developments in the history of religion in and under which revelatory experiences are going on — an event which, therefore, makes possible a concrete theology that has universalistic significance.

There is also a fifth presupposition. The history of religions in its essential nature does not exist alongside the history of culture. The sacred does not lie beside the secular, but it is its depths. The sacred is the creative ground and at the same time a critical judgment of the secular. But the religious can be this only if it is at the same time a judgment on itself, a judgment which must use the secular as a tool of its own religious self-criticism.

Only if the theologian is willing to accept these five presuppositions can he seriously and fully affirm the significance of the history of religions for theology against those who reject such significance in the name of a new or an old absolutism.

On the other hand, he who accepts the significance of the history of religions must stand against the no-God-language theology. He must also reject the exclusive emphasis on the secular or the idea that the sacred has, so to speak, been fully absorbed by the secular.

The last of the five points, the point about the relation of the sacred and the secular, has already reduced the threat of the "God is dead" oracle. Religion must use the secular as a critical tool against itself, but the decisive question is: *Why any religions at all?* Here one means religions in the sense of a realm of symbols, rites, and institutions. Can they not be neglected by a secular theologian in the same way he probably neglects the history of magic or astrology? If he has no use for the idea of God, what can bring him to attribute high significance to the history of religions?

In order to affirm religion against the attack from this side, the theologian must have one basic presupposition. He must assume that religion as a structure of symbols of intuition and action — that is, myths and rites within a social group — has lasting necessity for even the most secularized culture and the most demythologized theology. I derive this necessity, the lasting necessity of religion, from the fact that spirit requires embodiment in order to become real and effective. It is quite well to say that the Holy, or the Ultimate, or the Word is within the secular realm, and I myself have done so innumerable times. But in order to say that something is *in* something, it must have at least a possibility of being *outside* of it. In other words, that which is *in* and that *in* which it is, must be distinguishable. In some way their manifestations must differ. And this is the question: *In what does the merely secular differ from that secular which would be the object of a secular theology?*

Let me say the same thing in a well-known, popular form. The reformers were right when they said that every day is the Lord's Day and, therefore, devaluated the sacredness of the seventh day. But in order to say this, there must have been a Lord's Day, and that not only once upon a time but continuously in counterbalance against the overwhelming weight of the secular. This is what makes God-language necessary, however untraditional that language may be. This makes a serious affirmation in the history of religion possible.

Therefore, as theologians, we have to break through two barriers against a free approach to the history of religions: the orthodox-exclusive one and the secular-rejective one. The mere term "religion" still produces a flood of problems for the systematic theologian, and this is increased by the fact that the two fronts of resistance, though coming from opposite sides, involve an alliance. This has happened and *still* happens.

Both sides are reductionistic, and both are inclined to eliminate everything from Christianity except the figure of Jesus of Nazareth. The neo-orthodox group does this by making him the exclusive place where the word of revelation can be heard. The secular group does the same thing by making him the representative of a theologically relevant secularity. But this can be done only if the picture and message of Jesus is itself drastically reduced. He must be limited to an embodiment of the ethical call, especially in the social direction, and the ethical call is then the only thing which is left of the whole message of Christ. In *this* case, of course, history of religion is not needed any longer, not even the Jewish and Christian. Therefore, in order to have a valued, evaluated and significant understanding of the history of religions, one has to break through the Jesus-centered alliance of the opposite poles, the orthodox as well as the secular.

Now I come to my second consideration: a theology of the history of religions. The traditonal view of the history of religions is limited to the history that is told in the Old and New Testament, enlarged to include church history as the continuity of that history. Other religions are not qualitatively distinguished from each other. They all are perversions of

315

a kind of original revelation but without particular revelatory experiences of any value for Christian theology. They are pagan religions, religions of the nations, but they are not bearers of revelation and salvation. Actually, this principle was never fully carried through. Jews and Christians were both influenced religiously by the religions of conquered and conquering nations, and frequently these religions almost suffocated Judaism and Christianity and led to explosive reactions in both of them.

Therefore, what we need, if we want to accept the title of this lecture, "The Significance of the History of Religions for the Systematic Theologian", is a theology of the history of religions in which the positive valuation of universal revelation balances the critical valuation. Both are necessary. This theology of the history of religions can help systematic theologians to understand the present moment and the nature of our own historical place, both in the particular character of Christianity and in its universal claim.

I am still grateful, looking back on my own formative period of study and the time after it, to what in German is called the *religionsgeschichtliche Schule*, the School of History of Religions in biblical and church historical studies. These studies opened our eyes and demonstrated the degree to which the biblical tradition participates in the Asia Minor and Mediterranean traditions. I remember the liberating effect of the understanding of universal, human motives in the stories of Genesis or in Hellenistic existentialism and Persian eschatology, as they appeared in the late periods of the Old and New Testament.

From this point of view, all of the history of religions produced symbols for savior figures, which then supplied the framework for the New Testament understanding of Jesus and his work. This was liberating. These things did not fall from heaven like stones, but there was a long preparatory revelatory history, which finally, in the *kairos*, in the right time, in the fulfilled time, made possible the appearance of Jesus as the Christ. All this was done without hurting the uniqueness of the prophetic attack on religion in the Old Testament and the unique power of Jesus in the New Testament. Later on, in my own development, as in that of many other theologians, the significance was made clear of both the religions that surrounded the Old and New Testament situation and the religions farther removed from Biblical history.

The first question confronting a theology of the history of Israel and of the Christian Church is the history of salvation; but the history of salvation is something within the history. It is expressed in great symbolic movements, in *kairoi* such as the various efforts at reform in the history of the Church. In the same vein, nobody would identify history of religions and history of salvation, or revelation, but one searches for symbolic moments. If the history of religions is taken seriously, are there *kairoi* in the general history of religions? Attempts have been made to find such *kairoi*. There was the Enlightenment of the eighteenth century. Everything for these theologians was a preparation for the great *kairos*, the great moment, in which mature reason is reached in mankind. There are still religious elements in this reason: God, freedom, immortality. Kant developed it in his famous book *Religion within the Limits of Pure Reason*.

Another attempt was the romanticist understanding of history, which led to Hegel's famous effort. From his point of view, there is a progressive history of religion. It progresses according to the basic philosophical categories which give structure to all reality. Christianity is the highest and last point, and it is called "revealed religion", but this Christianity is philosophically demythologized. Such a view is a combination of Kantian philosphy and the message of the New Testament.

All earlier religions in Hegel's construction of the history of religions are *aufgehoben*, which can only be translated by two English verb forms, namely, "taken in" and "removed". In this construction, therefore, that which is past in the history of religion has lost its meaning. It is only an element in the later development. This means, for instance, that for Hegel the Indian religions are long, long past, long ago finished, and have no contemporary meaning. They belong to an early stage of history. Hegel's attempt to develop a theology of the history of religion resulted in the experiential theology which was very strong in America about thirty years ago. It was based on the idea of remaining open to new experiences of a religious character in the future. Today men like Toynbee point in this direction — or perhaps look for that in religious experience which leads to a union of the great religions. In any case, it is a post-Christian era that is looking for such a construction.

It is also necessary to mention Teilhard de Chardin, who stresses the development of a universal, divine-centered consciousness which is basically Christian. For him, Christianity takes in all spiritual elements of the future. I am dissatisfied with such an attempt. I am also dissatisfied with my own, but I will give it in order to induce you to try yourself, because that is what one should do if he takes the history of religions seriously.

My approach is dynamic-typological. There is no progressive

development which goes on and on, but there are elements in the experience of the Holy which are always there, if the Holy is experienced. These elements, if they are predominant in one religion, create a particular religious type. It is necessary to go into greater depth, but I will only mention a tentative scheme, which would appear as follows. The universal religious basis is the experience of the Holy within the finite. Universally in everything finite and particular, or in this and that finite, the Holy appears in a special way. I could call this the sacramental basis of all religions — the Holy here and now which can be seen, heard, dealt with, in spite of its mysterious character. We still have remnants of this in the highest religions, in their sacraments, and I believe that without it a religious group becomes an association of moral clubs, as much of Protestantism has, because it has lost the sacramental basis.

Then, there is a second element, namely, a critical movement against the demonization of the sacramental, that is, making it into an object that can be handled. This element is embodied in various critical ways. The first of these critical movements is mystical. The mystical movement indicates a dissatisfaction with any of the concrete expressions of the Ultimate, of the Holy. Man goes beyond them. He goes to the one beyond any manifoldness. The Holy as the Ultimate lies beyond any of its embodiments. The embodiments are justified. They are accepted, but they are secondary. Man must go beyond them in order to reach the highest, the Ultimate itself. The particular is denied for the Ultimate One. The concrete is devaluated.

Another element, or the third element in the religious experience, is the element of "ought to be". This is the ethical or prophetic element. Here the sacramental is criticized because of demonic consequences like the denial of justice in the name of holiness. This is the whole fight of the Jewish prophets against sacramental religion. In some of the words of Amos and Hosea the fight is carried so far that the whole cult is abrogated. This criticism of the sacramental basis is decisive for Judaism and is one element in Christianity. But again I would say, if religious experience is without the sacramental and the mystical element, it becomes moralistic and finally secular.

I would like to describe the unity of these three elements in a religion which one could call — I hesitate to do so, but I don't know a better word — "the religion of the concrete spirit". And it might well be that one can say the inner *telos*, which means the inner aim of a thing, such as the *telos* of the acorn is to become a tree — the inner aim of the history of religions is to become a religion of the concrete spirit. But we cannot identify this religion of the concrete spirit with any actual religion, not even Christianity as a religion. But I would dare to say — of course, dare as a Protestant theologian — that I believe that there is no higher expression of what I call the synthesis of these three elements than in Paul's doctrine of the Spirit. There we have the two fundamental elements, the ecstatic and the rational elements, united. There is ecstasy, but the highest creation of the ecstasy is love in the sense of *agape*. There is ecstasy, but the other creation of ecstasy is *gnosis*, the knowledge of God. It is knowledge, and it is not disorder and chaos.

The positive and negative relation of these elements or motives now gives the history of religions its dynamic character. The inner *telos* of which I spoke, the religion of the concrete spirit, is, so to speak, that toward which everything drives. But we cannot say that this is a merely futuristic expectation. It appears everywhere in the struggle against the demonic resistance of the sacramental basis and the demonic and secularistic distortion of the critics of the sacramental basis. It appears in a fragmentary way in many moments in the history of religions. Therefore, we have to absorb the past history of religions and annihilate it in this way; but we have a genuine living tradition that consists in the moments in which this great synthesis became, in a fragmentary way, reality. We can see the whole history of religions in this sense as a fight for the religion of the concrete spirit, a fight of God against religion within religion. And this phrase, a fight of God against religion within religion, could become the key for understanding the otherwise extremely chaotic, or at least seemingly chaotic, history of religions.

Now, as Christians we see in the appearance of Jesus as the Christ the decisive victory in this struggle. There is an old symbol for the Christ, Christus Victor, and this can be used again in this view of the history of religions. And thus it is already connected in the New Testament with the victory over the demonic powers and the astrological forces. It points to the victory on the cross as a negation of any demonic claim. And I believe we see here immediately that this symbol can give us a Christological approach which could liberate us from many of the dead ends into which the discussion of the Christological dogma has led the Christian churches from the very beginning. In this way, the continuation of critical moments in history, of moments of *kairoi* in which the religion of the concrete spirit is actualized fragmentarily, can happen here and there.

The criterion for us as Christians is the event of the cross. That which happened there in a symbolic way, which supplies the criterion, also happens fragmentarily in other places, in other moments, has happened and will happen even though they are not historically or empirically connected with the cross.

Now I come to a question which was very much in the center of this whole conference, namely, How are these dynamics of the history of religions related to the relationship of the religious and of the secular? The holy is not only open to demonization and to the fight of God against religion as a fight against the demonic implications of religion. But the holy is also open to secularization. And these two, demonization and secularization, are related to each other in so far as secularization is the third and most radical form of de-demonization. Now, this is a very important systematic idea.

You know the meaning of the term *profane,* "to be before the doors of the sanctuary", and the meaning of *secular,* "belonging to the world". In both cases, somebody leaves the ecstatic, mysterious fear of the Holy for the world of ordinary rational structures. It would be easy to fight against this, to keep the people in the sanctuary, if the secular had not been given a critical religious function by itself. And this makes the problem so serious. The secular is the rational, and the rational must judge the irrationality of the Holy. It must judge its demonization.

The rational structure of which I am speaking implies the moral, the legal, the cognitive, and the aesthetic. The consecration of life which the Holy gives is at the same time the domination of life by the ecstatic forms of the Holy and the repression of the intrinsic demands of goodness, of justice, of truth and of beauty. Secularization occurring in such a context is liberation.

In this sense, both the prophets and the mystics were predecessors of the secular. The Holy became slowly the morally good, or the philosophically true, and the later the scientifically true, or the aesthetically expressive. But then, a profound dialectic appears. The secular shows its inability to live by itself. The secular that is right in fighting against domination by the Holy becomes empty and becomes victim of what I call "quasi-religions". And these "quasi-religions" imply an oppressiveness like that of the demonic elements of the religions. But they are worse, as we have seen in our century, because they are without the depths and the richness of the genuine religious traditions.

And here, another *telos,* the inner aim of the history of religions, appears. I call it *theonomy,* from *theos* — God — and *nomos* — law. If the autonomous forces of knowledge, of aesthetics, of law and morals, point to the ultimate meaning of life, then we have theonomy. Then they are not dominated, but in their inner being they point beyond themselves to the Ultimate. In reality, there takes place another dynamic struggle, namely, between a consecration of life, which becomes heteronomous, and a self-actualization of all the cultural functions, which becomes autonomous and empty.

Theonomy appears in what I called the religion of the concrete spirit in fragments, never fully. Its fulfillment is eschatological; its end is expectation which goes beyond time to eternity. This theonomous element in the relation of the sacred and the secular is an element in the structure of the religion of the concrete spirit. It is certainly progressive, as every action is. Even to give a lecture has in itself the tendency to make progress in some direction, but it is not progressivistic — it doesn't imagine a temporal fulfillment. And here I differ from Teilhard de Chardin, to whom I feel very near in so many respects.

And now my third and last consideration: the interpretation of the theological tradition in the light of religious phenomena. Let me tell you about a great colleague, a much older colleague at the University of Berlin, Adolph Harnack. He once said that Christianity in its history embraces all elements of the history of religions. This was a partially true insight, but he did not follow it through. He did not see that, if this is so, then there must be a much more positive relationship between the whole history of religion and the history of the Christian Church. And so, he narrowed down his own constructive theology to a kind of high bourgeois, individualistic, moralistic theology.

I now want to return my thanks on this point to my friend Professor Eliade for the two years of seminars and the cooperation we had in them. In these seminars I experienced that every individual doctrinal statement or ritual expression of Christianity receives a new intensity of meaning. And in terms of a kind of apologia, yet also a self-accusation, I must say that my own *Systematic Theology* was written before these seminars and had another intention, namely, the apologetic discussion against and with the secular. Its purpose was the discussion or the answering of questions coming from the scientific and philosophical criticism of Christianity. But perhaps we need a longer, more intensive period of interpenetration of systematic theological study and religious historical studies. Under such circumstances, the structure of religious thought might develop in connection with another or different fragmentary manifestation of theonomy or of the religion of the concrete spirit. This is my hope for the future of theology.

To see this possibility, one should look to the example of the emphasis on the particular which the method of the history of religions gives to the systematic theologian. It is to be seen in two negations: against a supernatural theology and against a natural theology. First, there is the method of supranatural theology, which was the way classical Protestant orthodoxy formulated the idea of God in systematic theology. This concept of God appears in revelatory documents which are inspired but were not prepared for in history. For orthodoxy, these views are found in the biblical books, or for Islam, in the Koran. From there, dogmatic statements are prepared out of the material of the holy books by the Church, usually in connection with doctrinal struggles, formulated in creeds or official collections of doctrines, and theologically explained with the help of philosophy. All this is done without looking beyond the revelatory circle which one calls one's own religion or faith. This is the predominant method in all Christian churches.

Then there is the method of natural theology, the philosophical derivation of religious concepts from an analysis of reality encountered as a whole and especially from an analysis of the structure of the human mind. Often these concepts, God and others, are then related to the traditional doctrines; sometimes they are not related.

These are the two main methods traditionally used. The method of the history of religions takes the following steps: first, it uses the material of the tradition as existentially experienced by those who work theologically. But since the historian of religions works theologically, he must also have the detachment which is necessary to observe any reality. This is the first step.

In the second step, the historian of religions takes over from the naturalistic methodology the analysis of mind and reality to show where the religious question is situated in human experiences both within ourselves and within our world; for instance, the experience of finitude, the experience of concern about the meaning of our being, the experience of the Holy as Holy, and so on.

Then the third step is to present a phenomenology of religion, showing the phenomena, especially that which shows itself in the history of religion — the symbols, the rites, the ideas, and the various activities. And the fourth step consists in the attempt to point out the relation of these phenomena — their relatedness, their difference, their contradictions — to the traditional concepts and to the problems that emerge from this. Finally, the historian of religions tries to place the reinterpreted concepts into the framework of the dynamics of religious and secular history and especially into the framework of our present religious and cultural situation. Now these five steps include parts of the earlier methods, but they apply them in the context of the history of the human race and into the experiences of mankind as expressed in the great symbols of religious history.

The last point, namely, putting everything into the present situation, leads to another advantage or, if you wish to call it so, to a new element of truth. It provides the possibility of understanding religious symbols in relation to the social matrix within which they have grown and into which we have to reintroduce them today. This is an exceedingly important step. Religious symbols are not stones falling from heaven. They have their roots in the totality of human experience, including local surroundings in all their ramifications, both political and economic. And these symbols can then be understood partly as in revolt against these surroundings. And in both cases, this is very important for our way of using symbols and reintroducing them.

A second positive consequence of this method is that we can use religious symbolism as a language of the doctrine of man, as the language of anthropology, not in the empirical sense of this word, but in the sense of doctrine of man — man in his true nature. The religious symbols say something to us about the way in which men have understood themselves in their very nature. The discussion about the emphasis on sin in Christianity and the lack of such emphasis in Islam is a good example. This shows a fundamental difference in the self-interpretation of two great religions and cultures, of men as men. We enlarge our understanding of the nature of man in a way which is more embracing than any particular technical psychology.

But now my last word. What does this mean for the theologian's relationship to his own? His theology remains rooted in its experiential basis. Without this, no theology at all is possible. But he tries to formulate the basic experiences which are universally valid in universally valid statements. The universality of a religious statement does not lie in an all-embracing abstraction which would destroy religion as such but in the depths of every concrete religion. Above all, it lies in the openness to spiritual freedom both from one's own foundation and for one's own foundation.

# THE RIGHT TO HOPE: A SERMON

*Many considered Paul Tillich's sermons to be the most effective conveyors of his creative thought. For lay and clergy, men and women, as well as for himself, Tillich wrestled in his sermons with the themes of existential anguish, world affairs, political oppression, human pride and hope. German critical theorist, Theodore W. Adorno, considered Tillich's preaching more persuasive than his* Systematic Theology *(Wilhelm & Marion Pauck, pp. 232, 321). Poet and novelist, May Sarton, recorded her own appreciation of Tillich's sermon "Waiting" in her* The House by the Sea: A Journal *(New York: W.W. Norton, pp. 206-8). In contrast to so much sentimentalist, inspirational literature, she writes that "Tillich enters like a cleansing, ruthless wind", giving some "answer to my long anguish over the absence of God".\* The sermon appearing below is one given at the Memorial Church, Harvard University in Cambridge, Massachusetts, 1965. This sermon well displays the this-worldly kind of hope characteristic of his "self-transcending realism". Here he joins his listeners in searching for a genuine hope, thriving not only amid personal doubt and despair, but also amid national and world developments. His hope for nations and movements draws on the Exodus story and finds at least "fragmentary fulfillment" in historical realities such as democracy, the "social principle" in the dreams of the poor, and in the will and inner power to fight displayed by "suppressed races". Here, too, is Paul Tillich's vision of the only sort of "eternal life" consonant with his historical realism: the kind known in "the here and now". For Tillich's longer treatment of the symbol, "Eternal Life", see* Systematic Theology, *volume 3, pp. 394-423. The sermon included below was published in English translation in* Neue Zeitschrift für Systematische Theologie und Religionsphilosophie *7 (1965): 371-7.*

*Text: Romans 4, 18: "In hope he believed against hope"*

### I

A few years ago, the Humanist and Marxist philosopher Ernst Bloch became famous through a two-volume work about hope, the hopes of men in their personal lives and as members of social groups and movements. He recognized to what a degree hope is a permanent force in every man, a driving power as long as he lives. We must agree when we

---

\* I am indebted to Ms. Susan Halcomb Craig for calling my attention to Sarton's journal entries on Tillich. (M.K.T.)

look both into ourselves and at human history, and we may wonder why it is so seldom that philosophers and theologians speak about it, its roots and its justification. They don't ask what kind of force it is that creates and maintains hope, even if everything seems to contradict it. Instead, they devaluate hope by calling it wishful thinking or utopian fantasy.

But nobody can live without hope, even if it were only for the smallest things which give some satisfaction even under the worst of conditions, even in poverty, sickness and social failure. Without hope, the tension of our life toward the future would vanish, and with it, life itself. We would end in despair, a word that originally meant: "Without hope", or in deadly indifference. Therefore I want to ask the question today: Do we have a right to hope? Is there justified hope for each of us, for nations and movements, for mankind and perhaps for all life, for the whole universe? Do we have a *right to hope,* even against hope? Even against the transitoriness of everything that is? Even against the reality of death?

Our text: "In hope he believed against hope" refers to Abraham's faith in the divine promise that he would become the father of a large nation, although he had no son in his and his wife's old age. There is probably no book in which the struggle for hope is more drastically expressed than in the Old Testament. The men of the Old Testament tried to maintain the hope for Israel within the many catastrophes of its history. And later on, they struggled as individuals for their personal hope, and finally there grew a hope in them for the rebirth of the present world and a new state of all things. This double hope, for the universe and for the single person, became the faith of the early Christians, and it is the Christian hope up to today. It is the hope of the church for "the new heaven and the new earth" and of the individual to enter this new earth and new heaven.

But these hopes, in both Testaments, have to struggle with continuous attacks of hopelessness, attacks against the faith in a meaning of life and against the hope for life's fulfillment. There are in the Old Testament outcries of despair about life. There is the despair of Job, when he says: "For there is hope for a tree, if it be cut down, that it will sprout again and its shoots will not cease" — but as "the waters wear away the stones, and the torrents wash away the soil of the earth, so thou (God) destroyest the hope of man".

There is also a tremendous struggle about hope in the New Testament. It went on during the whole lifetime of Jesus. But it reached its height when after his arrest, the disciples fled to Galilee. Hopelessly they said to themselves — like the two in the beautiful story of the walk to

Emmaus — "We had hoped that he was the one to redeem Israel." "... we hoped, but he was crucified." In order to regain hope, they had — as is said in I Peter — "to be *reborn* to a living hope" namely by the Spiritual Appearances of Jesus which many of them experienced.

Later on, the church had to fight with hopelessness, because the expectations of the Christians for the early return of the Christ remained unfulfilled, year after year. So they became impatient and felt betrayed. To such members of his congregations, Paulus writes: "For in hope we are saved. Now hope that is seen is no hope. But if we hope for what we do not see, we wait for it with patience." We wait: That means we have not; but in some way we have, and this having gives us the power to wait.

The Christians learned to wait for the end. But slowly they ceased to wait. The tension of genuine waiting vanished and they were satisfied with what they had, the Christ who has founded the Church and given through it hope for Eternal Life. The expectation for a new state of things on earth became weak, although one prayed for it in every Lord's prayer: Thy will be done on earth as it is in heaven!

This has led to new attacks on hope, first from the side of the Jews who believe with the prophets of the Old Testament in the coming of a new eon, a new state of things in this world. They ask: How can Jesus be the Christ, the bringer of the new, if the world has remained as it was? The demonic powers which ruled the world in the time of Jesus, are ruling it still today. Our own century proves this irrefutably. Not only the Jews speak like this, but millions of critics of Christianity everywhere, awakening anxious response also in many Christians.

At the same time, the hope of the individual for participation in eternal life was more and more undercut by the present understanding of our world through science and philosophy. Imaginations of a heavenly place above and a hell below became symbols for the state of our inner life. The expectation of a simple continuation of life after death vanished in view of a sober acceptance of the seriousness of death and a deeper understanding of the difference between eternity and endless time by theology. In view of all this, most people today, including many Christians, have experienced the attacks of hopelessness and struggle for hope against hope. They — and "they" are also "*we*" — have learned how hard it is to preserve genuine hope. We know that one has to go ever again through the narrows of a painful and courageous "In-spite-of". For hope cannot be verified by sense experience or rational proof.

This leads to something else that makes hope so difficult. Hope is easy for every fool, but hard for the wise one. Everybody can lose himself into foolish hopes, but genuine hope is something rare and great. How then can we distinguish genuine from foolish hope?

## II

We often feel doubt not only about others but also about ourselves whether their own or our own hope is a foolish or a genuine hope. We may clearly calculate the future and think our expectations justified; but they are foolish. And we may tenaciously hope against hope and begin to feel foolish about it. But we were right in our hope — yet there is a difference which does not remain hidden, if we search for it. Where there is genuine hope, there that for which we hope, has already some presence. In some way, the hoped for is at the same time here and not here. It is not yet fulfilled and it may remain unfulfilled. But it is here, in the situation and in ourselves as a power which drives those who hope into the future. There is a beginning here and now. And this beginning drives towards an end. The hope itself, if it is rooted in the reality of something already given, becomes a driving power and makes fulfillment, not certain, but possible. Where such a beginning of what is hoped for is lacking, hope is foolishness.

If, for instance, a daydreamer expects to become something which has no relation to his present state, externally or internally, he is a fool. And he remains a fool, even if, by some strange accident, he gets what he has dreamed to get, such as sudden success, wealth, power, beauty, love. Fairytales know this. The beggar who becomes king is in the beggar's gown; but he is of royal blood. Those who dream for it without such present reality, never attain it, even if they try it, often by evil means.

But there are many things and events in which we can see reasons for genuine hope, namely the seed-like presence of that which is hoped for. In the seed of a tree, stem and leaves are already present, and this gives us the right to sow the seed in hope for the fruit. We have *no* assurance that it will develop. But our hope is genuine. There is a presence, a beginning of what is hoped for. And so it is with the child and our hope for his maturing; we hope, because maturing has already begun; but we don't know how far it will go. We hope for the fulfillment of our work, often against hope, because it is already in us as vision and driving force. We hope for a lasting love, because we feel the power of this love present. But it is hope, not certainty.

Hoping often implies waiting. "Be still before the Lord and wait patiently for him" says the psalmist (Ps. 37). Waiting demands patience and patience demands stillness within one's self. This aspect of hope is most important in the hope we have within ourselves and our own maturing and fulfilling what we essentially are and therefore ought to be.

There are two kinds of waiting, the passive waiting in laziness and the receiving waiting in openness. He who waits in laziness, passively, prevents the coming of what he is waiting for. He who waits in a quiet tension, open for what he may encounter, works for its coming. Such waiting in openness and hope does what no will power can do for our own inner development. The more seriously the great religious men took their own transformation, using their will to achieve it, the more they failed and were thrown into hopelessness about themselves. Desperately they ask, and many of us ask with them: Can we hope at all for such inner renewal? What gives us the right to such hope after all our failures? Again there is only one answer: Waiting in inner stillness, with poised tension and openness toward what we can only receive. Such openness is highest activity; it is the driving force which leads us toward the growth of something new in us. And the struggle between hope and despair in our waiting is a symptom that the new has already taken hold of us.

### III

Let us now, in brief consideration, turn to the hopes for nations, movements and mankind in human history and let us ask: What gives us the right to hope for them? A great example is the history of Israel from the exodus out of Egypt to the present day. There are few things in world history more astonishing than the preservation of hope for Israel by Israel and the continuous fulfillment and disastrous destruction of this hope. No fool's hope can give this power; if Israel's hope had been wishful thinking, Israel would have disappeared from history like all the nations surrounding them. But they had a reality in every period, an experience in their past, a divine guidance which saved them through overwhelming dangers, bound them together as a nation through the gift of the law by the God who is not a particular God, but the God of justice, whose justice shows itself when he judges his own nation and threatens to reject it, if it does not keep justice within itself.

For there was and is in Israel, as in every nation, much foolish hope:

National arrogance, will to power, ignorance about other nations, hate and fear of them, the use of God and his promises for the nation's own glory. Such hopes, present also in our own nation, are foolish hopes. They do not come out of what we truly are and cannot, therefore, become reality in history, but they are illusions about our own goodness and distortions of the image of others. Out of what we truly *are*, the hope for what we may *become* must grow. Otherwise, it will be defeated and die. World history is a cemetery of broken hopes, of utopias which had no foundation in reality.

But there is also fulfillment of historical hopes, however fragmentary it may be. The democratic form of life which has become reality is a fulfillment of old ideas about the equal dignity of men before God and under the law; and it could become reality because there were social groups in which the idea was already effective, so that it could grow into reality. The social principle which is powerful today is the fragmentary fulfillment of the dreams of the poor: that they may participate in the goods of life. But the dreams could become genuine hopes only when a social class appeared whose nature and destiny was one with this aspiration and which could make a successful fight for it. The belief in the original unity of all human races became a matter of genuine hope for reunion in the moment when suppressed races arose with the will and inner power to fight for a real reunion. In these three great events of modern history, in the midst of one of which we live, the presence of a beginning became the power driving towards fulfillment.

Is there a right to hope for mankind as a whole? There is one idea which has grasped the imagination of Western man, but which has already lost its power because of the horrors which have happened in our century: it is the idea of progress towards the fulfillment of the ages hold hopes of man. This is still a half conscious, half unconscious belief of many people today. It is often the only hope they have, and its breakdown is a profound shock for them. Is progress a justified hope for man? In some respects it is, because man has received the power to control nature almost without limits and there is daily progress in science and in technical production. But the question is: Does this progress justify the hope for a stage of fulfillment? Certainly: Progress is a justified hope in all moments, in which we work for a task and hope that something better and new will replace old goods and old evils. But whenever an evil is conquered, another appears, using the new which is good to support a new evil. The goal of mankind is not progress towards a final stage of perfection; but it is the creation of what is possible for man in each particular state of history; and it is the struggle against the forces of evil, old ones and new ones, which arise in each period in a different way. There will be victories as well as defeats in these struggles. There will be progress and regressions. But every victory, every particular progress from injustice to more justice, from suffering to more happiness, from hostility to more peace, from separation to more unity anywhere in mankind, is a manifestation of the eternal in time and space. It is, in the language of the men of the Old and New Testaments, the coming of the Kingdom of God. For the Kingdom of God does not come in one dramatic event sometime in the future. It is coming here and now in every act of love, in every manifestation of truth, in every moment of joy, in every experience of the holy. The hope of the Kingdom of God is not the expectation of a perfect stage at the end of history, in which only a few, in comparison with the innumerable generations of men, would participate, and the unimaginable amount of misery of all past generations would not be compensated. And it might even be that those who would live in it, as "blessed animals" would long for the struggles, the victories and defeats of the past. No! The hope of mankind lies in the here and now whenever the eternal appears in time and history. This hope is justified; for there is always a presence and a beginning of what is seriously hoped for.

IV

And now we ask the question of our personal participation in the eternal. Do we have a right to hope for it? The answer is: We have a right to such ultimate hope, even in view of the end of all others hopes, even in the face of death. For we experience the presence of the eternal in us and in our world here and now. We experience it in moments of silence and in hours of creativity. We experience it in the conflicts of our conscience and in the hours of peace with ourselves, we experience it in the unconditional seriousness of the moral command and in the ecstasy of love. We experience it when we discover a lasting truth and feel the need for a great sacrifice. We experience it in the beauty that life reveals as well as in the demonic darkness of it. We experience it in moments in which we feel: this is a holy place, a holy thing, a holy person, a holy time; it transcends the ordinary experiences: It gives more, it demands more, it points to the ultimate mystery of my existence, of all existence. It shows me that my finitude, my transitoriness, my being, surrendered to the flux of things, is only one side of my being and that man is both in and above finitude. Where this is experienced, there is awareness of the eternal, there is already, however, fragmentary, participation in the eternal. This is the basis of the hope for eternal life; it is the justification of our ultimate hope. And if as Christians we point to Good Friday and Easter, we point to the most powerful example of the same experience.

The hope for participation in eternity is hope for a continuation of the present life after death. It is not hope for endless time after the time given to us. Endless time is not eternity; no finite being can seriously hope for it. But every finite being can hope for return to the eternal from which it comes. And this hope has the more assurance, the deeper and more real the present participation in eternal life is.

And a last remark: Participation in the eternal is not given to the separated individual. It is given to him in unity with all others, with mankind, with everything living, with everything that has being and is rooted in the divine ground of being. All powers of creation are in us and we are in them. We do not hope for us alone or for those alone who share our hope; we hope also for those who had and have no hope, for those whose hopes for this life remain unfulfilled, for those who are disappointed and indifferent, for those who despair of life and even for those who have hurt or destroyed life. Certainly, if we could only hope each for himself, it would be a poor and foolish hope. Eternity is the ground and aim of every being for God shall be all in all. *Amen.*

# SELECTED BIBLIOGRAPHY

## I. BIBLIOGRAPHICAL RESOURCES

1  Jack Mouw and Robert P. Scharlemann, "Bibliography of the Publications of Paul Tillich", in *The Theology of Paul Tillich: A Revised and Updated Classic,* ed. Charles W. Kegley. New York: The Pilgrim Press, 1982: 395-423.

2  "Register, Bibliographie und Textgeschichte zu den Gesammelten Werken von Paul Tillich." *Gesammelte Werke* Band XIV. Stuttgart: Evangelisches Verlag, 1975.

3  *Paul Tillich: A Comprehensive Bibliography and Key Word Index of Primary and Secondary Writings in English.* Metuchen, New Jersey and London: The Scarecrow Press, 1983.

## II. TILLICH'S WORKS

### A.  From Tillich's Birth Through World War I (1886-1919)

4  *Die religionsgeschichtliche Konstruktion in Schellings positiver Philosophie, ihre Voraussetzungen und Prinzipien.* Breslau: Fleischmann, 1910. English translation (ET) − Lewisburg, PA: Bucknell University Press, 1974.

5  *Mystik und Schuldbewusstsein in Schellings philosophischer Entwicklung.* Beiträge zur Förderung christlicher Theologie, XVI, No. I. Gütersloh: Bertelsmann, 1912. ET − Lewisburg, PA: Bucknell University Press, 1974.

6  *Der Begriff des Übernatürlichen, sein dialektischer Charakter und das Prinzip der Identität, dargestellt an der supranaturalistischen Theologie vor Schleiermacher.* Königsberg: Madrasch, 1915.

### B.  The Struggle for a New Theonomy (1919-1923)

7  *Der Sozialismus als Kirchenfrage.* Leitsätze von Paul Tillich und Carl Richard Wegener. Berlin: Gracht, 1919.

8  *Masse und Geist.* Studien zur Philosophie der Masse. Berlin, Frankfurt: Verlag der Arbeitsgemeinschaft, 1922.

9  "Kairos", *Die Tat* XIV, 5 (August 1922): 330-350. ET − in *The Protestant Era,* edited by James L. Adams. Chicago: The University of Chicago Press, 1948.

10  *Das System der Wissenschaften nach Gegenständen und Methoden.* Ein Entwurf. Göttingen: Vandenhoeck und Ruprecht, 1923. ET − Lewisburg, PA: Bucknell University Press, 1981.

11  "Kritisches und positives Paradox. Eine Aufeinandersetzung mit Karl Barth und Friedrich Gogarten". *Theologische Blätter* II, 11 (November, 1923) 263-269. ET − in *The Beginnings of Dialectical Theology,* edited by James M. Robinson. Richmond, Virginia: John Knox Press, 1968.

## C. Protestant Theology Amid Socialist Crisis (1924-1933)

12 *Die Religiöse Lage der Gegenwart.* Berlin: Ullstein, 1926. ET — *The Religious Situation.* New York: Henry Holt, 1932.

13 *Das Dämonische. Ein Beitrag zur Sinndeutung der Geschichte.* Tübingen: J.C.B. Mohr, 1926. ET — in *The Interpretation of History.* New York: Scribner, 1936.

14 *Protestantisches Prinzip und proletarische Situation.* Bonn: Cohen, 1931. ET — in *The Protestant Era,* edited by James L. Adams. Chicago: The University of Chicago Press, 1948.

15 *Die sozialistische Entscheidung.* Potsdam: Protte, 1933. ET — *The Socialist Decision,* trans. Franklin Sherman. New York: Harper & Row, 1977.

## D. Early Years in America Through World War II (1933-1945)

16 "An Open Letter to Emmanuel Hirsch", October 1, 1934. ET — in *The Thought of Paul Tillich,* editors James Luther Adams, Wilhelm Pauck, Roger Lincoln Shinn. New York, San Francisco, Harper & Row, 1985: 353-388.

17 "Marx and the Prophetic Tradition." *Radical Religion* I, 4 (Autumn, 1935): 21-29.

18 *The Interpretation of History.* New York: Scribner, 1936.

19 "The Significance of the Historical Jesus for the Christian Faith." *Monday Forum Talks* (Union Theological Seminary, New York). 5 (February 28, 1938): 1, 4-5, 6.

20 "I am an American". *Protestant Digest* III, 12 (June-July, 1941): 24-26.

21 "Trends in Religious Thought That Affect Social Outlook", in *Religion and the World Order,* edited by F. Ernest Johnson. New York: Harper & Row, 1944.

22 "The World Situation", in *The Christian Answer,* edited by Henry P. Van Dusen. New York: Charles Scribner's Sons, 1945. (Also: Philadelphia: Fortress Press, 1965.)

23 "Nietzsche and the Bourgeois Spirit." *Journal of the History of Ideas.* Volume 6, 3 (June, 1945): 307-309.

## E. In the Sacred Void: Being and God (1946-1952)

24 "The Two Types of Philosophy of Religion." *Union Seminary Quarterly Review* I, 4 (May, 1946): 3-13.

25 *The Protestant Era.* Ed. James L. Adams. Chicago: The University of Chicago Press, 1948.

26 *The Shaking of the Foundations.* New York: Scribner, 1948.

27 "A Reinterpretation of the Doctrine of the Incarnation." *Church Quarterly Review* CXLVII, 294 (January-March, 1949): 133-148.

28 "Anxiety-Reducing Agencies in Our Culture", in *Anxiety,* eds. Paul H. Hoch and Joseph Zubin. New York: Grune and Stratton, 1950.

29 "Religion and the Intellectuals". *Partisan Review* XVII, 3 (March, 1950): 254-256.

30 *The Christian Conscience and Weapons of Mass Destruction.* New York: The Department of International Justice and Good Will, December, 1950.

31 "Autobiographical Reflections", in *The Theology of Paul Tillich.* Edited by Charles W. Kegley. New York: The Pilgrim Press, 1982.

32 "Being and Love", in *Moral Principles of Action,* ed. Ruth Nanda Anshen. New York: Harper and Brothers, 1952.

33 "Jewish Influences on Contemporary Christian Theology". *Cross Currents* II, 3 (Spring, 1952): 35-42.

### F. Amid Structures of Destruction: Christ as New Being (1952-1957)

34 "The Person in a Technical Society", in *Christian Faith and Social Action,* ed. John A. Hutchinson. New York: Charles Scribner's Sons, 1953.

35 *Love, Power, and Justice.* Ontological Analyses and Ethical Applications. New York, London: Oxford University Press, 1954.

36 "The Theology of Missions". *Occasional Bulletin of the Missionary Research Library* V, 10 (August 10, 1954): 6.

37 *Biblical Religion and the Search for Ultimate Reality.* Chicago: The University of Chicago Press, 1955.

38 *The New Being.* New York: Scribner, 1955.

39 "Psychoanalysis, Existentialism and Theology". *Faith and Freedom* IX, 125 (Autumn, 1955): 1-11.

40 "Existential Aspects of Modern Art", in *Christianity and the Existentialists,* ed. Carl Michalson. New York: Scribner, 1956.

41 "Reinhold Niebuhr's Doctrine of Knowledge", in *Reinhold Niebuhr: His Religious, Social, and Political Thought,* eds. Charles W. Kegley and Robert W. Bretall. New York: The Macmillan Co., 1956.

42 "Female Symbolism in the Trinity". 1956. Paul Tillich: Audiotape Collection, Tape No. 40. Produced by Union Theological Seminary in Virginia.

43 *Dynamics of Faith.* New York: Harper & Row, 1957.

44 "Theology of Education", in *The Church School in Our Time.* Concord: St. Paul's School, 1957.

### G. Among the Ambiguities of Life: Spirit and the Churches (1958-1963)

45 "The Riddle of Inequality". *Union Seminary Quarterly Review* XIII, 4 (May, 1958): 3-9.

46 *Theology of Culture,* ed. Robert C. Kimball. New York: Oxford University Press, 1959.

47 "The Relationship Today between Science and Religion", in *The Student Seeks an Answer.* Waterville, Maine: Colby College Press, 1960.

48 "The Relevance of the Ministry in Our Time and Its Theological Foundation", in *Making the Ministry Relevant*, ed. Hans Hofmann. New York: Scribner, 1960.

49 "Sin and Grace in the Theology of Reinhold Niebuhr", in *Reinhold Niebuhr: A Prophetic Voice in Our Time*, edited by Harold R. Landon. Greenwich, Conn.: The Seabury Press, 1962.

50 "The Philosophy of Social Work". *The Social Service Review* XXXVI, 1 (1962): 13-16.

51 *Christianity and the Encounter of the World Religions.* New York: Columbia University Press, 1963.

52 *The Eternal Now.* New York: Scribner, 1963.

53 *Morality and Beyond,* ed. Ruth Nanda Anshen. New York: Harper & Row, 1963.

## H. In the End: Revisioning and Hope (1964-1965)

54 "An Afterword. Appreciation and Reply", in *Paul Tillich in Catholic Thought.* Eds. Thomas A. O'Meara and Celestin D. Weisser. Dubuque, Iowa: Priory Press, 1964.

55 *Ultimate Concern: Tillich in Dialogue,* ed. D. Mackenzie Brown. New York: Harper & Row, 1965.

56 "from" *A Final Conversation with Paul Tillich,* ed. Albert H. Friedlander. *The Reconstructionist* XXXI, 14 (1965): 21-25.

## I. Posthumously Published Writings and Collections

57 *On the Boundary: An Autobiographical Sketch.* New York: Charles Scribner's Sons, 1966.

58 *The Future of Religion,* ed. Jerald C. Brauer. New York: Harper & Row, 1966.

59 *My Search for Absolutes,* ed. Ruth Nanda Anshen. New York: Simon and Schuster, 1967.

60 *A History of Christian Thought: From its Judaic and Hellenistic Origins to Existentialism,* ed. Carl E. Braaten. New York: Harper & Row, 1967-1968.

61 *What is Religion?* ed. James L. Adams. New York: Harper & Row, 1969.

62 *My Travel Diary: 1936. Between Two Worlds,* ed. Jerald C. Brauer. Translated by Maria Pelikan. New York: Harper & Row, 1970.

63 *Political Expectation,* ed. James L. Adams. New York: Harper & Row, 1971.

64 "Dialogues, East and West: Conversation between Dr. Paul Tillich and Dr. Hisamatsu Shin'ichi. Part I." *The Eastern Buddhist* (New Series) (Kyoto) IV, 2 (1971): 89-107. Part II. *Ibid.* V, 2 (1972): 108-128.

65 *The Meaning of Health: Essays in Existentialism, Psychoanalysis, and Religion,* ed. Perry LeFevre. Chicago: Exploration Press, 1984.

# III. LITERATURE ABOUT PAUL TILLICH'S LIFE AND THOUGHT

Adams, James L., "Introduction" in *Political Expectation*, ed. James L. Adams. New York: Harper & Row, 1971. Pp. vi-xx.

_____. *Paul Tillich's Philosophy of Culture, Science, and Religion.* New York: Harper & Row, 1965

_____. "Tillich's Concept of the Protestant Era". In *The Protestant Era.* Trans. James L. Adams. Chicago: The University of Chicago Press, 1948. Pp. 273-316.

Adams, J.L., Pauck, W., Shinn, R.L., eds. *The Thought of Paul Tillich.* San Francisco: Harper & Row, 1985.

Carey, John J., ed. *Theonomy and Autonomy: Studies in Paul Tillich's Engagements with Modern Culture.* Macon, Georgia: Mercer University Press, 1984.

Kegley, Charles, ed. *The Theology of Paul Tillich.* A Revised and Updated Classic. New York: The Pilgrim Press, 1982.

Kelsey, David. *The Fabric of Paul Tillich's Theology.* New Haven: Yale University Press, 1967.

Leibrecht, Walter. *Religion and Culture: Essays in Honor of Paul Tillich.* New York: Harper and Bros., 1959.

May, Rollo. *Paulus: Reminiscences of a Friendship.* New York: Harper & Row, 1973.

Mckelway, Alexander J. *The Systematic Theology of Paul Tillich: A Review and Analysis.* Richmond, Virginia: John Knox Press, 1964.

Newport, John P. *Paul Tillich.* Makers of the Modern Theological Mind series. Ed. Bob E. Patterson. Waco, TX.: Word Books, 1984.

O'Meara, Thomas A., and Weisser, C.D., eds. *Paul Tillich in Catholic Thought.* Dubuque, Iowa: Priory Press, 1964.

Pauck, Wilhelm and Marion. *Paul Tillich: His Life and Thought, Vol. I: Life.* New York: Harper & Row, 1976.

Palmer, Michael F. *Paul Tillich's Philosophy of Art.* Berlin: Walter de Gruyter, 1984.

Plaskow, Judith. *Sex, Sin and Grace: Women's Experience and the Theologies of Reinhold Niebuhr and Paul Tillich.* Lanham, Maryland: University Press of America, 1980.

Scharlemann, Robert P. *Reflections and Doubt in the Thought of Paul Tillich.* New Haven: Yale University Press, 1969.

Stone, Ronald H. *Paul Tillich's Radical Social Thought.* Atlanta: John Knox Press, 1980.

Stumme, John R. *Socialism in Theological Perspective: A Study of Paul Tillich, 1918-1933.* American Academy of Religion Dissertation Series, No. 21. Missoula, Montana: Scholars Press, 1978.

Tillich, Hannah. *From Time to Time.* New York: Stein and Day, 1973.

_____. *From Place to Place.* New York: Stein and Day, 1976.

# NOTES

[1] **Wilhelm and Marion Pauck.** *Paul Tillich: His Life and Thought, Vol. I: Life* (New York: Harper & Row, 1976), pp. 49-50.

[2] Paul Tillich, *On the Boundary: An Autobiographical Sketch* (New York: Charles Scribner's Sons, 1966), p. 14.

[3] Tillich, *On the Boundary*, p. 51.

[4] Wilhelm and Marion Pauck, p. 36.

[5] Claude Welch, *Protestant Thought in the Nineteenth Century, Volume 1, 1799-1870* (New Haven: Yale University Press, 1972), pp 269-273.

[6] Wilhelm and Marion Pauck, p. 14.

[7] For a summary of this varied literature, see John P. Newport, *Paul Tillich*, "Makers of Modern Theological Mind" Series, ed. Bob E. Patterson (Waco, Texas; Word Books, 1984) pp. 197-205.

[8] Paul Tillich, *My Search for Absolutes* (New York: Simon & Schuster, 1969), p. 32.

[9] Wilhelm and Marion Pauck, p. 41. For an alternative interpretation of World War I in Tillich's life, as a "bridge" instead of a "turning point", see Ronald H. Stone, *Paul Tillich's Radical Social Thought* (Richmond, VA: John Knox Press, 1980), pp. 37-38.

[10] See Keith Clements, *Friedrich Schleiermacher: Pioneer of Modern Theology* in, *The Making of Modern Theology: 19th and 20th Century Theological Texts*, General Editor: John W. de Gruchy (London and San Francisco: Collins, 1987).

[11] David Tracy, *The Analogical Imagination: Christian Theology and the Culture of Pluralism* (New York: Crossroad, 1981); Sallie McFague, *Metaphorical Theology: Models of God in Religious Language* (Philadelphia: Fortress, 1982).

[12] John B. Cobb, Jr. *Christ in a Pluralistic Age* (Philadelphia: Westminster, 1975).

[13] Langdon Gilkey, *Religion and Scientific Future: Reflections on Myth, Science and Theology* (New York: Harper & Row, 1970).

[14] Rosemary Radford Ruether, *Sexism and God-Talk: Toward a Feminist Theology* (Boston: Beacon Press, 1983).

[15] Gregory Baum, *Religion and Alienation: A Theological Reading of Sociology* (New York: Paulist, 1975); Gustavo Gutierrez, *A Theology of Liberation* (Maryknoll, NY: Orbis, 1975).

[16] Wolfhart Pannenberg, *Anthropology in Theological Perspective* (Philadelphia: Westminster, 1985).

[17] See the works of Hans W. Frei, *The Identity of Jesus Christ: The Hermeneutical Bases of Dogmatic Theology* (Philadelphia: Fortress, 1975); George A. Lindbeck *The Nature of Doctrine: Religion and Theology in a Postliberal Age* (Philadelphia: Westminster, 1984), and Stanley Hauerwas, *Character and the Christian Life* (San Antonio, TX.: Trinity University Press, 1975).

[18] Paul Tillich, *The Socialist Decision*, trans. Franklin Sherman (New York: Harper & Row, 1977), pp. 70-71.

[19] George Hunsinger, ed., *Karl Barth and Radical Politics* (Philadelphia: Westminster, 1976), pp. 19-45.

[20] Dietrich Bonhoeffer, *The Communion of Saints: A Dogmatic Inquiry into the Sociology of the Church* (New York and Evanston: Harper & Row, 1963), pp. 193-194.

[21] Reinhold Niebuhr, *An Interpretation of Christian Ethics* (New York: Seabury, 1979/1935), pp. 50, 62-83.

[22] Claude Welch, *Protestant Thought in the Nineteenth Century, Vol. 2, 1870-1914* (New Haven: Yale University Press, 1985), pp. 238-265.

[23] Paul Tillich, "Trends in Religious Thought that Affect Social Outlook", in *Religion and the World Order*, ed. F. Ernest Johnson (New York: Harper & Row, 1944), pp. 24-25.

[24] Paul Tillich, *The World Situation*, Social Ethics Series-2, ed. Franklin Sherman (Philadelphia: Fortress Press, 1965), p. 9.

[25] Tillich's example is interpreted negatively by the Brazilian theologian Clodovis Boff, *Theology and Praxis: Epistemological Foundations* (Maryknoll, NY: Orbis, 1987), p. 327, n. 46.

[26] Peter Berger, *The Capitalist Revolution: Fifty Propositions about Property, Equality and Liberty* (New York: Basic Books, 1986).

[27] Gutierrez, pp. 111-113, 265-279.

[28] James H. Cone, *For My People: Black Theology and the Black Church* (Maryknoll, NY: Orbis, 1984), Cornel West, *Prophesy Deliverance! An Afro-American Revolutionary Christianity* (Philadelphia: Westminster Press, 1982).

[29] As an example of a theological conversation with Jürgen Habermas, see Helmut Peukert, *Science, Action and Fundamental Theology: Toward a Theology of Communicative Action* (Cambridge, Mass: MIT Press, 1984).

[30] See the helpful discussion of this shift in Roger Shinn, "Tillich as Interpreter and Disturber of Contemporary Civilization", in James Luther Adams, Wilhelm Pauck, Roger Lincoln Shinn, eds., *The Thought of Paul Tillich* (New York: Harper & Row, 1985), pp. 58-60.

[31] See the discussions of "correlation" and "mutually critical correlation" in *Consensus in Theology? A Dialogue with Hans Küng and Edward Schillebeeckx*, ed. Leonard Swidler (Philadelphia: Westminster, 1980), esp. pp. 1-39, 63-68, 81-85.

[32] Paul Tillich, *The Courage to Be* (New Haven: Yale University Press, 1952), pp. 182-190.

[33] Malcolm L. Diamond, *Contemporary Philosophy and Religious Thought: An Introduction to the Philosophy of Religion* (New York: McGraw-Hill, 1974), pp. 378-381.

[34] As one example, see the reflections of Drew University theologian, Nelle Morton, *The Journey is Home* (Boston: Beacon, 1985).

[35] Tillich, *Systematic Theology*, vol. 3 (Chicago: The University of Chicago Press, 1983), pp. 293-94.

[36] For both an appreciative and also vigorously critical assessment of Tillich, see Mary Daly, *Pure Lust: Elemental Feminist Theology* (Boston: Beacon Press, 1984), pp. 155-160. For general discussion of relationships between Tillich and contemporary feminism, see Mary Ann Stenger "A Critical Analysis of the Influence of Paul Tillich on Mary Daly's Feminist Theology" *Encounter* 43 (Winter 1982): 219-238.

[37] Friedrich Schleiermacher, *The Christian Faith*, eds. H. R. Mackintosh and S. S. Stewart (Philadelphia: Fortress Press, 1976 [1822]), pp. 282-304. Schleiermacher could write about "original sinfulness" *and* "original perfection" as both co-inhering in the past and present forms of human nature.

[38] Tillich, "Reply to Interpretation and Criticism," in *The Theology of Paul Tillich*, ed. by Charles W. Kegley (New York: The Pilgrim Press, 1982), pp. 387-389.

[39] Tillich, *Systematic Theology*, vol. 3, p. 149.

[40] Cf. "Realism and Faith" above, pp. 67ff., and "Jesus as the Christ", above pp. 212ff.

[41] Arthur A. Cohen, *The Tremendum: A Theological Interpretation of the Holocaust* (New York: Crossroad, 1981).

[42] Jon Sobrino, *Christology at the Crossroads: A Latin American Approach* (Maryknoll, NY: Orbis, 1978).

[43] James H. Cone, *God of the Oppressed* (New York: Seabury, 1975), pp. 133-137, and Allan Boesak, *Black and Reformed* (Maryknoll, NY: Orbis, 1984), p. 15.

[44] Elisabeth Schüssler Fiorenza, *In Memory of Her: A Feminist Theological Reconstruction of Christian Origins* (New York: Crossroads, 1983), pp. 130-140; Caroline Walker Bynum, *Jesus as Mother: Studies in the Spirituality of the High Middle Ages* (Berkeley: University of California Press, 1982), and Susan Cady, Marian Ronan and Hal Taussig, *The Future of Feminist Spirituality* (San Francisco: Harper & Row, 1986), pp. 38-54.

[45] Raimundo Panikkar, *The Unknown Christ of Hinduism: Towards an Ecumenical Christophany* (Maryknoll, NY: Orbis, 1981); Douglas J. Elwood and Patricia Ling Magdamo, *Christ in a Philippine Context* (Quezon City: New Day, 1971).

[46] Tillich, *Systematic Theology*, vol. 2, pp. 150-51, and *Systematic Theology*, vol. 3, pp. 144-152.

[47] Wilhelm and Marion Pauck, p. 274.

[48] Paul Tillich, "The Divine Spirit in the Functions of Life", above pp. 233ff.

[49] For a summary of different groups' and disciplines' criticisms of structures of bureaucratic state socialism and state capitalism, see Matthew L. Lamb, *Solidarity with Victims: Toward a Theology of Social Transformation* (New York: Crossroad, 1982).

[50] Wilhelm and Marion Pauck, p. 279.

[51] Mircea Eliade, "Paul Tillich and the History of Religions", in *The Future of*

*Religions,* ed. Jerald C. Brauer (New York: Harper & Row, 1966), pp. 35-36.

[52]  E.g. Paul Tillich, "Kairos", in *The Protestant Era* (Chicago: The University of Chicago Press, 1948), pp. 32-51.

[53]  John Herman Randall, Jr., "The Ontology of Paul Tillich", in Kegley, p. 193.

[54]  Paul Tillich, "The Significance of the History of Religions for Systematic Theologian", above pp. 312ff.

[55]  Paul Tillich, "Dialogues, East and West: Conversation between Paul Tillich and Dr. Hisamatsu Shin'ichi. Part 1." *The Eastern Buddhist* (New Series) (Kyoto) IV, 2 (1971): 89-107. Part 2. *Ibid.* V, 2 (1972): 108-128.

[56]  Among evangelicals, see Mark Lau Branson and C. René Padilla, *Conflict and Context: Hermeneutics in the Americas* (Grand Rapids, MI: William B. Eerdmans, 1986).

[57]  For a particularly striking example of a theologian moving in these directions, see James Cone, *For My People,* pp. 78-98, 122-174.

[58]  See Ada Maria Isasi-Diaz in *God's Fierce Whimsy: Christian Feminism and Theological Education* (New York: Pilgrim Press, 1985), esp. pp. 106-108. For Delores Huerta, see Andrés G. Guerrero, *A Chicano Theology* (Maryknoll, NY: Orbis, 1987) pp. 35, 40-44, 105-106.

[59]  Katie Geneva Cannon, "Emergence of a Black Feminist Consciousness", in *Feminist Interpretation of the Bible,* ed. Letty M. Russell (Philadelphia: Westminster, 1985), pp. 30-40, and Delores S. Williams, "Womanist Theology: Black Women's Voices", *Christianity and Crisis* 27, No. 3 (March 2, 1987): 66-70.

[60]  In theology, see the discussions by The Mudflower Collective in *God's Fierce Whimsy: Christian Feminism and Theological Education* (New York: Pilgrim Press, 1985, pp. 180-195. On lesbian literature and readers, see Bonnie Zimmerman "What Has Never Been: An Overview of Lesbian Feminist Criticism" in *The New Feminist Criticism,* ed. Elaine Showalter (New York: Pantheon, 1985), pp. 200-224.

# SUBJECT INDEX

Page numbers in *italics* denote references in editorial sections,
those in ordinary type denote references in the Tillich texts.

343

# INDEX OF NAMES

Page numbers in *italics* denote references in editorial sections, those in ordinary type denote references in the Tillich texts.